# ESSAYS AND REVIEWS.

# ESSAYS AND REVIEWS.

LONDON:

JOHN W. PARKER AND SON, WEST STRAND

1860.

283.057H
Raise
C.2

178418

S.B.N.—0.576.02183.0.

Republished in 1970 by Gregg International Publishers Limited
Westmead, Farnborough, Hants, England.


Printed in England.

# TO THE READER.

———

IT will readily be understood that the Authors of the ensuing Essays are responsible for their respective articles only. They have written in entire independence of each other, and without concert or comparison.

The Volume, it is hoped, will be received as an attempt to illustrate the advantage derivable to the cause of religious and moral truth, from a free handling, in a becoming spirit, of subjects peculiarly liable to suffer by the repetition of conventional language, and from traditional methods of treatment.

# CONTENTS.

# THE EDUCATION OF THE WORLD.

IN a world of mere phenomena, where all events are
bound to one another by a rigid law of cause and
effect, it is possible to imagine the course of a long
period bringing all things at the end of it into exactly
the same relations as they occupied at the beginning.
We should, then, obviously have a succession of cycles
rigidly similar to one another, both in events and in
the sequence of them. The universe would eternally
repeat the same changes in a fixed order of recurrence,
though each cycle might be many millions of years in
length. Moreover, the precise similarity of these
cycles would render the very existence of each one of
them entirely unnecessary. We can suppose, without
any logical inconsequence, any one of them struck out,
and the two which had been destined to precede and
follow it brought into immediate contiguity.

This supposition transforms the universe into a
dead machine. The lives and the souls of men
become so indifferent, that the annihilation of a whole
human race, or of many such races, is absolutely
nothing. Every event passes away as it happens,
filling its place in the sequence, but purposeless for
the future. The order of all things becomes, not
merely an iron rule, from which nothing can ever
swerve, but an iron rule which guides to nothing and
ends in nothing.

Such a supposition is possible to the logical understanding: it is not possible to the spirit. The human

heart refuses to believe in a universe without a purpose. To the spirit, all things that exist must have a purpose, and nothing can pass away till that purpose be fulfilled. The lapse of time is no exception to this demand. Each moment of time, as it passes, is taken up in the shape of permanent results into the time that follows, and only perishes by being converted into something more substantial than itself. A series of recurring cycles, however conceivable to the logical understanding, is inconceivable to the spirit; for every later cycle must be made different from every earlier by the mere fact of coming after it and embodying its results. The material world may possibly be subject to such a rule, and may, in successive epochs, be the cradle of successive races of spiritual beings. But the world of spirits cannot be a mere machine.

In accordance with this difference between the material and the spiritual worlds, we ought to be prepared to find progress in the latter, however much fixity there may be in the former. The earth may still be describing precisely the same orbit as that which was assigned to her at the creation. The seasons may be precisely the same. The planets, the moon, and the stars, may be unchanged both in appearance and in reality. But man is a spiritual as well as a material creature, must be subject to the laws of the spiritual as well as to those of the material world, and cannot stand still because things around him do. Now, that the individual man is capable of perpetual, or almost perpetual, development from the day of his birth to that of his death, is obvious of course. But we may well expect to find something more than this in a spiritual creature who does not stand alone, but forms a part of a whole world of creatures like himself. Man cannot be considered as an individual. He is, in reality, only man by virtue of his being a member of the human race. Any other animal that we know would probably not be very different in its nature if

brought up from its very birth apart from all its
kind. A child so brought up becomes, as instances
could be adduced to prove, not a man in the full sense
at all, but rather a beast in human shape, with human
faculties, no doubt, hidden underneath, but with no
hope in this life of ever developing those faculties into
true humanity. If, then, the whole in this case, as in
so many others, is prior to the parts, we may conclude, that we are to look for that progress which is
essential to a spiritual being subject to the lapse of
time, not only in the individual, but also quite as
much in the race taken as a whole. We may expect
to find, in the history of man, each successive age incorporating into itself the substance of the preceding.

This power, whereby the present ever gathers into
itself the results of the past, transforms the human
race into a colossal man, whose life reaches from the
creation to the day of judgment. The successive
generations of men are days in this man's life. The
discoveries and inventions which characterize the different epochs of the world's history are his works.
The creeds and doctrines, the opinions and principles
of the successive ages, are his thoughts. The state of
society at different times are his manners. He grows
in knowledge, in self-control, in visible size, just as we
do. And his education is in the same way and for
the same reason precisely similar to ours.

All this is no figure but only a compendious statement of a very comprehensive fact. The child that
is born to-day may possibly have the same faculties
as if he had been born in the days of Noah; if it be
otherwise, we possess no means of determining the
difference. But the equality of the natural faculties
at starting will not prevent a vast difference in their
ultimate development. That development is entirely
under the control of the influences exerted by the
society in which the child may chance to live. If
such society be altogether denied, the faculties perish,

and the child (as remarked above) grows up a beast and not a man; if the society be uneducated and coarse, the growth of the faculties is early so stunted as never afterwards to be capable of recovery; if the society be highly cultivated, the child will be culti-vated also, and will show, more or less, through life the fruits of that cultivation. Hence each generation receives the benefit of the cultivation of that which preceded it. Not in knowledge only but in develop-ment of powers the child of twelve now stands at the level where once stood the child of fourteen, where ages ago stood the full-grown man. The discipline of manners, of temper, of thought, of feeling, is trans-mitted from generation to generation, and at each transmission there is an imperceptible but unfailing increase. The perpetual accumulation of the stores of knowledge is so much more visible than the change in the other ingredients of human progress, that we are apt to fancy that knowledge grows, and knowledge only. I shall not stop to examine whether it be true (as is sometimes maintained) that all progress in human society is but the effect of the progress of knowledge. For the present, it is enough to point out that knowledge is not the only possession of the human spirit in which progress can be traced.

We may, then, rightly speak of a childhood, a youth, and a manhood of the world. The men of the earliest ages were, in many respects, still children as compared with ourselves, with all the blessings and with all the disadvantages that belong to childhood. We reap the fruits of their toil, and bear in our characters the impress of their cultivation. Our characters have grown out of their history, as the character of the man grows out of the history of the child. There are matters in which the simplicity of childhood is wiser than the maturity of manhood, and in these they were wiser than we. There are matters in which the child is nothing, and the man everything, and in these we are the gainers. And the process by which we have either lost or gained corresponds, stage by stage, with the process by which the infant is trained for youth, and the youth for manhood.

This training has three stages. In childhood we are subject to positive rules which we cannot understand, but are bound implicitly to obey. In youth we are subject to the influence of example, and soon break loose from all rules unless illustrated and enforced by the higher teaching which example imparts. In manhood we are comparatively free from external restraints, and if we are to learn, must be our own instructors. First come Rules, then Examples, then Principles. First comes the Law, then the Son of Man, then the Gift of the Spirit. The world was once a child under tutors and governors until the time appointed by the Father. Then, when the fit season had arrived, the Example to which all ages should turn was sent to teach men what they ought to be. Then the human race was left to itself to be guided by the teaching of the Spirit within.

The education of the world, like that of the child, begins with Law. It is impossible to explain the reasons of all the commands that you give to a child, and you do not endeavour to do so. When he is to go to bed, when he is to get up, how he is to sit, stand, eat, drink, what answers he is to make when spoken to, what he may touch and what he may not, what prayers he shall say and when, what lessons he is to learn, every detail of manners and of conduct the careful mother teaches her child, and requires implicit obedience. Mingled together in her teaching are commands of the most trivial character and commands of the gravest importance ; their relative value marked by a difference of manner rather than by anything else, since to explain it is impossible. Meanwhile to the child obedience is the highest duty, affection the highest stimulus, the mother's word the highest sanction. The conscience is alive, but it is, like the other faculties at that age, irregular, undeveloped, easily deceived. The mother does not leave it uncultivated, nor refuse sometimes to explain her motives for commanding or forbidding ; but she never thinks of putting the judgment of the child against her own, nor of considering the child's conscience as having a right to free action.

As the child grows older the education changes its character, not so much in regard to the sanction of its precepts as in regard to their tenor. More stress is laid upon matters of real duty, less upon matters of mere manner. Falsehood, quarrelling, bad temper, greediness, indolence, are more attended to than times of going to bed, or fashions of eating, or postures in sitting. The boy is allowed to feel, and to show that he feels, the difference between different commands. But he is still not left to himself : and though points of manner are not put on a level with points of conduct, they are by no means neglected. Moreover, while much stress is laid upon his deeds, little is laid upon his opinions ; he is rightly supposed not to have any, and will not be allowed to plead them as a reason for disobedience.

After a time, however, the intellect begins to assert a right to enter into all questions of duty, and the intellect accordingly is cultivated. The reason is appealed to in all questions of conduct : the consequences of folly or sin are pointed out, and the punishment which, without any miracle, God invariably brings upon those who disobey His natural laws— how, for instance, falsehood destroys confidence and incurs contempt ; how indulgence in appetite tends to brutal and degrading habits ; how ill-temper may end in crime, and must end in mischief. Thus the conscience is reached through the understanding.

Now, precisely analogous to all this is the history of the education of the early world. The earliest commands almost entirely refer to bodily appetites and animal passions. The earliest wide-spread sin was brutal violence. That wilfulness of temper, —those germs of wanton cruelty, which the mother corrects so easily in her infant, were developed in the earliest form of human society into a prevailing plague of wickedness. The few notices which are given of that state of mankind do not present a picture of mere lawlessness, such as we find among the medieval nations of Europe, but of blind, gross ignorance of themselves and all around them. Atheism is possible now, but Lamech's presumptuous comparison of himself with God is impossible, and the thought of building a tower high enough to escape God's wrath could enter no man's dreams. We sometimes see in very little children a violence of temper which seems hardly human : add to such a temper the strength of a full-grown man, and we shall perhaps understand what is meant by the expression, that the earth was filled with violence.

Violence was followed by sensuality. Such was the sin of Noah, Ham, Sodom, Lot's daughters, and the guilty Canaanites. Animal appetites—the appetites which must be subdued in childhood if they are to be subdued at all—were still the temptation of mankind. Such sins are, it is true, prevalent in the world even now. But the peculiarity of these early forms of licentiousness is their utter disregard of every kind of restraint, and this constitutes their childish character.

The education of this early race may strictly be said to begin when it was formed into the various masses out of which the nations of the earth have sprung. The world, as it were, went to school, and was broken up into classes. Before that time it can hardly be said that any great precepts had been given. The only commands which claim an earlier date are the prohibitions of murder and of eating blood. And

these may be considered as given to all alike. But
the whole lesson of humanity was too much to be
learned by all at once. Different parts of it fell to the
task of different parts of the human race, and for a
long time, though the education of the world flowed
in parallel channels, it did not form a single stream.

The Jewish nation, selected among all as the
depository of what may be termed, in a pre-eminent
sense, religious truth, received, after a short preparation, the Mosaic system. This system is a mixture
of moral and positive commands : the latter, precise
and particular, ruling the customs, the festivals, the
worship, the daily food, the dress, the very touch ; the
former large, clear, simple, peremptory. There is
very little directly spiritual. No freedom of conduct
or of opinion is allowed. The difference between different precepts is not forgotten ; nor is all natural
judgment in morals excluded. But the reason for all
the minute commands is never given. Why they
may eat the sheep and not the pig they are not told.
The commands are not confined to general principles,
but run into such details as to forbid tattooing or dis-
figuring the person, to command the wearing of a
blue fringe, and the like. That such commands
should be sanctioned by divine authority is utterly
irreconcileable with our present feelings. But in the
Mosaic system the same peremptory legislation deals
with all these matters, whether important or trivial.
The fact is, that however trivial they might be in
relation to the authority which they invoked, they were
not trivial in relation to the people who were to be
governed and taught.

The teaching of the Law was followed by the comments of the Prophets. It is impossible to mistake
the complete change of tone and spirit. The ordinances indeed remain, and the obligation to observe
them is always assumed. But they have sunk to the
second place. The national attention is distinctly

fixed on the higher precepts. Disregard of the ordinances is, in fact, rarely noticed, in comparison with breaches of the great human laws of love and brotherly kindness, of truth and justice. There are but two sins against the ceremonial law which receive marked attention—idolatry and sabbath-breaking; and these do not occupy a third of the space devoted to the denunciation of cruelty and oppression, of maladministration of justice, of impurity and intemperance. Nor is the change confined to the precepts enforced: it extends to the sanction which enforces them. Throughout the Prophets there is an evident reference to the decision of individual conscience, which can rarely be found in the Books of Moses. Sometimes, as in Ezekiel's comment on the Second Commandment, a distinct appeal is made from the letter of the law to the voice of natural equity. Sometimes, as in the opening of Isaiah, the ceremonial sacrifices are condemned for the sins of those who offered them. Or, again, fasting is spiritualized into self-denial. And the tone taken in this teaching is such as to imply a previous breach, not so much of positive commands, as of natural morality. It is assumed that the hearer will find within himself a sufficient sanction for the precepts. It is no longer, as in the law, 'I am the Lord;' but, 'Hath not he showed thee, O man, what is good?' And hence the style becomes argumentative instead of peremptory, and the teacher pleads instead of dogmatizing. In the meanwhile, however, no hint is ever given of a permission to dispense with the ordinances even in the least degree. The child is old enough to understand, but not old enough to be left to himself. He is not yet a man. He must still conform to the rules of his father's house, whether or not those rules suit his temper or approve themselves to his judgment.

The comments of the Prophets were followed in their turn by the great Lesson of the Captivity. Then

for the first time the Jews learned, what that Law and
the Prophets had been for centuries vainly endeavouring to teach them, namely, to abandon for ever
polytheism and idolatry.   But though this change in
their national habits and character is unmistakeable,
it might seem at first sight as if it were no more than
an external and superficial amendment, and that their
growth in moral and spiritual clearness, though traceable with certainty up to this date, at any rate
received   a   check   afterwards.   For it is undeniable
that, in the time of our Lord, the Sadducees had
lost all depth of spiritual feeling, while the Pharisees
had   succeeded   in   converting   the   Mosaic   system
into so mischievous an idolatry of forms, that St.
Paul does not hesitate to call the law the strength
of sin.   But in spite of this it is nevertheless clear
that even the Pharisaic teaching contained elements
of a more spiritual religion than the original Mosaic
system.   Thus, for instance, the importance attached
by the Pharisees to prayer is not be found in the law.
The worship under the law consisted almost entirely
of sacrifices. With the sacrifices we may presume that
prayer was always offered, but it was not positively
commanded; and, as a regular and necessary part of
worship, it first appears in the later books of the Old
Testament, and is never even there so earnestly insisted
upon as afterwards by the Pharisees.   It was in fact
in the captivity, far from the temple and the sacrifices
of the temple, that the Jewish people first learned that
the spiritual part of worship could be separated from
the ceremonial, and that of the two the spiritual was
far the higher.   The first introduction of preaching
and the reading of the Bible in the synagogues
belong to the same date.   The careful study of the
law, though it degenerated into formality, was yet in
itself a more intellectual service than the earlier
records exhibit.   And this study also, though commencing earlier, attains its maximum after the cap-

tivity; the Psalmists who delight in the study of the law are all, or nearly all, much later than David; and the enthusiasm with which the study is praised increases as we come down. In short, the Jewish nation had lost very much when John the Baptist came to prepare the way for his Master; but time had not stood still, nor had that course of education whereby the Jew was to be fitted to give the last revelation to the world.

The results of this discipline of the Jewish nation may be summed up in two points—a settled national belief in the unity and spirituality of God, and an acknowledgment of the paramount importance of chastity as a point of morals.

The conviction of the unity and spirituality of God was peculiar to the Jews among the pioneers of civilization. Greek philosophers had, no doubt, come to the same conclusion by dint of reason. Noble minds may often have been enabled to raise themselves to the same height in moments of generous emotion. But every one knows the difference between an opinion and a practical conviction—between a scientific deduction or a momentary insight and that habit which has become second nature. Every one, also, knows the difference between a tenet maintained by a few intellectual men far in advance of their age, and a belief pervading a whole people, penetrating all their daily life, leavening all their occupations, incorporated into their very language. To the great mass of the Gentiles, at the time of our Lord, polytheism was the natural posture of the thoughts into which their minds unconsciously settled when undisturbed by doubt or difficulties. To every Jew, without exception, monotheism was equally natural. To the Gentile, even when converted, it was, for some time, still an effort to abstain from idols; to the Jew it was no more an effort than it is to us. The bent of the Jewish mind was, in fact, so fixed by their previous

training that it would have required a perpetual and
difficult strain to enable a Jew to join in such folly.
We do not readily realize how hard this was to
acquire, because we have never had to acquire it : and
in reading the Old Testament we look on the repeated
idolatries of the chosen people as wilful backslidings
from an elementary truth within the reach of children,
rather than as stumblings in learning a very difficult
lesson—difficult even for cultivated men. In reality,
elementary truths are the hardest of all to learn, unless we pass our childhood in an atmosphere
thoroughly impregnated with them ; and then we
imbibe them unconsciously, and find it difficult to
perceive their difficulty.

It was the fact that this belief was not the tenet of
the few, but the habit of the nation, which made the
Jews the proper instruments for communicating the
doctrine to the world. They supported it, not by
arguments, which always provoke replies, and rarely,
at the best, penetrate deeper than the intellect; but
by the unconscious evidence of their lives. They
supplied that spiritual atmosphere in which alone the
faith of new converts could attain to vigorous life.
They supplied forms of language and expression fit
for immediate and constant use. They supplied devotions to fill the void which departed idolatry left behind. The rapid spread of the Primitive Church,
and the depth to which it struck its roots into the
decaying society of the Roman empire, are unquestionably due, to a great extent, to the body of Jewish
proselytes already established in every important
city, and to the existence of the Old Testament as a
ready-made text-book of devotion and instruction.

Side by side with this freedom from idolatry there
had grown up in the Jewish mind a chaster morality
than was to be found elsewhere in the world. There
were many points, undoubtedly, in which the early
morality of the Greeks and Romans would well bear

a comparison with that of the Hebrews. In simplicity of life, in gentleness of character, in warmth
of sympathy, in kindness to the poor, in justice to all
men, the Hebrews could not have rivalled the best
days of Greece. In reverence for law, in reality of obedience, in calmness under trouble, in dignity of self-
respect, they could not have rivalled the best days of
Rome. But the sins of the flesh corrupted both these
races, and the flower of their finest virtues had
withered before the time of our Lord. In chastity
the Hebrews stood alone ; and this virtue, which had
grown up with them from their earliest days, was
still in the vigour of fresh life when they were commissioned to give the Gospel to the nations. The
Hebrew morality has passed into the Christian
church, and sins of impurity (which war against the
soul) have ever since been looked on as the type of
all evil ; and our Litany selects them as the example
of deadly sin. What sort of morality the Gentiles
would have handed down to us, had they been left
to themselves, is clear from the Epistles. The excesses
of the Gentile party at Corinth (1 Cor. v. 2), the first
warning given to the Thessalonians (1 Thes. iv. 3),
the first warning given to the Galatians (Gal. v. 19),
the description of the Gentile world in the Epistle to
the Romans, are sufficient indications of the prevailing Gentile sin. But St. James, writing to the
Hebrew Christians, says not a word upon the subject,
and St. Peter barely alludes to it.

The idea of monotheism and the principle of
purity might seem hardly enough to be the chief
results of so systematic a discipline as that of the
Hebrews. But, in reality, they are the cardinal points
in education. The idea of monotheism outtops all
other ideas in dignity and worth. The spirituality of
God involves in it the supremacy of conscience, the
immortality of the soul, the final judgment of the
human race. For we know the other world, and can

only know it, by analogy, drawn from our own experience. With what, then, shall we compare God? With the spiritual or the fleshly part of our nature? On the answer depends the whole bent of our religion and of our morality. For that in ourselves which we choose as the nearest analogy of God, will, of course, be looked on as the ruling and lasting part of our being. If He be one and spiritual, then the spiritual power within us, which proclaims its own unity and independence of matter by the universality of its decrees, must be the rightful monarch of our lives; but if there be Gods many and Lords many, with bodily appetites and animal passions, then the voice of conscience is but one of those wide-spread delusions which, some for a longer, some for a shorter period, have, before now, misled our race. Again, the same importance which we assign to monotheism as a creed, we must assign to chastity as a virtue. Among all the vices which it is necessary to subdue in order to build up the human character, there is none to be compared in strength, or in virulence, with that of impurity. It can outlive and kill a thousand virtues; it can corrupt the most generous heart; it can madden the soberest intellect; it can debase the loftiest imagination. But, besides being so poisonous in character, it is above all others most difficult to conquer. And the people whose extraordinary toughness of nature has enabled it to outlive Egyptian Pharaohs, and Assyrian kings, and Roman Cæsars, and Mussulman caliphs, was well matched against a power of evil which has battled with the human spirit ever since the creation, and has inflicted, and may yet inflict, more deadly blows than any other power we know of.

Such was the training of the Hebrews. Other nations meanwhile had a training parallel to and contemporaneous with theirs. The natural religions, shadows projected by the spiritual light within shining on the dark problems without, were all in reality systems of Law, given also by God, though not given by revelation but by the working of nature, and consequently so distorted and adulterated that in lapse of time the divine element in them had almost perished. The poetical gods of Greece, the legendary gods of Rome, the animal worship of Egypt, the sun worship of the East, all accompanied by systems of law and civil government springing from the same sources as themselves, namely, the character and temper of the several nations, were the means of educating these people to similar purposes in the economy of Providence to that for which the Hebrews were destined.

When the seed of the Gospel was first sown, the field which had been prepared to receive it may be divided into four chief divisions, Rome, Greece, Asia, and Judea. Each of these contributed something to the growth of the future Church. And the growth of the Church is, in this case, the development of the human race. It cannot indeed yet be said that all humanity has united into one stream; but the Christian nations have so unquestionably taken the lead amongst their fellows, that although it is likely enough the unconverted peoples may have a real part to play, that part must be plainly quite subordinate; subordinate in a sense in which neither Rome, nor Greece, nor perhaps even Asia, was subordinate to Judea.

It is not difficult to trace the chief elements of civilization which we owe to each of the four. Rome contributed her admirable spirit of order and organization. To her had been given the genius of government. She had been trained to it by centuries of difficult and tumultuous history. Storms which would have rent asunder the framework of any other polity only practised her in the art of controlling popular passions; and when she began to aim consciously at the Empire of the World, she had already learned her lesson. She had learned it as the Hebrews had learned theirs, by an enforced obedience to her own system. In no nation of antiquity had civil officers the same unquestioned authority during their term of office, or laws and judicial rules the same reverence. That which religion was to the Jew, including even the formalism which encrusted and fettered it, law was to the Roman. And law was the lesson which Rome was intended to teach the world. Hence the Bishop of Rome soon became the Head of the Church. Rome was, in fact, the centre of the traditions which had once governed the world; and their spirit still remained; and the Roman Church developed into the papacy simply because a head was wanted, and no better one could be found. Hence again in all the doctrinal disputes of the fourth and fifth centuries the decisive voice came from Rome. Every controversy was finally settled by her opinion, because she alone possessed the art of framing formulas which could hold together in any reasonable measure the endless variety of sentiments and feelings which the Church by that time comprised. It was this power of administering law which enabled the Western Church, in the time of Charlemagne, to undertake, by means of her bishops, the task of training and civilizing the new population of Europe. To Rome we owe the forms of local government which in England have saved liberty and elsewhere have mitigated despotism. Justinian's laws have penetrated into all modern legislation, and almost all improvements bring us only nearer to his code. Much of the spirit of modern politics came from Greece; much from the woods of Germany. But the skeleton and framework is almost entirely Roman. And it is not this framework only that comes from Rome. The moral sentiments and the moral force which lie at the back of all political life and are absolutely indispensable to its vigour are in great measure Roman too. It is true that the life and power of all

morality whatever will always be drawn from the New
Testament; yet it is in the history of Rome rather
than in the Bible that we find our models and precepts of political duty, and especially of the duty of
patriotism. St. Paul bids us follow whatsoever things
are lovely, whatsoever things are of good report. But
except through such general appeals to natural feeling
it would be difficult to prove from the New Testament
that cowardice was not only disgraceful but sinful,
and that love of our country was an exalted duty of
humanity. That lesson our consciences have learnt
from the teaching of Ancient Rome.

To Greece was entrusted the cultivation of the
reason and the taste. Her gift to mankind has
been science and art. There was little in her temper
of the spirit of reverence. Her morality and her
religion did not spring from the conscience. Her
gods were the creatures of imagination, not of spiritual
need. Her highest idea was, not holiness, as with the
Hebrews, nor law, as with the Romans, but beauty.
Even Aristotle, who assuredly gave way to mere
sentiment as little as any Greek that ever lived,
placed the Beautiful (τὸ καλόν) at the head of his moral
system, not the Right, nor the Holy. Greece, in fact,
was not looking at another world, nor even striving
to organize the present, but rather aiming at the
development of free nature. The highest possible
cultivation of the individual, the most finished perfection of the natural faculties, was her dream. It is
true that her philosophers are ever talking of subordinating the individual to the state. But in reality
there never has been a period in history nor a country
in the world, in which the peculiarities of individual
temper and character had freer play. This is not the
best atmosphere for political action; but it is better
than any other for giving vigour and life to the impulses of genius, and for cultivating those faculties, the
reason and taste, in which the highest genius can be

c

shown. Such a cultivation needs discipline less than any. And of all the nations Greece had the least of systematic discipline, least of instinctive deference to any one leading idea. But for the same reason the cultivation required less time than any other ; and the national life of Greece is the shortest of all. Greek history hardly begins before Solon, and it hardly continues after Alexander, barely covering 200 years. But its fruits are eternal. To the Greeks we owe the logic which has ruled the minds of all thinkers since. All our natural and physical science really begins with the Greeks, and indeed would have been impossible had not Greece taught men how to reason. To the Greeks we owe the corrective which conscience needs to borrow from nature. Conscience, startled at the awful truths which she has to reveal, too often threatens to withdraw the soul into gloomy and perverse asceticism : then is needed the beauty which Greece taught us to admire, to show us another aspect of the Divine Attributes. To the Greeks we owe all modern literature. For though there is other literature even older than the Greek, the Asiatic for instance, and the Hebrew, yet we did not learn this lesson from them ; they had not the genial life which was needed to kindle other nations with the communication of their own fire.

The discipline of Asia was the never-ending succession of conquering dynasties, following in each other's track like waves, an ever moving yet never advancing ocean. Cycles of change were successively passing over her, and yet at the end of every cycle she stood where she had stood before, and nearly where she stands now. The growth of Europe has dwarfed her in comparison, and she is paralysed in presence of a gigantic strength younger but mightier than her own. But in herself she is no weaker than she ever was. The monarchs who once led Assyrian, or Babylonian, or Persian armies across half the world, impose on us by the vast extent and rapidity of their conquests; but these conquests had in reality no substance, no inherent strength. This perpetual baffling of all earthly progress taught Asia to seek her inspiration in rest. She learned to fix her thoughts upon another world, and was disciplined to check by her silent protest the over-earthly, over-practical tendency of the Western nations. She was ever the one to refuse to measure Heaven by the standard of earth. Her teeming imagination filled the church with thoughts 'undreamt of in our philosophy.' She had been the instrument selected to teach the Hebrews the doctrine of the Immortality of the Soul; for whatever may be said of the early notions on this subject, it is unquestionable that in Babylon the Jews first attained the clearness and certainty in regard to it which we find in the teaching of the Pharisees. So again, Athanasius, a thorough Asiatic in sentiment and in mode of arguing, was the bulwark of the doctrine of the Trinity. The Western nations are always tempted to make reason not only supreme, but despotic, and dislike to acknowledge mysteries even in religion. They are inclined to confine all doctrines within the limits of spiritual utility, and to refuse to listen to dim voices and whispers from within, those instincts of doubt, and reverence, and awe, which yet are, in their place and degree, messages from the depths of our being. Asia supplies the corrective by perpetually leaning to the mysterious. When left to herself, she settles down to baseless dreams, and sometimes to monstrous and revolting fictions. But her influence has never ceased to be felt, and could not be lost without serious damage.

Thus the Hebrews may be said to have disciplined the human conscience, Rome the human will, Greece the reason and taste, Asia the spiritual imagination. Other races that have been since admitted into Christendom also did their parts. And others may yet have something to contribute; for though the time for discipline is childhood, yet there is no precise line beyond which all discipline ceases. Even the grey-haired man has yet some small capacity for learning like a child; and even in the maturity of the world the early modes of teaching may yet find a place. But the childhood of the world was over when our Lord appeared on earth. The tutors and governors had done their work. It was time that the second teacher of the human race should begin his labour. The second teacher is Example.

The child is not insensible to the influence of example. Even in the earliest years the manners, the language, the principles of the elder begin to mould the character of the younger. There are not a few of our acquirements which we learn by example without any, or with very little, direct instruction—as, for instance, to speak and to walk. But still example at that age is secondary. The child is quite conscious that he is not on such an equality with grown-up friends as to enable him to do as they do. He imitates, but he knows that it is merely play, and he is quite willing to be told that he must not do this or that till he is older. As time goes on, and the faculties expand, the power of discipline to guide the actions and to mould the character decreases, and in the same proportion the power of example grows. The moral atmosphere must be brutish indeed which can do deep harm to a child of four years. But what is harmless at four is pernicious at six, and almost fatal at twelve. The religious tone of a household will hardly make much impression on an infant; but it will deeply engrave its lessons on the heart of a boy growing towards manhood. Different faculties within us begin to feel the power of this new guide at different times. The moral sentiments are perhaps the first to expand to the influence; but gradually the example of those among whom the life is cast lays hold of all the soul,— of the tastes, of the opinions, of the aims, of the temper. As each restraint of discipline is successively cast off, the soul does not gain at first a real, but only an apparent freedom. The youth, when too old for discipline, is not yet strong enough to guide his life by fixed principles. He is led by his emotions and impulses. He admires and loves, he condemns and dislikes, with enthusiasm. And his love and admiration, his disapproval and dislike, are not his own, but borrowed from his society. He can appreciate a character, though he cannot yet appreciate a principle. He cannot walk by reason and conscience alone; he still needs those 'supplies to the imperfection of our nature' which are given by the higher passions. He cannot follow what his heart does not love as well as his reason approve; and he cannot love what is presented to him as an abstract rule of life, but requires a living person. He needs to see virtue in the concrete, before he can recognise her aspect as a divine idea. He instinctively copies those whom he admires, and in doing so imbibes whatever gives the colour to their character. He repeats opinions without really understanding them, and in that way admits their infection into his judgment. He acquires habits which seem of no consequence, but which are the channels of a thousand new impulses to his soul. If he reads, he treats the characters that he meets with in his book as friends or enemies, and so unconsciously allows them to mould his soul. When he seems most independent, most defiant of external guidance, he is in reality only so much the less master of himself, only so much the more guided and formed, not indeed by the will, but by the example and sympathy of others.

The power of example probably never ceases during life. Even old age is not wholly uninfluenced by society; and a change of companions acts upon the character long after the character would appear incapable of further development. The influence, in fact, dies out just as it grew; and as it is impossible to mark its beginning, so is it to mark its end. The child is governed by the will of its parents; the man by principles and habits of his own. But neither is insensible to the influence of associates, though neither finds in that influence the predominant power of his life.

This, then, which is born with our birth and dies with our death, attains its maximum at some point in the passage from one to the other. And this point is just the meeting point of the child and the man, the brief interval which separates restraint from liberty. Young men at this period are learning a peculiar lesson. They seem to those who talk to them to be imbibing from their associates and their studies principles both of faith and conduct. But the rapid fluctuations of their minds show that their opinions have not really the nature of principles. They are really learning, not principles, but the materials out of which principles are made. They drink in the lessons of generous impulse, warm unselfishness, courage, self-devotion, romantic disregard of worldly calculations, without knowing what are the grounds of their own approbation, or caring to analyse the laws and ascertain the limits of such guides of conduct. They believe, without exact attention to the evidence of their belief; and their opinions have accordingly the richness and warmth that belongs to sentiment, but not the clearness or firmness that can be given by reason. These affections, which are now kindled in their hearts by the contact of their fellows, will afterwards be the reservoir of life and light, with which their faith and their highest conceptions will be animated and coloured. The opinions now picked up, apparently not really, at random, must hereafter give reality to the clearer and more settled convictions of mature manhood. If it were not for these, the ideas and laws afterwards supplied by reason would be empty forms of thought, without body or substance; the faith would run a risk of being the form of godliness without the power thereof. And hence the lessons of this time have such an attractiveness in their warmth and life, that they are very reluctantly exchanged for the truer and profounder, but at first sight colder wisdom which is destined to follow them. To almost all men this period is a bright spot to which the memory ever afterwards loves to recur; and even those who can remember nothing but folly—folly too which they have repented and relinquished—yet find a nameless charm in recalling such folly as that. For indeed even folly itself at this age is sometimes the cup out of which men quaff the richest blessings of our nature—simplicity, generosity, affection. This is the seed time of the soul's harvest, and contains the promise of the year. It is the time for love and marriage, the time for forming life-long friendships. The after life may be more contented, but can rarely be so glad and joyous. Two things we need to crown its blessings—one is, that the friends whom we then learn to love, and the opinions which we then learn to cherish, may stand the test of time, and deserve the esteem and approval of calmer thoughts and wider experience; the other, that our hearts may have depth enough to drink largely of that which God is holding to our lips, and never again to lose the fire and spirit of the draught. There is nothing more beautiful than a manhood surrounded by the friends, upholding the principles, and filled with the energy of the spring-time of life. But even if these highest blessings be denied, if we have been compelled to change opinions, and to give up friends, and the cold experience of the world has extinguished the heat of youth, still the heart will instinctively recur to that happy time, to explain to itself what is meant by love and what by happiness.

Of course, this is only one side of the picture. This keen susceptibility to pleasure and joy implies a keen susceptibility to pain. There is, probably, no time of life at which pains are more intensely felt; no time at which the whole man more 'groaneth and travaileth in pain together.' Young men are prone to extreme melancholy, even to disgust with life. A young preacher will preach upon afflictions much more often than an old one. A young poet will write more sadly. A young philosopher will moralize more gloomily. And this seems unreal sentiment, and is

smiled at in after years.    But it is real at the time;
and, perhaps, is nearer the truth at all times than the
contentedness of those who ridicule it.    Youth, in
fact, feels everything more keenly; and as far as the
keenness of feeling contributes to its truth, the feeling,
whether it is pain or pleasure, is so much the truer.
But in after life it is the happiness, not the suffering
of youth, that most often returns to the memory, and
seems to gild all the past.

The period of youth in the history of the world,
when the human race was, as it were, put under the
teaching of example, corresponds, of course, to the
meeting point of the Law and the Gospel.    The
second stage, therefore, in the education of man was
the presence of our Lord upon earth.    Those few
years of His divine presence seem, as it were, to
balance all the systems and creeds and worships which
preceded, all the Church's life which has followed since.
Saints had gone before, and saints have been given
since; great men and good men had lived among the
heathen; there were never, at any time, examples
wanting to teach either the chosen people or any
other.    But the one Example of all examples came in
the ' fulness of time,' just when the world was fitted to
feel the power of His presence.    Had His revelation
been delayed till now, assuredly it would have been
hard for us to recognise His Divinity; for the faculty
of Faith has turned inwards, and cannot now accept
any outer manifestations of the truth of God.    Our
vision of the Son of God is now aided by the eyes
of the Apostles, and by that aid we can recognise the
Express Image of the Father.    But in this we are
like men who are led through unknown woods by
Indian guides.    We recognise the indications by
which the path was known, as soon as those indications are pointed out; but we feel that it would have
been quite vain for us to look for them unaided.    We,
of course, have, in our turn, counterbalancing advantages.    If we have lost that freshness of faith which

would be the first to say to a poor carpenter—Thou
art the Christ, the Son of the Living God—yet we
possess, in the greater cultivation of our religious understanding, that which, perhaps, we ought not to be
willing to give in exchange. The early Christians
could recognise, more readily than we, the greatness
and beauty of the Example set before them ; but it is
not too much to say, that we know better than they
the precise outlines of the truth. To every age is given
by God its own proper gift. They had not the same
clearness of understanding as we ; the same recognition that it is God and not the devil who rules
the world ; the same power of discrimination between
different kinds of truth ; they had not the same calmness, or fixedness of conduct ; their faith was not so
quiet, so little tempted to restless vehemence. But
they had a keenness of perception which we have not,
and could see the immeasurable difference between
our Lord and all other men as we could never have
seen it. Had our Lord come later, He would have
come to mankind already beginning to stiffen into the
fixedness of maturity. The power of His life would
not have sunk so deeply into the world's heart ; the
truth of His Divine Nature would not have been
recognised. Seeing the Lord, would not have been
the title to Apostleship. On the other hand, had our
Lord come earlier, the world would not have been
ready to receive Him, and the Gospel, instead of being
the religion of the human race, would have been the
religion of the Hebrews only. The other systems
would have been too strong to be overthrown by the
power of preaching. The need of a higher and purer
teaching would not have been felt. Christ would have
seemed to the Gentiles the Jewish Messiah, not the
Son of Man. But He came in the 'fulness of time,'
for which all history had been preparing, to which all
history since has been looking back. Hence the first
and largest place in the New Testament is assigned to
His Life four times told. This life we emphatically

call the Gospel. If there is little herein to be technically called doctrine, yet here is the fountain of all
inspiration. There is no Christian who would not
rather part with all the rest of the Bible than with
these four Books. There is no part of God's Word
which the religious man more instinctively remembers.
The Sermon on the Mount, the Parables and the Miracles, the Last Supper, the Mount of Olives, the Garden
of Gethsemane, the Cross on Calvary—these are the
companions alike of infancy and of old age, simple
enough to be read with awe and wonder by the one,
profound enough to open new depths of wisdom to
the fullest experience of the other.

Our Lord was the Example of mankind, and there
can be no other example in the same sense. But the
whole period from the closing of the Old Testament to
the close of the New was the period of the world's
youth—the age of examples ; and our Lord's presence
was not the only influence of that kind which has
acted upon the human race. Three companions were
appointed by Providence to give their society to this
creature whom God was educating; Greece, Rome,
and the Early Church. To these three mankind has
ever since looked back, and will ever hereafter look
back, with the same affection, the same lingering regret, with which age looks back to early manhood. In
these three mankind remembers the brilliant social
companion whose wit and fancy sharpened the intellect and refined the imagination ; the bold and clever
leader with whom to dare was to do, and whose very
name was a signal of success; and the earnest, heavenly-
minded friend, whose saintly aspect was a revelation
in itself.

Greece and Rome have not only given to us the
fruits of their discipline, but the companionship of
their bloom. The fruits of their discipline would
have passed into our possession, even if their memory
had utterly perished; and just as we know not the

man who first discovered arithmetic, nor the man who first invented writing—benefactors with whom no other captains of science can ever be compared—so, too, it is probable that we inherit from many a race, whose name we shall never hear again, fruits of long training now forgotten. But Greece and Rome have given us more than any results of discipline in the never-dying memory of their fresh and youthful life. It is this, and not only the greatness or the genius of the classical writers, which makes their literature pre-eminent above all others. There have been great poets, great historians, great philosophers in modern days. Greece can show few poets equal, none superior, to Shakspeare. Gibbon, in many respects, stands above all ancient historians. Bacon was as great a master of philosophy as Aristotle. Nor, again, are there wanting great writers of times older, as well as of times later, than the Greek, as, for instance, the Hebrew prophets. But the classics possess a charm quite independent of genius. It is not their genius only which makes them attractive. It is the classic life, the life of the people of that day. It is the image, there only to be seen, of our highest natural powers in their freshest vigour. It is the unattainable grace of the prime of manhood. It is the pervading sense of youthful beauty. Hence, while we have elsewhere great poems and great histories, we never find again that universal radiance of fresh life which makes even the most commonplace relics of classic days models for our highest art. The common workman of those times breathed the atmosphere of the gods. What are now the ornaments of our museums were then the every-day furniture of sitting and sleeping rooms. In the great monuments of their literature we can taste this pure inspiration most largely; but even the most commonplace fragments of a classic writer are steeped in the waters of the same fountain. Those who compare the moderns with the ancients, genius for genius, have no difficulty in claiming for the former equality, if not victory. But the issue is mistaken. To combine the highest powers of intellect with the freshness of youth was possible only once, and that is the glory of the classic nations. The inspiration which is drawn by the man from the memory of those whom he loved and admired in the spring-time of his life, is drawn by the world now from the study of Greece and Rome. The world goes back to its youth in hopes to become young again, and delights to dwell on the feats achieved by the companions of those days. Beneath whatever was wrong and foolish it recognises that beauty of a fresh nature which never ceases to delight. And the sins and vices of that joyous time are passed over with the levity with which men think of their young companions' follies.

The Early Church stands as the example which has most influenced our religious life, as Greece and Rome have most influenced our political and intellectual life. We read the New Testament, not to find there forms of devotion, for there are few to be found ; nor laws of church government, for there are hardly any ; nor creeds, for there are none ; nor doctrines logically stated, for there is no attempt at logical precision. The New Testament is almost entirely occupied with two lives—the life of our Lord and the life of the Early Church. Among the Epistles there are but two which seem, even at first sight, to be treatises for the future instead of letters for the time—the Epistle to the Romans and the Epistle to the Hebrews. But even these, when closely examined, appear, like the rest, to be no more than the fruit of the current history. That early church does not give us precepts, but an example. She says, Be ye followers of me, as I also am of Christ. This had never been said by Moses, nor by any of the prophets. But the world was now grown old enough to be taught by seeing

the lives of saints, better than by hearing the words
of prophets. When afterwards Christians needed
creeds, and liturgies, and forms of church government and systems of theology, they could not find
them in the New Testament. They found there only
the materials out of which such needs could be supplied. But the combination and selection of those
materials they had to provide for themselves. In
fact, the work which the early church had to do was
peculiar. Her circumstances were still more peculiar.
Had she legislated peremptorily for posterity, her
legislation must have been set aside, as, indeed, the
prohibition to eat things strangled and to eat blood
has been already set aside. But her example will live
and teach for ever. In her we learn what is meant
by zeal, what by love of God, what by joy in the
Holy Ghost, what by endurance for the sake of Christ.
For the very purpose of giving us a pattern, the chief
features in her character are, as it were, magnified
into colossal proportions. Our saints must chiefly be
the saints of domestic life, the brightness of whose
light is visible to very few. But their saintliness was
forced into publicity, and its radiance illumines the
earth. So on every page of the New Testament is
written, Go and do thou likewise. Transplant into
your modern life the same heavenly-mindedness, the
same fervour of love, the same unshaken faith, the
same devotion to your fellow-men. And to these
pages accordingly the church of our day turns for
renewal of inspiration. We even busy ourselves
in tracing the details of the early Christian life, and
we love to find that any practice of ours comes down
from apostolic times. This is an exaggeration. It is
not really following the early church, to be servile
copyists of her practices. We are not commanded to
have all things in common, because the church of
Jerusalem once had ; nor are we to make every supper
a sacrament, because the early Christians did so. To

copy the early church is to do as she did, not what
she did. Yet the very exaggeration is a testimony
of the power which that church has over us. We
would fain imitate even her outward actions as a step
towards imitating her inner life. Her outward actions
were not meant for our model. She, too, had her
faults: disorders, violent quarrels, licentious recklessness of opinion, in regard both to faith and practice.
But these spots altogether disappear in the blaze of light
which streams upon us when we look back towards
her. Nay, we are impatient of being reminded that
she had faults at all. So much does her youthful
holiness surpass all that we can show, that he who
can see her faults seems necessarily insensible to the
brightness of her glory. There have been great saints
since the days of the apostles. Holiness is as possible
now as it was then. But the saintliness of that time
had a peculiar beauty which we cannot copy; a
beauty not confined to the apostles or great leaders,
but pervading the whole church. It is not what they
endured, nor the virtues which they practised, that so
dazzle us. It is the perfect simplicity of the religious
life, the singleness of heart, the openness, the child-
like earnestness. All else has been repeated since,
but this never. And this makes the religious man's
heart turn back with longing to that blessed time
when the Lord's service was the highest of all
delights, and every act of worship came fresh from
the soul. If we compare degrees of devotion, it may
be reckoned something intrinsically nobler, to serve
God and love Him now when religion is colder than
it was, and when we have not the aid of those thril-
ling, heart-stirring sympathies which blessed the early
church. But even if our devotion be sometimes
nobler in itself, yet theirs still remains the more beautiful, the more attractive. Ours may have its own place
in the sight of God, but theirs remains the irresistible
example which kindles all other hearts by its fire.

It is nothing against the drift of this argument, that the three friends whose companionship is most deeply engraven on the memory of the world were no friends one to another. This was the lot of mankind, as it is the lot of not a few men. Greece, the child of nature, had come to full maturity so early as to pass away before the other two appeared; and Rome and the Early Church disliked each other. Yet that dislike makes little impression on us now. We never identify the Rome of our admiration with the Rome which persecuted the Christian, partly, indeed, because the Rome that we admire was almost gone before the church was founded; but partly, too, because we forget each of these while we are studying the other. We almost make two persons of Trajan, accordingly as we meet with him in sacred or profane history. So natural is it to forget in after life the faulty side of young friends' characters.

The susceptibility of youth to the impression of society wears off at last. The age of reflection begins. From the storehouse of his youthful experience the man begins to draw the principles of his life. The spirit or conscience comes to full strength and assumes the throne intended for him in the soul. As an accredited judge, invested with full powers, he sits in the tribunal of our inner kingdom, decides upon the past, and legislates upon the future without appeal except to himself. He decides not by what is beautiful, or noble, or soul-inspiring, but by what is right. Gradually he frames his code of laws, revising, adding, abrogating, as a wider and deeper experience gives him clearer light. He is the third great teacher and the last.

Now the education by no means ceases when the spirit thus begins to lead the soul; the office of the spirit is in fact to guide us into truth, not to give truth. The youth who has settled down to his life's work makes a great mistake if he fancies that because he is no more under teachers and governors his education is therefore at an end. It is only changed in form. He has much, very much, to learn, more perhaps than all which he has yet learned; and his new teacher will not give it to him all at once. The lesson of life is in this respect like the lessons whereby we learn any ordinary business. The barrister, who has filled his memory with legal forms and imbued his mind with their spirit, knows that the most valuable part of his education is yet to be obtained in attending the courts of law. The physician is not content with the theories of the lecture-room, nor with the experiments of the laboratory, nor even with the attendance at the hospitals; he knows that independent practice, when he will be thrown upon his own resources, will open his eyes to much which at present he sees through a glass darkly. In every profession, after the principles are apparently mastered, there yet remains much to be learnt from the application of those principles to practice, the only means by which we ever understand principles to the bottom. So too with the lesson which includes all others, the lesson of life.

In this last stage of his progress a man learns in various ways. First he learns unconsciously by the growth of his inner powers and the secret but steady accumulation of experience. The fire of youth is toned down and sobered. The realities of life dissipate many dreams, clear up many prejudices, soften down many roughnesses. The difference between intention and action, between anticipating temptation and bearing it, between drawing pictures of holiness or nobleness and realizing them, between hopes of success and reality of achievement, is taught by many a painful and many an unexpected experience. In short, as the youth puts away childish things, so does the man put away youthful things. Secondly, the full-grown man learns by reflection. He looks inwards

and not outwards only. He re-arranges the results of
past experience, re-examines by the test of reality the
principles supplied to him by books or conversation,
reduces to intelligible and practical formulas what he
has hitherto known as vague general rules. He not
only generalizes—youth will generalize with great
rapidity and often with great acuteness—but he learns
to correct one generalization by another. He gradually learns to disentangle his own thoughts, so as not
to be led into foolish inconsistency by want of clearness of purpose. He learns to distinguish between
momentary impulses and permanent determinations
of character. He learns to know the limits of his
own powers, moral and intellectual; and by slow
degrees and with much reluctance he learns to sus-
pend his judgment and to be content with ignorance
where knowledge is beyond his reach. He learns to
know himself and other men, and to distinguish in
some measure his own peculiarities from the leading
features of humanity which he shares with all men. He
learns to know both the worth and the worthlessness of
the world's judgment and of his own. Thirdly, he
learns much by mistakes, both by his own and by those
of others. He often persists in a wrong cause till it is
too late to mend what he has done, and he learns how
to use it and how to bear it. His principles, or what he
thought his principles, break down under him, and he
is forced to analyse them in order to discover what
amount of truth they really contain. He comes upon
new and quite unexpected issues of what he has done
or said, and he has to profit by such warnings as he
receives. His errors often force him, as it were, to go
back to school; not now with the happy docility of a
child, but with the chastened submission of a penitent.
Or, more often still, his mistakes inflict a sharp chastise-
ment which teaches him a new lesson without much
effort on his own part to learn. Lastly, he learns much
by contradiction. The collision of society compels him

to state his opinions clearly; to defend them; to modify
them when indefensible; perhaps to surrender them
altogether, consciously or unconsciously; still more
often to absorb them into larger and fuller thoughts,
less forcible but more comprehensive. The precision
which is thus often forced upon him always seems to
diminish something of the heartiness and power which
belonged to more youthful instincts. But he gains
in directness of aim, and therefore in firmness of resolution. But the greatest of his gains is what seems
a loss: for he learns not to attempt the solution of
insoluble problems, and to have no opinion at all on
many points of the deepest interest. Usually this
takes the form of an abandonment of speculation;
but it may rise to the level of a philosophical humility which stops where it can advance no further, and
confesses its own weakness in the presence of the mysteries of life.

But throughout all this it must not be supposed
that he has no more to do either with that law which
guided his childhood or with any other law of any
kind. Since he is still a learner, he must learn on the
one condition of all learning—obedience to rules; not
indeed, blind obedience to rules not understood, but
obedience to the rules of his own mind—an obedience
which he cannot throw off without descending below
the childish level. He is free. But freedom is not
the opposite of obedience, but of restraint. The free-
man must obey, and obey as precisely as the bond-
man; and if he has not acquired the habit of obedience
he is not fit to be free. The law in fact which God
makes the standard of our conduct may have one of
two forms. It may be an external law, a law which is
in the hands of others, in the making, in the applying, in the enforcing of which we have no share; a
law which governs from the outside, compelling our
will to bow even though our understanding be un-
convinced and unenlightened; saying you must, and

making no effort to make you feel that you ought; appealing not to your conscience, but to force or fear, and caring little whether you willingly agree or reluctantly submit. Or, again, the law may be an internal law; a voice which speaks within the conscience, and carries the understanding along with it; a law which treats us not as slaves but as friends, allowing us to know what our Lord doeth; a law which bids us yield not to blind fear or awe, but to the majesty of truth and justice; a law which is not imposed on us by another power, but by our own enlightened will. Now the first of these is the law which governs and educates the child; the second the law which governs and educates the man. The second is in reality the spirit of the first. It commands in a different way, but with a tone not one whit less peremptory; and he only who can control all appetites and passions in obedience to it can reap the full harvest of the last and highest education.

This need of law in the full maturity of life is so imperative that if the requisite self-control be lost or impaired, or have never been sufficiently acquired, the man instinctively has recourse to a self-imposed discipline if he desire to keep himself from falling. The Christian who has fallen into sinful habits often finds that he has no resource but to abstain from much that is harmless in itself because he has associated it with evil. He takes monastic vows because the world has proved too much for him. He takes temperance pledges because he cannot resist the temptations of appetite. There are devils which can be cast out with a word; there are others which go not out but by (not prayer only, but) fasting. This is often the case with the late converted. They are compelled to abstain from, and sometimes they are induced to denounce, many pleasures and many enjoyments which they find unsuited to their spiritual health. The world and its enjoyments have been to them a source of perpetual temptation, and they cannot conceive any religious life within such a circle of evil. Sometimes these men are truly spiritual enough and humble enough to recognise that this discipline is not essential in itself, but only for them and for such as they. The discipline is then truly subordinate. It is an instrument in the hands of their conscience. They know what they are doing and why they do it. But sometimes, if they are weak, this discipline assumes the shape of a regular external law. They look upon many harmless things, from which they have suffered mischief as absolutely, not relatively, hurtful. They denounce what they cannot share without danger, as dangerous, not only for them, but for all mankind, and as evil in itself. They set up a conventional code of duty founded on their own experience which they extend to all men. Even if they are educated enough to see that no conventional code is intellectually tenable, yet they still maintain their system, and defend it, as not necessary in itself, but necessary for sinful men. The fact is, that a merciful Providence, in order to help such men, puts them back under the dominion of the law. They are not aware of it themselves—men who are under the dominion of the law rarely are aware of it. But even if they could appeal to a revelation from heaven, they would still be under the law; for a revelation speaking from without and not from within is an external law and not a spirit.

For the same reason a strict and even severe discipline is needed for the cure of reprobates. Philanthropists complain sometimes that this teaching ends only in making the man say, 'the punishment of crime is what I cannot bear;' not, 'the wickedness of crime is what I will not do.' But our nature is not all will: and the fear of punishment is very often the foundation on which we build the hatred of evil. No convert would look back with any other feeling than deep gratitude on a severity which had set free his spirit by chaining down his grosser appetites.  It is true that the teaching of mere discipline, if there be no other teaching, is useless.  If you have *only* killed one selfish principle by another you have done nothing.  But if while thus killing one selfish prin-ciple by another you have also succeeded in awaking the higher faculty and giving it free power of self-exertion, you have done everything.

This return to the teaching of discipline in mature life is needed for the intellect even more than for the conduct.  There are many men who though they pass from the teaching of the outer law to that of the inner in regard to their practical life, never emerge from the former in regard to their speculative. They do not think; they are contented to let others think for them and to accept the results.  How far the average of men are from having attained the power of free independent thought is shown by the stagger-ing and stumbling of their intellects when a completely new subject of investigation tempts them to form a judgment of their own on a matter which they have not studied.  In such cases a really educated intel-lect sees at once that no judgment is yet within its reach, and acquiesces in suspense.  But the unedu-cated intellect hastens to account for the phenomenon ; to discover new laws of nature, and new relations of truth; to decide, and predict, and perhaps to demand a remodelling of all previous knowledge.  The dis-cussions on table-turning a few years ago, illustrated this want of intellects able to govern themselves. The whole analogy of physical science was not enough to induce that suspension of judgment which was effected in a week by the dictum of a known philo-sopher.

There are, however, some men who really think for themselves.  But even they are sometimes obliged, especially if their speculations touch upon practical life, to put a temporary restraint upon their intellects.

They refuse to speculate at all in directions where they cannot feel sure of preserving their own balance of mind. If the conclusions at which they seem likely to arrive are very strange, or very unlike the general analogy of truth, or carry important practical consequences, they will pause, and turn to some other subject, and try whether if they come back with fresh minds they still come to the same results. And this may go further, and they may find such speculations so bewildering and so unsatisfactory, that they finally take refuge in a refusal to think any more on the particular questions. They content themselves with so much of truth as they find necessary for their spiritual life; and, though perfectly aware that the wheat may be mixed with tares, they despair of rooting up the tares with safety to the wheat, and therefore let both grow together till the harvest. All this is justifiable in the same way that any self-discipline is justifiable. That is, it is justifiable if really necessary. But as is always the case with those who are under the law, such men are sometimes tempted to prescribe for others what they need for themselves, and to require that no others should speculate because they dare not. They not only refuse to think, and accept other men's thoughts, which is often quite right, but they elevate those into canons of faith for all men, which is not right. This blindness is of course wrong; but in reality it is a blindness of the same kind as that with which the Hebrews clung to their law; a blindness, provided for them in mercy, to save their intellects from leading them into mischief.

Some men, on the other hand, show their want of intellectual self-control by going back not to the dominion of law, but to the still lower level of intellectual anarchy. They speculate without any foundation at all. They confound the internal consistency of some dream of their brains with the reality of independent truth. They set up theories which have

no other evidence than compatibility with the few facts
that happen to be known ; and forget that many other
theories of equal claims might readily be invented.
They are as little able to be content with having no
judgment at all as those who accept judgments at
second hand.   They never practically realize that
when there is not enough evidence to justify a conclusion, it is wisdom to draw no conclusion.   They
are so eager for light that they will rub their eyes in
the dark and take the resulting optical delusions for
real flashes.   They need intellectual discipline—but
they have little chance of getting it, for they have
burst its bands.

There is yet a further relation between the inner
law of mature life and the outer law of childhood
which must be noticed.   And that is, that the outer
law is often the best vehicle in which the inner law
can be contained for the various purposes of life.
The man remembers with affection, and keeps up
with delight the customs of the home of his childhood ; tempted perhaps to over-estimate their value,
but even when perfectly aware that they are no more
than one form out of many which a well-ordered
household might adopt, preferring them because of
his long familiarity, and because of the memories with
which they are associated.   So, too, truth often seems to
him richer and fuller when expressed in some favourite
phrase of his mother's, or some maxim of his father's.
He can give no better reason very often for much that
he does every day of his life than that his father did
it before him ; and provided the custom is not a
bad one the reason is valid.   And he likes to go to
the same church.   He likes to use the same prayers.
He likes to keep up the same festivities.   There are
limits to all this.   But no man is quite free from the
influence ; and it is in many cases, perhaps in most,
an influence of the highest moral value.   There is
great value in the removal of many indifferent matters

out of the region of discussion into that of precedent.
There is greater value still in the link of sympathy
which binds the present with the past, and fills old
age with the fresh feelings of childhood.  If truth
sometimes suffers in form, it unquestionably gains
much in power ; and if its onward progress is retarded,
it gains immeasurably in solidity and in its hold on
men's hearts.

Such is the last stage in the education of a human
soul, and similar (as far as it has yet gone) has been
the last stage in the education of the human race.
Of course, so full a comparison cannot be made in this
instance as was possible in the two that preceded it.
For we are still within the boundaries of this third
period, and we cannot yet judge it as a whole.  But
if the Christian Church be taken as the representative
of mankind it is easy to see that the general law observable in the development of the individual may also
be found in the development of the Church.

Since the days of the Apostles no further revelation
has been granted, nor has any other system of religion
sprung up spontaneously within the limits which the
Church has covered.  No prophets have communicated messages from Heaven.  No infallible inspiration has guided any teacher or preacher.  The claim
of infallibility still maintained by a portion of Christendom has been entirely given up by the more
advanced section.  The Church, in the fullest sense,
is left to herself to work out, by her natural faculties,
the principles of her own action.  And whatever
assistance she is to receive in doing so, is to be through
those natural faculties, and not in spite of them or
without them.

From the very first, the Church commenced the
task by determining her leading doctrines and the
principles of her conduct.  These were evolved, as
principles usually are, partly by reflection on past experience, and by formularizing the thoughts embodied

in the record of the Church of the Apostles, partly by
perpetual collision with every variety of opinion.
This career of dogmatism in the Church was, in many
ways, similar to the hasty generalizations of early
manhood. The principle on which the controversies
of those days were conducted is that of giving an
answer to every imaginable question. It rarely
seems to occur to the early controversialists that there
are questions which even the Church cannot solve—
problems which not even revelation has brought within
the reach of human faculties. That the decisions
were right, on the whole—that is, that they always
embodied, if they did not always rightly define, the
truth—is proved by the permanent vitality of the
Church as compared with the various heretical bodies
that broke from her. But the fact that so vast a
number of the early decisions are practically obsolete,
and that even many of the doctrinal statements are
plainly unfitted for permanent use, is a proof that the
Church was not capable, any more than a man is
capable, of extracting, at once, all the truth and wisdom contained in the teaching of the earlier periods.
In fact, the Church of the Fathers claimed to do what
not even the Apostles had claimed—namely, not only
to teach the truth, but to clothe it in logical statements, and that not merely as opposed to then prevailing heresies (which was justifiable), but for all
succeeding time. Yet this was, after all, only an
exaggeration of the proper function of the time.
Those logical statements were necessary. And it
belongs to a later epoch to see ' the law within the law'
which absorbs such statements into something higher
than themselves.

Before this process can be said to have worked itself
out, it was interrupted by a new phenomenon, demanding essentially different management. A flood of new
and undisciplined races poured into Europe, on the one
hand supplying the Church with the vigour of fresh

life to replace the effete materials of the old Roman Empire, and, on the other carrying her back to the childish stage, and necessitating a return to the dominion of outer law. The Church instinctively had recourse to the only means that would suit the case— namely, a revival of Judaism. The Papacy of the Middle Ages, and the Papal Hierarchy, with all its numberless ceremonies and appliances of external religion, with its attention fixed upon deeds and not on thoughts, or feelings, or purposes, with its precise apportionment of punishments and purgatory, was, in fact, neither more nor less than the old schoolmaster come back to bring some new scholars to Christ. Of course, this was not the conscious intention of the then rulers of the Church; they believed in their own cere- monies as much as any of the people at large. The return to the dominion of law was instinctive, not inten- tional. But its object is now as evident as the object of the ancient Mosaic system. Nothing short of a real system of discipline, accepted as Divine by all alike, could have tamed the German and Celtish nature into the self-control needed for a truly spiritual religion. How could Chlovis, at the head of his Franks, have made any right use of absolute freedom of conscience? Nor was this a case in which the less disciplined race could have learned spirituality from the more disci- plined. This may happen when the more disciplined is much the more vigorous of the two. But the ex- hausted Roman Empire had not such strength of life left within it. There was no alternative but that all alike should be put under the law to learn the lesson of obedience.

When the work was done, men began to discover that the law was no longer necessary. And of course there was no reason why they should then discuss the question whether it ever had been necessary. The time was come when it was fit to trust to the conscience as the supreme guide, and the yoke of the medieval discipline was shaken off by a controversy which, in many respects, was a repetition of that between St. Paul and the Judaizers. But, as is always the case after a temporary return to the state of discipline, Christendom did not go back to the position or the duty from which she had been drawn by the influx of the barbarian races. The human mind had not stood still through the ages of bondage, though its motions had been hidden. The Church's whole energy was taken up in the first six centuries of her existence in the creation of a theology. Since that time it had been occupied in renewing by self-discipline the self-control which the sudden absorption of the barbarians had destroyed. At the Reformation it might have seemed at first as if the study of theology were about to return. But in reality an entirely new lesson commenced—the lesson of toleration. Toleration is the very opposite of dogmatism. It implies in reality a confession that there are insoluble problems upon which even revelation throws but little light. Its tendency is to modify the early dogmatism by substituting the spirit for the letter, and practical religion for precise definitions of truth. This lesson is certainly not yet fully learnt. Our toleration is at present too often timid, too often rash, sometimes sacrificing valuable religious elements, sometimes fearing its own plainest conclusions. Yet there can be no question that it is gaining on the minds of all educated men, whether Protestant or Roman Catholic, and is passing from them to be the common property of educated and uneducated alike. There are occasions when the spiritual anarchy which has necessarily followed the Reformation threatens for a moment to bring back some temporary bondage, like the Roman Catholic system. But on the whole the steady progress of toleration is unmistakeable. The mature mind of our race is beginning to modify and soften the hardness and severity of the principles which its early manhood had elevated into immutable statements of truth. Men are beginning to take a wider view than they did. Physical science, researches into history, a more thorough knowledge of the world they inhabit, have enlarged our philosophy beyond the limits which bounded that of the Church of the Fathers. And all these have an influence, whether we will or no, on our determinations of religious truth. There are found to be more things in heaven and earth than were dreamt of in the patristic theology. God's creation is a new book to be read by the side of His revelation, and to be interpreted as coming from Him. We can acknowledge the great value of the forms in which the first ages of the Church defined the truth, and yet refuse to be bound by them; we can use them, and yet endeavour to go beyond them, just as they also went beyond the legacy which was left us by the Apostles.

In learning this new lesson, Christendom needed a firm spot on which she might stand, and has found it in the Bible. Had the Bible been drawn up in precise statements of faith, or detailed precepts of conduct, we should have had no alternative but either permanent subjection to an outer law, or loss of the highest instrument of self-education. But the Bible, from its very form, is exactly adapted to our present want. It is a history; even the doctrinal parts of it are cast in a historical form, and are best studied by considering them as records of the time at which they were written, and as conveying to us the highest and greatest religious life of that time. Hence we use the Bible— some consciously, some unconsciously—not to override, but to evoke the voice of conscience. When conscience and the Bible appear to differ, the pious Christian immediately concludes that he has not really understood the Bible. Hence, too, while the interpretation of the Bible varies slightly from age to age, it varies always in one direction. The schoolmen found purgatory in it. Later students found enough to con-

demn Galileo. Not long ago it would have been held
to condemn geology, and there are still many who so
interpret it. The current is all one way—it evidently points to the identification of the Bible with the
voice of conscience. The Bible, in fact, is hindered by
its form from exercising a despotism over the human
spirit; if it could do that, it would become an outer
law at once; but its form is so admirably adapted to
our need, that it wins from us all the reverence of a
supreme authority, and yet imposes on us no yoke of
subjection. This it does by virtue of the principle of
private judgment, which puts conscience between us
and the Bible, making conscience the supreme interpreter, whom it may be a duty to enlighten, but whom
it can never be a duty to disobey.

This recurrence to the Bible as the great authority
has been accompanied by a strong inclination, common
to all Protestant countries, to go back in every detail
of life to the practices of early times, chiefly, no doubt,
because such a revival of primitive practices, wherever
possible, is the greatest help to entering into the very
essence, and imbibing the spirit of the days when the
Bible was written. So, too, the observance of the
Sunday has a stronger hold on the minds of all religious
men because it penetrates the whole texture of the
Old Testament. The institution is so admirable,
indeed so necessary in itself, that without this hold it
would deserve its present position. But nothing but
its prominent position in the Bible would have made
it, what it now is, the one ordinance which all Christendom alike agrees in keeping. In such an observance
men feel that they are, so far, living a scriptural life,
and have come, as it were, a step nearer to the inner
power of the book from which they expect to learn
their highest lessons. Some, indeed, treat it as
enjoined by an absolutely binding decree, and thus at
once put themselves under a law. But short of that,
those who defend it only by arguments of Christian

expediency, are yet compelled to acknowledge that those arguments are so strong that it would be difficult to imagine a higher authority for any ceremonial institution. And among those arguments one of the foremost is the sympathy which the institution fosters between the student of the Bible and the book which he studies.

This tendency to go back to the childhood and youth of the world has, of course, retarded the acquisition of that toleration which is the chief philosophical and religious lesson of modern days. Unquestionably as bigoted a spirit has often been shown in defence of some practice for which the sanction of the Bible had been claimed, as before the Reformation in defence of the decrees of the Church. But no lesson is well learned all at once. To learn toleration well and really, to let it become, not a philosophical tenet but a practical principle, to join it with real religiousness of life and character, it is absolutely necessary that it should break in upon the mind by slow and steady degrees, and that at every point its right to go further should be disputed, and so forced to logical proof. For it is only by virtue of the opposition which it has surmounted that any truth can stand in the human mind. The strongest argument in favour of tolerating all opinions is that our conviction of the truth of an opinion is worthless unless it has established itself in spite of the most strenuous resistance, and is still prepared to overcome the same resistance, if necessary. Toleration itself is no exception to the universal law; and those who must regret the slow progress by which it wins its way, may remember that this slowness makes the final victory the more certain and complete. Nor is that all. The toleration thus obtained is different in kind from what it would otherwise have been. It is not only stronger, it is richer and fuller. For the slowness of its progress gives time to disentangle from dogmatism the really valuable

principles and sentiments that have been mixed up
and entwined in it, and to unite toleration, not with
indifference and worldliness, but with spiritual truth
and religiousness of life.

Even the perverted use of the Bible has therefore
not been without certain great advantages. And
meanwhile how utterly impossible it would be in the
manhood of the world to imagine any other instructor
of mankind. And for that reason, every day makes
it more and more evident that the thorough study of
the Bible, the investigation of what it teaches and
what it does not teach, the determination of the
limits of what we mean by its inspiration, the determination of the degree of authority to be ascribed
to the different books, if any degrees are to be admitted, must take the lead of all other studies. He
is guilty of high treason against the faith who fears
the result of any investigation, whether philosophical,
or scientific, or historical. And therefore nothing
should be more welcome than the extension of knowledge of any and every kind—for every increase in
our accumulations of knowledge throws fresh light
upon these the real problems of our day. If geology
proves to us that we must not interpret the first
chapters of Genesis literally; if historical investigations shall show us that inspiration, however it may
protect the doctrine, yet was not empowered to protect the narrative of the inspired writers from occasional inaccuracy; if careful criticism shall prove that
there have been occasionally interpolations and forgeries
in that Book, as in many others; the results should
still be welcome. Even the mistakes of careful and
reverent students are more valuable now than truth
held in unthinking acquiescence. The substance of
the teaching which we derive from the Bible will
not really be affected by anything of this sort. While
its hold upon the minds of believers, and its power to
stir the depths of the spirit of man, however much

weakened at first, must be immeasurably strengthened in the end, by clearing away any blunders which may have been fastened on it by human interpretation.

The immediate work of our day is the study of the Bible. Other studies will act upon the progress of mankind by acting through and upon this. For while a few highly educated men here and there who have given their minds to special pursuits may think the study of the Bible a thing of the past, yet assuredly, if their science is to have its effect upon men in the mass, it must be by affecting their moral and religious convictions—in no other way have men been, or can men be, deeply and permanently changed. But though this study must be for the present and for some time the centre of all studies, there is meanwhile no study of whatever kind which will not have its share in the general effect. At this time, in the maturity of mankind, as with each man in the maturity of his powers, the great lever which moves the world is knowledge, the great force is the intellect. St. Paul has told us ' that though in malice we must be children, in understanding we ought to be men.' And this saying of his has the widest range. Not only in the understanding of religious truth, but in all exercise of the intellectual powers, we have no right to stop short of any limit but that which nature, that is, the decree of the Creator, has imposed on us. In fact, no knowledge can be without its effect on religious convictions; for if not capable of throwing direct light on some spiritual questions, yet in its acquisition knowledge invariably throws light on the process by which it is to be, or has been, acquired, and thus affects all other knowledge of every kind.

If we have made mistakes, careful study may teach us better. If we have quarrelled about words, the enlightenment of the understanding is the best means to show us our folly. If we have vainly puzzled our intellects with subjects beyond human cognizance, better knowledge of ourselves will help us to be humbler. Life, indeed, is higher than all else; and no service that man can render to his fellows is to be compared with the heavenly power of a life of holiness. But next to that must be ranked, whatever tends to make men think clearly and judge correctly. So valuable, even above all things (excepting only godliness) is clear thought, that the labours of the statesman are far below those of the philosopher in duration, in power, and in beneficial results. Thought is now higher than action, unless action be inspired with the very breath of heaven. For we are now men, governed by principles, if governed at all, and cannot rely any longer on the impulses of youth or the discipline of childhood.

E

# BUNSEN'S BIBLICAL RESEARCHES.

---

WHEN geologists began to ask whether changes in the earth's structure might be explained by causes still in operation, they did not disprove the possibility of great convulsions, but they lessened the necessity for imagining them. So, if a theologian has his eyes opened to the Divine energy as continuous and omnipresent, he lessens the sharp contrast of epochs in Revelation, but need not assume that the stream has never varied in its flow. Devotion raises time present into the sacredness of the past; while Criticism reduces the strangeness of the past into harmony with the present. Faith and Prayer (and great marvels answering to them), do not pass away: but, in prolonging their range as a whole, we make their parts less exceptional. We hardly discern the truth, for which they are anxious, until we distinguish it from associations accidental to their domain. The truth itself may have been apprehended in various degrees by servants of God, of old, as now. Instead of, with Tertullian, *what was first is truest*, we may say, what comes of God is true, and He is not only afar, but nigh at hand; though His mind is not changed.

Questions of miraculous interference do not turn merely upon our conceptions of physical law, as unbroken, or of the Divine Will, as all-pervading: but they include inquiries into evidence, and must abide by verdicts on the age of records. Nor should the distinction between poetry and prose, and the possi-

bility of imagination's allying itself with affection,
be overlooked. We cannot encourage a remorseless
criticism of Gentile histories and escape its contagion
when we approach Hebrew annals; nor acknowledge
a Providence in Jewry without owning that it may
have comprehended sanctities elsewhere. But the
moment we examine fairly the religions of India and of
Arabia, or even those of primæval Hellas and Latium,
we find they appealed to the better side of our nature,
and their essential strength lay in the elements of
good which they contained, rather than in any Satanic
corruption.

Thus considerations, religious and moral, no less
than scientific and critical, have, where discussion was
free, widened the idea of Revelation for the old world, and
deepened it for ourselves ; not removing the footsteps
of the Eternal from Palestine, but tracing them on
other shores ; and not making the saints of old orphans,
but ourselves partakers of their sonship. Conscience
would not lose by exchanging that repressive idea of
revelation, which is put over against it as an adversary,
for one to which the echo of its best instincts should
be the witness. The moral constituents of our nature,
so often contrasted with Revelation, should rather be
considered parts of its instrumentality. Those cases
in which we accept the miracle for the sake of the
moral lesson prove the ethical element to be the more
fundamental. We see this more clearly if we imagine
a miracle of cruelty wrought (as by Antichrist) for
immoral ends ; for then only the technically miraculous has its value isolated ; whereas by appealing to
*good* 'WORKS' (however wonderful) for his witness, Christ
has taught us to have faith mainly in goodness. This
is too much overlooked by some apologists. But there
is hardly any greater question than whether history
shows Almighty God to have trained mankind by a
faith which has reason and conscience for its kindred,
or by one to whose miraculous tests their pride must

bow; that is, whether His Holy Spirit has acted
through the channels which His Providence ordained,
or whether it has departed from these so signally
that comparative mistrust of them ever afterwards
becomes a duty. The first alternative, though invidiously termed philosophical, is that to which free
nations and Evangelical thinkers tend; the second has
a greater show of religion, but allies itself naturally
with priestcraft or formalism; and not rarely with
corruptness of administration or of life.

In this issue converge many questions anciently
stirred, but recurring in our daylight with almost
uniform[1] accession of strength to the liberal side.
Such questions turn chiefly on the law of growth,
traceable throughout the Bible, as in the world; and
partly on science, or historical inquiry : but no less on
the deeper revelations of the New Testament, as compared to those of the Old. If we are to retain the
old Anglican foundations of research and fair statement, we must revise some of the decisions provi-
sionally given upon imperfect evidence; or, if we
shrink from doing so, we must abdicate our ancient
claim to build upon the truth; and our retreat will
be either to Rome, as some of our lost ones have
consistently seen, or to some form, equally evil, of
darkness voluntary. The attitude of too many English scholars before the last Monster out of the Deep
is that of the degenerate senators before Tiberius.
They stand, balancing terror against mutual shame.
Even with those in our universities who no longer re-

---

[1] It is very remarkable that, amidst all our Biblical illustration from
recent travellers, Layard, Rawlinson, Robinson, Stanley, &c., no single
point has been discovered to tell in favour of an irrational supernaturalism;
whereas numerous discoveries have confirmed the more liberal (not to say,
rationalizing) criticism which traces Revelation historically within the
sphere of nature and humanity. Such is the moral, both of the Assyrian
discoveries, and of all travels in the East, as well as the verdict of philologers
at home. Mr. G. Rawlinson's proof of this is stronger, because undesigned.

peat fully the required Shibboleths, the explicitness of truth is rare.   He who assents most, committing himself least to baseness, is reckoned wisest.

Bunsen's enduring glory is neither to have paltered with his conscience nor shrunk from the difficulties of the problem; but to have brought a vast erudition, in the light of a Christian conscience, to unroll tangled records, tracing frankly the Spirit of God elsewhere, but honouring chiefly the traditions of His Hebrew sanctuary.   No living author's works could furnish so pregnant a text for a discourse on Biblical criticism.   Passing over some specialties of Lutheranism, we may meet in the field of research which is common to scholars; while even here, the sympathy, which justifies respectful exposition, need not imply entire agreement.

In the great work upon Egypt,[1] the later volumes of which are now appearing in English, we do not find that picture of home life which meets us in the pages of our countryman, Sir G. Wilkinson.   The interest for robust scholars is not less, in the fruitful comparison of the oldest traditions of our race, and in the giant shapes of ancient empires, which flit like dim shadows, evoked by a master's hand.   But for those who seek chiefly results, there is something wearisome in the elaborate discussion of authorities; and, it must be confessed, the German refinement of method has all the effect of confusion.   To give details here is impossible (though the more any one scrutinizes them, the more substantial he will find them), and this sketch must combine suggestions, which the author has scattered strangely apart, and sometimes repeated without perfect consistency. He dwells largely upon Herodotus, Eratosthenes, and their successors, from Champollion and Young to Lepsius.   Especially

---

[1] *Egypt's Place in Universal History*, by Christian C. J. Bunsen, &c. London.   1848, vol. i.   1854, vol. ii.

the dynastic records of the Ptolemaic priest, Manetho,[1] are compared with the accounts of the stone monuments. The result, if we can receive it, is to vindicate for the civilized kingdom of Egypt, from Menes downward, an antiquity of nearly four thousand years before Christ. There is no point in which archæologists of all shades were so nearly unanimous as in the belief that our Biblical chronology was too narrow in its limits; and the enlargement of our views, deduced from Egyptian records, is extended by our author's reasonings on the development of commerce and government, and still more of languages, and physical features of race. He could not have vindicated the unity of mankind if he had not asked for a vast extensior of time, whether his petition of twenty thousand years be granted or not. The mention of such a term may appear monstrous to those who regard six thousand years as a part of Revelation. Yet it is easier to throw doubt on some of the arguments than to show that the conclusion in favour of a vast length is improbable. If pottery in a river's mud proves little, its tendency may agree with that of the discovery of very ancient pre-historic remains in many parts of the world. Again, how many years are needed to develope modern French out of Latin, and Latin itself out of its original crude forms? How unlike is English to Welsh, and Greek to Sanskrit—yet all indubitably of one family of languages! What years were required to create the existing divergence of members of this family! How many more for other

---

[1] See an account of him, and his tables, in the Byzantine Syncellus, **pp. 72-145**, vol. i., ed. Dind., in the *Corpus Historiæ Byzantinæ*, Bonn. 1829. But with this is to be compared the Armenian version of Eusebius's Chronology, discovered by Cardinal Mai. The text, the interpretation, and the historical fidelity, are all controverted. Baron Bunsen's treatment of them deserves the provisional acceptance due to elaborate research, with no slight concurrence of probabilities; and if it should not ultimately win a favourable verdict from Egyptologers, no one who summarily rejects it as arbitrary or impossible can have a right to be on the jury.

families, separated by a wide gulf from this, yet retaining traces of a primæval aboriginal affinity, to have
developed themselves, either in priority or collate-
rally ?   The same consonantal roots, appearing either
as verbs inflected with great variety of grammatical form, or as nouns with case-endings in some
languages, and with none in others, plead as convincingly as the succession of strata in geology, for
enormous lapses of time.   When, again, we have
traced our Gaelic and our Sanskrit to their inferential
pre-Hellenic stem, and when reason has convinced
us that the Semitic languages which had as distinct
an individuality four thousand years ago as they
have now, require a cradle of larger dimensions
than Archbishop Ussher's chronology, what farther effort is not forced upon our imagination, if we
would guess the measure of the dim background in
which the Mongolian and Egyptian languages, older
probably than the Hebrew, became fixed, growing
early into the type which they retain?   Do we see
an historical area of nations and languages extending
itself over nearly ten thousand years : and can we
imagine less than another ten thousand, during which
the possibilities of these things took body and form?
Questions of this kind require from most of us a
special training for each : but Baron Bunsen revels
in them, and his theories are at least suggestive.
He shows what Egypt had in common with that
primæval Asiatic stock, represented by Ham, out of
which, as raw material, he conceives the divergent
families, termed Indo-European[1] and Semitic (or the
kindreds of Europe and of Palestine) to have been

---

[1] The common term was Indo-Germanic.  Dr. Prichard, on bringing the
Gael and Cymry into the same family, required the wider term Indo-
European.   Historical reasons, chiefly in connexion with Sanskrit, are
bringing the term Aryan (or Aryas) into fashion.   We may adopt which-
ever is intelligible, without excluding, perhaps, a Turanian or African
element surviving in South Wales.   Turanian means nearly Mongolian.

later developed. Nimrod is considered as the Biblical representative of the earlier stock, whose ruder language is continued, by affiliation or by analogy, in the Mongolian races of Asia and in the negroes of Africa.

The traditions of Babylon, Sidon, Assyria, and Iran, are brought by our author to illustrate and confirm, though to modify our interpretation of, Genesis. It is strange how nearly those ancient cosmogonies[1] approach what may be termed the philosophy of Moses, while they fall short in what Longinus called his 'worthy conception of the divinity.' Our deluge takes its place among geological phenomena, no longer a disturbance of law from which science shrinks, but a prolonged play of the forces of fire and water, rendering the primæval regions of North Asia uninhabitable, and urging the nations to new abodes. We learn approximately its antiquity, and infer limitation in its range, from finding it recorded in the traditions of Iran and Palestine (or of Japhet and Shem) but unknown to the Egyptians and Mongolians, who left earlier the cradle of mankind. In the half ideal half traditional notices[2] of the beginnings of our race, compiled in Genesis, we are bid notice the combination of documents, and the recurrence of barely consistent genealogies. As the man Adam begets Cain, the man Enos begets Cainan. Jared and Irad, Methuselah and Methusael, are similarly compared. Seth, like El, is an old deity's appellation, and MAN was the son of Seth in one record, as Adam was the son of God in the other. One could wish the puzzling circumstance, that the etymology of some of the earlier names seems strained to suit the present form of the narrative had been explained. That our author would

---

[1] *Aegypten's Stelle in der Weltgeschichte,* pp. 186-400; B. v. 1-3. Gotha. 1856.

[2] *Aegypten's Stelle,* &c., B. v. 4-5, pp. 50-142. Gotha. 1857.

not shrink from noticing this, is shown by the firmness
with which he relegates the long lives of the first
patriarchs to the domain of legend, or of symbolical
cycle. He reasonably conceives that the historical
portion begins with Abraham, where the lives become natural, and information was nearer. A sceptical criticism might, indeed, ask, by what right he
assumes that the moral dimensions of our spiritual
heroes can not have been idealized by tradition, as he
admits to have been the case with physical events
and with chronology rounded into epical shape. But
the first principles of his philosophy, which fixes on
personality (or what we might call force of character)
as the great organ of Divine manifestation in the
world, and his entire method of handling the Bible,
lead him to insist on the genuineness, and to magnify
the force, of spiritual ideas, and of the men who exem-
plified them. Hence, on the side of religion, he does
not intentionally violate that reverence with which
Evangelical thinkers view the fathers of our faith.
To Abraham and Moses, Elijah and Jeremiah, he
renders grateful honour. Even in archæology his
scepticism does not outrun the suspicions often betrayed in our popular mind; and he limits, while he
confirms these, by showing how far they have ground.
But as he says, with quaint strength, ' there is no
chronological element in Revelation.' Without bor-
rowing the fifteen centuries which the Greek Church
and the Septuagint would lend us, we see, from com-
paring the Bible with the Egyptian records and with
itself, that our common dates are wrong, though it is
not so easy to say how they should be rectified. The
idea of bringing Abraham into Egypt as early as 2876
B.C. is one of our author's most doubtful points, and
may seem hardly tenable. But he wanted time for
the growth of Jacob's family into a people of two
millions, and he felt bound to place Joseph under
a native Pharaoh, therefore, before the Shepherd

Kings. He also contends that Abraham's horizon in
Asia is antecedent to the first Median conquest of
Babylon in 2234. A famine, conveniently mentioned
under the twelfth dynasty of Egypt, completes his
proof. Sesortosis, therefore, is the Pharaoh to whom
Joseph was minister; the stay of the Israelites in
Egypt is extended to fourteen centuries; and the date
215 represents the time of oppression. Some of these
details are sufficiently doubtful to afford ground of
attack to writers whose real quarrel is with our author's
Biblical research, and its more certain, but not therefore
more welcome, conclusions. It is easier to follow him
implicitly when he leads us, in virtue of an overwhelm-
ing concurrence of Egyptian records and of all the
probabilities of the case, to place the Exodus as late as
1320 or 1314. The event is more natural in Egypt's
decline under Menephthah, the exiled son of the great
Ramses, than amidst the splendour of the eighteenth
dynasty. It cannot well have been earlier, or the
Book of Judges must have mentioned the conquest of
Canaan by Ramses; nor later, for then Joshua would
come in collision with the new empire of Ninus and
Semiramis. But Manetho places, under Menephthah,
what seems the Egyptian version of the event, and the
year 1314, one of our alternatives, is the date assigned
it by Jewish tradition. Not only is the historical
reality of the Exodus thus vindicated against the
dreams of the Drummonds and the Volneys, but a
new interest is given it by its connexion with the rise
and fall of great empires. We can understand how
the ruin on which Ninus rose made room in Canaan
for the Israelites, and how they fell again under the
satraps of the New Empire, who appear in the Book
of Judges as kings of the provinces. Only, if we
accept the confirmation, we must take all its parts.
Manetho makes the conquerors before whom Menephthah retreats into Ethiopia Syrian shepherds, and
gives the human side of an invasion, or war of libera-.

tion;[1] Baron Bunsen notices the 'high hand' with which Jehovah led forth his people, the spoiling of the Egyptians, and the lingering in the peninsula, as signs, even in the Bible, of a struggle conducted by human means. Thus, as the pestilence of the Book of Kings becomes in Chronicles the more visible angel, so the avenger who slew the firstborn may have been the Bedouin host, akin nearly to Jethro, and more remotely to Israel.

So in the passage of the Red Sea, the description may be interpreted with the latitude of poetry : though, as it is not affirmed that Pharaoh was drowned, it is no serious objection that Egyptian authorities continue the reign of Menephthah later. A greater difficulty is that we find but three centuries thus left us from the Exodus to Solomon's Temple. Yet less stress will be laid on this by whoever notices how the numbers in the Book of Judges proceed by the eastern round number of forty, what traces the whole book bears of embodying history in its most popular form, and how naturally St. Paul or St. Stephen would speak after received accounts.

It is not the importance severally, but the continual recurrence of such difficulties, which bears with ever-growing induction upon the question, whether the Pentateuch is of one age and hand, and whether subsequent books are contemporary with the events, or whether the whole literature grew like a tree rooted in the varying thoughts of successive generations, and whether traces of editorship, if not of composition, between the ages of Solomon and Hezekiah, are manifest to whoever will recognise them. Baron Bunsen

---

[1] νόμον ἔθετο μήτε προσκυνεῖν Θεοὺς . . . . συνάπτεσθαι δὲ μηδενὶ πλὴν τῶν συνωμοσμένων· αὐτὸς δὲ . . . . ἔπεμψε πρέσβεις πρὸς τοὺς ὑπὸ Τεθμώσεως ἀπελαθέντας ποιμένας . . . . καὶ ἠξίου συνεπιστρατεύειν κ.τ.λ. Manetho, apud Jos. c. Apion. The whole passage has the stamp of genuine history.

finds himself compelled to adopt the alternative of
gradual growth. He makes the Pentateuch Mosaic,
as indicating the mind and embodying the developed
system of Moses, rather than as written by the great
lawgiver's hand. Numerous fragments of genealogy,
of chronicle, and of spiritual song go up to a high
antiquity, but are imbedded in a crust of later narrative, the allusions of which betray at least a time
when kings were established in Israel. Hence the
idea of composition out of older materials must be
admitted; and it may in some cases be conceived that
the compiler's point of view differed from that of the
older pieces, which yet he faithfully preserved. If the
more any one scrutinizes the sacred text, the more he
finds himself impelled to these or like conclusions
respecting it, the accident of such having been alleged
by men more critical than devout should not make
Christians shrink from them. We need not fear that
what God has permitted to be true in history can be
at war with the faith in Himself taught us by His
Son.

As in his *Egypt* our author sifts the historical date
of the Bible, so in his *Gott in der Geschichte*,[1] he
expounds its directly religious element. Lamenting,
like Pascal, the wretchedness of our feverish being,
when estranged from its eternal stay, he traces, as a
countryman of Hegel, the Divine thought bringing
order out of confusion. Unlike the despairing school,
who forbid us trust in God or in conscience, unless we
kill our souls with literalism, he finds salvation for
men and States only in becoming acquainted with the
Author of our life, by whose reason the world stands
fast, whose stamp we bear in our forethought, and
whose voice our conscience echoes. In the Bible, as
an expression of devout reason, and therefore to be

---

[1] *Gott in der Geschichte* (i.e. the Divine Government in History).
Books i. and ii. Leipzig. 1857.

read with reason in freedom, he finds record of the
spiritual giants whose experience generated the religious atmosphere we breathe. For, as in law and
literature, so in religion we are debtors to our ancestors; but their life must find in us a kindred apprehension, else it would not quicken; and we must give
back what we have received, or perish by unfaithfulness
to our trust. Abraham, the friend of God, Moses the
inspired patriot, Elijah the preacher of the still small
voice, and Jeremiah the foreseer of a law written on
the conscience, are not ancestors of Pharisees who inherit their flesh and name, so much as of kindred spirits
who put trust in a righteous God above offerings of
blood, who build up free nations by wisdom, who
speak truth in simplicity though four hundred priests
cry out for falsehood, and who make self-examination
before the Searcher of hearts more sacred than the
confessional. When the fierce ritual of Syria, with the
awe of a Divine voice, bade Abraham slay his son, he
did not reflect that he had no perfect theory of the
absolute to justify him in departing from traditional
revelation, but trusted that the FATHER, whose
voice from heaven he heard at heart, was better pleased
with mercy than with sacrifice; and this trust was his
righteousness. Its seed was sown from heaven, but
it grew in the soil of an honest and good heart. So
in each case we trace principles of reason and right, to
which our heart perpetually responds, and our response
to which is a truer sign of faith than such deference
to a supposed external authority as would quench
these principles themselves.

It may be thought that Baron Bunsen ignores too
peremptorily the sacerdotal element in the Bible, forgetting how it moulded the form of the history. He
certainly separates the Mosaic institutions from
Egyptian affinity more than our Spencer and Warburton would permit; more, it seems, than Hengstenberg considers necessary. But the distinctively Mosaic

is with him, not the ritual, but the spiritual, which
generated the other, but was overlaid by it.   Moses,
he thinks, would gladly have founded a free religious
society, in which the primitive tables written by the
Divine finger on man's heart should have been law ;
but the rudeness or hardness of his people's heart
compelled him to a sacerdotal system and formal
tablets of stone.   In favour of this view, it may be
remarked, that the tone of some passages in Exodus
appears less sacerdotal than that of later books in the
Pentateuch.   But, be this as it may, the truly Mosaic
(according to our author) is not the Judaic, but the
essentially human; and it is not the Semitic form, often
divergent from our modes of conception, but the eternal truths of a righteous God, and of the spiritual
sacrifices with which He is pleased, that we ought to
recognise as most characteristic of the Bible; and
these truths the same Spirit which spoke of old
speaks, through all variety of phrase, in ourselves.

That there was a Bible before our Bible, and that
some of our present books, as certainly Genesis and
Joshua, and perhaps Job, Jonah, Daniel, are expanded
from simpler elements, is indicated in the book before
us rather than proved as it might be.   Fuller details
may be expected in the course of the revised *Bible
for the People*,[1] that grand enterprise of which three
parts have now appeared.   So far as it has gone,
some amended renderings have interest, but are
less important than the survey of the whole subject in the Introduction.   The word JEHOVAH has
its deep significance brought out by being rendered
THE ETERNAL.   The famous Shiloh (Gen. xlix. 10) is
taken in its local sense, as the sanctuary where the young
Samuel was trained ; which, if doctrinal perversions
did not interfere, hardly any one would doubt to be

---

[1] *Bibel-werk für die Gemeinde.*   I. and II.   Leipzig.   1858.

the true sense. The three opening verses of Genesis are treated as *side*-clauses (*when* God created, &c.), so that the first direct utterance of the Bible is in the fourth verse, ' *God said*, LET THERE BE LIGHT.' Striking as this is, the Hebrew permits, rather than requires it. Less admissible is the division after verse 4 of the 2nd chapter, as if ' This is the history' was a summary of what precedes, instead of an announcement of what follows. But the 1st verse of the 2nd chapter belongs properly to the preceding. Sometimes the translator seems right in substance but wrong in detail. He rightly rejects the perversions which make the cursing Psalms evangelically inspired; but he forgets that the bitterest curses of Psalm 109 (from verse 6 to 19) are not the Psalmist's own, but a speech in the mouth of his adversary. These are trifles, when compared with the mass of information, and the manner of wielding it, in the prefaces to the work. There is a grasp of materials and a breadth of view from which the most practised theologian may learn something, and persons least versed in Biblical studies acquire a comprehensive idea of them. Nothing can be more dishonest than the affectation of contempt with which some English critics endeavoured to receive this instalment of a glorious work. To sneer at demonstrated criticisms as ' old,' and to brand fresh discoveries as ' new,' is worthy of men who neither understand the Old Testament nor love the New. But they to whom the Bible is dear for the truth's sake will wish its illustrious translator life to accomplish a task as worthy of a Christian statesman's retirement as the Tusculans of Cicero were of the representative of Rome's lost freedom.

Already in the volume before-mentioned Baron Bunsen has exhibited the Hebrew Prophets as witnesses to the Divine Government. To estimate aright his services in this province would require from most Englishmen years of study. Accustomed to be told that modern history is expressed by the Prophets in a riddle, which requires only a key to it, they are disappointed to hear of moral lessons, however important. Such notions are the inheritance of days when Justin could argue, in good faith, that by the riches of Damascus and the spoil of Samaria were intended the Magi and their gifts, and that the King of Assyria signified King Herod (!);[1] or when Jerome could say, ' *No one doubts that by Chaldeans are meant Demons,*'[2] and the Shunammite Abishag could be no other than heavenly wisdom, for the honour of David's old age[3]—not to mention such things as Lot's daughters symbolizing the Jewish and Gentile Churches.[4] It was truly felt by the early fathers that Hebrew prophecy tended to a system more spiritual than that of Levi; and they argued unanswerably that circumcision and the Sabbath[5] were symbols for a time, or means to ends. But when, instead of using the letter as an instrument of the spirit, they began to accept the letter in all its parts as their law, and twisted it into harmony with the details of Gospel history, they fell into in-

---

[1] Isaiah viii. 4. Trypho § 77, 8, 9. Well might Trypho answer, that such interpretations are strained, if not blasphemous.

[2] On Isaiah xliii. 14-15, and again, on ch. xlviii. 12-16. He also shows on xlviii. 22, that the Jews of that day had not lost the historical sense of their prophecies; though mystical renderings had already shown themselves. But the later mysticists charitably prayed for Hillel, because his expositions had been historical. (See Pearson's Notes on Art. iii.) When will *our* mysticists show as Christian a temper as the Jewish ones? *Condonet Dominus hoc R. Hillel!*

[3] To Nepotian. Letter 52.

[4] Presbyteri apud Irenæum.

[5] Trypho § 41-43. This tract of Justin's shows strikingly a transition from the utmost evangelical freedom, with simplicity of thought, to a more learned, but confused speculation and literalism. He still thinks reason a revelation, Socrates a Christian, prophecy a necessary and perpetual gift of God's people, circumcision temporary, *because not natural;* and lustral washings, which he contrasts with mental baptism, superstitious. His view of the Sabbath is quite St. Paul's. His making a millennial resurrection the Christian doctrine, as opposed to the heathen immortality of the soul, is embarrassing, but perhaps primitive. But his Scriptural interpretations are dreams, and his charge against the Jews of corrupting the Prophets as suicidal as it is groundless.

extricable contradictions; the most rational interpreter among them is Jerome, and the perusal of his criticisms is their ample confutation.[1]  Nor could the strong intellect of Augustine compensate for his defect of little Greek, which he shared with half, and of less Hebrew, which he shared with most of the Fathers.  But with the revival of learning began a reluctant and wavering, yet inevitable, retreat from the details of patristic exposition, accompanied with some attempts to preserve its spirit.  Even Erasmus looked that way; Luther's and Calvin's strong sense impelled them some strides in the same direction; but Grotius, who outweighs as a critic any ten opposites, went boldly on the road.  In our own country each successive defence of the prophecies, in proportion as its author was able, detracted something from the extent of literal prognostication; and either laid stress on the moral element, or urged a second, as the spiritual sense.  Even Butler foresaw the possibility, that every prophecy in the Old Testament might have its elucidation in contemporaneous history; but literature was not his strong point, and he turned aside, endeavouring to limit it, from an unwelcome idea.  Bishop Chandler is said to have thought twelve passages in the Old Testament directly Messianic; others restricted this character to five.  Paley ventures to quote only one.  Bishop Kidder[2] conceded freely an historical sense in Old Testament texts remote from adaptations in the New.  The apostolic Middleton pronounced firmly for the same principle; Archbishop Newcome[3] and others proved in detail

---

[1] Thus he makes Isaac's hundredfold increase, Gen. xxvi. 12. mean 'multiplication of virtues,' because no grain is specified! *Quæst. Hebraic. in Gen.* ch. xxvi. When Jerome Origenises, he is worse than Origen, because he does not, like that great genius, distinguish the historical from the mystical sense.

[2] Collected in the *Boyle Lectures.*

[3] *A Literal Translation of the Prophets, from Isaiah to Malachi,* with

F

its necessity. Coleridge, in a suggestive letter, preserved in the memoirs of Cary, the translator of
Dante, threw secular prognostication altogether out
of the idea of prophecy.[1]  Dr. Arnold, and his truest
followers, bear, not always consistently, on the same
side.  On the other hand, the declamatory assertions,
so easy in pulpits or on platforms, and aided sometimes by powers, which produce silence rather than
conviction, have not only kept alive but magnified
with uncritical exaggeration, whatever the Fathers
had dreamt or modern rhetoric could add, tending to
make prophecy miraculous.  Keith's edition of Newton need not be here discussed.  Davison, of Oriel, with
admirable skill, threw his argument into a series as
it were of hypothetical syllogisms, with only the defect
(which some readers overlook) that his minor premise
can hardly in a single instance be proved.  Yet the
stress which he lays on the moral element of prophecy
atones for his sophistry as regards the predictive.
On the whole, even in England, there is a wide gulf
between the arguments of our genuine critics, with
the convictions of our most learned clergy, on the
one side, and the assumptions of popular declamation
on the other.  This may be seen on a comparison
of Kidder with Keith.[2]  But in Germany there has

---

Notes, by Lowth, Blayney, Newcome, Wintle, Horsley, &c.  London.
1836.  A book unequal, but useful for want of a better, and of which a
revision, if not an entire recast, with the aid of recent expositors, might
employ our Biblical scholars.

[1] 'Of prophecies in the sense of *prognostication* I utterly deny that there
is any instance delivered by one of the illustrious Diadoche, whom the Jewish church comprised in the name *Prophets*—and I shall regard *Cyrus* as
an exception, when I believe the 137th Psalm to have been composed by
David. . . . .

Nay, I will go farther, and assert that the contrary belief, the hypothesis
of prognostication, is in irreconcileable oppugnancy to our Lord's declaration, that the *times* hath the Father reserved to Himself.'—*Memoir of
Cary*, vol. ii. p. 180.

[2] Amongst recent authors, Dr. Palfrey, an American scholar, has
expounded in five learned volumes the difficulties in current traditions about
prophecy ; but instead of remedying these by restricting the idea of revela-

been a pathway streaming with light, from Eichhorn to Ewald, aided by the poetical penetration of Herder and the philological researches of Gesenius, throughout which the value of the moral element in prophecy has been progressively raised, and that of the directly predictive, whether secular or Messianic, has been lowered. Even the conservatism of Jahn amongst Romanists, and of Hengstenberg amongst Protestants, is free and rational, compared to what is often in this country required with denunciation, but seldom defended by argument.

To this inheritance of opinion Baron Bunsen succeeds. Knowing these things, and writing for men who know them, he has neither the advantage in

---

tion to Moses and the Gospels, he would have done better to seek a definition of revelation which should apply to the Psalms, and Prophets, and Epistles.

Mr. Francis Newman, in his *Hebrew Monarchy*, is historically consistent in his expositions, which have not been controverted by any serious argument; but his mind seems to fail in the *Ideal* element; else he would see, that the typical ideas (of patience or of glory) in the Old Testament, find their culminating fulfilment in the New.

Mr. Mansel's *Bampton Lectures* must make even those who value his argument, regret that to his acknowledged dialectical ability he has not added the rudiments of Biblical criticism. In all his volume not one text of Scripture is elucidated, nor a single difficulty in the evidences of Christianity removed. Recognised mistranslations, and misreadings, are alleged as arguments, and passages from the Old Testament are employed without reference to the illustration, or inversion, which they have received in the New. Hence, as the eristic arts of logic without knowledge of the subject-matter become powerless, the author is a mere gladiator hitting in the dark, and his blows fall heaviest on what it was his duty to defend. As to his main argument (surely a strange parody of Butler), the sentence from Sir W. Hamilton prefixed to his volume, seems to me its gem, and its confutation. Of the *reasoning*, which would bias our interpretation of Isaiah, by telling us Feuerbach was an atheist, I need not say a word.

We are promised from Oxford farther elucidations of the Minor Prophets by the Regius Professor of Hebrew, whose book seems launched sufficiently to catch the gales of friendship, without yet tempting out of harbour the blasts of criticism. Let us hope that, when the work appears, its interpretations may differ from those of a *Catena Aurea*, published under high auspices in the same university, in which the narrative of Uriah the Hittite is improved by making David represent Christ, and Uriah symbolize the devil; so that the grievous crime which 'displeased the Lord,' becomes a typical prophecy of Him who was harmless and undefiled!

argument of unique knowledge, nor of unique ignorance. He dare not say, though it was formerly said,
that David foretold the exile, because it is mentioned
in the Psalms. He cannot quote Nahum denouncing
ruin against Nineveh, or Jeremiah against Tyre,
without remembering that already the Babylonian
power threw its shadow across Asia, and Nebuchad-
nezzar was mustering his armies. If he would
quote the book of Isaiah, he cannot conceal, after
Gesenius, Ewald, and Maurer have written, that the
book is composed of elements of different eras. Finding Perso-Babylonian, or new-coined words, such as
*sagans* for officers, and Chaldaic forms of the Hebrew
verb, such as *Aphel* for *Hiphil*, in certain portions, and
observing that the political horizon of these portions
is that of the sixth century, while that of the elder or
more purely Hebraic portions belonged to the eighth, he
must accept a theory of authorship and of prediction,
modified accordingly. So, if under the head of
Zechariah he finds three distinct styles and aspects of
affairs, he must acknowledge so much, whether he is
right or wrong in conjecturing the elder Zechariah of
the age of Isaiah to have written the second portion,
and Uriah in Jeremiah's age the third. If he would
quote Micah, as designating Bethlehem for the birth-
place of the Messiah, he cannot shut his eyes to the
fact, that the Deliverer to come from thence was to be a
contemporary shield against the Assyrian. If he
would follow Pearson in quoting the second Psalm,
*Thou art my son;* he knows that Hebrew idiom convinced even Jerome[1] the true rendering was, *worship
purely.* He may read in Psalm xxxiv. that, ' not a
bone of the righteous shall be broken,' but he must
feel a difficulty in detaching this from the context, so

---

[1] Cavillatur  .  .  .  .  quod posuerim,  .  .  .  .  *Adorate purè*
.  .  .  .  ne violentus viderer interpres, et Jud. locum darem.—*Hieron.
c. Ruffin.* § 19.

as to make it a prophecy of the crucifixion. If he
accepts mere versions of Psalm xxii. 17, he may
wonder how 'piercing the hands and the feet' can fit
into the whole passage; but if he prefers the most
ancient Hebrew reading, he finds, instead of '*piercing*,'
the comparison 'like a lion,' and this corresponds sufficiently with the 'dogs' of the first clause; though a
morally certain emendation would make the parallel
more perfect by reading the word 'lions' in both
clauses.[1] In either case, the staring monsters are intended, by whom Israel is surrounded and torn. Again
he finds in Hosea that the Lord loved Israel when
he was young, and called him out of Egypt to be his
son; but he must feel, with Bishop Kidder, that such
a citation is rather accommodated to the flight of
Joseph into Egypt, than a prediction to be a ground
of argument. Fresh from the services of Christ-
mas, he may sincerely exclaim, *Unto us a child is born*;
but he knows that the Hebrew translated *Mighty God*,
is at least disputable, that perhaps it means only Strong
and Mighty One, Father of an Age; and he can never
listen to any one who pretends that the Maiden's
Child of Isaiah vii. 16, was not to be born in the
reign of Ahaz, as a sign against the Kings Pekah
and Rezin. In the case of Daniel, he may doubt
whether all parts of the book are of one age, or what
is the starting point of the seventy weeks; but two
results are clear beyond fair doubt, that the period of
weeks ended in the reign of Antiochus Epiphanes, and
that those portions of the book, supposed to be
specially predictive, are a history of past occurrences
up to that reign. When so vast an induction on the
destructive side has been gone through, it avails little
that some passages may be doubtful, one perhaps in
Zechariah, and one in Isaiah, capable of being made

---

[1] By reading כלביאים for כלבים. The Septuagint version may have
arisen from הקיפוני, taken as from נקף.

directly Messianic, and a chapter possibly in Deutero-
nomy foreshadowing the final fall of Jerusalem. Even
these few cases, the remnant of so much confident
rhetoric, tend to melt, if they are not already melted,
in the crucible of searching inquiry. If our German
had ignored all that the masters of philology have
proved on these subjects, his countrymen would have
raised a storm of ridicule, at which he must have
drowned himself in the Neckar.

Great then is Baron Bunsen's merit, in accepting
frankly the belief of scholars, and yet not despairing
of Hebrew Prophecy as a witness to the kingdom of
God. The way of doing so left open to him, was to
show, pervading the Prophets, those deep truths
which lie at the heart of Christianity, and to trace
the growth of such ideas, the belief in a righteous
God, and the nearness of man to God, the power of
prayer, and the victory of self-sacrificing patience,
ever expanding in men's hearts, until the fulness of
time came, and the ideal of the Divine thought was
fulfilled in the Son of Man. Such accordingly is the
course our author pursues, not with the critical finish
of Ewald, but with large moral grasp. Why he
should add to his moral and metaphysical basis of
prophecy, a notion of foresight by vision of particulars,
or a kind of *clairvoyance*, though he admits it to be[1]
a natural gift, consistent with fallibility, is not so easy
to explain. One would wish he might have intended
only the power of seeing the ideal in the actual, or of
tracing the Divine Government in the movements of
men. He seems to mean more than presentiment or

---

[1] 'Die Kraft des Schauens, die im Menschen verborgen liegt, und, von
der Naturnothwendigkeit befreit, im hebräischen Prophetenthum sich zur
wahren Weltanschauung erhoben hat . . . . ist der Schlüssel,' &c.
*Gott in der Geschichte*, p. 149.

'Jene Herrlichkeit besteht nicht in dem Vorhersagen . . . . Dieses
haben sie gemein mit manchen Aussprüchen der Pythia, . . . . und
mit vielen Weissagungen der Hellseherinnen dieses Jahrhunderts . . .
*id.* p. 151.

sagacity; and this element in his system requires proof.

The most brilliant portion of the prophetical essays is the treatment of the later Isaiah. With the insertion of four chapters concerning Hezekiah from the histories of the kings, the words and deeds of the elder Isaiah apparently close. It does not follow that all the prophecies arranged earlier in the book are from his lips; probably they are not; but it is clear to demonstration,[1] that the later chapters (xl., &c.,) are upon the stooping of Nebo, and the bowing down of Babylon, when the Lord took out of the hand of Jerusalem the cup of trembling; for the glad tidings of the decree of return were heard upon the mountains; and the people went forth, not with haste or flight, for their God went before them, and was their rereward (ch. lii). So they went forth with joy, and were led forth with peace (ch. liv). So the arm of the Lord was laid bare, and his servant who had foretold it was now counted wise, though none had believed his report. We cannot take a portion out of this continuous song, and by dividing it as a chapter, separate its primary meaning from what precedes and follows. The servant in chapters lii. and liii. must have relation to the servant in chapters xlii. and xlix. Who was this servant, that had foretold the exile and the return, and had been a man of grief, rejected of his people, imprisoned and treated as a malefactor? The oldest Jewish tradition, preserved in Origen,[2] and to be inferred from Justin,[3] said the chosen people—in opposition to heathen oppressors—an opinion which suits ch. xlix. ver. 3. Nor is the[4] later

---

[1] To prove this, let any one read Jerome's arguments against it; if the sacred text itself be not sufficient proof. ' *Go ye forth of Babylon,*' &c., ch. xlviii. 20.

[2] *C. Celsum,* i. 55. (Quoted by Pearson.)

[3] For, in making the Gentiles mean *Proselytes,* they must have made the servant Israel. ἀλλὰ τί; οὐ πρὸς τὸν νόμον λέγει, καὶ τοὺς φωτιζομένους ὑπ᾽ αὐτοῦ, κ.τ.λ.—*Trypho,* § 122.

[4] Later, because it implies the fall of Jerusalem. It is thought to have

exposition of the Targum altogether at variance; for though Jonathan speaks of the Messiah, it is in the character of a Judaic deliverer: and his expressions about ' *the holy people's being multiplied,*' and seeing their sanctuary rebuilt, especially when he calls the holy people a *remnant,*[1] may be fragments of a tradition older than his time. It is idle, with Pearson,[2] to quote Jonathan as a witness to the Christian interpretation, unless his conception of the Messiah were ours. But the idea of the Anointed One, which in some of the Psalms belongs to Israel, shifted from time to time, being applied now to people, and now to king or prophet, until at length it assumed a sterner form, as the Jewish spirit was hardened by persecutions into a more vindicative hope. The first Jewish expositor who loosened, without breaking Rabbinical fetters, R. Saadiah,[3] in the 9th century, named Jeremiah as the man of grief, and emphatically the prophet of the return, rejected of his people. Grotius, with his usual sagacity, divined the same clue; though Michaelis says upon it, *pessimè Grotius.* Baron Bunsen puts together, with masterly analysis, the illustrative passages of Jeremiah; and it is difficult to resist the conclusion to which they tend. Jeremiah compares his whole people to sheep going astray,[4] and himself to 'a lamb or an ox, brought to the slaughter.'[5] He was taken from prison;[6] and

---

been compiled in the fourth century of our era. It is very doubtful, whether the Jewish schools of the middle ages had (except in fragments) any Hermeneutic tradition so old as what we gather from the Church fathers, however unfairly this may be reported. My own belief is clear, that they had not.

[1] דעמיה ית שארא, and יסגון תולדת קודשא.—*Targum on Isaiah* liii.

[2] In Pearson's hands, even the Rabbins become more Rabbinical. His citations from Jonathan and from Jarchi are most unfair; and in general he makes their prose more prosaic.

[3] Titularly styled Gaon, as president of the Sora school.

[4] Jer. xxiii. 1-2; l. 6-17; xii. 3.

[5] Jer. xi. 19.

[6] Jer. xxxviii. 4-6, 13; xxxvii. 16.

his generation, or posterity, none took account of;[1] he interceded for his people in prayer:[2] but was not the less despised, and a man of grief, so that no sorrow was like his;[3] men assigned his grave with the wicked,[4] and his tomb with the oppressors; all who followed him seemed cut off out of the land of the living,[5] yet his seed prolonged their days;[6] his prophecy was fulfilled,[7] and the arm of the Eternal laid bare; he was counted wise on the return; his place in the book of Sirach[8] shows how eminently he was enshrined in men's thoughts as the servant of God; and in the book of Maccabees[9] he is the gray prophet, who is seen in vision, fulfilling his task of interceding for the people.

This is an imperfect sketch, but may lead readers to consider the arguments for applying Isaiah lii. and liii. to Jeremiah. Their weight (in the master's hand) is so great, that if any single person should be selected, they prove Jeremiah should be the one. Nor are they a slight illustration of the historical sense of that famous chapter, which in the original is a history.[10] Still the general analogy of the Old Testament which makes collective Israel, or the prophetic remnant, especially the servant of Jehovah, and the comparison of c. xlii., xlix. may permit us to think the oldest interpretation the truest; with only this admission, that

---

[1] Jer. xi. 19-23; xx. 10; xxxvi. 19; xlv. 2-3.
[2] Jer. xviii. 20; xiv. 11; xv. i.
[3] Jer. xviii. 18; xx. 9-17; Lam. iii. 1-13.
[4] Lam. iii. 52, 53, 54; Jer. xxvi. 11-15, 23; xliv. 15, 16; i, 18, 19.
[5] Jer. xlv. 1-3; xi. 19; xli. 2-3; with xli. 9-10.
[6] Psalm cxxvi. 1; Isaiah xliii. 1-5, 10-14.
[7] Lam. i. 17; Jer. xvi. 15; xxx. 1, 2, 3, 10, 18; xxxi. 6-12; Isaiah xliv. 7-8; xlvi. 1-9, 10; l. 5-6; lii. 10-13.
[8] Eccles. xlix. 6-7, and Jer. i.
[9] 2 Macc. xv. 13, 14.
[10] The tenses from verse 2 onward are rather historical than predictive; and in ver. 8, for *he was stricken*, the Hebrew is, נֶגַע לָמוֹ, the *stroke was upon them;* i.e. on the generation of the faithful, which was cut off; when the blood of the Prophets was shed on every side of Jerusalem.

the figure of Jeremiah stood forth amongst the Prophets, and tinged the delineation of the true Israel,
that is, *the faithful remnant* who had been disbelieved
—just as the figure of Laud or Hammond might
represent the Caroline Church in the eyes of her poet.

If this seems but a compromise, it may be justified by Ewald's phrase, '*Die wenigen Treuen im Exile,
Jeremjah und andre,*'[1] though he makes the servant
idealized Israel.

If any sincere Christian now asks, is not then our
Saviour spoken of in Isaiah; let him open his New
Testament, and ask therewith John the Baptist,
whether he was Elias? If he finds the Baptist
answering *I am not*, yet our Lord testifies that in
spirit and power this was Elias; a little reflexion will
show how the historical representation in Isaiah liii. is
of some suffering prophet or remnant, yet the truth
and patience, the grief and triumph, have their highest
fulfilment in Him who said, ' Father, not my will,
but thine.' But we must not distort the prophets,
to prove the Divine WORD incarnate, and then from
the incarnation reason back to the sense of prophecy.

Loudly as justice and humanity exclaim against
such traditional distortion of prophecy as makes their
own sacred writings a ground of cruel prejudice against
the Hebrew people, and the fidelity of this remarkable
race to the oracles of their fathers a handle for social
obloquy, the cause of Christianity itself would be the
greatest gainer, if we laid aside weapons, the use of
which brings shame. Israel would be acknowledged,
as in some sense still a Messiah, having borne centuries
of reproach through the sin of the nations; but the
Saviour who fulfilled in his own person the highest
aspiration of Hebrew seers and of mankind, thereby
lifting the ancient words, so to speak, into a new and

---

[1] *Die Propheten, d. A. B.* 2ter Band. pp. 438-453.

higher power, would be recognised as having eminently
the unction of a prophet whose words die not, of a
priest in a temple not made with hands, and of a king
in the realm of thought, delivering his people from a
bondage of moral evil, worse than Egypt or Babylon.
If already the vast majority of the prophecies are
acknowledged by our best authorities to require some
such rendering, in order to Christianize them, and if
this acknowledgment has become uniformly stronger
in proportion as learning was unfettered, the force of
analogy leads us to anticipate that our Isaiah too must
require a similar interpretation. No new principle is
thrust upon the Christian world, by our historical
understanding of this famous chapter; but a case
which had been thought exceptional, is shown to
harmonize with a general principle.

Whether the great prophet, whose triumphant
thanksgiving on the return from Babylon forms the
later chapters of our Isaiah, is to remain without a
name, or whether Baron Bunsen has succeeded in
identifying him with BARUCH, the disciple, scribe, and
perhaps biographer or editor of Jeremiah, is a question
of probability. Most readers of the argument for the
identity will feel inclined to assent; but a doubt may
occur, whether many an unnamed disciple of the prophetic school may not have burnt with kindred zeal, and
used diction not peculiar to any one; while such a
doubt may be strengthened by the confidence with
which our critic ascribes a recasting of Job, and
of parts of other books, to the same favourite Baruch.
Yet, if kept within the region of critical conjecture,
his reasons are something more than ingenious. It
may weigh with some Anglicans, that a letter ascribed
to St. Athanasius mentions Baruch among the canonical prophets.[1]

---

[1] Ἰερεμίας, καὶ σὺν αὐτῷ Βαρούχ, Θρῆνοι, Ἐπιστολὴ καὶ μετ' αὐτὸν Ἰεζεκιήλ,
κ.τ.λ.—*Ep. Fest.*

In distinguishing the man Daniel from our book of Daniel, and in bringing the latter as low as the reign of Epiphanes, our author only follows the admitted necessities of the case.[1]  Not only Macedonian words, such as *symphonia*[2] and *psanterion*, but the texture of the Chaldaic, with such late forms as דִּי, לְכוֹן and אִלֵּן the pronominal מ and ה having passed into נ, and not only minute description of Antiochus's reign, but the stoppage of such description at the precise date 169 B.C., remove all philological and critical doubt as to the age of the book.  But what seems peculiar to Baron Bunsen, is the interpretation of the four empires' symbols with reference to the original Daniel's abode in Nineveh : so that the winged lion traditionally meant the Assyrian empire ; the bear was the Babylonian symbol ; the leopard that of the Medes and Persians ; while the fourth beast represented, as is not uncommonly held, the sway of Alexander.  A like reference is traced in the mention of Hiddekel, or the Tigris, in ch. x ; for, if the scene had been Babylon under Darius, the river must have been the Euphrates.  The truth seems, that starting like many a patriot bard of our own, from a name traditionally sacred, the writer used it with no deceptive intention, as a dramatic form which dignified his encourage-ment of his countrymen in their great struggle against Antiochus.  The original place of the book,[3] amongst the later Hagiographa of the Jewish canon, and the absence of any mention of it by the son of Sirach, strikingly confirm this view of its origin ; and, if some obscurity rests upon details, the general conclusion, that the book contains no predictions, except by

---

[1] Auberlen indeed defends, but says, ' Die Unächtheit Daniels ist in der modernen Theologie zum Axiom geworden.'—*Der Prophet Daniel.* Basel. 1854.
[2] Compare ' Philosophy of Universal History' (part of the *Hippolytus*), vol i. pp. 217-219, with *Gott in der Geschichte*, 1str Theil. pp. 514-540.
[3] The saying that later Jews changed the place of the book in the canon, seems to rest on no evidence.

analogy and type, can hardly be gainsaid. But it may not the less, with some of the latest Psalms, have nerved the men of Israel, when they turned to flight the armies of the aliens; and it suggests, in the Godless invader, no slight forecast of Caligula again invading the Temple with like abomination, as well as of whatever exalts itself against faith and conscience, to the end of the world. It is time for divines to recognise these things, since, with their opportunities of study, the current error is as discreditable to them, as for the well-meaning crowd, who are taught to identify it with their creed, it is a matter of grave compassion.

It provokes a smile on serious topics to observe the zeal with which our critic vindicates the personality of Jonah, and the originality of his hymn (the latter being generally thought doubtful), while he proceeds to explain that the narrative of our book, in which the hymn is imbedded, contains a late legend,[1] founded on misconception. One can imagine the cheers which the opening of such an essay might evoke in some of our own circles, changing into indignation as the distinguished foreigner developed his views. After this, he might speak more gently of mythical theories.

But, if such a notion alarms those who think that, apart from omniscience belonging to the Jews, the proper conclusion of reason is atheism; it is not inconsistent with the idea that Almighty God has been pleased to educate men and nations, employing imagination no less than conscience, and suffering His lessons to play freely within the limits of humanity and its shortcomings. Nor will any fair reader rise from the prophetical disquisitions without feeling that he has been under the guidance of a master's hand.

---

[1] The present writer feels excused from repeating here the explanation given in the appendix to his *Sermon on Christian Freedom*. London, 1858.

The great result is to vindicate the work of the Eternal Spirit; that abiding influence, which as our church teaches us in the Ordination Service, under- lies all others, and in which converge all images of old time and means of grace now; temple, Scripture, finger, and hand of God; and again, preaching, sacra- ments, waters which comfort, and flame which burns. If such a Spirit did not dwell in the Church the Bible would not be inspired, for the Bible is, before all things, the written voice of the congregation. Bold as such a theory of inspiration may sound, it was the earliest creed of the Church, and it is the only one to which the facts of Scripture answer. The sacred writers acknowledge themselves men of like passions with ourselves, and we are promised illumination from the Spirit which dwelt in them. Hence, when we find our Prayer-book constructed on the idea of the Church being an inspired society, instead of ob- jecting that every one of us is fallible, we should define inspiration consistently with the facts of Scrip- ture, and of human nature. These would neither exclude the idea of fallibility among Israelites of old, nor teach us to quench the Spirit in true hearts for ever. But if any one prefers thinking the Sacred Writers passionless machines, and calling Luther and Milton 'uninspired,' let him co-operate in researches by which his theory, if true, will be triumphantly confirmed. Let him join in considering it a religious duty to print the most genuine text of those words which he calls Divine; let him yield no grudging assent to the removal of demonstrated interpolations in our text or errors in our translation; let him give English equivalents for its Latinisms, once natural, but now become deceptive; let him next trace fairly the growth of our complex doctrines out of scriptural germs, whether of simple thought or of Hebrew idiom; then, if he be not prepared to trust our Church with a larger freedom in incorporating into her language the results of such inquiry and adapting one-sided forms to wider experience, he will at least have acquired such a knowledge of this field of thought as may induce him to treat labourers in it with respect. A recurrence to first principles, even of Revelation, may, to minds prudent or timid, seem a process of more danger than advantage; and it is possible to defend our traditional theology, if stated reasonably, and with allowance for the accidents of its growth. But what is not possible, with honesty, is to uphold a fabric of mingled faith and speculation, and in the same breath to violate the instinct which believed, and blindfold the mind which reasoned. It would be strange if God's work were preserved, by disparaging the instruments which His wisdom chose for it.

On turning to the *Hippolytus*[1] we find a congeries of subjects, but yet a whole, pregnant and suggestive beyond any book of our time. To lay deep the foundations of faith in the necessities of the human mind, and to establish its confirmation by history, distinguishing the local from the universal, and translating the idioms of priesthoods or races into the broad speech of humanity, are amongst parts of the great argument. Of those wonderful aphorisms, which are further developed in the second volume of *Gott in der Geschichte*, suffice it here, that their author stands at the farthest pole from those who find no divine footsteps in the Gentile world. He believes in Christ, because he first believes in God and in mankind. In this he harmonizes with the church Fathers before Augustine, and with all our deepest Evangelical school. In handling the New Testament he remains faithful to his habit of exalting spiritual ideas,

---

[1] *Hippolytus and his Age*, by Chr. C. J. Bunsen, &c. London, 1852. 2nd edition, recast, London, 1854. The awakening freshness of the first edition is hardly replaced by the fulness of the second. It is to be wished that the Biblical portions of the *Philosophy of Universal History*, vol. ii. pp. 149-338, were reprinted in a cheap form.

and the leading characters by whose personal impulse
they have been stamped on the world. Other foundation for healthful mind or durable society he suffers
no man to lay, save that of Jesus, the Christ of God.
In Him he finds brought to perfection that religious idea, which is the thought of the Eternal, without conformity to which our souls cannot be saved
from evil. He selects for emphasis such sayings as,
'*I came to cast fire upon the earth, and how I would it
were already kindled! I have a baptism to be baptized
with, and how am I straitened until it be accomplished!*'
In these he finds the innermost mind of the Son of
Man, undimmed by the haze of mingled imagination
and remembrance, with which his awful figure should
scarcely fail to be at length invested by affection.
The glimpses thus afforded us into the depth of our
Lord's purpose, and his law of giving rather than
receiving, explain the wonder-working power with
which he wielded the truest hearts of his generation, and correspond to his life and death of self-
sacrifice.

This recognition of Christ as the moral Saviour of
mankind may seem to some Baron Bunsen's most
obvious claim to the name of Christian. For, though
he embraces with more than orthodox warmth New
Testament terms, he explains them in such a way,
that he may be charged with using Evangelical language in a philosophical sense. But in reply he would
ask, what proof is there that the reasonable sense of
St. Paul's words was not the one which the Apostle
intended? Why may not justification by faith have
meant the peace of mind, or sense of Divine approval,
which comes of trust in a righteous God, rather than
a fiction of merit by transfer? St. Paul would then
be teaching moral responsibility, as opposed to sacerdotalism; or that to obey is better than sacrifice.
Faith would be opposed, not to the good deeds which
conscience requires, **but to works** of appeasement

by ritual. Justification would be neither an arbitrary ground of confidence, nor a reward upon condition of our disclaiming merit, but rather a verdict of forgiveness upon our repentance, and of acceptance upon the offering of our hearts. It is not a fatal objection, to say that St. Paul would thus teach Natural Religion, unless we were sure that he was bound to contradict it; but it is a confirmation of the view, if it brings his hard sayings into harmony with the Gospels and with the Psalms, as well as with the instincts of our best conscience. If we had dreamed of our nearest kindred in irreconcilable combat, and felt anguish at the thought of opposing either, it could be no greater relief to awake, and find them at concord, than it would be to some minds to find the antagonism between Nature and Revelation vanishing[1] in a wider grasp and deeper perception of the one, or in a better balanced statement of the other.

If our philosopher had persuaded us of the moral nature of Justification, he would not shrink from adding that Regeneration is a correspondent giving of insight, or an awakening of forces of the soul. By Resurrection he would mean a spiritual quickening. Salvation would be our deliverance, not from the life-giving God, but from evil and darkness, which are His finite opposites, (ὁ ἀντικείμενος.) Propitiation would be the recovery of that peace, which cannot be while sin divides us from the Searcher of hearts. The eternal is what belongs to God, as spirit, therefore the negation of things finite and unspiritual, whether world, or letter, or rite of blood. The hateful fires of the vale of Hinnom, (Gehenna,) are hardly in the strict letter imitated by the God who has pronounced them cursed, but may serve as images of distracted remorse. Hea-

---

[1] 'The doctrine of the Fall, the doctrine of Grace, and the doctrine of the Atonement, *are grounded in the instincts of mankind.*'—Mozley *on Predestination,* chap. xi. p. 331.

G

ven is not a place, so much as fulfilment of the love
of God.   The kingdom of God is no more Romish
sacerdotalism than Jewish royalty, but the realization
of the Divine Will in our thoughts and lives.   This
expression of spirit, in deed and form, is generically
akin to creation, and illustrates the incarnation.   For
though the true substance of Deity took body in the
Son of Man, they who know the Divine Substance to
be Spirit, will conceive of such embodiment of the
Eternal Mind very differently from those who abstract
all Divine attributes, such as consciousness, forethought, and love, and then imagine a material
*residuum*, on which they confer the Holiest name.
The Divine attributes are[1] consubstantial with the
Divine essence.   He who abides in love, abides in
God, and God in him.   Thus the incarnation becomes
with our author as purely spiritual, as it was with St.
Paul.   The son of David by birth is the Son of God
by the spirit of holiness.   What is flesh, is born of
flesh, and what is spirit, is born of spirit.[2]

If we would estimate the truth of such views, the
full import of which hardly lies on the surface, we find
two lines of inquiry present themselves as criteria:
and each of these divides itself into two branches.
First, as regards the subject matter, both spiritual
affection and metaphysical reasoning forbid us to
confine revelations like those of Christ to the first
half century of our era, but show at least affinities of
our faith existing in men's minds, anterior to Christianity, and renewed with deep echo from living hearts
in many a generation.   Again, on the side of external
criticism, we find the evidences of our canonical books
and of the patristic authors nearest to them, are

[1] On this point, the summary of St. Augustine at the end of his 15th
book, ' *On the Trinity*,' is worth reading.
[2] ' Neque sermo aliud quam Deus neque caro aliud quam homo,' and ' ex
carne homo, ex spiritu Deus.'—Tertullian *adv. Prax.* c. xxvii.   Comp.
Romans i. 1-3.

sufficient to prove illustration in outward act of principles perpetually true ; but not adequate to guarantee
narratives inherently incredible, or precepts evidently
wrong. Hence we are obliged to assume in ourselves
a verifying faculty, not unlike the discretion which a
mathematician would use in weighing a treatise on
geometry, or the liberty which a musician would
reserve in reporting a law of harmony. Thus, as we
are expressly told, we are to have the witness in ourselves. It is not our part to dictate to Almighty God,
that He ought to have spared us this strain upon our
consciences; nor in giving us through His Son a
deeper revelation of His own presence, was He bound
to accompany His gift by a special form of record.[1]
Hence there is no antecedent necessity that the least
rational view of the gospel should be the truest, or
that our faith should have no human element, and its
records be exempt from historical law. Rather we
may argue, the more Divine the germ, the more human
must be the development.

Our author then believes St. Paul, because he understands him reasonably. Nor does his acceptance of
Christ's redemption from evil bind him to repeat
traditional fictions about our canon, or to read its
pages with that dulness which turns symbol and
poetry into materialism. On the side of history lies
the strength of his genius. His treatment of the
New Testament is not very unlike the acute criticism
of De Wette, tempered by the affectionateness of
Neander. He finds in the first three gospels divergent
forms of the tradition, once oral, and perhaps cate-
chetical, in the congregations of the apostles. He thus
explains the numerous traces characteristic of a traditional narrative. He does not ascribe the quadruple
division of record to the four churches of Jerusalem,
Rome, Antioch, and Alexandria, on the same principle

---

[1] Butler's *Analogy.* Part ii. ch. iii. Hooker, *Eccl. Pol.* Books i. ii.

as liturgical families are traced; but he requires time enough for some development, and for the passing of some symbol into story.   By making the fourth gospel the latest of all our genuine books, he accounts for its style (so much more Greek than the Apocalypse), and explains many passages.   The verse, 'And no man hath ascended up to Heaven, but he that came down,'[1] is intelligible as a free comment near the end of the first century; but has no meaning in our Lord's mouth at a time when the ascension had not been heard of.   So the Apocalypse, if taken as a series of poetical visions, which represent the outpouring of the vials of wrath upon the city where the Lord was slain, ceases to be a riddle.   Its horizon answers to that of Jerusalem already threatened by the legions of Vespasian, and its language is partly adapted from the older prophets, partly a repetition of our Lord's warnings as described by the Evangelists, or as deepened into wilder threatenings in the mouth of the later Jesus,[2] the son of Ananus.   The Epistle to the Hebrews, so different in its conception of faith, and in its Alexandrine rhythm, from the doctrine and the language of St. Paul's known Epistles, has its degree of discrepance explained by ascribing it to some[3] companion of the apostle's; and minute reasons are found for fixing with probability on Apollos. The second of the Petrine Epistles, having alike external and internal evidence against its genuineness, is necessarily surrendered as a whole; and our critic's good faith in this respect is more certain than the ingenuity with which he reconstructs a part of it. The second chapter may not improbably be a quotation; but its quoter, and the author of the rest of the epistle,

---

[1] John iii. 13.

[2] Josephus *B. J.* b. vi. c. v. § 3.

[3] In my own judgment, the Epistle bears traces of being *post*-apostolic. iii. 14; xiii. 7; ii. 3; x. 2, 25-32.

need not therefore have been St. Peter. Where so
many points are handled, fancifulness in some may be
pardoned ; and indulgence is needed for the eagerness
with which St. Paul is made a widower, because some
fathers[1] misunderstood the texts, ' true yoke-fellow,'
and ' leading about a sister.'

After a survey of the Canon ; the working as of
leaven in meal, of that awakening of mankind which
took its impulse from the life of Christ, is traced
through the first seven generations of Christendom.
After Origen, the first freedom of the Gospel grows
faint, or is hardened into a system more Ecclesiastical
in form, and more dialectical in speculation, the fresh
language of feeling or symbol being transferred to
the domain of logic, like Homer turned into prose by
a scholiast. It need not, to a philosophical observer,
necessarily follow that the change was altogether a
corruption ; for it may have been the Providential
condition of religious feeling brought into contact with
intellect, and of the heavenly kingdom's expansion in
the world. The elasticity with which Christianity
gathers into itself the elements of natural piety, and
assimilates the relics of Gentile form and usage, can
only be a ground of objection with those who have
reflected little on the nature of revelation. But
Baron Bunsen, as a countryman of Luther, and a
follower of those *Friends of God* whose profound
mysticism appears in the *Theologia Germanica*, takes
decided part with the first freshness of Christian freedom, against the confused thought and furious passions
which disfigure most of the great councils. Those
who imagine that the laws of criticism are arbitrary
(or as they say, subjective), may learn a different
lesson from the array of passages, the balance of
evidence, and the estimate of each author's point of
view, with which the picture of Christian antiquity

---

[1] Clement and Origen, amongst others.

is unrolled in the pages of the *Hippolytus.* Every triumph of our faith, in purifying life, or in softening and enlightening barbarism, is there expressed in the lively records of Liturgies and Canons ; and again the shadows of night approach, with monkish fanaticism and imperial tyranny, amidst intrigues of bishops who play the parts, alternately, of courtier and of demagogue.

The picture was too truly painted for that ecclesiastical school which appeals loudest to antiquity, and has most reason to dread it. While they imagine a system of Divine immutability, or one in which, at worst, holy fathers unfolded reverently Apostolic oracles, the true history of the Church exhibits the turbulent growth of youth ; a democracy, with all its passions, transforming itself into sacerdotalism, and a poetry, with its figures, partly represented by doctrine, and partly perverted. Even the text of Scripture fluctuated in sympathy, with the changes of the Church, especially in passages bearing on asceticism, and the fuller development of the Trinity. The first Christians held that the heart was purified by faith ; the accompanying symbol, water, became by degrees the instrument of purification. Holy baptism was at first preceded by a vow, in which the young soldier expressed his consciousness of spiritual truth ; but when it became twisted into a false analogy with circumcision, the rite degenerated into a magical form, and the Augustinian notion, of a curse inherited by infants, was developed in connexion with it. Sacrifice, with the Psalmist, meant not the goat's or heifer's blood-shedding, but the contrite heart expressed by it. So, with St. Paul, it meant the presenting of our souls and bodies, as an oblation of the reason, or worship of the mind. The ancient liturgies contain prayers that God would make our sacrifices 'rational,' that is spiritual. Religion was thus moralized by a sense of the righteousness of God ; and morality

transfigured into religion, by a sense of His holiness.
Vestiges of this earliest creed yet remain in our communion service. As in life, so in sacrament, the first
Christians offered themselves in the spirit of Christ;
therefore, in his name. But when the priest took the
place of the congregation, when the sacramental signs
were treated as the natural body, and the bodily
sufferings of Christ enhanced above the self-sacrifice
of his will even to the death of the cross, the centre
of Christian faith became inverted, though its form remained. Men forgot that the writer to the Hebrews
exalts the blood of an *everlasting,* that is, of a spiritual
covenant; for what is fleshly, vanishes away. The
angels who hover with phials, catching the drops from
the cross, are pardonable in art, but make a step in theology towards transubstantiation. Salvation from evil
through sharing the Saviour's spirit, was shifted into a
notion of purchase from God through the price of his
bodily pangs. The deep drama of heart and mind
became externalized into a commercial transfer, and this
effected by a form of ritual. So with the more speculative fathers, the doctrine of the Trinity was a profound metaphysical problem, wedded to what seemed
consequences of the incarnation. But in ruder hands,
it became a materialism almost idolatrous, or an
arithmetical enigma.[1] Even now, different accepters
of the same doctrinal terms hold many shades of conception between a philosophical view which recommends itself as easiest to believe, and one felt to
be so irrational, that it calls in the aid of terror.
'Quasi non unitas, *irrationaliter* collecta, hæresin
faciat; et Trinitas *rationaliter* expensa, veritatem
constituat,' said Tertullian.[2]

---

[1] See this shown, with just rebuke of some Oxford sophistries, in the
learned Bishop Kaye's *Council of Nicæa,* London, 1853; a book of
admirable moderation, though hardly of speculative power. See pp. 163,
168, 194, 199, 219, 226, 251, 252.
[2] *Adv. Prax.* c. iii.

The historian of such variations was not likely, with those whose theology consists of invidious terms, to escape the nickname of Pelagian or Sabellian. He evidently could not state Original Sin in so exaggerated a form as to make the design of God altered by the first agents in his creation, or to destroy the notion of moral choice and the foundation of ethics. Nor could his Trinity destroy by-inference that divine Unity which all acknowledge in terms. The fall of Adam represents with him ideally the circumscription of our spirits in limits of flesh and time, and practically the selfish nature with which we fall from the likeness of God, which should be fulfilled in man. So his doctrine of the Trinity ingenuously avoids building on texts which our Unitarian critics from Sir Isaac Newton to Gilbert Wakefield have impugned, but is a philosophical rendering of the first chapter of St. John's Gospel. The profoundest analysis of our world leaves the law of thought as its ultimate basis and bond of coherence. This thought is consubstantial with the Being of the Eternal I AM. Being, becoming, and animating, or substance, thinking, and conscious life, are expressions of a Triad, which may be also represented as will,[1] wisdom, and love, as light, radiance, and warmth, as fountain, stream, and united flow, as mind, thought, and consciousness, as person, word, and life, as Father, Son, and Spirit. In virtue of such identity of Thought with Being the primitive Trinity represented neither three originant principles nor three transient phases, but three eternal inherencies in one Divine Mind. 'The unity of God, as the eternal Father, is the [2] fundamental doctrine of Christianity.' But the Di-

---

[1] 'Anima hominis naturâ suâ in se habet Ss. Trinitatis simulacrum; in se enim tria complectitur, Mentem, Intellectum, et Voluntatem; . . . cogitat . . . percipit . . . vult.'—Bede i. 8. Copying almost verbally St. Augustine.

[2] *Hippolytus*, vol. ii. p. 46. 1st ed.

vine Consciousness or Wisdom, consubstantial with the
Eternal Will, becoming personal in the Son of man, is
the express image of the Father; and Jesus actually,
but also mankind ideally, is the Son of God.   If all
this has a Sabellian or almost a Brahmanical sound,
its impugners are bound, even on patristic grounds, to
show how it differs from the doctrine of Justin Martyr, Tertullian, Hippolytus, Origen, and the historian
Eusebius.   If the language of those very fathers who
wrote against different forms of Sabellianism, would,
if now first used, be condemned as Sabellian, are we
to follow the ancient or the modern guides?   May
not a straining after orthodoxy, with all the confusion
incident to metaphysical terms, have led the scholars
beyond their masters?   We have some authorities,
who, if Athanasius himself were quoted anonymously,
would neither recognise the author nor approve his
doctrine.   They would judge him by the creed bearing his name, the sentiments of which are as difficult
to reconcile with his genuine works as its Latin terms
are with his Greek language.   Baron Bunsen may admire that creed as little as Jeremy Taylor[1] and Tillotson did, without necessarily contradicting the great
Father to whom it is ascribed.   Still more, as a philosopher, sitting loose to our Articles, he may delibe-
rately assign to the conclusions of councils a very subordinate value; and taking his stand on the genuine
words of Holy Scripture, and the immutable laws of
God to the human mind, he may say either the doctrine of the Trinity agrees with these tests, or, if you
make it disagree, you make it false.   If he errs in his
speculation, he gives us in his critical researches the
surest means of correcting his errors; and his polemic
is at least triumphant against those who load the
church with the conclusions of patristic thought, and

---

[1] '*Liberty of Prophesying,*' pp. 491-2; vol. vii. ed. Heber.   Burnet's
'*Own Times.*'   Letter from Tillotson at the end.

forbid our thinking sufficiently to understand them.
As the coolest heads at Trent said, Take care lest in
condemning Luther you condemn St. Augustine; so
if our defenders of the faith would have men believe
the doctrine of the Trinity, they had better not forbid
metaphysics, nor even sneer at Realism.

The strong assertions in the *Hippolytus* concerning
the freedom of the human will, may require some
balance from the language of penitence and of prayer.
They must be left here to comparison with the
constant language of the Greek Church, with the
doctrine of the first four centuries, with the schoolmen's
practical evasions of the Augustinian standard which
they professed, and with the guarded, but earnest
protests and limitations of our own ethical divines from
Hooker and Jeremy Taylor to Butler and Hampden.

On the great hope of mankind, the immortality of
the soul, the *Hippolytus* left something to be desired.
It had a Brahmanical, rather than a Christian, or
Platonic, sound. But the second volume of *Gott in
der Geschichte* seems to imply that, if the author
recoils from the fleshly resurrection and Judaic
millennium of Justin Martyr, he still shares the aspiration of the noblest philosophers elsewhere, and of
the firmer believers among ourselves, to a revival
of conscious and individual life, in such a form of
immortality as may consist with union with the
Spirit of our Eternal life-giver. Remarkable in the
same volume is the generous vindication of the first
Buddhist Sakya against the misunderstandings which
fastened on him a doctrine of atheism and of annihilation. The penetrating prescience of Neander seems
borne out on this point by genuine texts against the
harsher judgment of recent Sanskrit scholars. He
judged as a philosopher, and they as grammarians.

It would be difficult to say on what subject Baron
Bunsen is not at home. But none is handled by him
with more familiar mastery than that of Liturgies,

ancient and modern. He has endeavoured to enlarge the meagre stores of the Lutheran Church by a collection of evangelical songs and prayers.[1] Rich in primitive models, yet adapted to Lutheran habits, this collection might be suggestive to any Nonconformist congregations which desire to enrich or temper their devotions by the aid of common prayers. Even our own Church, though not likely to recast her ritual in a foreign mould, might observe with profit the greater calmness and harmony of the older forms, as compared with the amplifications, which she has in some cases adopted. Our Litany is hardly equal to its germ. Nor do our collects exhaust available stores. Yet if it be one great test of a theology, that it shall bear to be prayed, our author has hardly satisfied it. Either reverence, or deference, may have prevented him from bringing his prayers into entire harmony with his criticisms ; or it may be that a discrepance, which we should constantly diminish, is likely to remain between our feelings and our logical necessities. It is not the less certain, that some reconsideration of the polemical element in our Liturgy, as of the harder scholasticism in our theology, would be the natural offspring of any age of research in which Christianity was free ; and if this, as seems but too probable, is to be much longer denied us, the consequence must be a lessening of moral strength within our pale, and an accession to influences which will not always be friendly. But to estrange our doctrinal teaching from the convictions, and our practical administration from the influence, of a Protestant Laity, are parts of one policy, and that not always a blind one. Nor is doctrinal narrowness of view without practical counterpart in the rigidity which excludes the breath of prayer from our churches for six days in seven, rather than permit a clergyman to select such portions as devotion suggests, and average strength permits.

---

[1] *Gesang-und Gebet-buch.* Hamburgh. 1846.

It did not fall within the scope of this Essay to define the extent of its illustrious subject's obligations (which he would no doubt largely acknowledge) to contemporary scholars, such as Mr. Birch, or others. Nor was it necessary to touch questions of ethnology and politics which might be raised by those who value Germanism so far as it is human, rather than so far as it is German. Sclavonians might notice the scanty acknowledgment of the vast contributions of their race to the intellectual wealth of Germany.[1] Celtic scholars might remark that triumph in a discovery which has yet to be proved, regarding the law of initial mutations in their language, is premature.[2] Nor would they assent to our author's ethical description of their race. So, when he asks : ' How long shall we bear this fiction of an *external* revelation,'—that is, of one violating the heart and conscience, instead of expressing itself through them— or when he says, ' All this is delusion for those who believe it ; but what is it in the mouths of those who teach it?'—or when he exclaims, ' Oh the fools ! who, if they do see the imminent perils of this age, think to ward them off by narrow-minded persecution !' and when he repeats, ' Is it not time, in truth, to withdraw the veil from our misery? to tear off the mask from hypocrisy, and destroy that sham which is undermining all real ground under our feet? to point out the dangers which surround, nay, threaten already to engulf us?'—there will be some who think his language too vehement for good taste. Others will think burning words needed by the disease of our time. They will not quarrel on points of taste with a man

---

[1] One might ask, whether the experience of our two latest wars encourages our looking to Germany for any unselfish sympathy with the rights of nations ? Or has she not rather earned the curse of Meroz ?

[2] So the vaunted discovery of Professor Zeuss, deriving CYMRY from an imaginary word ' Combroges,' is against the testimony of the best Greek geographers.

who in our darkest perplexity has reared again the banner of truth, and uttered thoughts which give courage to the weak, and sight to the blind. If Protestant Europe is to escape those shadows of the twelfth century, which with ominous recurrence are closing round us, to Baron Bunsen will belong a foremost place among the champions of light and right. Any points disputable, or partially erroneous, which may be discovered in his many works, are as dust in the balance, compared with the mass of solid learning, and the elevating influence of a noble and Christian spirit. Those who have assailed his doubtful points are equally opposed to his strong ones. Our own testimony is, where we have been best able to follow him, we have generally found most reason to agree with him. But our little survey has not traversed his vast field, nor our plummet sounded his depth.

Bunsen, with voice, like sound of trumpet born,
　Conscious of strength, and confidently bold,
Well feign the sons of Loyola the scorn
　Which from thy books would scare their startled fold—
To thee our Earth disclosed her purple morn,
　And Time his long-lost centuries unrolled ;
Far Realms unveiled the mystery of their Tongue ;
Thou all their garlands on the CROSS hast hung.

My lips but ill could frame thy Lutheran speech,
　Nor suits thy Teuton vaunt our British pride—
But ah ! not dead my soul to giant reach,
　That envious Eld's vast interval defied ;
And when those fables strange, our hirelings teach,
　I saw by genuine learning cast aside,
Even like Linnæus kneeling on the sod,
For faith from falsehood severed, thank I GOD.

# ON THE STUDY OF THE EVIDENCES OF CHRISTIANITY.

THE investigation of that important and extensive
subject which includes what have been usually
designated as 'The Evidences of Revelation,' has pre-
scriptively occupied a considerable space in the field
of theological literature, especially as cultivated in
England.  There is scarcely one, perhaps, of our more
eminent divines who has not in a greater or less degree distinguished himself in this department, and
scarcely an aspirant for theological distinction who
has not thought it one of the surest paths to that
eminence, combining so many and varied motives of
ambition, to come forward as a champion in this
arena.  At the present day it might be supposed the
discussion of such a subject, taken up as it has been
successively in all its conceivable different bearings,
must be nearly exhausted.  It must, however, be
borne in mind, that, unlike the *essential doctrines* of
Christianity, ' the same yesterday, to-day, and for ever,'
these *external accessories* constitute a subject which
of necessity is perpetually taking somewhat at least of
a new form, with the successive phases of opinion and
knowledge.  And it thus becomes not an unsatisfactory
nor unimportant object, from time to time, to review the
condition in which the discussion stands, and to comment on the peculiar features which at any particular
epoch it most prominently presents, as indicative of
strength or weakness—of the advance and security of
the cause—if, in accordance with the real progress of
enlightenment, its advocates have had the wisdom to
rescind what better information showed defective, and

to substitute views in accordance with higher knowledge; or, on the other hand, inevitable symptoms of weakness and inefficiency, if such salutary cautions have been neglected. To offer some general remarks of this kind on the existing state of these discussions will be the object of the present Essay.

Before proceeding to the main question we may, however, properly premise a brief reflection on the spirit and temper in which it should be discussed. In writings on these subjects it must be confessed we too often find indications of a polemical acrimony on questions where a calm discussion of arguments would be more becoming, as well as more consistent with the proposed object; the too frequent assumption of the part of the special partisan and ingenious *advocate,* when the character to be sustained should be rather that of the unbiassed *judge;* too much of hasty and captious objection on the one hand, or of settled and inveterate prejudice on the other; too strong a tendency not fairly to appreciate, or even to keep out of sight, the broader features of the main question, in the eagerness to single out particular salient points for attack; too ready a disposition to triumph in lesser details, rather than steadily to grasp more comprehensive principles, and leave minor difficulties to await their solution, or to regard this or that particular argument as if the entire credit of the cause were staked upon it.

And if on the one side there is often a just complaint that objections are urged in a manner and tone offensive to religious feeling and conscientious prepossessions, which are, at least, entitled to respectful consideration; so, on the other, there is too often evinced a want of sympathy with the difficulties which many so seriously feel in admitting the alleged evidences, and which many habitual believers do not appreciate, perhaps because they have never thought or enquired deeply on the subject; or, what is more, have believed it wrong and impious to do so.

Any appeal to *argument* must imply perfect freedom of conviction. It is a palpable absurdity to put *reasons* before a man, and yet wish to *compel* him to adopt them, or to anathematize him if he find them unconvincing; to repudiate him as an unbeliever, because he is careful to find satisfactory grounds for his belief; or to denounce him as a sceptic, because he is scrupulous to discriminate the truth; to assert that his honest doubts evince a moral obliquity; in a word, that he is no judge of his own mind; while it is obviously implied that his instructor is so—or, in other words, is omniscient and infallible. When serious difficulties have been felt and acknowledged on any important subject, and a writer undertakes the task of endeavouring to obviate them, it is but a fair demand that, if the reader be one of those who do not feel the difficulties, or do not need or appreciate any further argument to enlighten or support his belief, he should not cavil at the introduction of topics, which may be valuable to others, though needless, or distasteful to himself. Such persons are in no way called upon to enter into the discussion, but they are unfair if they accuse those who do so of agitating questions of whose existence *they* have been unconscious; and of unsettling men's minds, because their *own* prepossessions have been long settled, and they do not perceive the difficulties of others, which it is the very aim of such discussion to remove.

Perhaps most of the various parties who have at all engaged in the discussion of these subjects are agreed in admitting a wide distinction between the influences of feeling and those of reason; the impressions of conscience and the deductions of intellect; the dictations of moral and religious sense, and the conclusions from evidence; in reference especially to the questions agitated as to the grounds of belief in Divine revelation. Indeed, when we take into account the nature of the *objects* considered, the distinction is manifest and undeniable ; when a reference is made to matters of *external fact* (insisted on as such) it is obvious that reason and intellect can alone be the proper judges of the evidence of such facts.   When, on the other hand, the question may be as to points of moral or religious doctrine, it is equally clear, other and higher grounds of judgment and conviction must be appealed to.

In the questions now under consideration, *both* classes of arguments are usually involved.   It is the professed principle of at least a large section of those who discuss the subject, that the question is materially connected with the truth and evidence of certain external alleged historical facts : while again, all will admit that the most essential and vital portion of the inquiry refers to matters of a higher—of a more internal, moral, and spiritual kind.

But while this distinction is clearly implied and even professedly acknowledged by the disputants, it is worthy of careful remark,  how extensively it is overlooked and kept out of sight in practice ; how commonly—almost universally, we find writers and reasoners taking up the question, even with much ability and eloquence, and arguing it out sometimes on the one, sometimes on the other ground, forgetful of their own professions, and in a way often quite inconsistent with them.

Thus we continually find the professed advocates of an external revelation and historical evidence, nevertheless making their appeal to conscience and feeling, and decrying the exercise of reason ; and charging those who find critical objections in the evidence with spiritual blindness and moral perversity ; and on the other hand we observe the professed upholders of faith and internal conviction as the only sound basis of religion, nevertheless regarding the external facts as not less essential truth which it would be profane to question.   It often seems to be rather the want of clear apprehension in the first instance of the distinct

H

kind and character of such inquiries, when on the one side directed to the *abstract* question of evidence, and when on the other pointing to the *practical* object of addressing the moral and religious feelings and affections, which causes so many writers on these subjects to betray an inconsistency between *their professed purpose* and their *mode* of carrying it out. They avow matter-of-fact inquiry—a question of the critical evidence for alleged events—yet they pursue it as if it were an appeal to moral sentiments ; in which case it would be a virtue to assent, and a crime to deny : if it be the one, it should not be proposed as the other.

Thus it is the common language of orthodox writings and discourses to advise the believer, when objections or difficulties arise, not to attempt to offer a precise answer, or to argue the point, but rather to look at the whole subject as of a kind which ought to be exempt from critical scrutiny and be regarded with a submission of judgment, in the spirit of humility and faith. This advice may be very just in reference to practical impressions ; yet if the question be one (as is so much insisted on) of external facts, it amounts to neither more nor less than a tacit surrender of the claims of external evidence and historical reality. We are told that we ought to investigate such high questions rather with our affections than with our logic, and approach them rather with good dispositions and right motives, and with a desire to find the doctrine true ; and thus shall discover the real assurance of its truth in obeying it; suggestions which, however good in a *moral* and *practical sense*, are surely inapplicable if it be made a question of *facts*.

If we were inquiring into historical evidence in any other case (suppose *e.g.* of Cæsar's landing in Britain) it would be little to the purpose to be told that we must look at the case through our desires rather than our reason, and exercise a believing disposition rather than rashly scrutinize testimony by critical cavils. Those

who speak thus on the question of religious belief, in
fact shift the basis of all belief from the alleged evidence
of facts to the influence of an internal persuasion ;
they virtually give up the evidential proof so strongly
insisted on, and confess that the whole is, after all, a
mere matter of feeling and sentiment, just as much as
those to whose views they so greatly object as openly
avowing the very same thing.

We find certain forms of expression commonly
stereotyped among a very large class of Divines,
whenever a critical difficulty or a sceptical exception
is urged, which are very significant as to the prevalent view of religious evidence. Their reply is
always of this tenor : ' These are not subjects on
which you can expect demonstrative evidence ; you
must be satisfied to accept such general proof or
probability as the nature of the question allows : you
must not inquire too curiously into these things ; it is
sufficient that we have a general moral evidence of the
doctrines ; exact critical discussion will always rake
up difficulties, to which perhaps no satisfactory answer
can be at once given. A precise sceptical caviller will
always find new objections as soon as the first are
refuted. It is in vain to seek to convince reason
unless the conscience and the will be first well-disposed
to accept the truth.' Such is the constant language
of orthodox theologians. What is it but a mere translation into other phraseology, of the very assertions of
the sceptical transcendentalist ?

Indeed, with many who take up these questions,
they are almost avowedly placed on the ground of
practical expediency rather than of abstract truth.
Good and earnest men become alarmed for the
*dangerous* consequences they think likely to result
from certain speculations on these subjects, and
thence in arguing against them, are led to assume
a tone of superiority, as the guardians of virtue
and censors of right, rather than as unprejudiced in-

quirers into the matters-of-fact on which, nevertheless,‍ they professedly make the case rest. And thus a disposition has been encouraged to regard any such question as one of *right or wrong*, rather than one of *truth or error :* to treat all objections as profane, and to discard exceptions unanswered as shocking and immoral.

If indeed the discussion were carried on upon the professed ground of spiritual impression and religious feeling, there would be a consistency in such a course; but when *evidential* arguments are avowedly addressed to the *intellect*, it is especially preposterous to shift the ground, and charge the rejection of them on *moral* motives; while those who impute such bad motives fairly expose themselves to the retort, that their own belief may be dictated by other considerations than the love of truth.

Again, in such inquiries there is another material distinction very commonly lost sight of; the difference between discussing the *truth* of a conclusion, or opinion, and the *mode* or *means* of arriving at it; or the *arguments* by which it is supported. Either may clearly be impugned or upheld without implicating the other. We may have the best evidence, but draw a wrong conclusion from it; or we may support an incontestible truth by very fallacious arguments.

The present discussion is not intended to be of a controversial kind, it is purely contemplative and theoretical; it is rather directed to a calm and unprejudiced survey of the various opinions and arguments adduced, whatever may be their ulterior tendency, on these important questions; and to the attempt to state, analyse, and estimate them just as they may seem really conducive to the high object professedly in view.

The idea of *a positive external Divine revelation* of some kind has formed the very basis of all hitherto received systems of Christian belief. The Romanist indeed regards that revelation as of the nature of a standing oracle accessible in the living voice of the Church; which being infallible, of course sufficiently accredits all the doctrines it announces, and constitutes them Divine. A more modified view has prevailed among a considerable section of Anglican theologians, who ground their faith on the same principles of Church authority, divested of its divine and infallible character. Most Protestants, with more or less difference of meaning, profess to regard revelation as once for all announced, long since finally closed, permanently recorded, and accessible only in the written Divine word contained in the Scriptures. And the discussion with those outside the pale of belief has been entirely one as to the validity of those external marks and attestations by which the truth of the alleged fact of such communication of the Divine will, was held to be substantiated.

The scope and character of the various discussions raised on 'the evidences of religion,' have varied much in different ages, following of course both the view adopted of revelation itself, the nature of the objections which for the time seemed most prominent, or most necessary to be combated, and stamped with the peculiar intellectual character, and reasoning tone, of the age to which they belonged.

The early apologists were rather defenders of the Christian cause generally; but when they entered on evidential topics, naturally did so rather in accordance with the prevalent modes of thought, than with what would now be deemed a philosophic investigation of alleged facts and critical appreciation of testimony in support of them.

In subsequent ages, as the increasing claims of infallible Church authority gained ground, to discuss evidence became superfluous, and even dangerous and impious; accordingly, of this branch of theological

literature (unless in the most entire subjection to
ecclesiastical dictation) the mediæval church presented
hardly any specimens.

It was not perhaps till the 15th century, that any
works bearing the character of what are now called
treatises on 'the evidences' appeared; and these were
probably elicited by the sceptical spirit which had
already begun to show itself, arising out of the sub-
tilties of the schoolmen.[1]

But in modern times, and under Protestant auspices, a greater disposition to follow up this kind of
discussion has naturally been developed. The sterner
genius of Protestantism required definition, argument,
and proof, where the ancient church had been content
to impress by the claims of authority, veneration, and
prescription, and thus left the conception of truth to
take the form of a mere impression of devotional feeling or exalted imagination.

Protestantism sought something more definite and
substantial, and its demands were seconded and supported, more especially by the spirit of metaphysical
reasoning which so widely extended itself in the 17th
century, even into the domains of theology; and divines, stirred up by the allegations of the Deists, aimed
at formal refutations of their objections, by drawing out
the idea and the proofs of revelation into systematic
propositions supported by logical arguments. In that
and the subsequent period the same general style of
argument on these topics prevailed among the advocates
of the Christian cause. The appeal was mainly to the
miracles of the Gospels, and here it was contended we
want merely the same testimony of eye-witnesses
which would suffice to substantiate any ordinary
matter of fact; accordingly, the narratives were to be
traced to writers at the time, who were either them-

---

[1] Several such treatises are enumerated and described by Eichhorn. See
Hallam's *Lit. of Europe*, i. p. 190.

selves eye-witnesses, or recorded the testimony of those who were so, and the direct transmission of the evidence being thus established, everything was held to be demonstrated. If any antecedent question was raised, a brief reference to the Divine Omnipotence to work the miracles, and to the Divine goodness to vouchsafe the revelation and confirm it by such proofs, was all that could be required to silence sceptical cavils.

It is true, indeed, that some consideration of the *internal* evidence derived from the excellence of the doctrines and morality of the Gospel was allowed to enter the discussion, but it formed only a subordinate branch of the evidences of Christianity. The main and essential point was always the consideration of external facts, and the attestations of testimony offered in support of them. Assuming Christianity to be essentially connected with certain outward and sensible events, the main thing to be inquired into and established, was the historical evidence of those events, and the genuineness of the records of them; if this were satisfactorily made out, then it was considered the object was accomplished. The external facts simply substantiated, the intrinsic doctrines and declarations of the Gospel must by necessary consequence be Divine truths.

If we compare the general tone, character, and pretensions of those works which, in our schools and colleges, have been regarded as the standard authorities on the subject of 'the evidences,' we must acknowledge a great change in the taste or opinions of the times from the commencement of the last century to the present day; which has led the student to turn from the erudite folios of Jackson and Stillingfleet, or the more condensed arguments of Clarke *On the Attributes*, Grotius *de Veritate*, and Leslie's *Method with the Deists*, the universal text-books of a past generation, to the writings of Lardner and Paley; the latter of whom, in the beginning of the present century, reigned supreme, the acknowledged champion of revelation, and the head of a school to which numerous others, as Campbell, Watson, and Douglas, contributed their labours. But more recently, these authors have been in an eminent degree superseded, by a recurrence to the once comparatively neglected resources furnished by Bishop Butler; of so much less formal, technical, and positive a kind, yet offering wider and more philosophical views of the subject; still, however, confessedly not supplying altogether that comprehensive discussion which is adapted to the peculiar tone and character of thought and existing state of knowledge in our own times.

The state of opinion and information in different ages is peculiarly shown in the tone and character of those discussions which have continually arisen, affecting the *grounds* of religious belief. The particular species of difficulty or objection in the reception of Christianity, and especially of its external manifestations, which have been found most formidable, have varied greatly in different ages according to the prevalent modes of thought and the character of the dominant philosophy. Thus, the difficulties with respect to miraculous evidence in particular, will necessarily be very differently viewed in different stages of philosophical and physical information. Difficulties in the idea of suspensions of natural laws, in former ages were not at all felt, canvassed, or thought of. But in later times they have assumed a much deeper importance. In an earlier period of our theological literature, the critical investigation of the question of *miracles* was a point scarcely at all appreciated. The attacks of the Deists of the 17th and early part of the 18th century were almost wholly directed to other points. But the speculations of Woolston, and still more the subsequent influence of the celebrated Essay of Hume, had the effect of directing the attention of divines more pointedly to the precise topic of miraculous evidence ; and to these causes was added the agitation of the question of the ecclesiastical miracles, giving rise to the semi-sceptical discussions of Middleton, which called forth a more exact spirit of examination into such distinctions as were needed to preserve the miracles of the Gospels from the criticisms applied to those of the Church. This distinction, in fact, involves a large part of the entire question; and towards márking it out effectually, various precautionary rules and principles were laid down by several writers. Thus, Bishop Warburton suggested as a criterion the *necessity* of the miracles to the ends of the dispensation,[1] which he conceived answered the demands of Middleton. Bishop Douglas made it the test—to connect miracles with inspiration in those who wrought them ; this, he thought, would exclude the miracles of the Church.[2]

But it was long since perceived that the argument from *necessity* of miracles is at best a very hazardous one, since it implies the presumption of constituting ourselves judges of such necessity, and admits the fair objection—when were miracles more needed than at the present day, to indicate the truth amid manifold error, or to propagate the faith ? And again, in the other case, how is the inspiration to be ascertained apart from the miracles ? or, if it be, what is the use of the miracles ? In fact, in proportion as external evidence to facts is made the professed demand, it follows that we can only recur to those grounds and rules by which the intellect always proceeds in the satisfactory investigation of any questions of fact and evidence, especially those of *physical* phenomena. By an adherence to those great principles on which

---

[1] *Div. Leg.* ix. 5.    [2] *Criterion*, pp. 239, 241.

all knowledge is acquired—by a reference to the fixed laws of belief, and our convictions of established order and analogy—we estimate the credibility of alleged events and the value of testimony, and weigh them more carefully in proportion as the matter may appear of greater moment or difficulty.

In appreciating the evidence for *any* events of a striking or wonderful kind, we must bear in mind the extreme difficulty which always occurs in eliciting the truth, dependent not on the uncertainty in the transmission of testimony, but even in cases where we were ourselves witnesses, on the enormous influence exerted by our prepossessions previous to the event, and by the momentary impressions consequent upon it. We look at all events, through the medium of our prejudices, or even where we may have no prepossessions, the more sudden and remarkable any occurrence may be, the more unprepared we are to judge of it accurately or to view it calmly; our after representations, especially of any extraordinary and striking event, are always at the best mere recollections of our impressions, of ideas dictated by our emotions at the time, of surprise and astonishment which the suddenness and hurry of the occurrence did not allow us time to reduce to reason, or to correct by the sober standard of experience or philosophy.

Questions of this kind are often perplexed for want of due attention to the laws of human thought and belief, and of due distinction in ideas and terms. The proposition 'that an event may be so incredible intrinsically as to set aside any degree of testimony,' in no way applies to or affects the *honesty* or *veracity* of that testimony, or the reality of the *impressions* on the minds of the witnesses, so far as it relates to the matter of *sensible fact* simply. It merely means this: that from the nature of our antecedent convictions, the probability of *some* kind of mistake or deception *somewhere*, though we know not *where*, is greater than the probability of the event really happening in *the way* and from the *causes* assigned.

This of course turns on the general grounds of our antecedent convictions. The question agitated is not that of mere testimony, of its value, or of its failures. It refers to those *antecedent* considerations which must govern our entire view of the subject, and which being dependent on higher laws of belief, must be paramount to all *attestation*, or rather belong to a province distinct from it. What is alleged is a case of the supernatural; but no testimony can reach to the supernatural; testimony can apply only to apparent sensible facts; testimony can only prove an extraordinary and perhaps inexplicable occurrence or phenomenon: that it is due to supernatural causes is entirely dependent on the previous belief and assumptions of the parties.

If at the present day any very extraordinary and unaccountable fact were exhibited before the eyes of an unbiassed, educated, well-informed individual, and supposing all suspicion of imposture put out of the question, his only conclusion would be that it was something he was unable at present to explain; and if at all versed in physical studies, he would not for an instant doubt either that it was really due to some natural cause, or that if properly recorded and examined, it would at some future time receive its explanation by the advance of discovery.

It is thus the prevalent conviction that at the present day miracles are not to be expected, and consequently alleged marvels are commonly discredited.

But as exceptions proving the rule, it cannot be denied that amid the general scepticism, instances sometimes occur of particular persons and parties who, on peculiar grounds, firmly believe in the occurrence of certain miracles even in our own times. But we invariably find that this is only in connexion with their own particular tenets, and restricted to the com-

munion to which they are attached.   Such manifestations of course are believed to have a religious object,
and afford to the votaries a strong confirmation of their
belief, or are regarded as among the high privileges
vouchsafed to an earnest faith.   Yet even such persons,
almost as a matter of course, utterly discredit all
such wonders alleged as occurring within the pale of
any religion except their own; while those of other
communions as unhesitatingly reject the belief in
theirs.

To take a single instance, we may refer to the
alleged miraculous 'tongues' among the followers of
the late Mr. Irving some years ago.   It is not, and
was not, a question of *records* or *testimony*, or fallibility of *witnesses*, or exaggerated or fabulous *narratives*.
*At the time*, the matter was closely scrutinized and inquired into, and many perfectly unprejudiced, and
even sceptical persons, themselves witnessed the effects,
and were fully convinced, as, indeed, were most candid
inquirers at the time, that after all reasonable or
possible allowance for the influence of delusion or
imposture, beyond all question, *certain extraordinary
manifestations did occur*.   But just as little as the
*mere fact* could be disputed, did any sober-minded
person, except those *immediately interested*, or *influenced
by peculiar views*, for a moment believe those effects to
be *miraculous*.   Even granting that they could not be
explained by any known form of nervous affection,
or on the like physiological grounds, still that they
were in some way to be ascribed to natural causes, as
yet perhaps little understood, was what no one of
ordinarily cultivated mind, or dispassionate judgment,
ever doubted.

On such questions we can only hope to form just
and legitimate conclusions from an extended and unprejudiced study of the laws and phenomena of the
natural world.   The entire range of the inductive
philosophy is at once based upon, and in every

instance tends to confirm, by immense accumulation of evidence, the grand truth of the universal order and constancy of natural causes, as a primary law of belief; so strongly entertained and fixed in the mind of every truly inductive inquirer, that he can hardly even conceive the possibility of its failure. Yet we sometimes hear language of a different kind. There are still some who dwell on the idea of Spinoza, and contend that it is idle to object to miracles as violations of natural laws, because we know not the extent of nature; that all inexplicable phenomena are, in fact, miracles, or at any rate mysteries; that we are surrounded by miracles in nature, and on all sides encounter phenomena which baffle our attempts at explanation, and limit the powers of scientific investigation; phenomena whose causes or nature we are not, and probably never shall be, able to explain.

Such are the arguments of those who have failed to grasp the positive scientific idea of the power of the inductive philosophy, or the *order of nature.* The boundaries of nature exist only where our *present* knowledge places them; the discoveries of to-morrow will alter and enlarge them. The inevitable progress of research must, within a longer or shorter period, unravel all that seems most marvellous, and what is at present least understood will become as familiarly known to the science of the future, as those points which a few centuries ago were involved in equal obscurity, but are now thoroughly understood.

None of these, or the like instances, are at all of the same kind, or have any characteristics in common with the idea of what is implied by the term 'miracle,' which is asserted to mean something at variance with nature and law; there is not the slightest analogy between an unknown or inexplicable phenomenon, and a supposed suspension of a known law: even an exceptional case of a known law is included in some larger law. Arbitrary interposition is wholly different in kind; no argument from the one can apply to the other.

The enlarged critical and inductive study of the natural world, cannot but tend powerfully to evince the inconceivableness of imagined interruptions of natural order, or supposed suspensions of the laws of matter, and of that vast series of dependent causation which constitutes the legitimate field for the investigation of science, whose constancy is the sole warrant for its generalizations, while it forms the substantial basis for the grand conclusions of natural theology. Such would be the grounds on which our convictions would be regulated as *to marvellous events at the present day;* such the rules which we should apply to *the like cases narrated in ordinary history.*

But though, perhaps, the more general admission at the present day of critical principles in the study of history, as well as the extension of physical knowledge, has done something to diffuse among the better informed class more enlightened notions on this subject, taken abstractedly, yet they may be still much at a loss to apply such principles in all cases : and readily conceive that there are possible instances in which *large exceptions must be made.*

The above remarks may be admitted in respect to events at the *present day* and those narrated in *ordinary history;* but it will be said there may be, and there are, cases which are *not like those of* the present times nor of *ordinary history.*

Thus if we attempt any uncompromising, rigid scrutiny of the Christian miracles, on the same grounds on which we should investigate any ordinary narrative of the supernatural or marvellous, we are stopped by the admonition not to make an irreverent and profane intrusion into what ought to be held sacred and exempt from such unhallowed criticism of human reason.

Yet the champions of the 'Evidences' of Christianity have professedly rested the discussion of the miracles of the New Testament on the ground of precise evidence of witnesses, insisting on the *historical* character of the Gospel records, and urging the investigation of the truth of the facts on the strict principles of criticism, as they would be applied to any other historical narrative. On these grounds, it would seem impossible to exempt the miraculous parts of those narratives, from such considerations as those which must be resorted to in regard to marvellous or supposed supernatural events in general. Yet there seems an unwillingness to concede the propriety of such examination, and a disposition to regard this as altogether an *exceptional case.* But in proportion as it is so regarded, it must be remembered its strictly *historical* character is forfeited, or at least tampered with ; and those who would shield it from the criticisms to which history and fact are necessarily amenable, cannot in consistency be offended at the alternative involved, of a more or less mythical interpretation.

In history generally our attention is often called to narratives of the marvellous : and there is a sense in which they may be viewed with reference to its general purport and in connexion with those influences on human nature which play so conspicuous a part in many events. Thus it has been well remarked by Dean Milman—' History to be true must condescend to speak the language of legend ; the belief of the times is part of the record of the times ; and though there may occur what may baffle its more calm and searching philosophy, it must not disdain that which was the primal, almost universal motive of human life.' [1]

Yet in a more general point of view, when we consider the strict office of the critical historian, it is obvious that such cases are fair subjects of analysis, conducted with the view of ascertaining their real relation to nature and fact.

---

[1] *Latin Christianity*, vol. i. p. 388.

From the general maxim that all history is open to criticism as to its grounds of evidence, no *professed history* can be exempt without forfeiting its *historical* character; and in its contents, what is properly historical, is, on the same grounds, fairly to be distinguished from what may appear to be introduced on other authority and with other objects.   Thus, the general credit of an historical narrative does not exclude the distinct scrutiny into any statements of a supernatural kind which it may contain ; nor supersede the careful estimation of the value of the testimony on which they rest—the directness of its transmission from eye-witnesses, as well as the possibility of misconception of its tenor, or of our not being in possession of all the circumstances on which a correct judgment can be formed.

It must, however, be confessed that the propriety of such dispassionate examination is too little appreciated, or the fairness of weighing well the improbabilities on one side, against possible openings to misapprehension on the other.

The nature of the laws of all human belief, and the broader grounds of probability and credibility of events, have been too little investigated, and the great extent to which all testimony must be modified by antecedent credibility as determined by such general laws, too little commonly understood to be readily applied or allowed.

Formerly (as before observed) there was no question as to general credibility.   But in later times the most orthodox seem to assume that interposition would be *generally* incredible ; yet endeavour to lay down rules and criteria by which it may be rendered probable, in cases of great emergency.   Miracles were formerly the *rule*, latterly the *exception.*

The arguments of Middleton and others, all assume the antecedent incredibility of miracles in general, in order to draw more precisely the distinction that in certain cases of a very special nature that improbability may be removed, as in the case of authenticating a revelation. Locke[1] expressly contends that it is the very extraordinary nature of such an emergency which renders an extraordinary interposition requisite and therefore credible.

The belief in Divine interposition must be essentially dependent on what we *previously* admit or believe with respect to the *Divine attributes.*

It was formerly argued that every Theist must admit the credibility of miracles ; but this, it is now seen, depends on the *nature* and *degree* of his Theism, which may vary through many shades of opinion. It depends, in fact, on the precise view taken of the Divine attributes ; such, of course, as is attainable *prior* to our admission of revelation, or we fall into an argument in a vicious circle. The older writers on natural theology, indeed, have professed to deduce very exact conclusions as to the Divine perfections, especially *Omnipotence ;* conclusions which, according to the physical argument already referred to, appear carried beyond those limits to which reason or science are competent to lead us ; while, in fact, all our higher and more precise ideas of the Divine perfections are really derived from that very revelation, whose evidence is the point in question. The Divine Omnipotence is entirely an inference *from the language of the Bible,* adopted *on the assumption* of a belief in revelation. That 'with God nothing is impossible,' is the very declaration of Scripture ; yet on this, the whole belief in miracles is built, and thus, with the many, that belief is wholly the *result,* not the *antecedent* of faith.

But were these views of the Divine attributes, on the other hand, ever so well established, it must be considered that the Theistic argument requires to be applied with much caution ; since most of those, who have adopted such theories of the Divine perfections,

---

[1] *Essay,* Book i. ch. xvi. § 13.

I

on abstract grounds, have made them the basis of a precisely opposite belief, rejecting miracles altogether; on the plea, that our ideas of the Divine perfections must directly discredit the notion of occasional interposition; that it is derogatory to the idea of Infinite power and wisdom, to suppose an order of things so imperfectly established that it must be occasionally interrupted and violated when the necessity of the case compelled, as the emergency of a revelation was imagined to do.   But all such Theistic reasonings are but one-sided, and if pushed further must lead to a denial of all active operation of the Deity whatever; as inconsistent with unchangeable, infinite perfection.[1] Such are the arguments of Theodore Parker,[2] who denies miracles *because* 'everywhere I find law the constant mode of *operation of an infinite God,*' or that of Wegscheider,[3] that the belief in miracles is irreconcilable with the idea of an *eternal God consistent with himself,* &c.

Paley's grand resource is 'once believe in a God, and all is easy.'   Now, no men have evinced a more deep-seated and devout belief in the Divine perfections than the writers just named, or others differing from them by various shades of opinion, as the late J. Sterling, Mr. Emerson, and Professor F. W. Newman.   Yet these writers have agreed in the inference that the entire view of Theistic principles, in their highest spiritual purity, is utterly at variance with all conception of suspensions of the laws of nature, or with the idea of any kind of external manifestation addressed to the senses, as overruling the higher, and as they conceive, sole worthy and fitting convictions of moral sense and religious intuition.

We here speak impartially and disinterestedly, since we are far from agreeing in their reasonings, or even

---

[1] See Mansel, *Bampt. Lect.* p. 185.

[2] *Theism,* &c. p. 263, comp. p. 113.

[3] Persuasio de supernaturali et miraculosa eademque immediata Dei revelatione, haud bene conciliari videtur cum idea Dei æterni, semper sibi constantis, &c.'—Wegscheider, *Instit. Theol.* § 12.

their first principles. But we think it deeply incumbent on all who would fairly reason out the case of miraculous evidence at the present day, to give a full and patient discussion to this entire class of arguments which now command so many adherents.

In advancing from the argument *for* miracles to the argument *from* miracles; it should, in the first instance, be considered that the evidential force of miracles (to whatever it may amount) is wholly *relative* to the apprehensions of the parties addressed.

Thus, in an 'evidential' point of view, it by no means follows, supposing we at this day were able to explain what in an ignorant age was regarded as a miracle, that therefore that event was not equally *evidential* to those immediately addressed. Columbus's prediction of the eclipse to the native islanders was as true an argument *to them* as if the event had really been supernatural.

It is a consideration adopted by some eminent divines that in the very language of the Gospels the distinction is always kept up between mere 'wonders' (τέρατα) and 'miracles' or 'signs' (σημεῖα); that is to say, the latter were occurrences not viewed as mere matters of wonder or astonishment, but regarded as indications of other truths, specially adapted to convince those to whom they were addressed in their existing stage of enlightenment.

Archbishop Whately, besides dwelling on this distinction, argues that 'the apostles would not only not have been believed but not even *listened* to, if they had not first *roused men's attention* by working, as we are told they did, special (remarkable) miracles.'[1] (Acts xix. 11.)

Some have gone further, and have considered the application of miracles as little more than is expressed in the ancient proverb, ' θαύματα μώροις '—which is

---

[1] *Lessons on Evidences,* vii. § 5.

supposed to be nearly equivalent to the rebuke, 'an evil generation seeketh a sign, &c.'[1]   (Matt. xii. 38.)

Schleiermacher regards the miracles as only relatively or apparently such, to the apprehensions of the age. By the Jews we know such manifestations, especially the power of healing, were held to constitute the distinctive marks of the Messiah, according to the prophecies of their Scriptures. Signs of an improper or irrelevant kind were refused, and even those which were granted were not necessarily nor universally conclusive. With some they were so, but with the many the case was different. The Pharisees set down the miracles of Christ to the power of evil spirits; and in other cases no conviction[2] was produced, not even on the apostles.[3]   Even Nicodemus, notwithstanding his logical reasoning, was but half convinced. While Jesus himself, especially to his disciples in private, referred to his works as only secondary and subsidiary to the higher evidence of his character and doctrine,[4] which was so conspicuous and convincing even to his enemies as to draw forth the admission, 'Never man spake like this man.'

The later Jews adopted the strange legend of the '*Sepher Toldeth Yehsu*' (Book of the Generation of Jesus), which describes his miracles substantially as in the Gospels, but says that he obtained his power by hiding himself in the Temple, and possessing himself of the secret ineffable name, by virtue of which such wonders could be wrought.[5]

---

[1] *Letter and Spirit*, by Rev. J. Wilson, 1852, p. 21.
[2] As, *e. g.*, John xi. 46; vi. 2-30; Matt. xii. 39.
[3] Matt. xvi. 9; Luke xxiv. 21-25.        [4] John xiv. 11.
[5] Orobio, a Jewish writer, quoted by Limborch (*De Verit.* p. 12-156), observes :—'Non crediderunt Judæi non quia opera illa quæ in Evangelio, narrantur a Jesu facta esse negabant; sed quia iis se persuaderi non sunt passi ut Jesum crederent Messiam.' Celsus ascribed the Christian miracles to magic (Origen *cont. Cels.* i. 38; ii. 9.) as Julian did those of St. Paul to superior knowledge of nature. (*Ap. Cyr.* iii. 100.) The general charge of magic is noticed by Tertullian, *Ap.* 23. See also Dean Lyall, *Propædia Prophetica*, 439. Neander, *Hist.* i. 67.

All moral evidence must essentially have respect to the parties to be convinced. 'Signs' might be adapted peculiarly to the state of moral or intellectual progress of one age, or one class of persons, and not be suited to that of others. With the cotemporaries of Christ and the Apostles, it was not a question of testimony or credibility; it was not the mere occurrence of what they all regarded as a supernatural event, as such, but the particular character to be assigned to it, which was the point in question. And it is to the entire difference in the ideas, prepossession, modes, and grounds of belief in those times that we may trace the reason why miracles, which would be incredible *now*, were not so in the age and under the circumstances in which they are stated to have occurred.

The force and function of all moral evidence is nullified and destroyed if we seek to apply that *kind* of argument which does not find a response in the previous views or impressions of the individual addressed; all evidential reasoning is essentially an adaptation to the conditions of mind and thought of the parties addressed, or it fails in its object. An evidential appeal which in a long past age was convincing as made to the state of knowledge in that age, might have not only no effect, but even an injurious tendency, if urged in the present, and referring to what is at variance with existing scientific conceptions; just as the arguments of the present age would have been unintelligible to a former.

In his earlier views of miracles Dr. J. H. Newman[1] maintained (agreeing therein with Paulus and Rosenmüller,) that most of the Christian miracles could only be evidential *at the time* they were wrought, and are not so at present, a view in which a religious writer of a very different school, Athanase Coquerel,[2]

---

[1] *Essay on Miracles*, &c. p. 107.
[2] *Christianity*, &c. Davison's transl. 1847, p. 226.

seems to concur, alleging that they can avail only in
founding a faith—not in preserving it.

This was also the argument of several of the
Reformers, as Luther, Huss, and others[1] have reasonably contemplated the miracles as a part of the
peculiarities of the first outward manifestation and
development of Christianity ; like all other portions
of the Divine dispensations specially adapted to the age
and the condition of those to whom they were immediately addressed : but restricted apparently to those
ages, and at any rate, not in the same form continued
to subsequent times, when the application of them
would be inappropriate.

The force of the appeal to miracles must ever be essentially dependent on the preconceptions of the parties
addressed.    Yet even in an age, or among a people,
entertaining an indiscriminate belief in the supernatural, the allegation of particular miracles as evidential may be altogether .vain ; the very extent of
their belief may render it ineffective in furnishing
proofs to authenticate the communications of any
teacher as a Divine message.    The constant belief in
the miraculous may neutralize all evidential distinctions which it may be attempted to deduce.    Of this
we have a striking instance on record, in the labours
of the missionary, Henry Martyn, among the Persian
Mahometans.    They believed readily all that he told
them of the Scripture miracles, but directly paralleled
them by wonders of their own ; they were proof
against any argument from the resurrection, because
they held that their own Sheiks had the power of
raising the dead.

It is also stated that the later Jewish Rabbis, on
the same plea that miracles were believed to be
wrought by so many teachers, of the most different
doctrines, denied their evidential force altogether.[2]

---

[1] See Seckendorf's *Hist. Luther.*, iii. 633.
[2] For some instances of this class of objections, see Dean Lyall's *Propædia Prophetica*, p. 437 *et seq.*

By those who take a more enlarged survey of the subject, it cannot fail to be remarked how different has been the spirit in which miracles were contemplated as they are exhibited to us in the earlier stages of ecclesiastical literature, from that in which they have been regarded in modern times ; and this especially in respect to that particular view which has so intimately connected them with precise 'evidential arguments;' and by a school of writers, of whom Paley may be taken as the type, and who regard them as the sole external proof and certificate of a Divine revelation.

But at the present day this 'evidential' view of miracles as the sole or even the principal external attestation to the claims of a Divine revelation, is a species of reasoning which appears to have lost ground even among the most earnest advocates of Christianity. It is now generally admitted that Paley took too exclusive a view in asserting that we cannot conceive a revelation substantiated in any other way. And it has been even more directly asserted by some zealous supporters of Christian doctrine that the external evidences are altogether inappropriate and worthless.

Thus by a school of writers of the most highly orthodox pretensions, it is elaborately argued, to the effect, that revelation ought to be believed though destitute of strict evidence, either internal or external ; and though we neither see it nor know it.[1] And again, 'We must be as sure that the bishop is Christ's appointed representative, as if we actually saw him work miracles as St. Peter and St. Paul did.'[2] Another writer of the same school exclaims, 'As if *evidence* to the Word of God were a thing to be tolerated by a Christian ; except as an additional condemnation for those who reject it, or as a sort of exercise and in-

---

[1] See *Tracts for the Times*, No. lxxxv. pp. 85-100.
[2] *Tract* No. x. p. 4.

dulgence for a Christian understanding.'[1] Thus while the highest section of Anglican orthodoxy does not hesitate openly to disavow the old evidential argument; referring everything to the authority of the Church, the more moderate virtually discredit it by a general tone of vacillation between the antagonistic claims of reason and faith;—intuition and evidence;—while the extreme 'evangelical' school, strongly asserting the literal truth of the Bible, seeks its evidence wholly in spiritual impressions, regarding all exercise of the reason as partaking in the nature of sin. But even among less prejudiced thinkers, we find indications of similar views;[2] thus a very able critic writing in *express defence* of the Christian cause, speaks of ' that accumulation of historical testimonies,' ' which the last age erroneously denominated the evidences of Christianity.' And the poet Coleridge, than whom no writer has been more earnest in upholding and defending Christianity, even in its most orthodox form, in speaking of its external attestations, impatiently exclaims, ' Evidences of Christianity! I am weary of the word: make a man feel the want of it . . . and you may safely trust it to its own evidence.'[3]

But still further: Paley's well-known conclusion to the 5th book of his *Moral Philosophy*, pronounced by Dr. Parr to be the finest prose passage in English literature, more especially his final summing up of the evidential argument in the words, ' He alone discovers who proves: and no man can prove this point (a future retribution), but the teacher who testifies by miracles that his doctrine comes from God,'—calls forth from Coleridge an emphatic protest against the entire principle, as being at variance with that moral election which he would make the essential basis of religious

---

[1] *British Critic*, No. xlviii. p. 304.
[2] *Edin. Rev.* No. cxli.
[3] *Aids to Reflexion*, i. p. 333.

belief;[1] to which he adds, in another place, 'The cordial admiration with which I peruse the preceding passage as a masterpiece of composition would, could I convey it, serve as a measure of the vital importance I attach to the convictions which impelled me to animadvert on the same passage as doctrine.'[2]

Some of the most strenuous assertors of miracles have been foremost to disclaim the notion of their being the *sole certificate* of Divine communication, and have maintained that the true force of the Christian evidences lies in the *union* and *combination* of the *external* testimony of miracles, with the *internal* excellence of the doctrine; thus, in fact, practically making *the latter the real test of the admissibility of the former*.

The necessity for such a combination of the evidence of miracles with the test of the doctrine inculcated is acknowledged in the Bible, both under the old and the new dispensations. We read of false prophets who might predict signs and wonders, which might come to pass; but this was to be of no avail if they led their hearers 'after other gods.'[3]

In like manner, 'if an angel from heaven' preached any other gospel to the Galatians, they were to reject it.[4] And even according to Christ's own admonitions, *false* Christs and false prophets should show signs and wonders such as might 'deceive, if possible, the very elect.'[5]

According to this view, the main ground of the admissibility of external attestations is the worthiness of their object—the doctrine; its unworthiness will discredit even the most distinctly alleged apparent miracles, and such worthiness or unworthiness appeals solely to our moral judgment.

---

[1] *Aids to Reflexion*, p. 278.    [2] *Ib.* p. 338.
[3] Deut. xiii. 1.        [4] Gal. i. 8.        [5] Matt. xxiv. 24.

No man has dwelt more forcibly on miraculous evidence than Archbishop Whately; yet in relation to the character of Christ as conspiring with the external attestations of his mission, he strongly remarks (speaking of some who would ascribe to Christ an unworthy doctrine, an equivocal mode of teaching), ' If I could believe Jesus to have been guilty of such subterfuges . . . . . . I not only could not acknowledge him as sent from God, but should reject him with the deepest moral indignation.'[1]

Dean Lyall enters largely into this important qualification in his defence of the miraculous argument, applying it in the most unreserved manner to the ecclesiastical miracles,[2] which he rejects at once as having no connexion with doctrine. We have also on record the remark of Dr. Johnson :—' Why, sir, Hume, taking the proposition simply, is right; but the Christian revelation is not proved by miracles alone, but as connected with prophecies and with the doctrines in confirmation of which miracles were wrought.'[3]

This has, indeed, been the common argument of the most approved divines : it is that long ago urged by Dr. S. Clarke,[4] and recently supported by Dean Trench.[5]    Yet what is it but to acknowledge the right of an appeal, superior to that of all miracles, to our own moral tribunal, to the principle that ' the human mind is competent to sit in moral and spiritual tribunal on a professed revelation,' in virtue of which Professor F. Newman, as well as many other inquirers, have come to so very opposite a conclusion.

Again, it has been strongly urged by the last-

---

[1] *Kingdom of Christ,* Essay i. § 12.
[2] *Propædia Prophetica,* p. 441.
[3] Boswell's *Life,* iii. 169.  Ed. 1826.
[4] *Evidences of Natural and Revealed Religion,* § xiv.
[5] *Notes on Miracles,* p. 27.

named writer, if miracles are made the sole criterion, then amid the various difficulties attending the scrutiny of evidence, and the detection of imposture, an advantage is clearly given to the shrewd sceptic over the simple-minded and well-disposed disciple, utterly fatal to the purity of faith.[1]

The view of miraculous evidence which allows it to be taken only in connexion with, and in fact in subserviency to, the moral and internal proof derived from the character of the doctrine, has been pushed to a greater extent by the writer last named; who asks, What is the value of ' faith at second hand ?'—Ought any external testimony to overrule internal conviction ? Ought any *moral* truth to be received in mere obedience to a miracle of *sense ?*[2] and observes that a miracle can only address itself to our external senses, and that *internal and moral impressions* must be deemed of a kind paramount to *external* and *sensible*.

If it be alleged that this internal sense may be delusive, not less so, it is replied, may the external senses deceive us as to the world of sense and external evidence. The same author however expressly allows that the claims of 'the historical' and 'the spiritual,' the proofs addressed to ' reason' and to the ' internal sense,' may each be properly entertained in their respective provinces—the danger lies in confounding them or mistaking the one for the other.

Even in the estimation of external evidence, everything depends on our *preliminary* moral convictions, and upon deciding in the first instance whether, on the one hand, we are ' to abandon moral conviction at the bidding of a miracle,' or, on the other, to make conformity with moral principles the sole test both of the evidences and of the doctrines of revelation.

In point of fact, he contends that the main actual

---

[1] See *Phases of Faith*, p. 154.
[2] *Ib.* pp. 82, 108, 201, 1st Ed.

appeal of the Apostles, especially of St. Paul, was not to outward testimony or logical argument, but to spiritual assurances:—that even when St. Paul does enter on a sort of evidential discussion, his reasoning is very unlike what a Paley would have exacted :—that all real evidence is of the spirit—which alone can judge of spiritual things ; that the Apostles did not go about proclaiming *an infallible book*, but the convert was to be convinced by his own internal judgment, not called on to resign it to a systematized and dogmatic creed. And altogether the reasoning of the Apostles (wherever they enter upon the department of reasoning), was not according to our logic, but only in accordance with the knowledge and philosophy of the age.

Thus in this fundamental assumption of internal evidence, some of the most orthodox writers are in fact in close agreement with those nominally of a very opposite school.

It was the argument of Döderlein, that ' the truth of the doctrine does not depend on the miracles, but we must *first* be convinced of the doctrine by its internal evidence.'

De Wette and others of the rationalists expressly contend, that the real evidence of the divinity of any doctrine can only be its accordance with the dictations of this moral sense, and this, Wegscheider further insists, was in fact the actual appeal of Christ in his teaching.[1]

In a word, on this view, it would follow that all external attestation would seem superfluous if it concur with, or to be rejected if it oppose, these moral

---

[1] Jesus ipse doctrinam quam tradidit divinam esse professus est, quantum divina ejus indoles ab homine vere religioso proboque bene cognosci potest atque dijudicari.—Wegscheider, *in Joh.* vii. 17.

Nulla alia ratio et via eas [doctrinas] examinandi datur quam ut illarum placita cum iis quæ via naturali rectæ rationis de Deo ejusque voluntate ipsi innotuerint diligenter componat et ad normam sine omni superstitione examinet.—Wegscheider, *Instit. Theol. Chris. Dogm.*, § 11, p. 38.

convictions.[1] Thus a considerable school have been disposed to look to the intrinsic evidence *only*, and to accept the declarations of the Gospel *solely* on the ground of their intrinsic excellence and *accordance* with our best and highest moral and religious convictions; a view which would approach very nearly to rejecting its peculiarities altogether.

Thus considerations of a very different nature are now introduced from those formerly entertained; and of a kind which affect the *entire primary conception* of 'a revelation' and its authority, and not merely any alleged *external* attestations of its truth. Thus any discussion of the 'evidences' at the present day, must have a reference equally to the influence of the various systems whether of ancient precedent or of modern illumination, which so widely and powerfully affect the state of opinion or belief.

In whatever light we regard the 'evidences' of religion, to be of any effect, whether external or internal, they must always have a special reference to the *peculiar capacity and apprehension of the party addressed.* Points which may be seen to involve the greatest difficulty to more profound inquirers, are often such as do not occasion the least perplexity to ordinary minds, but are allowed to pass without hesitation. To them all difficulties are smoothed down, all objections (if for a moment raised) are at once answered by a few plausible commonplace generalities, which to their minds are invested with the force of axiomatic truths, and to question which they would regard as at once idle and impious.

On the other hand, exceptions held forth as fatal by the shallow caviller are seen by the more deeply reflecting in all their actual littleness and fallacy. But for the sake of all parties, at the present day, especially

---

[1] Such was the argument of the *Characteristics*, vol. ii. p. 334. Ed. 1727.

those who at least profess a disposition for pursuing
the serious discussion of such momentous subjects, it
becomes imperatively necessary, that such views of it
should be suggested as may be really suitable to
better informed minds, and may meet the increasing
demands of an age pretending at least to greater enlightenment.

Those who have reflected most deeply on the nature
of the argument from external evidence, will admit
that it would naturally possess very different degrees
of force as addressed to different ages; and in a period of advanced physical knowledge the reference to
what was believed in past times, if at variance with
principles now acknowledged, could afford little ground
of appeal : in fact, would damage the argument rather
than assist it.

Even some of the older writers assign a much lower
place to the *evidence of miracles*, contrasting it with
the conviction of *real faith*, as being merely a preparatory step to it.    Thus, an old divine observes :—

'Adducuntur primum ratione exteri ad fidem,
et quasi præparantur; . . . . . . . signis
ergo et miraculis via fidei per sensus et rationem
sternitur.'[1]

And here it should be especially noticed, as characteristic of the ideas of his age, that this writer classes
the *sensible* evidence of miracles along with the convictions of *reason*, the very opposite to the view which
would now be adopted, indicative of the difference in
physical conceptions, which connects miracles rather
with faith as they are seen to be inconceivable to
reason.

These prevalent tendencies in the opinions of the
age cannot but be regarded as connected with the increasing admission of those broader views of physical
truth and universal order in nature, which have been

---

[1] Melchior Canus, *Loci Theol.* ix. 6. about 1540.

followed out to higher contemplations, and point to the acknowledgment of an overruling and all-pervading supreme intelligence.

In advancing beyond these conclusions to the doctrines of revelation, we must recognise both the due claims of science to decide on points properly belonging to the world of *matter*, and the independence of such considerations which characterizes the disclosure of *spiritual* truth, as such.

All reason and science conspire to the confession that beyond the domain of physical causation and the possible conceptions of *intellect* or *knowledge*, there lies open the boundless region of spiritual things, which is the sole dominion of *faith*. And while intellect and philosophy are compelled to disown the recognition of anything in the world of matter at variance with the first principle of the laws of matter—the universal order and indissoluble unity of physical causes—they are the more ready to admit the higher claims of divine mysteries in the invisible and spiritual world. Advancing knowledge, while it asserts the dominion of science in physical things, confirms that of faith in spiritual; we thus neither impugn the generalizations of philosophy, nor allow them to invade the dominion of faith, and admit that what is not a subject for a problem may hold its place in a creed.

In an evidential point of view it has been admitted by some of the most candid divines that the appeal to miracles, however important in the early stages of the Gospel, has become less material in later times, and others have even expressly pointed to this as the reason why they have been withdrawn; whilst at the present day the most earnest advocates of evangelical faith admit that outward marvels are needless to spiritual conviction, and triumph in the greater moral miracle of a converted and regenerate soul.

They echo the declaration of St. Chrysostom— 'If you are a believer as you ought to be, and love

128 *Study of the Evidences of Christianity.*

Christ as you ought to love him, you have no need
of miracles, for these are given to unbelievers.'[1]

After all, the *evidential* argument has but little
actual weight with the generality of believers. The
high moral convictions often referred to for internal
evidence are, to say the least, probably really felt by
very few, and the appeal made to miracles as *proofs*
of *revelation* by still fewer; a totally different feeling
actuates the many, and the spirit of faith is acknowledged where there is little disposition to reason at all,
or where moral and philosophical considerations are
absolutely rejected on the highest religious grounds,
and everything referred to the sovereign power of
divine grace.

Matters of clear and positive fact, investigated on
critical grounds and supported by exact evidence, are
properly matters of knowledge, not of faith. It is
rather in points of less definite character that any
exercise of faith can take place; it is rather with
matters of religious belief belonging to a higher and
less conceivable class of truths, with the mysterious
things of the unseen world, that faith owns a connexion, and more readily associates itself with spiritual
ideas, than with external evidence, or physical events:
and it is generally admitted that many points of important religious instruction, even conveyed under the form
of fictions (as in the instances of doctrines inculcated
through parables) are more congenial to the spirit of
faith than any relations of historical events could be.

The more knowledge advances, the more it has
been, and will be, acknowledged that Christianity, as
a real religion, must be viewed apart from connexion
with physical things.

---

[1]  . . . εἰ γὰρ πίστος εἶ ὡς εἶναι χρὴ καὶ φιλεῖς τὸν Χρίστον ὡς φιλεῖν
δεῖ, οὐ χρείαν ἔχεις τῶν σημείων· ταῦτα γὰρ ἀπίστοις δέδοται.—*Hom.* xxiii.
*in Johan.*  To the same effect also S. Isidore, 'Tunc oportebat mundum
miraculis credere,—nunc vero credentem oportet bonis operibus coruscare,'
cited in Huss in defence of Wickliff.

The first dissociation of the spiritual from the physical was rendered necessary by the palpable contradictions disclosed by astronomical discovery with the letter of Scripture. Another still wider and more material step has been effected by the discoveries of geology. More recently the antiquity of the human race, and the development of species, and the rejection of the idea of 'creation,' have caused new advances in the same direction.

In all these cases there is, indeed, a direct discrepancy between what had been taken for revealed truth and certain undeniable existing monuments to the contrary.

But these monuments were interpreted by science and reason, and there are other deductions of science and reason referring to alleged events, which, though they have left no monuments or permanent effects behind them, are not the less legitimately subject to the conclusions of positive science, and require a similar concession and recognition of the same principle of the independence of spiritual and of physical truth.

Thus far our observations are general: but at the present moment some recent publications on the subject seem to call for a few more detailed remarks. We have before observed that the style and character of works on 'the evidences,' has of necessity varied in different ages. Those of Leslie and Grotius have, by common consent, been long since superseded by that of Paley. Paley was long the text-book at Cambridge; his work was never so extensively popular at Oxford— it has, of late, been entirely disused there. By the public at large however once accepted, we do not hesitate to express our belief, that before another quarter of a century has elapsed it will be laid on the shelf with its predecessors; not that it is a work destitute of high merit—as is pre-eminently true also of those it superseded, and of others again anterior to

K

them; but they have all followed the irreversible des-tiny that a work, suited to convince the public mind at any one particular period, must be accommodated to the actual condition of knowledge, of opinion, and mode of thought of that period. It is not a question of *abstract excellence*, but of *relative adaptation*.

Paley caught the prevalent tone of thought in his day. Public opinion has now taken a different turn; and, what is more important, the style and class of difficulties and objections *honestly* felt has become wholly different. New modes of speculation—new forms of scepticism—have invaded the domain of that settled belief which a past age had been ac-customed to rest on the Paleyan syllogism. Yet, among several works which have of late appeared on the subject, we recognise few which at all meet these requirements of existing opinion. Of some of the chief of these works, even appearing under the sanction of eminent names, we are constrained to remark that they are altogether behind the age; that amid much learned and acute remark on matters of detail, those material points on which the modern difficulties chiefly turn, as well as the theories advanced to meet them, are, for the most part, not only ignored and passed over without examination or notice, but the entire school of those writers who, with infinitely varied shades of view, have dwelt upon these topics and put forth their attempts, feeble or powerful as the case may be—to solve the difficulties—to improve the tone of discussion, to reconcile the difficulties of reason with the high aspirations and demands of faith—are all indiscriminately confounded in one common cate-gory of censure; their views dismissed with ridicule as sophistical and fallacious, abused as infinitely dan-gerous, themselves denounced as heretics and infidels, and libelled as scoffers and atheists.

In truth, the majority of these champions of the evidential logic betray an almost entire unconsciousness of the advance of opinion around them. Having their own ideas long since cast in the stereotyped mould of the past, they seem to expect that a progressing age ought still to adhere to the same type, and bow implicitly to a solemn and pompous, but childish parade and reiteration, of the one-sided dogmas of an obsolete school, coupled with awful denunciations of heterodoxy on all who refuse to listen to them.

Paley clearly, as some of his modern commentators do *avowedly*, occupied the position of an *advocate*, not of a *judge*. They professedly stand up on one side, and challenge the counsel on the other to reply. Their object is not truth, but their client's case. The whole argument is one of special pleading; we may admire the ingenuity, and confess the adroitness with which favourable points are seized, unfavourable ones dropped, evaded, or disguised; but we do not find ourselves the more impressed with those high and sacred convictions of truth, which ought to result rather from the wary, careful, dispassionate summing-up on both sides, which is the function of the impartial and inflexible judge.

The one topic constantly insisted on as essential to the grounds of belief, considered as based on outward historical evidence, is that of *the credibility of external facts as supported by testimony*. This has always formed the most material point in the reasonings of the evidential writers of former times, however imperfectly and unsatisfactorily to existing modes of thought they treated it. And to this point, their more recent followers have still almost as exclusively directed their attention.

In the representations which they constantly make, we cannot but notice a strong apparent tendency and desire to uphold the mere assertion of *witnesses* as the *supreme* evidence of *fact*, to the utter disparagement of all general grounds of reasoning, analogy, and an-

tecedent credibility, by which that testimony may be
modified or discredited. Yet we remark, that all the
*instances* they adduce, when carefully examined, *really
tend* to the very conclusion they are so anxious to set
aside. Arguments of this kind are sometimes deduced
from such cases as, *e. g.*, the belief accorded on very
slight ground of probability in all commercial trans-
actions dependent on the assumed credit and character of the negotiating parties; from the conclusions
acted upon in life assurances, notwithstanding the
proverbial instability of life;—and the like : in all which
we can see no other real drift or tendency than to
*substantiate* instead of *disparage* the necessity for
*some* deeply-seated conviction of *permanent order* as
the basis of all probability.

A great source of misapprehension in this class of
arguments has been the undue confusion between the
force of *testimony* in regard to *human* affairs and events
in *history*, and in regard to *physical* facts. It may be
true that some of the most surprising occurrences in
ordinary history are currently, and perhaps correctly
accepted, on but slight grounds of real testimony;
but then they relate to events of a kind which,
however singular in their particular concomitant
circumstances, are not pretended to be beyond natural causes, or to involve higher questions of intervention.

The most seemingly improbable events in *human* history may be perfectly credible, on sufficient testimony,
however contradicting ordinary experience of human
motives and conduct—simply because we cannot assign
any limits to the varieties of human dispositions,
passions, or tendencies, or the extent to which they
may be influenced by circumstances of which, perhaps,
we have little or no knowledge to guide us. But no
such cases would have the remotest applicability to
alleged violations of the laws of *matter*, or interruptions
of the course of *physical* causes.

The case of the alleged external attestations of Revelation, is one essentially involving considerations of *physical* evidence. It is not one in which such reflexions and habits of thought as arise out of a familiarity with human history, and moral argument, will suffice. These no doubt and other kindred topics, with which the scholar and the moralist are familiar, are of great and fundamental importance to our general views of the whole subject of Christian evidence ; but the particular case of *miracles*, as such, is one specially bearing on purely *physical* contemplations, and on which no general moral principles, no common rules of evidence or logical technicalities, can enable us to form a correct judgment. It is not a question which can be decided by a few trite and commonplace generalities as to the moral government of the world and the belief in the Divine Omnipotence—or as to the validity of human testimony, or the limits of human experience. It involves, and is essentially built upon, those grander conceptions of the order of nature, those comprehensive primary elements of all physical know-ledge, those ultimate ideas of universal causation, which can only be familiar to those thoroughly versed in cosmical philosophy in its widest sense.

In an age of physical research like the present, all highly cultivated minds and duly advanced intellects have imbibed, more or less, the lessons of the inductive philosophy, and have at least in some measure learned to appreciate the grand foundation conception of universal law—to recognise the impossibility even of *any two material atoms* subsisting together without a determinate relation—of any action of the one on the other, whether of equilibrium or of motion, without reference to a physical cause—of any modification whatsoever in the existing conditions of material agents, unless through the invariable operation of a series of eternally impressed consequences, following in some necessary chain of orderly connexion—however imper-

fectly known to us.  So clear and indisputable indeed
has this great truth become—so deeply seated has it
been now admitted to be, in the essential nature of
sensible things and of the external world, that not
only do all philosophical inquirers adopt it, as a
primary principle and guiding maxim of all their
researches—but, what is most worthy of remark,
minds of a less comprehensive capacity, accustomed to reason on topics of another character, and
on more contracted views, have at the present day
been constrained to evince some concession to this
grand principle, even when seeming to oppose it.

Among writers on these questions, Dean Trench has
evinced a higher view of physical philosophy than we
might have expected from the mere promptings of philology and literature, when he affirms that ' we continually behold lower laws held in restraint by higher ;
mechanic by dynamic—chemical by vital, physical by
moral ;' remarks which, if only followed out, entirely
accord with the conclusion of universal subordination
of causation ; though we must remark in passing that
the meaning of 'moral laws controlling physical,' is
not very clear.

It is for the most part hazardous ground for any
general moral reasoner to take, to discuss subjects of
evidence which essentially involve that higher appreciation of *physical truth* which can be attained only from
an accurate and comprehensive acquaintance-with the
connected series of the physical and mathematical
sciences.  Thus, for example, the simple but grand
truth of the law of conservation, and the stability of
the heavenly motions, now well understood by all sound
cosmical philosophers, is but the type of the universal
self-sustaining and self-evolving powers which pervade
all nature.  Yet the difficulty of conceiving this truth
in its simplest exemplification was formerly the chief
hindrance to the acceptance of the solar system—from
the prepossession of the peripatetic dogma that there

must be a constantly acting moving force to keep it going. This very exploded chimera, however, by a singular infatuation, is now actually revived as the ground of argument for miraculous interposition by redoubtable champions who, to evince their profound knowledge of mechanical philosophy, inform us that ' the whole of nature is like a mill, which cannot go on without the continual application of a moving power !'

Of these would-be philosophers, we find many anxiously dwelling on the topic, so undeniably just in itself, of the danger of incautious conclusions—of the gross errors into which men fall by over-hasty generalizations. They recount with triumph the absurd mistakes into which some even eminent philosophers have fallen in prematurely denying what experience has since fully shown to be true, because in the then state of knowledge it seemed incredible.[1] They feel an elevating sense of superiority in putting down the arrogance of scientific pretensions by alleging the short-sighted dogmatism with which men of high repute in science have evinced a scepticism in points of vulgar belief, in which, after all, the vulgar belief has proved right. They even make a considerable display of reasoning on such cases; but we cannot say that those reasonings are particularly distinguished for consistency, force, or originality. The philosopher (for example) denies the credibility of alleged events professedly in their nature *at variance with all physical analogy.* These writers, in reply, affect to make a solemn appeal to the bar of analogy, and support it by instances which precisely defeat their own conclusion. Thus they advance the novel and profoundly instructive story of an Indian who denied the existence of ice as at variance with

[1] Numerous instances of the kind referred to will be found cited in Mr. R. Chambers's *Essay on Testimony,* &c. Edinburgh Papers, 1859; and in Abp. Whately's Edition of Paley's *Evidences.*

experience ; and still more from the contradiction that being solid, it could not float in water. In like manner they dwell upon other equally interesting stories of a butterfly, who from the experience of his ephemeral life in summer, denied that the leaves were ever brown or the ground covered with snow ; of a child who watched a clock made to strike *only* at noon, through many hours, and therefore concluded it could never strike ; of a person who had observed that fish are organized to *swim*, and therefore concluded there could be no such animals as *flying* fish.

These, with a host of other equally recondite, novel, startling, and conclusive instances are urged in a tone of solemn wisdom, to prove—what ? That water is converted into ice by a regular *known law ;* that it has a specific gravity less than water by *some law* at present but imperfectly understood ; that without *violation of analogy*, fins may be modified into wings ; that it is part of the *great law* of climate that in winter leaves are brown and the ground sometimes white—that machinery may be made with action intermitting by *laws as regular* as those of its more ordinary operation. In a word, that the philosopher who looks to an endless subordinating series of laws of successively higher generality, is inconsistent in denying events at variance with that subordination !

It is indeed curious to notice the elaborate multiplication of instances adduced by some of the writers referred to, all really tending to prove the subordination of *facts* to *laws*, clearly evinced as soon as the cases were well understood, though, till then, often regarded in a sceptical spirit ; while of that scepticism they furnish the real and true refutation in the principle of *law* ultimately established, under whatever primary appearance and semblance of marvellous discordance from all law. It would be beyond our limits to notice in detail such instances as are thus dwelt upon, and apparently regarded as of sovereign

value and importance, to discredit philosophical generalization :—such as the disbelief in the marvels recounted by Marco Polo ; of the miracle of the martyrs
who spoke articulately after their tongues were cut
out ; the angel seen in the air by 2000 persons at
Milan ; the miraculous balls of fire on the spires at
Plausac ; Herodotus's story of the bird in the mouth
of the crocodile ; narratives of the sea-serpent, marvels
of mesmerism and electro-biology ; all discredited
formerly as fables ; vaccination observed and attested
by peasants, but denied and ridiculed by medical
men :—

These and the like cases are all urged as triumphant
proofs, of what ?—that some men have always been
found of unduly sceptical tendencies ; and sometimes
of a rationally cautious turn ; who have heard strange,
and, perhaps, exaggerated narratives, and have maintained sometimes a wise, sometimes an unwise, degree
of reserve and caution in admitting them ; though they
have since proved in accordance with *natural causes*.

Hallam and Rogers are cited as veritable witnesses
to the truth of certain effects of mesmerism in their
day generally disbelieved ; and for asserting which
they were met with all but an imputation of 'the lie
direct.' They admitted, however, that their assertion
was founded on 'experience so rare as to be had only
once in a century ;' but that experience has been
since universally borne out by all who have candidly
examined the question, and the *apparently isolated and
marvellous cases* have settled down into examples of
*broad and general laws*, now fully justified by experience
and analogy.

Physiological evidence is adduced (which we will
suppose well substantiated) to show that the excision
of the *whole tongue* does not take away the power of
speech, though that of the *extremity* does so ; hence
the denial of the story from imperfect experience.
So of other cases : the angel at Milan was the

aerial reflexion of an image on a church; the balls of fire, at Plausac, were electrical; the sea-serpent was a basking shark, or a stem of sea-weed. A committee of the French Academy of Sciences, with Lavoisier at its head, after a grave investigation, pronounced the alleged fall of aërolites to be a superstitious fable. It is, however, now substantiated, *not* as a miracle, but as a well-known *natural* phenomenon. Instances of undue philosophical scepticism are unfortunately common; but they are the errors, not the correct processes, of inductive inquiry.

Granting all these instances, we merely ask—what do they prove?—except the real and paramount dominion of the rule of *law* and *order*, of *universal subordination* of *physical causes*, as the sole principle and criterion of proof and evidence in the region of physical and sensible truth; and nowhere more emphatically than in the history of marvels and prodigies, do we find a verification of the truth, ' opinionum· commenta delet dies, naturæ judicia confirmat.'

This in fact is the sole real result of all the profound parallelisms and illustrative anecdotes so confidently but unconsciously adduced by these writers with an opposite design.

What is the *real* conclusion from the far-famed *Historic Doubts* and the *Chronicles of Ecnarf?* but simply this—*there is a rational solution*, a *real* conformity to *analogy and experience*, to whatever extent a partially informed inquirer might be led to reject the recounted apparent wonders on imperfect knowledge, and from too hasty inference; these delightful parodies on Scripture (if they prove anything), would simply prove that the Bible narrative is no more properly *miraculous* than the marvellous exploits of Napoleon I., or the paradoxical events of recent history.

Just a similar scepticism *has been* evinced by nearly all the first physiologists of the day, who have joined in rejecting the development theories of Lamarck and the *Vestiges;* and while they have strenuously maintained successive creations, have denied and denounced the alleged production of organic life by Messrs. Crosse and Weekes, and stoutly maintained the impossibility of spontaneous generation, on the alleged ground of contradiction to experience. Yet it is now acknowledged under the high sanction of the name of Owen,[1] that 'creation' is only another name for our ignorance of the mode of production ; and it has been the unanswered and unanswerable argument of another reasoner that new species *must* have originated *either* out of their inorganic elements, *or* out of previously organized forms ; *either* development *or* spontaneous generation *must be* true : while a work has now appeared by a naturalist of the most acknowledged authority, Mr. Darwin's masterly volume on *The Origin of Species* by the law of 'natural selection,'—which now substantiates on undeniable grounds the very principle so long denounced by the first naturalists,—*the origination of new species by natural causes :* a work which must soon bring about an entire revolution of opinion in favour of the grand principle of the self-evolving powers of nature.

By parity of reason it might just as well be objected to Archbishop Whately's theory of civilization, we have only for a few centuries known anything of savages ; how then can we pretend to infer that they have *never* civilized themselves ? never, in all that enormous length of time which modern discovery has now indisputably assigned to the existence of the human race ! This theory, however, is now introduced as a comment on Paley in support of the credibility of revelation ; and an admirable argument no doubt it is, though perhaps many would apply it in a sense somewhat different from that of the author. If the use of fire, the cultivation of the soil, and the like, were

---

[1] *British Association Address,* 1858.

Divine revelations, the most obvious inference would be that so likewise are printing and steam. If the boomerang was divinely communicated to savages ignorant of its principle, then surely the disclosure of that principle in our time by the gyroscope, was equally so. But no one denies revelation in this sense; the philosophy of the age does not discredit the inspiration of Prophets and Apostles, though it may sometimes believe it in poets, legislators, philosophers, and others gifted with high genius. At all events, the revelation of civilization does not involve the question of *external miracles*, which is here the sole point in dispute. The main assertion of Paley is that it is impossible to conceive a revelation given except by means of miracles. This is his primary axiom ; but this is precisely the point which the modern turn of reasoning most calls in question, and rather adopts the belief that a revelation is then most credible, when it appeals least to violations of natural causes. Thus, if miracles were in the estimation of a former age among the chief *supports* of Christianity, they are at present among the main *difficulties*, and hindrances to its acceptance.

One of the first inductive philosophers of the age, Professor Faraday, has incurred the unlimited displeasure of these profound intellectualists, because he has urged that the mere contracted experience of the senses is liable to deception, and that we ought to be guided in our conclusions—and, in fact, can only correct the errors of the senses—by a careful recurrence to the consideration of natural laws and extended analogies.[1] In opposition to this heretical proposition, they[2] set in array the dictum of two great authorities of the Scottish school, Drs. Abercrombie and Chalmers, that 'on a certain amount of testimony we might believe

---

[1] *Lecture on Mental Education.* 1854.
[2] See *Edinburgh Papers,* 'Testimony,' &c., by R. Chambers, Esq., F.R.S.E., &c.

any statement, however improbable;' so that if a number of respectable witnesses were to concur in asseverating that on a certain occasion they had seen two and two make five, we should be bound to believe them!

This, perhaps it will be said, is an extreme case. Let us suppose another :—if a number of veracious witnesses were to allege a *real* instance of witchcraft at the present day, there might no doubt be found some infatuated persons who would believe it; but the strongest of such assertions to any educated man would but prove either that the witnesses were cunningly imposed upon, or the wizard himself deluded. If the most numerous ship's company were all to asseverate that they had seen a mermaid, would any rational persons at the present day believe them? That they saw something which *they believed* to be a mermaid, would be easily conceded. No amount of attestation of innumerable and honest witnesses, would ever convince any one versed in mathematical and mechanical science, that a person had squared the circle or discovered perpetual motion. Antecedent credibility depends on antecedent knowledge, and enlarged views of the connexion and dependence of truths; and the value of any testimony will be modified or destroyed in different degrees to minds differently enlightened.

Testimony, after all, is but a second-hand assurance; —it is but a blind guide; testimony can avail nothing against reason. The essential question of miracles stands quite apart from any consideration of *testimony;* the question would remain the same, if we had the evidence of our own senses to an alleged miracle, that is, to an extraordinary or inexplicable fact. It is not the *mere fact*, but the *cause* or *explanation* of it, which is the point at issue.

The case, indeed, of the *antecedent* argument of miracles is very clear, however little some are inclined to perceive it. In nature and from nature, by science and by reason, we neither have nor can possibly have any evidence of a *Deity working miracles ;*—for that, we must go out of nature and beyond reason.  If we could have any such evidence *from nature*, it could only prove extraordinary *natural* effects, which would not be *miracles* in the old theological sense, as isolated, unrelated, and uncaused ; whereas no *physical* fact can be conceived as unique, or without analogy and relation to others, and to the whole system of natural causes.

To conclude, an alleged miracle can only be regarded in one of two ways ;—either (1) abstractedly as a physical event, and therefore to be investigated by reason and physical evidence, and referred to physical causes, possibly to *known* causes, but at all events to some higher cause or law, if at present unknown ; it then ceases to be supernatural, yet still might be appealed to in support of religious truth, especially as referring to the state of knowledge and apprehensions of the parties addressed in past ages ; or (2) as connected with religious doctrine, regarded in a sacred light, asserted on the authority of inspiration. In this case it ceases to be capable of investigation by reason, or to own its dominion ; it is accepted on religious grounds, and can appeal only to the principle and influence of faith.

Thus miraculous narratives become invested with the character of articles of faith, if they be accepted in a less positive and certain light, or perhaps as involving more or less of the parabolic or mythic character ; or at any rate as received in connexion with, and for the sake of the doctrine inculcated.

Some of the most strenuous advocates of the Christian 'evidences' readily avow, indeed expressly contend, that the attestation of miracles is, after all, not irresistible ; and that in the very uncertainty which confessedly remains lies the 'trial of faith,'[1] which it is

---

[1] See, *e.g.*, Butler's *Analogy*, pt. ii. ch. 6.

thus implied must really rest on some other independent moral conviction.

In the popular acceptation, it is clear the Gospel miracles are always *objects*, not *evidences* of faith; and when they are connected specially with doctrines, as in several of the higher mysteries of the Christian faith, the sanctity which invests the point of faith itself is extended to the external narrative in which it is embodied; the reverence due to the mystery renders the external events sacred from examination, and shields them also within the pale of the sanctuary; the *miracles* are merged in the *doctrines* with which they are connected, and associated with the declarations of spiritual things which are, as such, exempt from those criticisms to which physical statements would be necessarily amenable.

But even in a reasoning point of view, those who insist most on the positive external proofs, allow that *moral* evidence is distinguished from *demonstrative*, not only in that it admits of *degrees*, but more especially in that the *same* moral argument is of *different force* to *different minds*. And the advocate of Christian evidence triumphs in the acknowledgment that the strength of Christianity lies in the *variety* of its evidences, suited to all varieties of apprehension; and, that, amid all the diversities of conception, those who cannot appreciate some one class of proofs, will always find some other satisfactory, is itself the crowning evidence.

With a firm belief in constant supernatural interposition, the cotemporaries of the Apostles were as much blinded to the reception of the gospel, as, with an opposite persuasion, others have been at a later period. Those who had access to living Divine instruction were not superior to the prepossessions and ignorance of their times. There never existed an 'infallible age' of exemption from doubt or prejudice. And if to later times records written in the characters of a long past epoch are left to be deciphered by the advancing light of learning and science,—the spirit of faith discovers continually increasing attestation of the Divine authority of the truths they include.

The '*reason* of the hope that is in us' is not restricted to *external* signs, nor to any one kind of evidence, but consists of such assurance as may be most satisfactory to each earnest individual inquirer's own mind. And the true acceptance of the entire revealed manifestation of Christianity will be most worthily and satisfactorily based on that assurance of 'faith,' by which the Apostle affirms 'we stand,' (2 Cor. ii. 24), and which, in accordance with his emphatic declaration, must rest, 'not in the wisdom of man, but in the power of God.' (1 Cor. ii. 5.)

# SEANCES HISTORIQUES DE GENÈVE—
## THE NATIONAL CHURCH.

IN the city of Geneva, once the stronghold of the severest creed of the Reformation, Christianity itself has of late years received some very rude shocks. But special attempts have been recently made to counteract their effects and to re-organize the Christian congregations upon Evangelical principles. In pursuance of this design, there have been delivered and published during the last few years a series of addresses by distinguished persons holding Evangelical sentiments, entitled *Séances Historiques*. The attention of the hearers was to be conciliated by the concrete form of these discourses; the phenomenon of the historical Christianity to be presented as a fact which could not be ignored, and which must be acknowledged to have had some special source; while, from time to time, as occasion offered, the more peculiar views of the speakers were to be instilled. But before this panorama of historic scenes had advanced beyond the period of the fall of heathenism in the West, there had emerged a remarkable discrepancy between the views of two of the authors, otherwise agreeing in the main.

It fell to the Comte Léon de Gasparin to illustrate the reign of Constantine. He laid it down in the strongest manner, that the individualist principle supplies the true basis of the Church, and that by inaugurating the union between Church and State

Constantine introduced into Christianity the false
and pagan principle of Multitudinism.   M. Bungener
followed in two lectures upon the age of Ambrose and
Theodosius.   He felt it necessary, for his own satisfaction and that of others, to express his dissent from
these opinions.   He agreed in the portraiture drawn by
his predecessor of the so-called first Christian emperor,
and in his estimate of his personal character.   But he
maintained, that the multitudinist principle was not,
unlawful, nor essentially pagan; that it was recognised and consecrated in the example of the Jewish
theocracy; that the greatest victories of Christianity
have been won by it; that it showed itself under
Apostolic sanction as early as the day of Pentecost;—
for it would be absurd to suppose the three thousand
who were joined to the Church on the preaching of
Peter to have been all 'converted' persons in the
modern Evangelical sense of the word.   He especially
pointed out, that the Churches which claim to be
founded upon Individualism, fall back themselves,
when they become hereditary, upon the multitudinist principle.   His brief, but very pertinent observations on that subject were concluded in these
words:—

'Le multitudinisme est une force qui peut, comme
toute force, être mal dirigée, mal exploitée, mais qui
peut aussi l'être au profit de la vérité, de la piété, de
la vie.   Les Eglises fondées sur un autre principe ont
aidé à rectifier celui-là; c'est un des incontestables
services qu'elles ont rendus, de nos jours, à la cause de
l'Evangile.   Elles ont droit à notre reconnaissance;
mais à Genève, qu'elles ne nous demandent pas ce que
nous ne pouvons faire, et qu'on me permette de le
dire, ce qu'elles ne font pas elles-mêmes.   Oui! le
multitudinisme genevois est resté vivant chez elles, et
certainement elles lui doivent une portion notable de
leur consistance au dedans, de leur influence au dehors.
Elles font appel, comme nous, à ses souvenirs et à ses

gloires; elles forment, avec nous, ce que le monde chrétien appelle et appellera toujours *l'Eglise de Genève.* Nous ne la renions, au fond, pas plus les uns que les autres. Elle a été, elle est, elle restera notre mère à tous.'[1]

Such are the feelings in favour of Nationalism on the part of M. Bungener, a member of the Genevan Church; a Church to which many would not even concede that title, and of which the ecclesiastical renown centres upon one great name; while the civil history of the country presents but little of interest either in ancient or modern times. But the questions at issue between these two Genevans are of wide Christian concern, and especially to ourselves. If the Genevans cannot be proud of their Calvin, as they cannot in all things—and even he is not truly their own—they have little else of which to speak before Christendom. Very different are the recollections which are awakened by the past history of such a Church as ours. Its roots are found to penetrate deep into the history of the most freely and fully developed nationality in the world, and its firm hold upon the past is one of its best auguries for the future. It has lived through Saxon rudeness, Norman rapine, baronial oppression and bloodshed; it has survived the tyranny of Tudors, recovered from fanatical assaults, escaped the treachery of Stuarts; has not perished under coldness, nor been stifled with patronage, nor sunk utterly in a dull age, nor been entirely depraved in a corrupt one. Neither as a spiritual society, nor as a national institution, need there be any fear that the Church of this country, which has passed through so many ordeals, shall succumb, because we may be on the verge of some political and ecclesiastical changes. We, ourselves, cohere with those who have preceded us, under very different forms of civil constitution, and

---

[1] *Séances Historiques de Genève—Le Christianisme au 4ième Siècle,* p. 153.

under a very different creed and externals of worship.
The 'rude forefathers,' whose mouldering bones, layer
upon layer, have raised the soil round the foundations
of our old churches, adored the Host, worshipped the
Virgin, signed themselves with the sign of the cross,
sprinkled themselves with holy water, and paid money
for masses for the relief of souls in purgatory.  But it
is no reason, because we trust that spiritually we are
at one with the best of those who have gone before us
in better things than these, that we should revert to
their old-world practices; nor should we content ourselves with simply transmitting to those who shall
follow us, traditions which have descended to ourselves,
if we can transmit something better.  There is a time
for building up old waste places, and a time for raising
fresh structures; a time for repairing the ancient
paths, and a time for filling the valleys and lowering
the hills in the constructing of new.  The Jews, contemporaries of Jesus and his Apostles, were fighters
against God, in refusing to accept a new application
of things written in the Law, the Prophets, and the
Psalms; the Romans in the time of Theodosius were
fighters against Him, when they resisted the new
religion with an appeal to old customs; so were the
opponents of Wycliffe and his English Bible, and the
opponents of Cranmer and his Reformation.  Meddle
not with them that are given to change is a warning
for some times, and self-willed persons may 'bring in
damnable heresies;' at others, 'old things are to pass
away,' and that is erroneously 'called heresy' by the
blind, which is really a worshipping the God of the
Fathers in a better way.

When signs of the times are beheld, foretelling
change, it behoves those who think they perceive
them to indicate them to others, not in any spirit of
presumption or of haste; and, in no spirit of presumption, to suggest inquiries as to the best method of
adjusting old things to new conditions.

Many evils are seen in various ages, if not to have issued directly, to have been intimately linked with the Christian profession—such as religious wars, persecutions, delusions, impositions, spiritual tyrannies; many goods of civilization in our own day, when men have run to and fro and knowledge has been increased, have apparently not the remotest connexion with the Gospel. Hence grave doubts arise in the minds of really well-meaning persons, whether the secular future of humanity is necessarily bound up with the diffusion of Christianity—whether the Church is to be hereafter the life-giver to human society. It would be idle on the part of religious advocates to treat anxieties of this kind as if they were forms of the old Voltairian anti-Christianism. They are not those affectations of difficulties whereby vice endeavours to lull asleep its fears of a judgment to come; nor are they the pretensions of ignorant and presumptuous spirits, making themselves wise beyond the limits of man's wisdom. Even if such were, indeed, the sources of the wide-spread doubts respecting traditional Christianity which prevail in our own day, it would be very injudicious polemic which should content itself with denouncing the wickedness, or expressing pity for the blindness, of those who entertain them. An imputation of evil motives may embitter an opponent and add gall to controversy, but can never dispense with the necessity for replying to his arguments, nor with the advisableness of neutralizing his objections.

If anxieties respecting the future of Christianity, and the office of the Christian Church in time to come, were confined to a few students or speculative philosophers, they might be put aside as mere theoretical questions; if rude criticisms upon the Scriptures, of the Tom Paine kind, proceeding from agitators of the masses, or from uninstructed persons, were the only assaults to which the letter of the Bible was exposed, it might be thought, that further instruction would impart a more reverential and submissive spirit : if lay people only entertained objections to established formularies in some of their parts, a self-satisfied sacerdotalism, confident in a supernaturally transmitted illumination, might succeed in keeping peace within the walls of emptied churches. It may not be very easy, by a statistical proof, to convince those whose preconceptions indispose them to admit it, of the fact of a very wide-spread alienation, both of educated and uneducated persons, from the Christianity which is ordinarily presented in our churches and chapels. Whether it be their reason or their moral sense which is shocked by what they hear there, the ordinances of public worship and religious instruction provided for the people of England, alike in the endowed and unendowed churches, are not used by them to the extent we should expect, if they valued them very highly, or if they were really adapted to the wants of their nature as it is. And it has certainly not hitherto received the attention which such a grave circumstance demanded, that a number equal to five millions and a quarter of persons, should have neglected to attend means of public worship within their reach on the census Sunday in 1851; these five millions and a quarter being forty-two per cent. of the whole number able and with opportunity of then attending. As an indication, on the other hand, of a great extent of dissatisfaction on the part of the clergy to some portion, at least, of the formularies of the Church of England, may be taken the fact of the existence of various associations to procure their revision, or some liberty in their use, especially that of omitting one unhappy creed.

It is generally the custom of those who wish to ignore the necessity for grappling with modern questions concerning Biblical interpretation, the construction of the Christian Creed, the position and prospects

of the Christian Church, to represent the disposition
to entertain them as a disease contracted by means
of German inoculation.  At other times, indeed, the
tables are turned, and theological inquirers are to be
silenced with the reminder, that in the native land of
the modern scepticism, Evangelical and High Lutheran
reactions have already put it down.  It may be, that
on these subjects we shall in England be much in-
debted, for some time to come, to the patience of
German investigators; but we are by no means likely
to be mystified by their philosophical speculations, nor
to be carried away by an inclination to force all facts
within the sweep of some preconceived comprehensive
theory.  If the German biblical critics have gathered
together much evidence, the verdict will have to be
pronounced by the sober English judgment.  But, in
fact, the influence of this foreign literature extends to
comparatively few among us, and is altogether insufficient to account for the wide spread of that
which has been called the negative theology.  This
is rather owing to a spontaneous recoil, on the
part of large numbers of the more acute of our
population, from some of the doctrines which are to
be heard at church and chapel; to a distrust of the old
arguments for, or proofs of, a miraculous Revelation;
and to a misgiving as to the authority, or extent of
the authority, of the Scriptures.  In the presence of
real difficulties of this kind, probably of genuine
English growth, it is vain to seek to check that open
discussion out of which alone any satisfactory settlement of them can issue.

There may be a certain amount of literature circulating among us in a cheap form, of which the purpose,
with reference to Christianity, is simply negative and
destructive, and which is characterized by an absence
of all reverence, not only for beliefs, but for the best
human feelings which have gathered round them,
even when they have been false or superstitious.  But

if those who are old enough to do so would compare the tone generally of the sceptical publications of the present day with that of the papers of Hone and others about forty years ago, they would be reminded, that assaults were made then upon the Christian religion in far grosser form than now, and long before opinion could have been inoculated by German philosophy—long before the more· celebrated criticisms upon the details of the Evangelical histories had appeared.  But it was attacked then as an institution, or by reason of the unpopularity of institutions and methods of government connected, or supposed to be connected, with it.  The anti-christian agitation of that day in England was a phase of radicalism, and of a radicalism which was a terrific and uprooting force, of which the counterpart can scarcely be said to exist among us now.

The sceptical movements in this generation are the result of observation and. thought, not of passion. Things come to the knowledge of almost all persons, which were unknown a generation ago, even to the well informed.  Thus the popular knowledge, at that time, of the surface of the earth, and of the populations which cover it, was extremely incomplete.  In our own boyhood the world as known to the ancients was nearly all which was known to ourselves.  We have recently become acquainted—intimate—with the teeming regions of the far East, and with empires, pagan or even atheistic, of which the origin runs far back beyond the historic records of Judæa or of the West, and which were more populous than all Christendom now is, for many ages before the Christian era.  Not any book learning—not any proud exaltation of reason —not any dreamy German metaphysics—not any minute and captious Biblical criticism—suggest questions to those who on Sundays hear the reading and exposition of the Scriptures as they were expounded to our forefathers, and on Monday peruse the news of a world of which our forefathers little dreamed;—descriptions of great nations, in some senses barbarous compared with ourselves, but composed of men of flesh and blood like our own—of like passions, marrying and domestic, congregating in great cities, buying and selling and getting gain, agriculturists, merchants, manufacturers, making wars, establishing dynasties, falling down before objects of worship, constituting priesthoods, binding themselves by oaths, honouring the dead. In what relation does the Gospel stand to these millions? Is there any trace on the face of its records that it even contemplated their existence? We are told, that to know and believe in Jesus Christ is in some sense necessary to salvation. It has not been given to these. Are they—will they be, hereafter, the worse off for their ignorance? As to abstruse points of doctrine concerning the Divine Nature itself, those subjects may be thought to lie beyond the range of our faculties; if one says, aye, no other is entitled to say no to his aye; if one says, no, no one is entitled to say aye to his no. Besides, the best approximative illustrations of those doctrines must be sought in metaphysical conceptions, of which few are capable, and in the history of old controversies, with which fewer still are acquainted. But with respect to the moral treatment of His creatures by Almighty God, all men, in different degrees, are able to be judges of the representations made of it, by reason of the moral sense which He has given them. As to the necessity of faith in a Saviour to these peoples, when they could never have had it, no one, upon reflection, can believe in any such thing—doubtless they will be equitably dealt with. And when we hear fine distinctions drawn between covenanted and uncovenanted mercies, it seems either to be a distinction without a difference, or to amount to a denial of the broad and equal justice of the Supreme Being. We cannot be content to wrap this question up and leave it for a mystery, as to what shall become of those myriads upon myriads of non-christian races. First, if our traditions tell us, that they are involved in the curse and perdition of Adam, and may justly be punished hereafter individually for his transgression, not having been extricated from it by saving faith, we are disposed to think, that our traditions cannot herein fairly declare to us the words and inferences from Scripture; but if on examination it should turn out that they have, we must say, that the authors of the Scriptural books have, in those matters, represented to us their own inadequate conceptions, and not the mind of the Spirit of God; for we must conclude with the Apostle, 'Yea, let God be true and every man a liar.'

If, indeed, we are at liberty to believe, that all shall be equitably dealt with according to their opportunities, whether they have heard or not of the name of Jesus, then we can acknowledge the case of the Christian and non-Christian populations to be one of difference of advantages. And, of course, no account can be given of the principle which determines the unequal distribution of the divine benefits. The exhibition of the divine attributes is not to be brought to measure of numbers or proportions. But human statements concerning the dealings of God with mankind, hypotheses and arguments about them, may very usefully be so tested. Truly, the abstract or philosophical difficulty may be as great concerning a small number of persons unprovided for, or, as might be inferred from some doctrinal statements, not equitably dealt with, in the divine dispensations, as concerning a large one; but it does not so force itself on the imagination and heart of the generality of observers. The difficulty, though not new in itself, is new as to the great increase in the numbers of those who feel it, and in the practical urgency for discovering an answer, solution, or neutralization for it, if we would set many unquiet souls at rest.

From the same source of the advance of general knowledge respecting the inhabitancy of the world issues another inquiry concerning a promise, prophecy, or assertion of Scripture. For the commission of Jesus to his Apostles was to preach the gospel to ' all nations,' ' to every creature ;' and St. Paul says of the gentile world, ' But I say have they not heard ? Yes, verily, their sound went into all the earth, and their words unto the ends of the world,' (Rom. x. 18), and speaks of the gospel ' which was preached to every nation under Heaven,' (Col. i. 23), when it has never yet been preached even to the half. Then, again, it has often been appealed to as an evidence of the supernatural origin of Christianity, and as an instance of supernatural assistance vouchsafed to it in the first centuries, that it so soon overspread the world. It has seemed but a small leap of about three hundred years to the age of Constantine, if in that time, not to insist upon the letter of the texts already quoted, the conversion of the civilized world could be accomplished. It may be known only to the more learned, that it was not accomplished with respect to the Roman empire even then; that the Christians of the East cannot be fairly computed at more than half the population, nor the Christians of the West at so much as a third, at the commencement of that emperor's reign. But it requires no learning to be aware that neither then nor subsequently have the Christians amounted to more than a fourth part of the people of the earth; and it is seen to be impossible to appeal any longer to the wonderful spread of Christianity in the three first centuries, as a special evidence of the wisdom and goodness of God.

So likewise a very grave modification of an 'evidence' heretofore current must ensue in another respect, in consequence of an increased knowledge of other facts connected with the foregoing. It has been customary to argue that, *a priori*, a supernatural revelation was to be expected at the time when Jesus Christ was manifested upon the earth, by reason of the exhaustion of all natural or unassisted human efforts for the amelioration of mankind. The state of the world, it has been customary to say, had become so utterly corrupt and hopeless under the Roman sway, that a necessity and special occasion was presented for an express divine intervention. Our recently enlarged ethnographical information shows such an argument to be altogether inapplicable to the case. If we could be judges of the necessity for a special divine intervention, the stronger necessity existed in the East. There immense populations, like the Chinese, had never developed the idea of a personal God, or had degenerated from a once pure theological creed, as in India, from the religion of the Vedas. Oppressions and tyrannies, caste-distinctions, common and enormous vices, a polluted idolatrous worship, as bad as the worst which disgraced Rome, Greece, or Syria, had prevailed for ages.

It would not be very tasteful, as an exception to this description, to call Buddhism the gospel of India, preached to it five or six centuries before the Gospel of Jesus was proclaimed in the nearer East. But on the whole it would be more like the realities of things, as we can now behold them, to say that the Christian revelation was given to the western world, because it deserved it better and was more prepared for it than the East. Philosophers, at least, had anticipated in speculation some of its dearest hopes, and had prepared the way for its self-denying ethics.

There are many other sources of the modern questionings of traditional Christianity which cannot now be touched upon, originating like those which have been mentioned, in a change of circumstances wherein observers are placed; whereby their thoughts are turned in new directions, and they are rendered dissatisfied with old modes of speaking. But such a difficulty as that respecting the souls of heathendom, which must now come closely home to multitudes among us, will disappear, if it be candidly acknowledged that the words of the New Testament, which speak of the preaching of the Gospel to the whole world, were limited to the understanding of the times when they were spoken; that doctrines concerning salvation, to be met with in it, are for the most part applicable only to those to whom the preaching of Christ should come; and that we must draw our conclusions respecting a just dealing hereafter with the individuals who make up the sum of heathenism, rather from reflections suggested by our own moral instincts than from the express declarations of Scripture writers, who had no such knowledge, as is given to ourselves, of the amplitude of the world, which is the scene of the divine manifestations.

Moreover, to our great comfort, there have been preserved to us words of the Lord Jesus himself, declaring that the conditions of men in another world will be determined by their moral characters in this, and not by their hereditary or traditional creeds; and both many words and the practice of the great Apostle Paul, within the range which was given him, tend to the same result. He has been thought even to make an allusion to the Buddhist *Dharmma*, or law, when he said, 'When the gentiles which have not the law do by nature the things contained in the law, these having not the law are a law unto themselves, which show the work of the law written in their hearts,' &c. (Rom. i. 14, 15.) However this may be, it is evident that if such a solution as the above is accepted, a variety of doctrinal statements hitherto usual, Calvinistic and Lutheran theories on the one hand, and sacramental and hierarchical ones on the other, must be thrown into the background, if not abandoned.

There may be a long future during which the present course of the world shall last. Instead of its drawing near the close of its existence, as repre-

sented in Millennarian or Rabbinical fables, and with
so many more souls, according to some interpretations of the Gospel of Salvation, lost to Satan in
every age and in every nation, than have been won
to Christ, that the victory would evidently be on the
side of the Fiend, we may yet be only at the commencement of the career of the great Spiritual Con-
queror even in this world.  Nor have we any right to
say that the effects of what He does upon earth shall
not extend and propagate themselves in worlds to
come.  But under any expectation of the duration
of the present secular constitution, it is of the deepest
interest to us, both as observers and as agents, placed
evidently at an epoch when humanity finds itself
under new conditions, to form some definite conception to ourselves of the way in which Christianity
is henceforward to act upon the world which is our
own.

Different estimates are made of the beneficial effects
already wrought by Christianity upon the secular aspect of the world, according to the different points of
view from which it is regarded.  Some endeavour,
from an impartial standing point, to embrace in one
panorama the whole religious history of mankind, of
which Christianity then becomes the most important
phase; others can only look at such a history from
within some narrow chamber of doctrinal and ecclesiastical prepossessions.  And anticipations equally
different for like reasons will be entertained by persons differently imbued, as to the form under which,
and the machinery by which, it shall hereafter be
presented with success, either to the practically un-
christianized populations of countries like our own,
or to peoples of other countries never as yet even
nominally christianized.

Although the consequences of what the Gospel does
will be carried on into other worlds, its work is to be
done here; although some of its work here must be un-

seen, yet not all; nor much even of its unseen work without at least some visible manifestation and effects. The invisible Church is to us a mere abstraction. Now it is acknowledged on all hands, that to the multitudinist principle are due the great external victories which the Christian name has hitherto won. On the other hand, it is alleged by the advocates of Individualism, that these outward acquisitions and numerical accessions have always been made at the expense of the purity of the Church; and, also, that Scriptural authority and the earliest practice is in favour of Individualism. Moreover, almost all the corruptions of Christianity are attributed by individualists to the effecting by the Emperor Constantine of an unholy alliance between Church and State. Yet a fair review, as far as there are data for it, of the state of Christianity before the time of that emperor will leave us in at least very great doubt, whether the Christian character was really, in the anterior period, superior on the average to what it has subsequently been. We may appeal to the most ancient records extant, and even to the Apostolic Epistles themselves, to show, that neither in doctrine nor in morals did the primitive Christian communities at all approach to the ideal which has been formed of them. The moral defects of the earliest converts are the subject of the gravest expostulation on the part of the Apostolic writers: and the doctrinal features of the early Church are much more undetermined than would be thought by those who read them only through the ecclesiastical creeds.

Those who belong to very different theological schools acknowledge at times, that they cannot with any certainty find in the highest ecclesiastical antiquity the dogmas which they consider most important. It is customary with Lutherans to represent their doctrine of justification by subjective faith as having died out shortly after the Apostolic age. In fact, it never was the doctrine of any considerable portion of the Church

till the time of the Reformation. It is not met with
in the immediately post-Apostolic writings, nor in the
Apostolic writings, except those of St. Paul, not even
in the Epistle to the Hebrews, which is of the Pauline
or Paulo-Johannean school. The faith at least of that
Epistle, 'the substance of things hoped for,' is a very
different faith from the faith of the Epistle to the
Romans,—if the Lutherans are correct in representing
that to be, a conscious apprehending of the benefits
to the individual soul, of the Saviour's merits and
passion. Then, on the other hand, it is admitted,
even maintained, by a very different body of theologians, as by the learned Jesuit Petavius and many
others, that the doctrine afterwards developed into the
Nicene and Athanasian, is not to be found explicitly
in the earliest Fathers, nor even in Scripture, although
provable by it. One polemical value of this view to
those who uphold it, is to show the necessity of an
inspired Church to develope Catholic truth.

But although the primitive Christians fell far short
both of a doctrinal and ethical ideal, there is this
remarkable distinction to be noted between the primitive aspects of doctrine and of ethics. The morals of
the first Christians were certainly very far below
the estimate which has been formed of them ; but
the standard by which they were measured was un-
varying, lofty, and peculiar ; moreover, the nearer we
approach to the fountain head, the more definite do
we find the statement of the Christian principle, that
the source of religion is in the heart. On the contrary,
the nearer we come to the original sources of the
history, the less definite do we find the statements of
doctrines, and even of the facts from which the doctrines were afterwards inferred. And, at the very first,
with our Lord Himself and His Apostles, as represented to us in the New Testament, morals come
before contemplation, ethics before theoretics. In the
patristic writings, theoretics assume continually an

increasingly disproportionate value. Even within
the compass of our New Testament there is to be
found already a wonderful contrast between the words
of our Lord and such a discourse as the Epistle
to the Hebrews. There is not wanting, indeed, to
this Epistle an earnest moral appeal, but the greater
part of it is illustrative, argumentative, and controversial. Our Lord's discourses have almost all of
them a direct moral bearing. This character of His
words is certainly more obvious in the three first
Gospels than in the fourth; and the remarkable
unison of those Gospels, when they recite the Lord's
words, notwithstanding their discrepancies in some
matters of fact, compel us to think, that they embody
more exact traditions of what He actually said than
the fourth does.[1]

As monuments or witnesses, discrepant in a certain
degree as to other particulars, the evidence afforded
by the three Synoptics to the Lord's own words is
the most precious element in the Christian records.
We are thereby placed at the very root of the Gospel
tradition. And these words of the Lord, taken in conjunction with the Epistle of St. James, and with the
first, or genuine, Epistle of St. Peter, leave no reasonable doubt of the general character of His teaching

---

[1] The fourth Gospel has always been supposed to have been written with
a controversial purpose, and not to have been composed till from sixty to
seventy years after the events which it undertakes to narrate; some critics,
indeed, think it was not of a date anterior to the year 140, and that it pre-
supposes opinions of a Valentinian character, or even Montanist, which would
make it later still. At any rate it cannot, by external evidence, be attached
to the person of St. John as its author, in the sense wherein moderns understand the word author: that is, there is no proof that St. John gives his
voucher as an eye and ear witness of all which is related in it. Many
persons shrink from a *bonâ fide* examination of the 'Gospel question,'
because they imagine, that unless the four Gospels are received as perfectly
genuine and authentic—that is, entirely the composition of the persons
whose names they bear, and without any admixture of legendary matter
or embellishment in their narratives, the only alternative is to suppose a
fraudulent design in those who did compose them. This is a supposition
from which common sense, and the moral instinct, alike revolt; but it is
happily not an only alternative.

**M**

having been what, for want of a better word, we must perhaps call moral. But to represent the Spirit of Christ as a moral Spirit is not merely to proclaim Him as a Lawgiver, enacting the observance of a set of precepts, but as fulfilled with a Spirit given to Him 'without measure,' of which, indeed, all men are partakers who have a sense of what they 'ought' to be and do; yet flowing over from Him, especially on those who perceive in His words, and in His life, principles of ever-widening application to the circumstances of their own existence; who learn from Him to penetrate to the root of their conscience, and to recognise themselves as being active elements in the moral order of the universe.

We may take an illustration of the relative value in the Apostolic age of the doctrinal and moral principles, by citing a case which will be allowed to be extreme enough. It is evident there were among the Christian converts in that earliest period, those who had no belief in a corporeal resurrection. Some of these had, perhaps, been made converts from the sect of the Sadducees, and had brought with them into the Christian congregation the same doubts or negative beliefs which belonged to them before their conversion. The Jewish church embraced in its bosom both Pharisees and Sadducees: but our Lord, although he expressly taught a resurrection, and argued with the Sadducees on the subject, never treated them as aliens from Israel because they did not hold that doctrine; is much more severe on the moral defects and hypocrisies of the Pharisees than upon the doctrinal defects of the Sadducees. The Christian Church was recruited in its Jewish branch chiefly from the sect of the Pharisees, and it is somewhat difficult for us to realize the conversion of a Sadducee to Christianity, retaining his Sadducee disbelief or scepticism. But, the 'some among you who say that there is no resurrection of the dead,' (1 Cor. xv. 12, comp. 2 Tim.

ii. 18), can leave us in no doubt upon the matter, that there were Christians of Sadducee or Gentile prejudices, like those who mocked or those who hesitated when Paul preached at Athens the resurrection of the dead. But St. Paul argues with such elaborately in that chapter, without expelling them from the Church, although he always represents faith in the resurrection as the corner-stone of the Christian belief. He endeavours rather to conciliate and to remove objections. First, he represents the rising to life again, not as miraculous or exceptional, but as a law of humanity, or at least of Christian and spiritualized humanity; and he treats the resurrection of Christ, not as a wonder, but as a prerogative instance. Secondly, he shows, upon the doctrine of a spiritual body, how the objections against a resurrection from the gross conception of a flesh and blood body, fall to the ground.[1] Now, if there might thus be Sadducee, or quasi-Sadducee, Christians in the Church, their Christianity must have consisted in an appreciation of the moral spirit of Jesus, and in an obedience, such as it might be, to the Christian precepts; they could have been influenced by no expectation of a future recompense. Their obedience might or might not be of as high an order as that which is so motived; it might have been a mere legal habit, or an exalted disinterested life. Now, let us compare a person of this description with such as those who are indicated, (1 Cor. xv. 19, 32); and we cannot think that St. Paul is there speaking of himself personally, but of the general run of persons reluctant to exercise self-restraint and to expose themselves to persecution for the Gospel's sake, yet induced to do so by the hope of a

---

[1] So in Luke xx. 27-35, the Sadducees are dealt with in a like argumentative manner. They understood the doctrine of the resurrection to imply the rising of men with such bodies as they now have; the case supposed by them loses its point when the distinction is revealed between the animal and the angelic bodies.

future recompense. Let us consider these two descriptions of persons. The one class is defective in
the Christian doctrine, and in the most fundamental
article of the Apostle's preaching, the other in the
Christian moral life ; can we say that the one defect
was more fatal than the other? We do not find the
Apostle excommunicating these Corinthians, who said
there was no resurrection of the dead.[1] On the other
hand, we know it was only in an extreme case that
he sanctioned excommunication for the cause of
immorality. And upon the whole, if we cannot
effectually compare the person deficient in a
true belief of the resurrection, with an immoral
or evil liver— if we can only say they were both bad
Christians—at least we have no reason to determine
that the good liver who disbelieved the resurrection
was treated by St. Paul as less of a Christian than the
evil liver who believed it. We cannot suppose the
evil life always to have brought on the disbelief in the
doctrine, nor the disbelief in the doctrine to have issued
always in an evil life.

Now, from what has been said we gather two important conclusions :—first, of the at least equal value
of the Christian life, as compared with the Christian
doctrine ; and, secondly, of the retaining within the
Church, both of those who were erroneous and defective in doctrine, and of those who were by their lives
unworthy of their profession ; they who caused di-

---

[1] St. Paul 'delivered to Satan' (whatever that may mean), Hymenæus,
who maintained the resurrection to be past already, most likely meaning
it was only a moral one ; but it does not appear it was for this offence he
is so mentioned in conjunction with Alexander, and their provocation is not
described : where he is said to have taught that the resurrection is past
already, he is in companionship with Philetus, and nothing is added of any
punishment of either. These strange opinions afterwards hardened into
heretical doctrine. Tertull. *de Præscriptione Hær.* c. xxxiii. Paulus in
1mâ ad Corinthios notat negatores et dubitatores resurrectionis. Hæc
opinio propria Sadducæorum : partem ejus usurpat Marcion et Apelles, et
Valentinus et si qui alii resurrectionem carnis infringunt—æque tangit eos
qui dicerent factam jam resurrectionem : id de se Valentini adseverant.

visions and heresies were to be marked and avoided but not expelled, and if any called a brother were a notoriously immoral person, the rest were enjoined, no not to eat with him, but he was not to be refused the name of brother or Christian. (1 Cor. v. 11.)

It would be difficult to devise a description of a multitudinist Church, exhibiting more saliently the worst defects which can attend that form, than this which is taken from the evidence of the Apostolic Epistles. We find the Pauline Churches to have comprised, not only persons of the truest doctrinal insight, of the highest spiritual attainments, of martyr-like self-devotion, but of the strangest and most incongruous beliefs, and of the most unequal and inconsistent practice. The individualist could say nothing more derogatory of any multitudinist Church, not even of a national one; unless, perhaps, he might say this, that less distinction is made within such a Church itself, and within all modern Churches, between their better and worse members, than was made in the Apostolic Churches. Any judicial sentence of excommunication was extremely rare in the Apostolic age, as we have seen, and the distinction between the worthy and unworthy members of the Church was to be marked, not by any public and authoritative act, but by the operation of private conduct and opinion.

The Apostolic Churches were thus multitudinist, and they early tended to become National Churches; from the first they took collective names from the localities where they were situate. And it was natural and proper they should, except upon the Calvinistic theory of conversion. There is some show of reasonable independence, some appearance of applying the Protestant liberty of private judgment, in maintaining the Christian unlawfulness of the union of Church and State, corruption of national establishments, and like propositions. But it will be found, that where they are maintained by serious and religious people, they are parts of a Calvinistic system, and are held in connexion with peculiar theories of grace, immediate conversion, and arbitrary call. It is as merely a Calvinistic and Congregational commonplace to speak of the unholy union of Church and State accomplished by Constantine, as it is a Romish commonplace to denounce the unholy schism accomplished by Henry the Eighth. But in fact both those sovereigns only carried out, chiefly for their own purposes, that which was already in preparation by the course of events; even Henry would not have broken with the Pope if he had not seen the public mind to be in some degree ripe for it, nor would Constantine have taken the first steps towards an establishment of Christianity, unless the empire had already been growing Christian.

Unhappily, together with his inauguration of Multitudinism, Constantine also inaugurated a principle essentially at variance with it, the principle of doctrinal limitation. It is very customary to attribute the necessity of stricter definitions of the Christian creed from time to time to the rise of successive heresies. More correctly, there succeeded to the fluid state of Christian opinion in the first century after Christ, a gradual hardening and systematizing of conflicting views; and the opportunity of reverting to the freedom of the Apostolic and immediately succeeding periods, was finally lost for many ages by the sanction given by Constantine to the decisions of Nicæa. We cannot now be very good judges, whether it would have been possible, together with the establishment of Christianity as the imperial religion, to enforce forbearance between the great antagonisms which were then in dispute, and to have insisted on the maxim, that neither had a right to limit the common Christianity to the exclusion of the other. At all events a principle at variance with a true Multitudinism was then recognised. All parties it must be acknowledged were equally exclusive. And exclusion and definition

have since been the rule for almost all Churches, more
or less, even when others of their principles might
seem to promise a greater freedom.

That the members of a Calvinistic Church, as in the
Geneva of Calvin and Beza, or in the Church of Scotland,
should coincide with the members of the State—that
' election' and ' effectual call' should be hereditary, is, of
course, too absurd to suppose ; and the congregational
Calvinists are more consistent than the Calvinists of
Established Churches. Of Calvinism, as a system of
doctrine, it is not here proposed to say anything,
except, that it must of necessity be hostile to every
other creed ; and the members of a Calvinistic Church
can never consider themselves but as parted by an insuperable distinction from all other professors of the
Gospel ; they cannot stand on a common footing, in
any spiritual matter, with those who belong to the
world, that is, with all others than themselves. The
exclusiveness of a multitudinist Church, which makes,
as yet, the ecclesiastical creeds the terms of its communion, may cease when that test or limitation is
repealed. But the exclusiveness of a Calvinistic
Church, whether free from the creeds or not, is inherent in its principles. There is no insuperable
barrier between Congregationalists not being Calvinists, and a multitudinist Church which should
liberate itself sufficiently from the traditional symbols.
Doctrinal limitations in the multitudinist form of
Church are not essential to it ; upon larger knowledge
of Christian history, upon a more thorough acquaintance with the mental constitution of man, upon an
understanding of the obstacles they present to a true
Catholicity, they may be cast off. Nor is a multitudinist Church necessarily or essentially hierarchical,
in any extreme or superstitious sense ; it can well
admit, if not pure congregationalism, a large admixture of the congregational spirit. Indeed, a combination of the two principles will alone keep any

Church in health and vigour. Too great importance attached to a hierarchical order will lead into superstitions respecting Apostolical succession, ministerial illumination, supernatural sacramental influence; mere congregationalism tends to keep ministers and people at a dead spiritual level. A just recognition and balance of the two tendencies, allows the emerging of the most eminent of the congregation into offices for which they are suited; so that neither are the true hierarchs and leaders of thought and manners drawn down and made to succumb to a mere democracy, nor those clothed in the priests' robe who have no true unction from above. And this just balance between the hierarchy and the congregation would be at least as attainable in the national form of Church as in any other, if it were free from dogmatical tests and similar intellectual bondage. But there are some prejudices against Nationalism which deserve to be farther considered.

It was natural for a Christian in the earliest period to look upon the heathen State in which he found himself as if it belonged to the kingdom of Satan and not to that of God; and consecrated as it was, in all its offices, to the heathen divinities, to consider it a society having its origin from the powers of darkness, not from the Lord of light and life. In the Apostolic writers this view appears rather in the First Epistle of St. John than with St. Paul. The horizon which St. John's view embraced was much narrower than St. Paul's;

*Qui mores hominum multorum vidit et urbes.*

If the love felt and inculcated by St. John towards the brethren was the more intense, the charity with which St. Paul comprehended all men was the more ample; and it is not from every point of view we should describe St. John as pre-eminently the Apostle of love. With St. John, 'the whole world lieth in

wickedness,' while St. Paul exhorts 'prayers and sup-
plications to be made for all men, for kings, and for all
that are in authority.' Taking a wide view of the world
and its history, we must acknowledge political constitu-
tions of men to be the work of God Himself; they are
organizations into which human society grows by
reason of the properties of the elements which generate
it. But the primitive Christians could scarcely be expected to see, that ultimately the Gospel was to have
sway in doing more perfectly that which the heathen
religions were doing imperfectly; that its office should
be, not only to quicken the spirit of the individual and
to confirm his future hopes, but to sanctify all social
relations and civil institutions, and to enter into the
marrow of the national life; whereas heathenism had
only decorated the surface of it.

Heathendom had its national Churches. Indeed,
the existence of a national Church is not only a per-
missible thing, but is necessary to the completion of
a national life, and has shown itself in all nations,
when they have made any advance in civilization. It
has been usual, but erroneous, to style the Jewish constitution a theocracy in a peculiar and exclusive sense,
as if the combination of the religious and civil life
had been confined to that people. Even among barbarous tribes the fetish-man establishes an authority
over the rest, quite as much from the yearning of others
after guidance as from his own superior cunning.
Priesthoods have always been products. Priests have
neither been, as some would represent, a set of delibe-
rate conspirators against the free thoughts of mankind; nor, on the other hand, have they been the sole
divinely commissioned channels for communication of
spiritual truth. If all priests and ministers of religion
could at one moment be swept from the face of the
earth, they would soon be reproduced. If the human
race, or a given people—and a recent generation
saw an instance of something like it in no distant

nation—were resolved into its elements, and all its social and religious institutions shattered to pieces, it would reconstruct a political framework, and a spiritual organization, re-constituting governors, laws, and magistrates, educators, and ministers of religion.

The distinction between the Jewish people and the other nations, in respect of this so-called theocracy, is but feebly marked on both sides. For the religious element was much stronger than has been supposed in other nationalities, and the priesthood was by no means supreme in the Hebrew State.[1]

Constantly the title occurs in the Hebrew Scriptures, of 'the Lord's people,' with appeals to Jehovah as their Supreme Governor, Protector, and Judge. And so it is with polytheistic nations; they are the offspring of the gods; the deities are their guides and guardians, the authors of their laws and customs; their worship is interwoven with the whole course of political and social life. It will of course be said, the entire difference is no more than this—the object of worship in the one case was the true God, in the other

---

[1] Previous to the time of the divided kingdom, the Jewish history presents little which is thoroughly reliable. The taking of Jerusalem by 'Shishak' is for the Hebrew history that which the sacking of Rome by the Gauls is for the Roman. And from no facts ascertainable is it possible to infer there was any early period during which the Government by the priesthood was attended with success. Indeed the greater probability seems on the side of the supposition, that the priesthood, with its distinct offices and charge, was constituted by Royalty, and that the higher pretensions of the priests were not advanced till the reign of Josiah. There is no evidence of the priesthood ever having claimed a supremacy over the kings, as if it had been in possession of an oracular power; in the earlier monarchy the kings offer sacrifice, and the rudiments of a political and religious organization, which prevailed in the period of the Judges, cannot be appealed to as pre-eminently a theocracy. At any rate, nothing could be more unsuccessful, as a government, whatever it might be called. Indeed, the theory of the Jewish theocracy, seems built chiefly upon some expressions in 1 Sam. viii., xii. Samuel, however, with whose government the Israelites were dissatisfied, was not a priest but a prophet; and the whole of that part of the narrative is conceived in the prophetical, not in the priestly interest.

cases idols or demons. But it is very clear to unprejudiced persons, that the conceptions which the
Hebrews formed of Jehovah, though far superior to
the conceptions embodied in any other national religion, were obscured by figurative representations of
Him in accordance with the character of His worship-
pers. The passions ascribed to Him were not those
most base and degrading ones attributed to their deities
by the pagans; and on that account it has been less easy
to separate the figurative description from the true idea
of Him. The better pagans could easily perceive the
stories of their gods to have been, at the best, allegories, poetical embellishments, inventions of some
kind or other. Jews did not perceive, that the attribution of wrath and jealousy to their God could only
be by a figure of speech; and what is worse, it is difficult to persuade many Christians of the same thing,
and solemn inferences from the figurative expressions
of the Hebrew literature have been crystallized into
Christian doctrine.

All things sanctioned among the Jews are certainly
not to be imitated by us, nor all pagan institutions to
be abhorred. In respect of a State religion, Jew and
Gentile were more alike than has been thought. All
nations have exhibited, in some form or another, the
development of a public religion, and have done so by
reason of tendencies inherent in their nationality.
The particular form of the religion has been due to
various causes. Also in periods of transition there
would, for a time, be a breaking in upon this feature
of national life. While prophets, philosophers, reformers, were at work, or some new principle winning
its way, the national uniformity would be disturbed.
So it was at the first preaching of the Gospel; St.
Paul and the Lord Jesus himself offered it to the
Jews as a nation, on the multitudinist principle; but
when they put it from them, it must make progress by kindling a fire in the earth, even to the

dividing families, two against three and three against two. Thereupon Christians appear for a while to be aliens from their countries and commonwealths, but only for a while. We must not confound with an essential principle of Christianity that which only resulted from a temporary necessity. The individualist principle may have been the right one for a time, and under certain circumstances, not consequently the right one, under all circumstances, nor even the possible one. In this question, as in that of hierarchy, and in various ceremonial discussions, the appeal to a particular primitive antiquity is only an appeal from the whole experience of Christendom to a partial experience limited to a short period. Moreover, as to the mind of Jesus himself with respect to Nationalism it is fully revealed in those touching words, preserved both in the first and third Gospels, 'How often would I have gathered thy children together, even as a hen gathereth her chickens under her wings, and ye would not.'

Christianity was therefore compelled, as it were against its will, and in contradiction to its proper design, to make the first steps in its progress by cutting across old societies, filtering into the world by individual conversions, showing, nevertheless, from the very first, its multitudinist tendencies; and before it could comprehend countries or cities, embracing families and households, the several members of which must have been on very different spiritual levels (Acts xvi. 31-34). The Roman world was penetrated in the first instance by an individual and domestic Christianity, to which was owing the first conversion of our own country; in the second or Saxon conversion, the people were Christianized *en masse.* Such conversions as this last may not be thought to have been worth much, but they were worth the abolition of some of the grossness of idolatry; they effected all of which the subjects of them were for the time capable, and prepared the way for something better in another generation. The conversions operated by the German Apostle, Boniface, were of the same multitudinous kind as those of Austin and Paulinus in Britain, and for a like reason; in both cases the development of Christianity necessarily followed the forms of the national life.

In some parts of the West this national and natural tendency was counteracted by the shattering which ensued upon the breaking up of the Roman empire. And in those countries especially which had been longest and most closely connected with Pagan Rome, such as Italy itself, Spain, France, the people felt themselves unable to stand alone in their spiritual institutions, and were glad to lean on some other prop and centre, so far as was still allowed them. The Teutonic Churches were always more free than the Churches of the Latinized peoples, though they themselves had derived their Christianity from Roman Missionaries; and among the Teutonic Churches alone has a freedom from extraneous dominion as yet established itself. For a time even these could only adopt the forms of doctrine and practice which were current in other parts of the West. But those forms were neither of the essence of a national Church, nor even of the essence of a Christian Church. A national Church need not, historically speaking, be Christian, nor, if it be Christian, need it be tied down to particular forms which have been prevalent at certain times in Christendom. That which is essential to a national Church is, that it should undertake to assist the spiritual progress of the nation and of the individuals of which it is composed, in their several states and stages. Not even a Christian Church should expect all those who are brought under its influence to be, as a matter of fact, of one and the same standard, but should endeavour to raise each according to his capacities, and should give no occasion for a reaction against itself, nor provoke the individualist element into separatism. It would do this if it submitted to define itself otherwise than by its own nationality—if it represented itself as a part rather than a whole, as deriving authority and not claiming it, as imitative and not original.

It will do this also, if while the civil side of the nation is fluid, the ecclesiastical side of it is fixed; if thought and speech are free among all other classes, and not free among those who hold the office of leaders and teachers of the rest in the highest things; if they are to be bound to cover up instead of opening; and having, it is presumed, possession of the key of knowledge, are to stand at the door with it, permitting no one to enter, unless by force. A national Church may also find itself in this position, which, perhaps, is our own. Its ministers may become isolated between two other parties—between those on the one hand who draw fanatical inferences from formularies and principles which they themselves are not able or are unwilling to repudiate; and on the other, those who have been tempted, in impatience of old fetters, to follow free thought heedlessly wherever it may lead them. If our own Churchmen expect to discourage and repress a fanatical Christianity, without a frank appeal to reason, and a frank criticism of Scripture, they will find themselves without any effectual arms for that combat; or if they attempt to check inquiry by the repetition of old forms and denunciations, they will be equally powerless, and run the especial risk of turning into bitterness the sincerity of those who should be their best allies, as friends of truth. They should avail themselves of the aid of all reasonable persons for enlightening the fanatical religionist, making no reserve of any seemingly harmless or apparently serviceable superstitions of their own; they should also endeavour to supply to the negative theologian some positive elements in Christianity, on grounds more sure to him than the assumption of an objective 'faith once delivered to the saints,' which he cannot identify with the creed of any Church as yet known to him.

It has been matter of great boast within the Church of England, in common with other Protestant Churches, that it is founded upon the 'Word of God,' a phrase which begs many a question when applied to the canonical books of the Old and New Testaments, a phrase which is never applied to them by any of the Scriptural authors, and which, according to Protestant principles, never could be applied to them by any sufficient authority from without. In that which may be considered the pivot Article of the Church this expression does not occur, but only 'Holy Scripture,' 'Canonical Books,' 'Old and New Testaments.' It contains no declaration of the Bible being throughout supernaturally suggested, nor any intimation as to which portions of it were owing to a special divine illumination, nor the slightest attempt at defining inspiration, whether mediate or immediate, whether through, or beside, or overruling the natural faculties of the subject of it,—not the least hint of the relation between the divine and human elements in the composition of the Biblical books. Even if the Fathers have usually considered 'canonical' as synonymous with 'miraculously inspired,' there is nothing to show that their sense of the word must necessarily be applied in our own sixth Article. The word itself may mean either books ruled and determined by the Church, or regulative books; and the employment of it in the Article hesitates between these two significations. For at one time 'Holy Scripture' and canonical books are those books 'of whose authority never was any doubt in the Church,'[1] that is, they are 'de-

---

[1] This clause is taken from the Wirtemburg Confession (1552), which proceeds: 'Hanc Scripturam credimus et confitemur esse oraculum Spi.itus Sancti, cælestibus testimoniis ita confirmatum, ut *Si Angelus de cælo aliud prædicaverit, anathema sit.*'

termined' books; and then the other, or uncanonical books, are described as those which 'the Church doth not apply to establish any doctrine,' that is, they are not 'regulative' books. And if the other principal Churches of the Reformation have gone farther in definition in this respect than our own, that is no reason we should force the silence of our Church into unison with their expressed declarations, but rather that we should rejoice in our comparative freedom.[1]

The Protestant feeling among us has satisfied itself in a blind way with the anti-Roman declaration, that 'Holy Scripture containeth all things necessary to salvation, so that whatsoever is not read therein, nor may be proved thereby, is not to be required of any man, that it should be believed as an article of the faith,' &c., and without reflecting how very much is wisely left open in that Article. For this declaration itself is partly negative and partly positive; as to its negative part it declares that nothing—no clause of creed, no decision of council, no tradition or exposition—is to be required to be believed on peril of salvation, unless it be Scriptural; but it does not lay down, that everything which is contained in Scripture must be believed on the same peril. Or it may be expressed thus:—the Word of God is contained in Scripture, whence it does not follow that it is co-extensive with it. The Church to which we belong does not put that stumbling-block before the feet of her members; it is their own fault if they place it there for themselves, authors of their own offence. Under the terms of the sixth Article one may accept literally, or allegorically, or as

---

[1] Thus the Helvetic Confession states: 'We believe and profess that the Canonical Scriptures of the Holy Prophets and Apostles, of the Old and New Testaments, *are* the very Word of God, and have sufficient authority from themselves and not from men.' The Saxon Confession refers to the creeds as interpreters of Scripture—nos vera fide amplecti omnia scripta Prophetarum et Apostolorum; et quidem in hac ipsa nativa sententia, quæ expressa est in Symbolis, Apostolico, Nicæno et Athanasiano.—*De Doctrina.*

parable, or poetry, or legend, the story of a serpent tempter, of an ass speaking with man's voice, of an arresting of the earth's motion, of a reversal of its motion, of waters standing in a solid heap, of witches, and a variety of apparitions. So, under the terms of the sixth Article, every one is free in judgment as to the primeval institution of the Sabbath, the universality of the deluge, the confusion of tongues, the corporeal taking up of Elijah into Heaven, the nature of angel⸗, the reality of demoniacal possession, the personality of Satan, and the miraculous particulars of many events. So the dates and authorship of the several books received as canonical are not determined by any authority, nor their relative value and importance.

Many evils have flowed to the people of England, otherwise free enough, from an extreme and too exclusive Scripturalism. The rudimentary education of a large number of our countrymen has been mainly carried on by the reading of the Scriptures. They are read by young children in thousands of cases, where no attempt could be made, even if it were desired, to accompany the reading with the safeguard of a reasonable interpretation. A Protestant tradition seems to have prevailed, unsanctioned by any of our formularies, that the words of Scripture are imbued with a supernatural property, by which their true sense can reveal itself even to those who, by intellectual or educational defect, would naturally be incapable of appreciating it. There is no book indeed, or collection of books, so rich in words which address themselves intelligibly to the unlearned and learned alike. But those who are able to do so ought to lead the less educated to distinguish between the different kinds of words which it contains, between the dark patches of human passion and error which form a partial crust upon it, and the bright centre of spiritual truth within.

Some years ago a vehement controversy was carried on, whether the Scripture ought to be distributed in this

N

country with or without note and comment. It was a question at issue between two great parties and two great organized societies. But those who advocated the view which was the more reasonable in itself, did so in the interest of an unreasonable theory; they insisted on the authority of the Church in an hierarchical sense, and carried out their commentations in dry catenas of doctrine and precept. On the other side, the views of those who were for circulating the Bible without note or comment were partly superstitious, and partly antagonistic in the way of a protest against the hierarchical claim. The Scriptures have no doubt been received with sufficient readiness by all classes of English people, for there has been something very agreeable to some of the feelings of the Englishman in the persuasion that he possesses, independently of priest or clergyman, the whole matter of his religion bound up in the four corners of a portable book, furnishing him, as he thinks, with an infallible test of the doctrine which he hears from his preacher, with a substitute for all teaching, if he so pleases, and 'with the complete apparatus necessary, should he desire to become the teacher of others in his turn. But the result of this immense circulation of the Scriptures for many years by all parties, has been little adequate to what might have been expected beforehand, from the circulation of that which is in itself so excellent and divine.

It is ill to be deterred from giving expression to the truth or from prosecuting the investigation of it, from a fear of making concessions to revolutionary or captious dispositions. For the blame of this captiousness, when it exists, lies in part at the door of those who ignore the difficulties of others, because they may not feel any for themselves. To this want of wisdom on the part of the defenders of old opinions is to be attributed, that the noting of such differences as are to be found in the Evangelical narratives, or in the

books of Kings and Chronicles, takes the appearance
of an attack upon a holy thing.   The like ill consequences follow from not acknowledging freely the extent of
the human element in the sacred books ; for if this were
freely acknowledged on the one side, the divine element
would be frankly recognised on the other.   Good men—
and they cannot be good without the Spirit of God—
may err in facts, be weak in memory, mingle imagination with memory, be feeble in inferences, confound
illustration with argument, be varying in judgment
and opinion.   But the Spirit of absolute Truth cannot
err or contradict Himself, if He speak immediately, even
in small things, accessories, or accidents.   Still less can
we suppose Him to suggest contradictory accounts, or
accounts only to be reconciled in the way of hypothesis
and conjecture.   Some things indited by the Holy
Spirit may appear to relate to objects of which the
whole cannot be embraced by the human intellect,
and it may not, as to such objects, be possible to
reconcile opposite sides of Divine truth.   Whether
this is the general character of Scripture revelations
is not now the question ; but the theory is suppo-
sable and should be treated with respect, in regard to
some portions of Scripture.   To suppose, on the other
hand, a supernatural influence to cause the record of
that which can only issue in a puzzle, is to lower
infinitely our conception of the Divine dealings in
respect of a special revelation.

Thus it may be attributed to the defect of our
understandings, that we should be unable altogether
to reconcile the aspects of the Saviour as presented to
us in the three first Gospels, and in the writings of St.
Paul and St. John.   At any rate, there were current
in the primitive Church very distinct Christologies.
But neither to any defect in our capacities, nor to
any reasonable presumption of a hidden wise design,
nor to any partial spiritual endowments in the narra-
tors, can we attribute the difficulty, if not impossi-

bility, of reconciling the genealogies of St. Matthew and St. Luke, or the chronology of the Holy Week, or the accounts of the Resurrection ; nor to any mystery in the subject-matter can be referred the uncertainty in which the New Testament writings leave us, as to the descent of Jesus Christ according to the flesh, whether by his mother He were of the tribe of Judah, or of the tribe of Levi.

If the national Church is to be true to the multitudinist principle, and to correspond ultimately to the national character, the freedom of opinion which belongs to the English citizen should be conceded to the English Churchman ; and the freedom which is already practically enjoyed by the members of the congregation, cannot without injustice be denied to its ministers. A minister may rightly be expected to know more of theology than the generality, or even than the best informed of the laity ; but it is a strange ignoring of the constitution of human minds, to expect all ministers, however much they may know, to be of one opinion in theoreticals, or the same person to be subject to no variation of opinion at different periods of his life. And it may be worth while to consider how far a liberty of opinion is conceded by our existing laws, civil and ecclesiastical. Along with great openings for freedom it will be found there are some restraints, or appearances of restraints, which require to be removed.

As far as opinion privately entertained is concerned, the liberty of the English clergyman appears already to be complete. For no ecclesiastical person can be obliged to answer interrogations as to his opinions, nor be troubled for that which he has not actually expressed, nor be made responsible for inferences which other people may draw from his expressions.[1]

Still, though there may be no power of inquisition

---

[1] The oath *ex officio* in the ecclesiastical law, is defined to be an oath whereby any person may be obliged to make any presentment of any crime or offence, or to confess or accuse himself or herself of any criminal matter or thing, whereby he or she may be liable to any censure, penalty,

into the private opinions either of ministers or people in the Church of England, there may be some interference with the expression of them; and a great restraint is supposed to be imposed upon the clergy by reason of their subscription to the Thirty-nine Articles. Yet it is more difficult than might be expected, to define what is the extent of the legal obligation of those who sign them; and in this case the strictly legal obligation is the measure of the moral one. Subscription may be thought even to be inoperative upon the conscience by reason of its vagueness. For the act of subscription is enjoined, but its effect or meaning nowhere plainly laid down; and it does not seem to amount to more than an acceptance of the Articles of the Church as the formal law to which the subscriber is in some sense subject. What that subjection amounts to, must be gathered elsewhere, for it does not appear on the face of the subscription itself.

The ecclesiastical authority on the subject is to be found in the Canons of 1603, the fifth and the thirty-

---

or punishment whatsoever. 4 Jac. 'The lords of the council at Whitehall demanded of Popham and Coke, chief justices, upon motion made by the Commons in Parliament, in what cases the ordinary may examine any person *ex officio* upon oath.' They answered—1. That the ordinary cannot constrain any man, ecclesiastical or temporal, to swear generally to answer such interrogations as shall be administered to him, &c. 2. That no man, ecclesiastical or temporal, shall be examined upon the secret thoughts of his heart, or of his secret opinion, but something ought to be objected against him, which he hath spoken or done. Thus 13 Jac. *Dighton* and *Holt* were committed by the high commissioners because they being convented for slanderous words against the book of Common Prayer and the government of the Church, and being tendered the oath to be examined, they refused. The case being brought before the K.B. on *habeas corpus*, Coke, C.J., gave the determination of the Court. 'That they ought to be delivered, because their examination is made to cause them to accuse themselves of a breach of a penal law, which is against law, for they ought to proceed against them by witnesses, and not inforce them to take an oath to accuse themselves.' Then by 13 Car. 2, c. 12, it was enacted, 'that it shall not be lawful for any person, exercising ecclesiastical jurisdiction, to tender or administer to any person whatsoever the oath usually called the oath *ex-officio*, or any other oath, whereby such person to whom the same is tendered, or administered, may be charged, or compelled to confess, or accuse, or to purge himself, or herself, of any criminal matter or thing,' &c.—Burn's *Eccl. Law*, iii. 14, 15. Ed. Phillimore.

sixth. The fifth, indeed, may be applicable theoretically both to lay and to ecclesiastical persons; practically it can only concern those of whom subscription is really required. It is entitled, *Impugners of the Articles of Religion established in this Church of England censured.* 'Whosoever shall hereafter affirm, that any of the nine and thirty articles, &c., are in any part superstitious or erroneous, or such as he may not with a good conscience subscribe unto, let him be excommunicated, &c.' We need not stay to consider what the effects of excommunication might be, but rather attend to the definition which the canon itself supplies of 'impugning.' It is stated to be the affirming, that any of the Thirty-nine Articles are in any part 'superstitious or erroneous.' Yet an Article may be very inexpedient, or become so; may be unintelligible, or not easily intelligible to ordinary people; it may be controversial, and such as to provoke controversy and keep it alive when otherwise it would subside; it may revive unnecessarily the remembrance of dead controversies—all or any of these, without being 'erroneous;' and though not 'superstitious,' some expressions may appear so, such as those which seem to impute an occult operation to the Sacraments. The fifth canon does not touch the affirming any of these things, and more especially, that the Articles present truths disproportionately, and relatively to ideas not now current.

The other canon which concerns subscription is the thirty-sixth, which contains two clauses explanatory to some extent, of the meaning of ministerial subscription, 'That he *alloweth* the Book of Articles, &c.' and 'that he *acknowledgeth* the same to be agreeable to the Word of God.' We 'allow' many things which we do not think wise or practically useful; as the less of two evils, or an evil which cannot be remedied, or of which the remedy is not attainable, or is uncertain in its operation, or is not in our power, or concerning which there is much difference of opinion, or where

the initiation of any change does not belong to ourselves, nor the responsibility belong to ourselves,
either of the things as they are, or of searching for
something better. Many acquiesce in, submit to,
'allow,' a law as it operates upon themselves which
they would be horror-struck to have enacted; yet
they would gladly and in conscience, 'allow' and
submit to it, as part of a constitution under which
they live, against which they would never think of
rebelling, which they would on no account undermine,
for the many blessings of which they are fully grateful—they would be silent and patient rather than
join, even in appearance, the disturbers and breakers
of its laws. Secondly, he 'acknowledgeth' the same
to be agreeable to the Word of God. Some distinctions may be founded upon the word 'acknowledge.'
He does not maintain, nor regard it as self-evident, nor
originate it as his own feeling, spontaneous opinion,
or conviction; but when it is suggested to him, put
in a certain shape, when the intention of the framers
is borne in mind, their probable purpose and design
explained, together with the difficulties which surrounded them, he is not prepared to contradict, and
he acknowledges. There is a great deal to be said,
which had not at first occurred to him; many other
better and wiser men than himself have acknowledged
the same thing—why should he be obstinate? Besides,
he is young, and has plenty of time to reconsider it;
or he is old and continues to submit out of habit, and
it would be too absurd, at his time of life, to be setting
up as a Church reformer.

But after all, the important phrase is, that the
Articles are 'agreeable to the Word of God.' This
cannot mean that the Articles are precisely co-extensive with the Bible, much less of equal authority
with it as a whole. Neither separately, nor altogether, do they embody all which is said in it, and
inferences which they draw from it are only good
relatively and *secundum quid* and *quatenus concordant*.

If their terms are Biblical terms, they must be presumed to have the same sense in the Articles which they have in the Scripture; and if they are not all Scriptural ones, they undertake in the pivot Article not to contradict the Scripture. The Articles do not make any assumption of being interpretations of Scripture or developments of it. The greater must include the less, and the Scripture is the greater.

On the other hand, there may be some things in the Articles which could not be contained, or have not been contained, in the Scripture—such as propositions or clauses concerning historical facts more recent than the Scripture itself; for instance, that there never has been any doubt in the Church concerning the books of the New Testament. For without including such doubts as a fool might have, or a very conceited person, without carrying doubts founded upon mere criticism and internal evidence only, to such an extent as a Baur or even an Ewald, there was a time when certain books existed and certain others were not as yet written;—for example, the Epistles of St. Paul were anterior, probably to all of the Gospels, certainly to that of St. John, and of course the Church could not receive without doubt books not as yet composed. But as the canon grew, book after book emerging into existence and general reception, there were doubts as to some of them, for a longer or shorter period, either concerning their authorship or their authority. The framers of the Articles were not deficient in learning, and could not have been ignorant of the passages in Eusebius where the different books current in Christendom in his time are classified as genuine or acknowledged, doubtful and spurious. If there be an erroneousness in such a statement, as that there never was any doubt in the Church concerning the book of the Revelation, the Epistle to the Hebrews, or the second of St. Peter, it cannot be an erroneousness in the sense of the fifth canon, nor can it be at variance with the Word of God according to the thirty-sixth. Such things in the Articles as are beside the Scripture are not in the contemplation of the canons. Much less can historical questions not even hinted at in the Articles be excluded from free discussion—such as concern the dates and composition of the several books, the compilation of the Pentateuch, the introduction of Daniel into the Jewish canon, and the like with some books of the New Testament—the date and authorship, for instance, of the fourth Gospel.

Many of those who would themselves wish the Christian theology to run on in its old forms of expression, nevertheless deal with the opinions of others, which they may think objectionable, fairly as opinions. There will always, on the other hand, be a few whose favourite mode of warfare it will be, to endeavour to gain a victory over some particular person who may hold opinions they dislike, by entangling him in the formularies. Nevertheless, our formularies do not lend themselves very easily to this kind of warfare— *Contra retiarium baculo.*

We have spoken hitherto of the signification of subscription which may be gathered from the canons; there is, also, a statute, a law of the land, which forbids, under penalties, the advisedly and directly contradicting any of them by ecclesiastics, and requires subscription with declaration of 'assent' from beneficed persons. This statute (13 Eliz. c. 12), three hundred years old, like many other old enactments, is not found to be very applicable to modern cases; although it is only about fifty years ago that it was said by Sir William Scott to be *in viridi observantiá.* Nevertheless, its provisions would not easily be brought to bear on questions likely to be raised in our own days. The meshes are too open for modern refinements. For not to repeat concerning the word 'assent' what has been said concerning 'allow' and 'acknowledge,' let the Articles be taken according to an obvious classification. Forms of expression, partly derived from modern modes of thought on metaphysical sub-

jects, partly suggested by a better acquaintance than
heretofore with the unsettled state of Christian opinion
in the immediately post-apostolic age, may be adopted
with respect to the doctrines enunciated in the five
first Articles, without directly contradicting, impugning, or refusing assent to them, but passing by the
side of them—as with respect to the humanifying of the
Divine Word and to the Divine Personalities.   Then
those which we have called the pivot Articles, concerning the rule of faith and the sufficiency of Scripture,
are, happily, found to make no effectual provision for
an absolute uniformity, when once the freedom of
interpretation of Scripture is admitted; they cannot
be considered as interpreting their own interpreter;
this has sometimes been called a circular proceeding;
it might be resembled to a lever becoming its own
fulcrum.   The Articles, again, which have a Lutheran
and Calvinistic sound, are found to be equally open,
because they are, for the most part, founded on the
very words of Scripture, and these, while worthy of
unfeigned assent, are capable of different interpretations.   Indeed, the Calvinistic and Arminian views
have been declared by a kind of authority to be both
of them tenable under the seventeenth Article; and if
the Scriptural terms of 'election' and 'predestination' may be interpreted in an anti-Calvinistic sense,
'faith,' in the tenth and following Articles, need not
be understood in the Lutheran.   These are instances
of legitimate affixing different significations to terms
in the Articles, by reason of different interpretations
of Scriptural passages.

If, however, the Articles of religion and the law of
the Church of England be in effect liberal, flexible, or
little stringent, is there any necessity for expressing
dissatisfaction with them, any sufficient provocation to
change?   There may be much more liberty in a Church
like our own, the law of which is always interpreted,
according to the English spirit, in the manner most

favourable to those who are subject to its discipline, than in one which, whether free or not from Articles, might be empowered to develope doctrine and to denounce new heresies. Certainly the late Mr. Irving, if he had been a clergyman of the Church of England, could scarcely have been brought under the terms of any ecclesiastical law of ours, for the expression of opinions upon an abstruse question respecting the humanity of Jesus Christ, which subjected him to degradation in the Presbyterian Church of Scotland. And this transition state may be a state of as much liberty as the Church of England could in any way as yet have been enabled to attain, a state of greater practical liberty than has been attained in Churches supposed to be more free; it is a state of safety and protection to those who use it wisely, under which a farther freedom may be prepared.

But it is not a state which ought to be considered final, either by the Church itself or by the nation. It is very well for provisions which cease to be easily applicable to modern cases to be suffered to fall into desuetude, but after falling into desuetude they should be repealed. Desuetude naturally leads to repeal. Obsolete tests are a blot upon a modern system, and there is always some danger lest an antiquated rule may be unexpectedly revived for the sake of an odious individual application; when it has outlived its general regulative power, it may still be a trap for the weaker consciences; or when it has become powerless as to penal consequences, it may serve to give a point to invidious imputations.

And farther than this, the present apparent stringency of subscription as required of the clergy of the Church of England does not belong to it as part of its foundation, is not even coeval with its reconstruction at the period of the Reformation. For the Canons are of the date of 1603, and the Act requiring the public reading of the Thirty-nine Articles, with declaration

of assent by a beneficed person after his induction,
is the 13th Elizabeth. An enactment prohibiting the
bishops from requiring the subscriptions under the
third article of the thirty-sixth canon, together with
the repeal of 13th Elizabeth, except as to its second
section, would relieve many scruples, and make the
Church more national, without disturbing its ultimate
law. The Articles would then obviously become for
the clergy that which they are for the laity of the
Church, 'articles of peace, not to be contradicted
by her sons,' as the wise and liberal Burnet described them : and there is forcible practical reason for leaving the Thirty-nine Articles as the
ultimate law of the Church, not to be contradicted, and for confining relaxation to the abolition
of subscription.

A large portion of the Articles were originally
directed against the corruptions of the Church of Rome,
and whatever may be thought of the unadvisableness of
retaining tests to exclude opinions which few think
of reviving in their old shape, these Roman doctrines
and practices are seen to be flourishing in full life and
vigour. And considering the many grievous provo-
cations which the people of England have suffered
from the Papacy both in ancient and modern times, they
would naturally resist any change which might by
possibility weaken the barriers between the National
Church and the encroachments of the Church of Rome.
It is evident, moreover, that the act of signature to the
Thirty-nine Articles contributes nothing to the exclusion from the Church of Romish views. For, as it is,
opinions and practices prevail among some of the clergy,
which are extremely distasteful to the generality of
the people, by reason of their Romish character.
Those of the Articles which condemn the Romish
errors, cannot themselves be made so stringent as to
bar altogether the intrusion of some opinion of a
Roman tone, which the Reformers, if they could have
foreseen it, might have desired to exclude, and which

is equally strange and repugnant to the common sense
of the nation. No act of subscription can supply
this defect of stringency in the formulas themselves.
Now it would be impossible to secure the advantages
of freedom in one direction without making it equal
as far as it goes. We must endeavour to liberate
ourselves from the dominion of an unwise and really
unchristian principle with the fewest possible risks and
inconveniences.

Considering therefore the practical difficulties which
would beset any change, and especially those which
would attend, either the excepting of the anti-Romish
Articles from repeal or including them in it; any
attempt at a relaxation of the clerical test should
prudently confine itself in our generation, to an abolition of the act of subscription, leaving the Articles
themselves protected by the second section of the
Statute of Elizabeth and by the canons, against direct
contradiction or impugning.

For, the act of subscription being abolished, there
would disappear the invidious distinction between
the clergy and laity of the same communion, as if
there were separate standards for each of belief and
morals. There would disappear also a semblance of
a promissory oath on a subject which a promise
is incapable of reaching. No promise can reach
fluctuations of opinion and personal conviction. Open
teaching can, it is true, if it be thought wise, be
dealt with by the law and its penalties; but the law
should content itself with saying, you shall not
teach or proclaim in derogation of my formularies;
it should not require any act which appears to
signify 'I think.' Let the security be either the
penal or the moral one, not a commingling of the
two. It happens continually, that able and sincere
persons are deterred from entering the ministry of
the national Church by this consideration; they
would be willing to be subject to the law forbidding
them to teach Arianism or Pelagianism — as what

sensible man in our day would desire to teach them?
— but they do not like to say, or be thought to
say, that they assent to a certain number of anti-
Arian and anti-Pelagian propositions. And the absence
of vigorous tone—not confined to one party in the
Church, which is to be lamented of late years in its
ministry, is to be attributed to the reluctance of the
stronger minds to enter an Order in which their intellects may not have free play. The very course of
preparation for ordination, tied down as it is in one
department to the study of the Articles, which must
perforce be proved consentaneous to the 'Word of God'
according to some, and to 'Catholic antiquity' according
to others, has an enervating effect upon the mind,
which is compelled to embrace much scholastic matter,
not as a history of doctrine, but as a system of truth
of which it ought to be convinced.

It may be easy to urge invidiously, with respect to
the impediments now existing to undertaking office
in the national Church, that there are other sects,
which persons dissatisfied with her formularies may
join, and where they may find scope for their activity
with little intellectual bondage. Nothing can be said
here, whether or not there might be elsewhere bondage
at least as galling, of a similar or another kind. But
the service of the national Church may well be regarded in a different light from the service of a sect.
It is as properly an organ of the national life as a
magistracy, or a legislative estate. To set barriers
before the entrance upon its functions, by limitations
not absolutely required by public policy, is to infringe
upon the birthright of the citizens. And to lay down
as an alternative to striving for more liberty of thought
and expression within the Church of the nation, that
those who are dissatisfied may sever themselves and
join a sect, would be paralleled by declaring to political reformers, that they are welcome to expatriate
themselves, if they desire any change in the existing

forms of the constitution. The suggestion of the alternative is an insult; if it could be enforced, it would be a grievous wrong.

There is another part of the subject which may be slightly touched upon in this place — that of the endowment of the national Church. This was well described by Mr. Coleridge as the Nationalty. In a certain sense, indeed, the nation or state is lord paramount over all the property within its boundaries. But it provides for the usufruct of the property in two different ways. The usufruct of private property, as it is called, descends, according to our laws, by inheritance or testamentary disposition, and no specific services are attached to its enjoyment. The usufruct of that which Coleridge called the Nationalty circulates freely among all the families of the nation. The enjoyment of it is subject to the performance of special services, is attainable only by the possession of certain qualifications. In accordance with the strong tendency in England to turn every interest into a right of so-called private property, the nominations to the benefices of the national Church have come, by an abuse, to be regarded as part of the estates of patrons, instead of trusts, as they really are. No trustee of any analogous property, of a grammar-school for instance, would think of selling his right of appointment; he would consider the proper exercise of the trust his duty; much less would any court of law acknowledge that a beneficial interest in the trust property was an asset belonging to the estate of the trustee. If the nomination to the place of a schoolmaster ought to be considered as purely fiduciary, much more should the nomination of a spiritual person to his parochial charge. Objections are made against our own national Church founded upon these anomalies, which may in time be rectified. Others are made against the very principle of endowment.

It is said, that a fixed support of the minister

tends to paralyse both him and his people—making him independent of his congregation, and drying up their liberality. It would be difficult, perhaps, to say which would be the greater evil, for a minister to be in all things independent of his people, or in all things dependent upon them. But the endowed minister is by no means independent of all restraints, as, for instance, of the law of his Church and, which is much more, of public opinion, especially of the opinion of his own people. The unendowed minister is dependent in all things, both upon the opinion of his people and upon their liberality; and frequent complaints transpire among Nonconformists of the want of some greater fixity in the position and sustentation of their ministers. In the case of a nationally endowed Church, the people themselves contribute little or nothing to its support. The Church of England is said to be the richest Church in Europe, which is probably not true; but its people contribute less to its support than the members of any other Church in Christendom, whether established or voluntary. And if the contributing personally to the support of the ministry were the only form which Christian liberality could take, the stopping up the outflow of it would be an incalculable evil. But it is not so; there are a multitude of other objects, even though the principal minister in a parish or other locality were sufficiently provided for, to give an outlet for Christian liberality. It may flow over from more favoured localities where Churches are sufficiently endowed, into more destitute districts and into distant lands. This is so with ourselves; and those who are familiar with the statistics of the numerous voluntary societies in England for Christian and philanthropic purposes, know to how great an extent the bulk of the support they meet with is derived from the contributions of churchmen. There is reason to think on the other hand, that the means and willingness to give on the part of nonconforming congregations are already mainly exhausted in making provision for their ministers.

Reverting to the general interest in the *Nationalty*, it is evidently twofold. First, in the free circulation of a certain portion of the real property of the country, inherited not by blood, nor through the accident of birth, but by merit and in requital for certain performances. It evidently belongs to the popular interest, that this circulation should be free from all unnecessary limitations and restraints—speculative, antiquarian, and the like, and be regulated, as far as attainable, by fitness and capacity for a particular public service. Thus by means of the national endowment there would take place a distribution of property to every family in the country, *unencumbered by family provisions at each succession*—a distribution in like manner of the best kind of education, of which the effects would not be worn out in one or two generations. The Church theoretically is the most popular, it might be said, the most democratic of all our institutions; its ministers—as a spiritual magistracy—true tribunes of the people. Secondly, the general interest in the *Nationalty* as the material means whereby the highest services are obtained for the general good, requires, that no artificial discouragements should limit the number of those who otherwise would be enabled to become candidates for the service of the Church—that nothing should prevent the choice and recruiting of the Church ministers from the whole of the citizens. As a matter of fact we find that nearly one-half of our population are at present more or less alienated from the communion of the national Church, and do not, therefore, supply candidates for its ministry. Instead of securing the excellences and highest attainments from the whole of the people, it secures them, by means of the national reserve, only from one-half; the rest are either not drawn up into the Christian ministry at all, or undertake it in connexion with schismatical bodies, with as much detriment to the national unity, as to the ecclesiastical.

We all know how the inward moral life—or spiritual life on its moral side, if that term be preferred—is nourished into greater or less vigour by means of the conditions in which the moral subject is placed. Hence, if a nation is really worthy of the name, conscious of its own corporate life, it will develop itself on one side into a Church, wherein its citizens may grow up and be perfected in their spiritual nature. If there is within it a consciousness that as a nation it is fulfilling no unimportant office in the world, and is, under the order of Providence, an instrument in giving the victory to good over evil and to happiness over misery, it will not content itself with the rough adjustments and rude lessons of law and police, but will throw its elements, or the best of them, into another mould, and constitute out of them a society, which is in it, though in some sense not of it—which is another, yet the same.

That each one born into the nation is, together with his civil rights, born into a membership or privilege, as belonging to a spiritual society, places him at once in a relation which must tell powerfully upon his spiritual nature. For the sake of the reaction upon its own merely secular interests, the nation is entitled to provide from time to time, that the Church teaching and forms of one age do not traditionally harden, so as to become exclusive barriers in a subsequent one, and so the moral growth of those who are committed to the hands of the Church be checked, or its influences confined to a comparatively few. And the objects of the care of the State and of the Church will nearly coincide; for the former desires all its people to be brought under the improving influence, and the latter is willing to embrace all who have even the rudiments of the moral life.

And if the objects of the care of each nearly coincide, when the office of the Church is properly understood, so errors and mistakes in defining Church-membership, or in constituting a repulsive mode of Church teaching, are fatal to the purposes both of Church and State alike.

It is a great misrepresentation to exhibit the State as allying itself with one out of many sects—a misrepresentation, the blame of which does not rest wholly with political persons, nor with the partisans of sects adverse to that which is supposed to be unduly preferred. It cannot concern a State to develop as part of its own organization a machinery or system of relations founded on the possession of speculative truth. Speculative doctrines should be left to philosophical schools. A national Church must be concerned with the ethical development of its members. And the wrong of supposing it to be otherwise, is participated by those of the clericalty who consider the Church of Christ to be founded, as a society, on the possession of an abstractedly true and supernaturally communicated speculation concerning God, rather than upon the manifestation of a divine life in man.

It has often been made matter of reproach to the heathen State religions, that they took little concern in the moral life of the citizens. To a certain extent this is true, for the heathens of classical history had not generally the same conceptions of morals as we have. But as far as their conceptions of morals reached, their Church and State were mutually bound together, not by a material alliance, nor by a gross compact of pay and preferment passing between the civil society and the priesthood, but by the penetrating of the whole public and domestic life of the nation with a religious sentiment. All the social relations were consecrated by the feeling of their being entered into and carried on under the sanction—under the very impulse of Deity. Treaties and boundaries, buying and selling, marrying, judging, deliberating on affairs of State, spectacles and all popular amusements, were under the

protection of Divinity ; all life was a worship.   It can
very well be understood how philosophers should be
esteemed atheists, when they began to speculate upon
origins, causes, abstract being, and the like.

Certainly the sense of the individual conscience was
not sufficiently developed under those old religions.
Their observances, once penetrated with a feeling of
present Deity, became, in course of time, mere dry and
superstitious forms.   But the glory of the Gospel
would only be partial and one-sided, if, while quickening the individual conscience and the expectation of
individual immortality, it had no spirit to quicken the
national life.   An isolated salvation, the rescuing of
one's self, the reward, the grace bestowed on one's own
labours, the undisturbed repose, the crown of glory in
which so many have no share, the finality of the
sentence on both hands—reflections on such expectations as these may make stubborn martyrs and sour
professors, but not good citizens; rather tend to unfit
men for this world, and in so doing prepare them very
ill for that which is to come.

But in order to the possibility of recruiting any
national ministry from the whole of the nation, in
order to the operation upon the nation at large of the
special functions of its Church, no needless intellectual
or speculative obstacles should be interposed.   It is
not to be expected that terms of communion could
be made so large, as by any possibility to comprehend
in the national Church the whole of such a free nation
as our own.   There will always be those who, from
a conscientious scruple, or from a desire to define, or
from peculiarities of temper, will hold aloof from the
religion and the worship of the majority ; and it is not
desirable that it should be otherwise, so long as the national unity and the moral action of society are not thereby seriously impaired.   No doubt, speaking politically,
and regarding merely the peacefulness with which the
machinery of ordinary executive government can be carried on, it has proved very advantageous to the State,

that an Established Church has existed in this country, to receive the shafts which otherwise might have been directed against itself. Ill-humour has evaporated harmlessly in Dissent, which might otherwise have materially deranged the body politic; and village Hampdens have acquired a parochial renown, sufficient to satisfy their ambition, in resistance to a Church-rate, whose restlessness might have urged them to dispute, even to prison and spoiling of their goods, the lawfulness of a war-tax. But whatever root of conscientiousness and truth-seeking there has been in non-conformity, whatever amount of indirect good is produced by the emulation of the different religious bodies, whatever safety to social order by the escapement for temper so provided—the moral influence of the better people in their several neighbourhoods is neutralized or lost for want of harmony and concentration, when the alienation from the national Church reaches the extent which it has done in our country. Even in the more retired localities, industry, cleanliness, decency in the homes of the poor, school discipline and truthfulness, are encouraged far less than they might otherwise be, by reason of the absence of religious unanimity in the superior classes. And if the points of speculation and of form which separate Dissenters from the Church of England were far more important than they are, and the approximative truth preponderatingly upon the side of Dissent, it would do infinitely more harm by the dissension which it creates, than it possibly could accomplish of good, by a greater correctness in doctrine and ecclesiastical constitution. If this statement concerns Dissent itself on one side, it concerns the Church on the other, or rather those who so limit the terms of its communion as to provoke, and—as human beings are constituted—to necessitate separation from it. It is stated by Neal,[1] that if the alterations in the Prayer-book, recommended

---

[1] *Hist. Pur.* iv. p. 618.

by the Commissioners of 1689 had been adopted, it would ' in all probability have brought in three parts in four of the Dissenters.' No such result could be expected from any 'amendments' or 'concessions' now. Much less could anything be hoped for, by means of a ' Conference.' But it concerns the State, on the highest grounds of public policy, to rectify, as far as possible, the mistakes committed in former times by itself or by the Church under its sanction; and without aiming at an universal comprehension, which would be Utopian, to suffer the perpetuation of no unnecessary barriers excluding from the communion or the ministry of the national Church.

There are, moreover, besides those who have joined the ranks of Dissent, many others holding aloof from the Church of England, by reason of its real or supposed dogmatism—whose co-operation in its true work would be most valuable to it—and who cannot become utterly estranged from it, without its losing ultimately its popular influence and its national character. If those who distinguish themselves in science and literature cannot, in a scientific and literary age, be effectually and cordially attached to the Church of their nation, they must sooner or later be driven into a position of hostility to it. They may be as indisposed to the teaching of the majority of Dissenters as to that which they conceive to be the teaching of the Church ; but the Church, as an organization, will of necessity appear to be the most damaged by a scientific criticism of a supposed Christianity common to it with other bodies. Many personal and social bonds have retarded hitherto an issue which from time to time has threatened a controversy between our science and our theology. It would be a deplorable day, when the greatest names on either side should be found in conflict ; and theology should only learn to acknowledge, after a defeat, that there are no irreconcileable differences between itself and its opponents.

It is sometimes said with a sneer, that the scientific men and the men of abstractions will never change the religions of the world; and yet Christianity has certainly been very different from what it would have been without the philosophies of a Plato and an Aristotle; and a Bacon and a Newton exercise an influence upon ·the Biblical theology of Englishmen. They have modified, though they have not made it. The more diffused science of the present day will farther modify it. And the question seems to narrow itself to this—How can those who differ from each other intellectually in such variety of degrees as our more educated and our less educated classes, be comprised under the same formularies of one national Church—be supposed to follow them, assent to them, appropriate them, in one spirit? If such formularies embodied only an ethical result addressed to the individual and to society, the speculative difficulty would not arise. But as they present a fair and substantial representation of the Biblical records, incorporating their letter and presupposing their historical element, precisely the same problem is presented to us intellectually, as English Churchmen or as Biblical Christians.

It does not seem to be contradicted, that when Church formularies adopt the words of Scripture, these must have the same meaning, and be subject to the same questions, in the formularies, as in the Scripture. And we may go somewhat farther and say, that the historical parts of the Bible, when referred to or presupposed in the formularies, have the same *value* in them which they have in their original seat; and this *value* may consist, rather in their significance, in the ideas which they awaken, than in the scenes themselves which they depict. And as Churchmen, or as Christians, we may vary as to their value in particulars—that is, as to the extent of the verbal accuracy of a history, or of its spiritual significance, without breaking with our communion, or denying our sacred name. These varieties will be determined partly by the peculiarities of men's mental constitution, partly by the nature of their education, circumstances, and special studies. And neither should the idealist condemn the literalist, nor the literalist assume the right of excommunicating the idealist. They are really fed with the same truths; the literalist unconsciously, the idealist with reflection. Neither can justly say of the other that he undervalues the Sacred Writings, or that he holds them as inspired less properly than himself.

The application of ideology to the interpretation of Scripture, to the doctrines of Christianity, to the formularies of the Church, may undoubtedly be carried to an excess—may be pushed so far as to leave in the sacred records no historical residue whatever. On the other side, there is the excess of a dull and unpainstaking acquiescence, satisfied with accepting in an unquestioning spirit, and as if they were literally facts, all particulars of a wonderful history, because in some sense it is from God. Between these extremes lie infinite degrees of rational and irrational interpretation.

It will be observed that the ideal method is applicable in two ways; both to giving account of the origin of parts of Scripture, and also in explanation of Scripture. It is thus either critical or exegetical. An example of the critical ideology carried to excess is that of Strauss, which resolves into an ideal the whole of the historical and doctrinal person of Jesus; so again, much of the allegorizing of Philo and Origen is an exegetical ideology, exaggerated and wild. But it by no means follows, because Strauss has substituted a mere shadow for the Jesus of the Evangelists, and has frequently descended to a minute captiousness in details, that there are not traits in the scriptural person of Jesus, which are better explained by referring them to an ideal than an historical origin : and without falling into fanciful exegetics, there are parts of Scrip-

ture more usefully interpreted ideologically than in
any other manner—as, for instance, the history of
the temptation of Jesus by Satan, and accounts of
demoniacal possessions. And liberty must be left to
all as to the extent in which they apply the principle,
for there is no authority, through the expressed determination of the Church, nor of any other kind, which
can define the limits within which it may be reasonably
exercised.

Thus some may consider the descent of all mankind
from Adam and Eve as an undoubted historical fact;
others may rather perceive in that relation a form of
narrative, into which in early ages tradition would
easily throw itself spontaneously. Each race naturally
—necessarily, when races are isolated—supposes itself
to be sprung from a single pair, and to be the first, or
the only one, of races. Among a particular people this
historical representation became the concrete expression
of a great moral truth—of the brotherhood of all
human beings, of their community, as in other things,
so also in suffering and in frailty, in physical pains
and in moral 'corruption.' And the force, grandeur,
and reality of these ideas are not a whit impaired in
the abstract, nor indeed the truth of the concrete history as their representation, even though mankind
should have been placed upon the earth in many pairs
at once, or in distinct centres of creation. For the
brotherhood of men really depends, not upon the
material fact of their fleshly descent from a single
stock, but upon their constitution, as possessed in
common, of the same faculties and affections, fitting
them for mutual relation and association; so that the
value of the history, if it were a history strictly so
called, would lie in its emblematic force and application.
And many narratives of marvels and catastrophes in
the Old Testament are referred to in the New, as
emblems, without either denying or asserting their
literal truth—such as the destruction of Sodom and

Gomorrah by fire from heaven, and the Noachian deluge. And especially if we bear in mind the existence of such a school as that which produced Philo, or even the author of the Epistle to the Hebrews, we must think it would be wrong to lay down, that whenever the New Testament writers refer to Old Testament histories, they imply of necessity that the historic truth was the first to them. For their purposes it was often wholly in the background, and the history, valuable only in its spiritual application. The same may take place with ourselves, and history and tradition be employed emblematically, without, on that account, being regarded as untrue. We do not apply the term 'untrue' to parable, fable, or proverb, although their words correspond with ideas, not with material facts; as little should we do so, when narratives have been the spontaneous product of true ideas, and are capable of reproducing them.

The ideologian is evidently in possession of a principle which will enable him to stand in charitable relation to persons of very different opinions from his own, and of very different opinions mutually. And if he has perceived to how great extent the history of the origin itself of Christianity rests ultimately upon *probable* evidence, his principle will relieve him from many difficulties which might otherwise be very disturbing. For relations which may repose on doubtful grounds as matter of history, and, as history, be incapable of being ascertained or verified, may yet be equally suggestive of true ideas with facts absolutely certain. The spiritual significance is the same of the transfiguration, of opening blind eyes, of causing the tongue of the stammerer to speak plainly, of feeding multitudes with bread in the wilderness, of cleansing leprosy, whatever links may be deficient in the traditional record of particular events. Or, let us suppose one to be uncertain, whether our Lord were born of the house and lineage of David, or of the tribe of Levi, and even to be driven to conclude that the genealogies of Him have little historic value; nevertheless, in idea, Jesus is both Son of David and Son of Aaron, both Prince of Peace and High Priest of our profession; as He is, under another idea, though not literally, 'without father and without mother.' And He is none the less Son of David, Priest Aaronical, or Royal Priest Melchizedecan, in idea and spiritually, even if it be unproved, whether He were any of them in historic fact. In like manner it need not trouble us, if, in consistency, we should have to suppose both an ideal origin and to apply an ideal meaning to the birth in the city of David, and to other circumstances of the infancy. So, again, the incarnification of the divine Immanuel remains, although the angelic appearances which herald it in the narratives of the Evangelists may be of ideal origin according to the conceptions of former days. The ideologian may sometimes be thought sceptical, and be sceptical or doubtful, as to the historical value of related facts; but the historical value is not always to him the most important; frequently it is quite secondary. And, consequently, discrepancies in narratives, scientific difficulties, defects in evidence, do not disturb him as they do the literalist.

Moreover, the same principle is capable of application to some of those inferences which have been the source, according to different theologies, of much controversial acrimony and of wide ecclesiastical separations; such as those which have been drawn from the institution of the sacraments. Some, for instance, cannot conceive a presence of Jesus Christ in His institution of the Lord's Supper, unless it be a corporeal one, nor a spiritual influence upon the moral nature of man to be connected with baptism, unless it be supernatural, quasi-mechanical, effecting a psychical change then and there. But within these concrete conceptions there lie hid the truer ideas of the virtual presence of the Lord Jesus everywhere that He is preached, remembered, and represented, and of the continual force of His spirit in His words, and especially in the ordinance which indicates the separation of the Christian from the world.

The same may be said of the concrete conceptions of an hierarchy described by its material form and descent; also of millenarian expectations of a personal reign of the saints with Jesus upon earth, and of the many embodiments in which from age to age has reappeared the vision of a New Jerusalem shining with mundane glory here below. These gross conceptions, as they seem to some, may be necessary to others, as approximations to true ideas. So, looking for redemption in Israel was a looking for a very different redemption, with most of the Jewish people, from that which Jesus really came to operate, yet it was the only expectation which they could form, and was the shadow to them of a great reality.

> 'Lo, the poor Indian, whose untutored mind,
>   Sees God in clouds, or hears Him in the wind.'

Even to the Hebrew Psalmist, He comes flying upon the wings of the wind; and only to the higher Prophet is He not in the wind, nor in the earthquake, nor in the fire, but in 'the still small voice.' Not the same thoughts—very far from the same thoughts—pass through the minds of the more and the less instructed on contemplating the same face of the natural world. In like manner are the thoughts of men various, in form at least, if not in substance, when they read the same Scripture histories and use the same Scripture phrases. Histories to some, become parables to others; and facts to those, are emblems to these. The 'rock' and the 'cloud' and the 'sea' convey to the Christian admonitions of spiritual verities; and so do the ordinances of the Church and various parts of its forms of worship.

Jesus Christ has not revealed His religion as a theology of the intellect, nor as an historical faith; and it is a stifling of the true Christian life, both in the individual and in the Church, to require of many men a unanimity in speculative doctrine, which is unattainable, and a uniformity of historical belief, which can never exist. The true Christian life is the consciousness of bearing a part in a great moral order, of which the highest agency upon earth has been committed to the Church. Let us not oppress this work nor complicate the difficulties with which it is surrounded; 'not making the heart of the righteous sad, whom the Lord hath not made sad, nor strengthening the hands of the wicked by promising him life.'

There is enough indeed to sadden us in the doubtful warfare which the good wages with the evil, both within us and without us. How few, under the most favourable conditions, learn to bring themselves face to face with the great moral law, which is the manifestation of the Will of God! The greater part can only detect the evil when it comes forth from them, nearly as when any other might observe it. We cannot, in the matter of those who are brought under the highest influences of the Christian Church, any more than in the case of mankind viewed in their ordinary relations, give any account of the apparently useless expenditure of power—of the apparent overbearing generally of the higher law by the lower—of the apparent poverty of result from the operation of a wonderful machinery—of the seeming waste of myriads of germs, for the sake of a few mature growths. 'Many are called but few chosen'—and under the privileges of the Christian Church, as in other mysteries,—

πολλοὶ μὲν ναρθηκοφόροι, βάκχοι δέ γε παῦροι.

Calvinism has a keen perception of this truth; and we shrink from Calvinism and Augustinianism, not because of their perceiving how few, even under Christian privileges, attain to the highest adoption of sons; but because of the inferences with which they clog that truth—the inferences which they draw respecting the rest, whom they comprehend in one mass of perdition.

The Christian Church can only tend on those who are committed to its care, to the verge of that abyss which parts this world from the world unseen. Some few of those fostered by her are now ripe for entering on a higher career: the many are but rudimentary spirits—germinal souls. What shall become of them? If we look abroad in the world and regard the neutral character of the multitude, we are at a loss to apply to them, either the promises, or the denunciations of revelation. So, the wise heathens could anticipate a reunion with the great and good of all ages; they could represent to themselves, at least in a figurative manner, the punishment and the purgatory of the wicked; but they would not expect the reappearance in another world, for any purpose, of a Thersites or an Hyperbolos—social and poetical justice had been sufficiently done upon them. Yet there are such as these, and no better than these, under the Christian name—babblers, busy-bodies, livers to get gain, and mere eaters and drinkers. The Roman Church has imagined a *limbus infantium;* we must rather entertain a hope that there shall be found, after the great adjudication, receptacles suitable for those who shall be infants, not as to years of terrestrial life, but as to spiritual development—nurseries as it were and seed-grounds, where the undeveloped may grow up under new conditions—the stunted may become strong, and the perverted be restored. And when the Christian Church, in all its branches, shall have fulfilled its sublunary office, and its Founder shall have surrendered His kingdom to the Great Father—all, both small and great, shall find a refuge in the bosom of the Universal Parent, to repose, or be quickened into higher life, in the ages to come, according to his Will.

# MOSAIC COSMOGONY.

ON the revival of science in the 16th century, some of the earliest conclusions at which philosophers arrived were found to be at variance with popular and long-established belief. The Ptolemaic system of astronomy, which had then full possession of the minds of men, contemplated the whole visible universe from the earth as the immovable centre of things. Copernicus changed the point of view, and placing the beholder in the sun, at once reduced the earth to an inconspicuous globule, a merely subordinate member of a family of planets, which the terrestrials had until then fondly imagined to be but pendants and ornaments of their own habitation. The Church naturally took a lively interest in the disputes which arose between the philosophers of the new school and those who adhered to the old doctrines, inasmuch as the Hebrew records, the basis of religious faith, manifestly countenanced the opinion of the earth's immobility and certain other views of the universe very incompatible with those propounded by Copernicus. Hence arose the official proceedings against Galileo, in consequence of which he submitted to sign his celebrated recantation, acknowledging that ' the proposition that the sun is the centre of the world and immovable from its place is absurd, philosophically false, and formally heretical, because it is expressly contrary to the Scripture;' and that 'the proposition that the earth is not the centre of the world, nor immovable, but that it moves and also with a diurnal motion, is absurd, philosophically false, and at least erroneous in faith.'

The Romish Church, it is presumed, adheres to the old views to the present day. Protestant instincts, however, in the 17th century were strongly in sympathy with the augmentation of science, and consequently Reformed Churches more easily allowed themselves to be helped over the difficulty, which, according to the views of inspiration then held and which have survived to the present day, was in reality quite as formidable for them as for those of the old faith. The solution of the difficulty offered by Galileo and others was, that the object of a revelation or divine unveiling of mysteries, must be to teach man things which he is unable and must ever remain unable to find out for himself; but not physical truths, for the discovery of which he has faculties specially provided by his Creator. Hence it was not unreasonable that, in regard to matters of fact merely, the Sacred Writings should use the common language and assume the common belief of mankind, without purporting to correct errors upon points morally indifferent. So, in regard to such a text as, 'The world is established, it cannot be moved,' though it might imply the sacred penman's ignorance of the fact that the earth does move, yet it does not put forth this opinion as an indispensable point of faith. And this remark is applicable to a number of texts which present a similar difficulty.

It might be thought to have been less easy to reconcile in men's minds the Copernican view of the universe with the very plain and direct averments contained in the opening chapter of Genesis. It can scarcely be said that this chapter is not intended in part to teach and convey at least some physical truth, and taking its words in their plain sense it manifestly gives a view of the universe adverse to that of modern science. It represents the sky as a watery vault in which the sun, moon, and stars are set. But the discordance of this description with facts does not appear to have been so palpable to the minds of the seventeenth century as it is to us. The mobility of the earth was a proposition startling not only to faith but to the senses. The difficulty involved in this belief having been successfully got over, other discrepancies dwindled in importance. The brilliant progress of astronomical science subdued the minds of men; the controversy between faith and knowledge gradually fell to slumber; the story of Galileo and the Inquisition became a school commonplace, the doctrine of the earth's mobility found its way into children's catechisms, and the limited views of the nature of the universe indicated in the Old Testament ceased to be felt as religious difficulties.

It would have been well if theologians had made up their minds to accept frankly the principle that those things for the discovery of which man has faculties specially provided are not fit objects of a divine revelation. Had this been unhesitatingly done, either the definition and idea of divine revelation must have been modified, and the possibility of an admixture of error have been allowed, or such parts of the Hebrew writings as were found to be repugnant to fact must have been pronounced to form no part of revelation. The first course is that which theologians have most generally adopted, but with such limitations, cautels, and equivocations as to be of little use in satisfying those who would know how and what God really has taught mankind, and whether anything beyond that which man is able and obviously intended to arrive at by the use of his natural faculties.

The difficulties and disputes which attended the first revival of science have recurred in the present

P

century in consequence of the growth of geology. It is in truth only the old question over again—precisely the same point of theology which is involved,—although the difficulties which present themselves are fresh. The school-books of the present day, while they teach the child that the earth moves, yet assure him that it is a little less than six thousand years old, and that it was made in six days. On the other hand, geologists of all religious creeds are agreed that the earth has existed for an immense series of years,—to be counted by millions rather than by thousands; and that indubitably more than six days elapsed from its first creation to the appearance of man upon its surface. By this broad discrepancy between old and new doctrine is the modern mind startled, as were the men of the sixteenth century when told that the earth moved.

When this new cause of controversy first arose, some writers more hasty than discreet, attacked the conclusions of geologists, and declared them scientifically false. This phase may now be considered past, and although school-books probably continue to teach much as they did, no well-instructed person now doubts the great antiquity of the earth any more than its motion. This being so, modern theologians, forsaking the maxim of Galileo, or only using it vaguely as an occasional make-weight, have directed their attention to the possibility of reconciling the Mosaic narrative with those geological facts which are admitted to be beyond dispute. Several modes of doing this have been proposed which have been deemed more or less satisfactory. In a text-book of theological instruction widely used,[1] we find it stated in broad terms, ' Geological investigations, it is now known, all prove the perfect harmony between scripture and geology, in reference to the history of creation.'

---

[1] Horne's *Introduction to the Holy Scriptures* (1856, tenth Edition.)

In truth, however, if we refer to the plans of conciliation proposed, we find them at variance with each other and mutually destructive. The conciliators are not agreed among themselves, and each holds the views of the other to be untenable and unsafe. The ground is perpetually being shifted, as the advance of geological science may require. The plain meaning of the Hebrew record is unscrupulously tampered with, and in general the pith of the whole process lies in divesting the text of all meaning whatever. We are told that Scripture not being designed to teach us natural philosophy, it is in vain to attempt to make out a cosmogony from its statements. If the first chapter of Genesis convey to us no information concerning the origin of the world, its statements cannot indeed be contradicted by modern discovery. But it is absurd to call this harmony. Statements such as that above quoted are, we conceive, little calculated to be serviceable to the interests of theology, still less to religion and morality. Believing, as we do, that if the value of the Bible as a book of religious instruction is to be maintained, it must be not by striving to prove it scientifically exact, at the expense of every sound principle of interpretation, and in defiance of common sense, but by the frank recognition of the erroneous views of nature which it contains, we have put pen to paper to analyse some of the popular conciliation theories. The inquiry cannot be deemed a superfluous one, nor one which in the interests of theology had better be let alone. Physical science goes on unconcernedly pursuing its own paths. Theology, the science whose object is the dealing of God with man as a moral being, maintains but a shivering existence, shouldered and jostled by the sturdy growths of modern thought, and bemoaning itself for the hostility which it encounters. Why should this be, unless because theologians persist in clinging to theories of God's procedure towards man, which have long been seen to be untenable ? If, relinquishing theories, they would be content to inquire from the history of man what this procedure has actually been, the so-called difficulties of theology would, for the most part, vanish of themselves.

The account which astronomy gives of the relations of our earth to the rest of the universe, and that which geology gives of its internal structure and the development of its surface, are sufficiently familiar to most readers. But it will be necessary for our purpose to go over the oft-trodden ground, which must be done with rapid steps. Nor let the reader object to be reminded of some of the most elementary facts of his knowledge. The human race has been ages in arriving at conclusions now familiar to every child.

This earth apparently so still and stedfast, lying in majestic repose beneath the ætherial vault, is a globular body of comparatively insignificant size, whirling fast through space round the sun as the centre of its orbit, and completing its revolution in the course of one year, while at the same time it revolves daily once about its own axis, thus producing the changes of day and night. The sun, which seems to leap up each morning from the east, and traversing the skyey bridge, slides down into the west, is relatively to our earth motionless. In size and weight it inconceivably surpasses it. The moon, which occupies a position in the visible heavens only second to the sun, and far beyond that of every other celestial body in conspicuousness, is but a subordinate globe, much smaller than our own, and revolving round the earth as its centre, while it accompanies it in yearly revolutions about the sun. Of itself it has no lustre, and is visible to us only by the reflected sunlight. Those beautiful stars which are perpetually changing their position in the heavens, and shine with a soft and moon-like light, are bodies, some much larger, some less, than our earth, and like it revolve round the sun, by the reflection of whose rays we see them. The telescope has revealed to us the fact that several of these are attended by moons of their own, and that besides those which the unassisted eye can see, there are others belonging to the same family coursing round the sun. As for the glittering dust which emblazons the nocturnal sky, there is reason to believe that each spark is a self-luminous body, perhaps of similar material to our sun, and that the very nearest of the whole tribe is at an incalculable distance from us, the very least of them of enormous size compared with our own humble globe. Thus has modern science reversed nearly all the *primâ facie* views to which our senses lead us as to the constitution of the universe; but so thoroughly are the above statements wrought into the culture of the present day, that we are apt to forget that mankind once saw these things very differently, and that but a few centuries have elapsed since such views were startling novelties.

Our earth then is but one of the lesser pendants of a body which is itself only an inconsiderable unit in the vast creation. And now if we withdraw our thoughts from the immensities of space, and look into the construction of man's obscure home, the first question is whether it has ever been in any other condition than that in which we now see it, and if so, what are the stages through which it has passed, and what was its first traceable state. Here geology steps in and successfully carries back the history of the earth's crust to a very remote period, until it arrives at a region of uncertainty, where philosophy is reduced to mere guesses and possibilities, and pronounces nothing definite. To this region belong the speculations which have been ventured upon as to the original concretion of the earth and planets out of nebular matter of which the sun may have been the nucleus. But the first clear view which we obtain of the early condition of the earth, presents to us a ball of matter, fluid with intense heat, spinning on its own axis and revolving round the sun. How long it may have continued in this state is beyond calculation or surmise. It can only be believed that a prolonged period, beginning and ending we know not when, elapsed before the surface became cooled and hardened and capable of sustaining organized existences. The water which now enwraps a large portion of the face of the globe, must for ages have existed only in the shape of steam, floating above and enveloping the planet in one thick curtain of mist. When the cooling of the surface allowed it to condense and descend, then commenced the process by which the lowest stratified rocks were formed, and gradually spread out in vast layers. Rains and rivers now acted upon the scoriaceous integument, grinding it to sand and carrying it down to the depths and cavities. Whether organized beings co-existed with this state of things we know not, as the early rocks have been acted upon by interior heat to an extent which must have destroyed all traces of animal and vegetable life, if any such ever existed. This period has been named by geologists the Azoic, or that in which life was not. Its duration no one presumes to define.

It is in the system of beds which overlies these primitive formations that the first records of organisms present themselves. In the so-called Silurian system we have a vast assemblage of strata of various kinds, together many thousands of feet thick, and abounding in remains of animal life. These strata were deposited at the bottom of the sea, and the remains are exclusively marine. The creatures whose exuviæ have been preserved belong to those classes which are placed by naturalists the lowest with respect to organization, the mollusca, articulata, and radiata. Analogous beings exist at the present day, but not their lineal descendants, unless time can effect transmutation of species, an hypothesis not generally accepted by naturalists. In the same strata with these inhabitants of the early seas are found remains of fucoid or seaweed-like plants, the lowest of the vegetable tribe, which may have been the first of this kind of existences introduced into the world. But, as little has yet been discovered to throw light upon the state of the dry land and its productions at this remote period, nothing can be asserted positively on the subject.[1]

In the upper strata of the Silurian system is found the commencement of the race of fishes, the lowest creatures of the vertebrate type, and in the succeeding beds they become abundant. These monsters clothed in mail who must have been the terror of the seas they inhabited, have left their indestructible coats behind them as evidence of their existence.

Next come the carboniferous strata, containing the remains of a gigantic and luxuriant vegetation, and here reptiles and insects begin to make their appearance. At this point geologists make a kind of artificial break, and for the sake of distinction, denominate the whole of the foregoing period of animated existences the Palæozoic, or that of antique life.

In the next great geological section, the so-called Secondary period, in which are comprised the oolitic and cretaceous systems, the predominant creatures are different from those which figured conspicuously in the preceding. The land was inhabited by gigantic animals, half-toad, half-lizard, who hopped about, leaving often their foot-prints like those of a clumsy human hand, upon the sandy shores of the seas they frequented. The waters now abounded with monsters, half-fish, half-crocodile, the well-known saurians, whose bones have been collected in abundance. Even the air had its tenantry from the same

---

[1] It has been stated that a coal-bed, containing remains of land-plants, underlying strata of the lower Silurian class, has been found in Portugal.

family type, for the pterodactyls were creatures, half-lizard, half-vampyre, provided with membranous appendages which must have enabled them to fly. In an early stage of this period traces of birds appear, and somewhat later those of mammals, but of the lowest class belonging to that division, namely, the marsupial or pouch-bearing animals, in which naturalists see affinities to the oviparous tribes. The vegetation of this period seems to have consisted principally of the lower classes of plants, according to the scale of organization accepted by botanists, but it was luxuriant and gigantic.

Lastly, comes the Tertiary period, in which mammalia of the highest forms enter upon the scene, while the composite growths of the Secondary period in great part disappear, and the types of creatures approach more nearly to those which now exist. During long ages this state of things continued, while the earth was the abode principally of mastodons, elephants, rhinoceroses, and their thick-hided congeners, many of them of colossal proportions, and of species which have now passed away. The remains of these creatures have been found in the frozen rivers of the north, and they appear to have roamed over regions of the globe where their more delicate representatives of the present day would be unable to live. During this era the ox, horse, and deer, and perhaps other animals, destined to be serviceable to man, became inhabitants of the earth. Lastly, the advent of man may be considered as inaugurating a new and distinct epoch, that in which we now are, and during the whole of which the physical conditions of existence cannot have been very materially different from what they are now. Thus, the reduction of the earth into the state in which we now behold it has been the slowly continued work of ages. The races of organic beings which have populated its surface have from time to time passed away, and been supplanted by others, introduced we know not certainly by what means, but evidently according to a fixed method and order, and with a gradually increasing complexity and fineness of organization, until we come to man as the crowning point of all. Geologically speaking, the history of his first appearance is obscure, nor does archæology do much to clear this obscurity. Science has, however, made some efforts towards tracing man to his cradle, and by patient observation and collection of facts much more may perhaps be done in this direction. As for history and tradition, they afford little upon which anything can be built. The human race, like each individual man, has forgotten its own birth, and the void of its early years has been filled up by imagination, and not from genuine recollection. Thus much is clear, that man's existence on earth is brief, compared with the ages during which unreasoning creatures were the sole possessors of the globe.

We pass to the account of the creation contained in the Hebrew record. And it must be observed that in reality two distinct accounts are given us in the book of Genesis, one being comprised in the first chapter and the first three verses of the second, the other commencing at the fourth verse of the second chapter and continuing till the end. This is so philologically certain that it were useless to ignore it. But even those who may be inclined to contest the fact that we have here the productions of two different writers, will admit that the account beginning at the first verse of the first chapter, and ending at the third verse of the second, is a complete whole in itself. And to this narrative, in order not to complicate the subject unnecessarily, we intend to confine ourselves. It will be sufficient for our purpose to enquire, whether this account can be shown to be in accordance with our astronomical and geological knowledge. And for the right understanding of it the whole must be set out, so that the various parts may be taken in connexion with one another.

We are told that 'in the beginning God created the heaven and the earth.' It has been matter of discussion amongst theologians whether the word 'created' (Heb. *bara*) here means simply shaped or formed, or shaped or formed out of nothing. From the use of the verb *bara* in other passages, it appears that it does not necessarily mean to make out of nothing,[1] but it certainly might impliedly mean this in a case so peculiar as the present. The phrase 'the heaven and the earth,' is evidently used to signify the universe of things, inasmuch as the heaven in its proper signification has no existence until the second day. It is asserted then that God shaped the whole material universe, whether out of nothing, or out of pre-existing matter. But which sense the writer really intended is not material for our present purpose to enquire, since neither astronomical nor geological science affects to state anything concerning the first origin of matter.

In the second verse the earliest state of things is described; according to the received translation, 'the earth was without form and void.' The prophet Jeremiah[2] uses the same expression to describe the desolation of the earth's surface occasioned by God's wrath, and perhaps the words 'empty and waste' would convey to us at present something more nearly approaching the

---

[1] This appears at once from verse 21, where it is said that God created (*bara*) the great whales; and from verses 26 and 27, in the first of which we read, 'God said, Let us make (*hasah*) man in our image,' and in the latter, 'So God created (*bara*) man in his image.' In neither of these cases, can it be supposed to be implied that the whales, or man, were made out of nothing. In the second narrative, another word is used for the creation of man, *itzer*—to mould; and his formation out of the dust is circumstantially described.

[2] Chap. iv. 33.

meaning of *tohu va-bohu,* than those which the translators have used.

The earth itself is supposed to be submerged under the waters of the deep, over which the breath of God —the air or wind—flutters while all is involved in darkness. The first special creative command is that which bids the light appear, whereupon daylight breaks over the two primæval elements of earth and water—the one lying still enveloped by the other; and the space of time occupied by the original darkness and the light which succeeded, is described as the first day. Thus light and the measurement of time are represented as existing before the manifestation of the sun, and this idea, although repugnant to our modern knowledge, has not in former times appeared absurd. Thus we find Ambrose (*Hexaemeron* lib. 4, cap. 3) remarking:—'We must recollect that the light of day is one thing, the light of the sun, moon, and stars another,—the sun by his rays appearing to add lustre to the daylight. For before sunrise the day dawns, but is not in full refulgence, for the midday sun adds still further to its splendour.' We quote this passage to show how a mind unsophisticated by astronomical knowledge understood the Mosaic statement; and we may boldly affirm that those for whom it was first penned could have taken it in no other sense than that light existed before and independently of the sun, nor do we misrepresent it when we affirm this to be its natural and primary meaning. How far we are entitled to give to the writer's words an enigmatical and secondary meaning, as contended by those who attempt to conciliate them with our present knowledge, must be considered further on.

The work of the second day of creation is to erect the vault of Heaven (Heb. *rakia;* Gr. στερέωμα; Lat. *firmamentum*) which is represented as supporting an ocean of water above it. The waters are said to be divided, so that some are below, some above the vault.

That the Hebrews understood the sky, firmament, or heaven to be a permanent solid vault, as it appears to the ordinary observer, is evident enough from various expressions made use of concerning it. It is said to have pillars (Job xxvi. 11), foundations (2 Sam. xxii. 8), doors (Ps. lxxviii. 23), and windows (Gen. vii. 11). No quibbling about the derivation of the word *rakia*, which is literally something beaten out,[1] can affect the explicit description of the Mosaic writer, contained in the words 'the waters that are above the firmament,' or avail to show that he was aware that the sky is but transparent space.

On the third day, at the command of God, the waters which have hitherto concealed the earth are gathered together in one place—the sea,—and the dry land emerges. Upon the same day the earth brings forth grass, herb yielding seed and fruit trees, the destined food of the animals and of man (v. 29). Nothing is said of herbs and trees which are not serviceable to this purpose, and perhaps it may be contended, since there is no vegetable production which may not possibly be useful to man, or which is not preyed upon by some animal, that in this description the whole terrestrial flora is implied. We wish, however, to call the attention of the reader to the fact, that trees and plants destined for food are those which are particularly singled out here as the earliest productions of the earth, as we shall have occasion to refer to this again presently.

On the fourth day, the two great lights, the sun and moon, are *made* (Heb. *hasah*) and *set* in the firmament of heaven to give light to the earth, but more particularly to serve as the means of measuring time, and of marking out years, days, and seasons. This is the most prominent office assigned to them (v. 14-18).

---

[1] The root is generally applied to express the hammering or beating out of metal plates; hence something beaten or spread out. It has been pretended that the word *rakia* may be translated *expanse*, so as merely to mean empty space. The context sufficiently rebuts this.

The formation of the stars is mentioned in the most cursory manner. It is not said out of what materials all these bodies were made, and whether the writer regarded them as already existing, and only waiting to have a proper place assigned them, may be open to question. At any rate, their allotted receptacle—the firmament—was not made until the second day, nor were they set in it until the fourth; vegetation, be it observed, having already commenced on the third, and therefore independently of the warming influence of the sun.

On the fifth day 'the waters are called into productive activity, and bring forth fishes and marine animals, as also the birds of the air.[1] It is also said that God created or formed (*bara*) great whales and other creatures of the water and air. On the sixth day the earth brings forth living creatures, cattle, and reptiles, and also 'the beast of the field,' that is, the wild beasts. And here also it is added that God made (*hasah*) these creatures after their several kinds. The formation of man is distinguished by a variation of the creative fiat. ' Let us make man in our image after our likeness.' Accordingly, man is made and formed (*bara*) in the image and likeness of God, a phrase which has been explained away to mean merely ' perfect, sinless,' although the Pentateuch abounds in passages showing that the Hebrews contemplated the Divine being in the visible form of a man.[2] Modern spiritualism has so entirely banished this idea, that probably many may not without an effort be able to accept the plain language of the Hebrew writer in its obvious sense in the 26th verse of the 1st chapter of Genesis, though they will have no difficulty in doing so in the 3rd verse of the 5th chapter, where the same words ' image' and ' likeness' are used. Man is said to have been created male and female, and the narrative contains

---

[1] In the second narrative of creation, in which no distinction of days is made, the birds are said to have been formed out of the ground. Gen. ii.

[2] See particularly the narrative in Genesis xviii.

nothing to show that a single pair only is intended.[1]
He is commanded to increase and multiply, and to
assume dominion over all the other tribes of beings.
The whole of the works of creation being complete,
God gives to man, beast, fowl, and creeping thing,
the vegetable productions of the earth as their appointed food.   And when we compare the verses
Gen. i. 29, 30, with Gen. ix. 3, in which, after the
Flood, animals are given to man for food in addition to
the green herb, it is difficult not to come to the conclusion that in the earliest view taken of creation, men
and animals were supposed to have been, in their original condition, not carnivorous.   It is needless to say
that this has been for the most part the construction
put upon the words of the Mosaic writer, until a clear
perception of the creative design which destined the
tiger and lion for flesh-eaters, and latterly the geological proof of flesh-eating monsters having existed
among the pre-adamite inhabitants of the globe, rendered it necessary to ignore this meaning.

The 1st, 2nd, and 3rd verses of the second chapter
of Genesis, which have been most absurdly divided
from their context, conclude the narrative.[2]   On the
seventh day God rests from His work, and blesses
the day of rest, a fact which is referred to in the
Commandment given from Sinai as the ground of the
observance of Sabbatic rest imposed upon the Hebrews.

Remarkable as this narrative is for simple grandeur,
it has nothing in it which can be properly called
poetical.   It bears on its face no trace of mystical or
symbolical meaning.   Things are called by their right
names with a certain scientific exactness widely differ-

---

[1] It is in the second narrative of creation that the formation of a single
man, out of the dust of the earth, is described, and the omission to create
a female at the same time, is stated to have been repaired by the subsequent formation of one from the side of the man.

[2] The common arrangement of the Bible in chapters is of comparatively modern origin, and is admitted, on all hands, to have no authority
or philological worth whatever.   In many cases, the division is most preposterous, and interferes greatly with an intelligent perusal of the text.

ent from the imaginative cosmogonies of the Greeks, in which the powers and phenomena of nature are invested with personality, and the passions and qualities of men are represented as individual existences.

The circumstances related in the second narrative of creation are indeed such as to give at least some ground for the supposition that a mystical interpretation was intended to be given to it. But this is far from being the case with the first narrative, in which none but a professed mystifier of the school of Philo could see anything but a plain' statement of facts. There can be little reasonable dispute then as to the sense in which the Mosaic narrative was taken by those who first heard it, nor is it indeed disputed that for centuries, putting apart the Philonic mysticism, which after all did not exclude a primary sense, its words have been received in their genuine and natural meaning. That this meaning is *primá facie* one wholly adverse to the present astronomical and geological views of the universe is evident enough. There is not a mere difference through deficiency. It cannot be correctly said that the Mosaic writer simply leaves out details which modern science supplies, and that, therefore, the inconsistency is not a real but only an apparent one. It is manifest that the whole account is given from a different point of view from that which we now unavoidably take; that the order of things as we now know them to be, is to a great extent reversed, although here and there we may pick out some general analogies and points of resemblance. Can we say that the Ptolemaic system of astronomy is not at variance with modern science, because it represents with a certain degree of correctness some of the apparent motions of the heavenly bodies?

The task which sundry modern writers have imposed upon themselves is to prove, that the Mosaic narrative, however apparently at variance with our knowledge, is essentially, and in fact true, although never understood properly until modern science supplied the necessary commentary and explanation.

Two modes of conciliation have been propounded which have enjoyed considerable popularity, and to these two we shall confine our attention.

The first is that originally brought into vogue by Chalmers and adopted by the late Dr. Buckland in his Bridgewater Treatise, and which is probably still received by many as a sufficient solution of all difficulties. Dr. Buckland's treatment of the case may be taken as a fair specimen of the line of argument adopted, and it shall be given in his own words. 'The word *beginning*,' he says, ' as applied by Moses in the first verse of the book of Genesis, expresses an undefined period of time which was antecedent to the last great change that affected the surface of the earth, and to the creation of its present animal and vegetable inhabitants, during which period a long series of operations may have been going on; which as they are wholly unconnected with the history of the human race, are passed over in silence by the sacred historian, whose only concern was barely to state, that the matter of the universe is not eternal and self-existent, but was originally created by the power of the Almighty.'    'The Mosaic narrative commences with a declaration that ' in the beginning God created the heaven and the earth.'    These few first words of Genesis may be fairly appealed to by the geologist as containing a brief statement of the creation of the material elements, at a time distinctly preceding the operations of the first day; it is nowhere affirmed that God created the heaven and the earth in the *first day*, but in the *beginning;* this beginning may have been an epoch at an unmeasured distance, followed by periods of undefined duration during which all the physical operations disclosed by geology were going on.'

'The first verse of Genesis, therefore, seems explicitly to assert the creation of the universe; the heaven, including the sidereal systems; and the earth, more especially specifying our own planet, as the subsequent scene of the operations of the six days about to be described; no information is given as to events which may have occurred upon this earth, unconnected with the history of man, between the creation of its component matter recorded in the first verse, and the era at which its history is resumed in the second verse; nor is any limit fixed to the time during which these intermediate events may have been going on: millions of millions of years may have occupied the indefinite interval, between the beginning in which God created the heaven and the earth, and the evening or commencement of the first day of the Mosaic narrative.'

'The second verse may describe the condition of the earth on the evening of this first day (for in the Jewish mode of computation used by Moses each day is reckoned from the beginning of one evening to the beginning of another evening). This first evening may be considered as the termination of the indefinite time which followed the primeval creation announced in the first verse, and as the commencement of the first of the six succeeding days in which the earth was to be filled up, and peopled in a manner fit for the reception of mankind. We have in this second verse, a distinct mention of earth and waters, as already existing and involved in darkness; their condition also is described as a state of confusion and emptiness (*tohu bohu*), words which are usually interpreted by the vague and indefinite Greek term chaos, and which may be geologically considered as designating the wreck and ruins of a former world. At this intermediate point of time the preceding undefined geological periods had terminated, a new series of events commenced, and the work of the first morning of this new creation was the calling forth of light from a temporary darkness, which had overspread the ruins of the ancient earth.'

With regard to the formation of the sun and moon, Dr. Buckland observes, p. 27, 'We are not told that the substance of the sun and moon was first called into existence on the fourth day; the text may equally imply that these bodies were then prepared and appointed to certain offices, of high importance to mankind, 'to give light upon the earth, and to rule over the day, and over the night, to be for signs, and for seasons, and for days, and for years.' The fact of their creation had been stated before in the first verse.'

The question of the meaning of the word *bara*, create, has been previously touched upon; it has been acknowledged by good critics that it does not of itself necessarily imply 'to make out of nothing,' upon the simple ground that it is found used in cases where such a meaning would be inapplicable. But the difficulty of giving to it the interpretation contended for by Dr. Buckland, and of uniting with this the assumption of a six days' creation, such as that described in Genesis, at a comparatively recent period, lies in this, that the heaven itself is distinctly said to have been formed by the division of the waters on the second day. Consequently during the indefinite ages which elapsed from the primal creation of matter until the first Mosaic day of creation, there was no sky, no local habitation for the sun, moon, and stars, even supposing those bodies to have been included in the original material. Dr. Buckland does not touch this obvious difficulty, without which his argument that the sun and moon might have been contemplated as pre-existing, although they are not stated to have been set in the heaven until the fourth day, is of no value at all.

Dr. Buckland appears to assume that when it is said that the heaven and the earth were created in the beginning, it is to be understood that they were created in their present form and state of completeness, the heaven raised above the earth as we see it, or seem to see it now. This is the fallacy of his argument. The circumstantial description of the framing of the heaven out of the waters, proves that the words 'heaven and earth,' in the first verse, must be taken either proleptically, as a general expression for the universe, the matter of the universe in its crude and unformed shape, or else the word *bara* must mean formed, not created, the writer intending to say 'God formed the heaven and earth in manner following,' in which case heaven is used in its distinct and proper sense. But these two senses cannot be united in the manner covertly assumed in Dr Buckland's argument.

Having, however, thus endeavoured to make out that the Mosaic account does not negative the idea that the sun, moon, and stars had 'been created at the indefinitely distant time designated by the word beginning,' he is reduced to describe the primæval darkness of the first day as 'a temporary darkness, produced by an accumulation of dense vapours upon the face of the deep.' 'An incipient dispersion of these vapours may have readmitted light to the earth, upon the first day, whilst the exciting cause of light was obscured, and the further purification of the atmosphere upon the fourth day, may have caused the sun and moon and stars to re-appear in the firmament of heaven, to assume their new relations to the newly modified earth and to the human race.'

It is needless to discuss the scientific probability of this hypothesis, but the violence done to the grand and simple words of the Hebrew writer must strike every mind. 'And God said, Let there be light—and there was light—and God saw the light that it was good. And God divided the light from the darkness, and God called the light day, and the darkness called he night; and the evening and the morning were the first day.' Can any one sensible of the value of words suppose, that nothing more is here described, or intended to be described, than the partial clearing

away of a fog? Can such a manifestation of light have
been dignified by the appellation of day? Is not this
reducing the noble description which has been the
admiration of ages to a pitiful *caput mortuum* of
empty verbiage?

What were the *new relations* which the heavenly bodies
according to Dr. Buckland's view, assumed to the
newly modified earth and to the human race? They
had, as we well know, marked out seasons, days and
years, and had given light for ages before to the earth,
and to the animals which preceded man as its inhabitants, as is shown, Dr. Buckland admits, by the eyes
of fossil animals, optical instruments of the same construction as those of the animals of our days, and also
by the existence of vegetables in the early world, to the
development of which light must have been as essential
then as now.

The hypothesis adopted by Dr. Buckland was first
promulgated at a time when the gradual and regular
formation of the earth's strata was not seen or admitted so clearly as it is now. Geologists were more
disposed to believe in great catastrophes and sudden
breaks. Buckland's theory supposes that previous to
the appearance of the present races of animals and
vegetables there was a great gap in the globe's history,
—that the earth was completely depopulated, as well
of marine as land animals ; and that the creation of all
existing plants and animals was coæval with that of
man. This theory is by no means supported by
geological phenomena, and is, we suppose, now rejected
by all geologists whose authority is valuable. Thus
writes Hugh Miller in 1857—' I certainly did once
believe with Chalmers and with Buckland that the six
days were simply natural days of twenty-four hours each
—that they had comprised the entire work of the
existing creation—and that the latest of the geologic
ages was separated by a great chaotic gap from our
own. My labours at the time as a practical geologist

had been very much restricted to the palæozoic and secondary rocks, more especially to the old red and carboniferous systems of the one division, and the oolitic system of the other; and the long-extinct organisms which I found in them certainly did not conflict with the view of Chalmers. All I found necessary at the time to the work of reconciliation was some scheme that would permit me to assign to the earth a high antiquity, and to regard it as the scene of many succeeding creations. During the last nine years, however, I have spent a few weeks every autumn in exploring the late formations, and acquainting myself with their particular organisms. I have traced them upwards from the raised beaches and old coast lines of the human period, to the brick clays, Clyde beds, and drift and boulder deposits of the Pleistocene era; and again from them, with the help of museums and collections, up through the mammaliferous crag of England to its red and coral crags; and the conclusion at which I have been compelled to arrive is, that for many long ages ere man was ushered into being, not a few of his humbler contemporaries of the fields and woods enjoyed life in their present haunts, and that for thousands of years anterior to even *their* appearance, many of the existing molluscs lived in our seas. That *day* during which the present creation came into being, and in which God, when he had made 'the beast of the earth after his kind, and the cattle after their kind,' at length terminated the work by moulding a creature in His own image, to whom He gave dominion over them all, was not a brief period of a few hours' duration, but extended over, mayhap, millenniums of centuries. No blank chaotic gap of death and darkness separated the creation to which man belongs from that of the old extinct elephant, hippopotamus, and hyæna; for familiar animals, such as the red deer, the roe, the fox, the wild cat, and the badger, lived throughout the period which connected their time with our own; and so I have been compelled to hold that the days of creation were not natural but prophetic days, and stretched far back into the bygone eternity.'[1]

Hugh Miller will be admitted by many as a competent witness to the untenability of the theory of Chalmers and Buckland on mere geological grounds. He had, indeed, a theory of his own to propose, which we shall presently consider; but we may take his word that it was not without the compulsion of what he considered irresistible evidence that he relinquished a view which would have saved him infinite time and labour, could he have adhered to it.

But whether contemplated from a geological point of view, or whether from a philological one, that is, with reference to the value of words, the use of language, and the ordinary rules which govern writers whose object it is to make themselves understood by those to whom their works are immediately addressed, the interpretation proposed by Buckland to be given to the Mosaic description will not bear a moment's serious discussion. It is plain, from the whole tenor of the narrative, that the writer contemplated no such representation as that suggested, nor could any such idea have entered into the minds of those to whom the account was first given. Dr. Buckland endeavours to make out that we have here simply a case of leaving out facts which did not particularly concern the writer's purpose, so that he gave an account true so far as it went, though imperfect. 'We may fairly ask,' he argues, 'of those persons who consider physical science a fit subject for revelation, what point they can imagine short of a communication of Omniscience at which such a revelation might have stopped without imperfections of omission, less in degree, but

---

[1] *Testimony of the Rocks*, p. 10.

similar in kind, to that which they impute to the existing narrative of Moses? A revelation of so much only of astronomy as was known to Copernicus would have seemed imperfect after the discoveries of Newton; and a revelation of the science of Newton would have appeared defective to La Place : a revelation of all the chemical knowledge of the eighteenth century would have been as deficient in comparison with the information of the present day, as what is now known in this science will probably appear before the termination of another age ; in the whole circle of sciences there is not one to which this argument may not be extended, until we should require from revelation a full development of all the mysterious agencies that uphold the mechanism of the material world.' Buckland's question is quite inapplicable to the real difficulty, which is, not that circumstantial details are omitted—that might reasonably be expected,—but that what is told, is told so as to convey to ordinary apprehensions an impression at variance with facts. We are indeed told that certain writers of antiquity had already anticipated the hypothesis of the geologist, and two of the Christian fathers, Augustine and Episcopius, are referred to as having actually held that a wide interval elapsed between the first act of creation, mentioned in the Mosaic account, and the commencement of the six days' work.[1] If, however, they arrived at such a conclusion, it was simply because, like the modern geologist, they had theories of their own to support, which led them to make somewhat similar hypotheses.

' After all,' says Buckland, ' it should be recollected that the question is not respecting the correctness of the Mosaic narrative, but of our interpretation of it,' a proposition which can hardly be sufficiently re-

---

[1] See Dr. Pusey's note—Buckland's *Bridgewater Treatise*, pp. 24, 25.

probated. Such a doctrine, carried out unreservedly, strikes at the root of critical morality. It may, indeed, be sometimes possible to give two or three different interpretations to one and the same passage, even in a modern and familiar tongue, in which case this may arise from the unskilfulness of the writer or speaker who has failed clearly to express his thought. In a dead or foreign language the difficulty may arise from our own want of familiarity with its forms of speech, or in an ancient book we may be puzzled by allusions and modes of thought the key to which has been lost. But it is no part of the commentator's or interpreter's business to introduce obscurity or find difficulties where none exist, and it cannot be pretended that, taking it as a question of the use of words to express thoughts, there are any peculiar difficulties about understanding the first chapter of Genesis, whether in its original Hebrew or in our common translation, which represents the original with all necessary exactness. The difficulties arise for the first time, when we seek to import a meaning into the language which it certainly never could have conveyed to those to whom it was originally addressed. Unless we go the whole length of supposing the simple account of the Hebrew cosmogonist to be a series of awkward equivocations, in which he attempted to give a representation widely different from the facts, yet, without trespassing against literal truth, we can find no difficulty in interpreting his words. Although language may be, and often has been, used for the purpose, not of expressing, but concealing thought, no such charge can fairly be laid against the Hebrew writer.

'It should be borne in mind,' says Dr. Buckland, 'that the object of the account was, not to state *in what manner*, but *by whom* the world was made.' Every one must see that this is an unfounded assertion, inasmuch as the greater part of the narrative consists in a minute and orderly description of the manner in which things were made. We can know nothing as to the *object* of the account, except from the account itself. What the writer meant to state is just that which he has stated, for all that we can know to the contrary. Or can we seriously believe that if appealed to by one of his Hebrew hearers or readers as to his intention, he would have replied, My only object in what I have written is to inform you that God made the world; as to the manner of His doing it, of which I have given so exact an account, I have no intention that my words should be taken in their literal meaning.

We come then to this, that if we sift the Mosaic narrative of all definite meaning, and only allow it to be the expression of the most vague generalities, if we avow that it admits of no certain interpretation, of none that may not be shifted and altered as often as we see fit, and as the exigencies of geology may require, then may we reconcile it with what science teaches. This mode of dealing with the subject has been broadly advocated by a recent writer of mathematical eminence, who adopts the Bucklandian hypothesis, a passage from whose work we shall quote.[1]

'The Mosaic account of the six days' work is thus harmonized by some. On the first day, while the earth was 'without form and void,' the result of a previous convulsion in nature, 'and darkness was upon the face of the deep,' God commanded light to shine upon the earth. This may have been effected by such a clearing of the thick and loaded atmosphere, as to allow the light of the sun to penetrate its mass with a suffused illumination, sufficient to dispel the total darkness which had prevailed, but proceeding from a source not yet apparent on the earth. On the second day a separation took place in

---

[1] *Scripture and Science not at Variance.* By J. H. Pratt, M.A., Archdeacon of Calcutta, 1859. Third edition, p. 34.

the thick vapoury mass which lay upon the earth,
dense clouds were gathered up aloft and separated by
*an expanse* from the waters and vapours below. On
the third day these lower vapours, or fogs and mists
which hitherto concealed the earth, were condensed
and gathered with the other waters of the earth into
seas, and the dry land appeared. Then grass and
herbs began to grow. On the fourth day the clouds
and vapours so rolled into separate masses, or were so
entirely absorbed into the air itself, that the sun shone
forth in all its brilliancy, the visible source of light
and heat to the renovated earth, while the moon and
stars gave light by night, and God appointed them
henceforth for signs, and for seasons, and for days,
and for years, to his creatures whom he was about to
call into existence, as he afterwards set or appointed
his bow in the clouds, which had appeared ages before,
to be a sign to Noah and his descendants. The fifth
and sixth days' work needs no comment.

  ' According to this explanation, the first chapter of
Genesis does not pretend (as has been generally
assumed) to be a cosmogony, or an account of the
original creation of the material universe. The only
cosmogony which it contains, in that sense at least, is
confined to the sublime declaration of the first verse,
' In the beginning God created the heavens and the
earth.' The inspired record thus stepping over an
interval of indefinite ages with which man has no
direct concern, proceeds at once to narrate the events
preparatory to the introduction of man on the scene ;
employing phraseology strictly faithful to the *appear-*
*ances* which would have met the eye of man, could he
have been a spectator on the earth of what passed
during those six days. All this has been commonly
supposed to be a more detailed account of the general
truth announced in the first verse, in short, a cosmogony : such was the idea of Josephus ; such probably
was the idea of our translators ; for their version,

without form and void, points to the primæval chaos, out of which all things were then supposed to emerge; and these words standing *in limine,* have tended, perhaps more than anything else, to foster the idea of a cosmogony in the minds of general readers to this very day.

'The foregoing explanation many have now adopted. It is sufficient for my purpose, if it be a possible explanation, and if it meet the difficulties of the case. That it is possible in itself, is plain from the fact above established, that the Scriptures wisely speak on natural things according to their *appearances* rather than their *physical realities.* It meets the difficulties of the case, because all the difficulties hitherto started against this chapter on scientific grounds proceeded on the principle that it is a cosmogony; which this explanation repudiates, and thus disposes of the difficulties. It is therefore an explanation satisfactory to my own mind. I may be tempted to regret that I can gain no certain scientific information from Genesis regarding the process of the original creation; but I resist the temptation, remembering the great object for which the Scripture was given—to tell man of his origin and fall, and to draw his mind to his Creator and Redeemer. Scripture was not designed to teach us natural philosophy, and it is vain to attempt to make a cosmogony out of its statements. The Almighty declares himself the originator of all things, but he condescends not to describe the process or the laws by which he worked. All this he leaves for reason to decipher from the phenomena which his world displays.

'This explanation, however, I do not wish to impose on Scripture; and am fully prepared to surrender it, should further scientific discovery suggest another better fitted to meet all the requirements of the case.'

We venture to think that the world at large will continue to consider the account in the first chapter of

Genesis to be a cosmogony. But as it is here admitted that it does not describe physical realities, but only outward appearances, that is, gives a description false in fact, and one which can teach us no scientific truth whatever, it seems to matter little what we call it. If its description of the events of the six days which it comprises be merely one of appearances and not of realities, it can teach us nothing regarding them.

Dissatisfied with the scheme of conciliation which has been discussed, other geologists have proposed to give an entirely mythical or enigmatical sense to the Mosaic narrative, and to consider the creative days described as vast periods of time. This plan was long ago suggested, but it has of late enjoyed a high degree of popularity, through the advocacy of the Scotch geologist Hugh Miller, an extract from whose work has been already quoted. Dr. Buckland gives the following account of the first form in which this theory was propounded, and of the grounds upon which he rejected it in favour of that of Chalmers :[1]—

'A third opinion has been suggested both by learned theologians and by geologists, and on grounds independent of one another—viz., that the days of the Mosaic creation need not be understood to imply the same length of time which is now occupied by a single revolution of the globe, but successive periods each of great extent ; and it has been asserted that the order of succession of the organic remains of a former world accords with the order of creation recorded in Genesis. This assertion, though to a certain degree apparently correct, is not entirely supported by geological facts, since it appears that the most ancient marine animals occur in the same division of the lowest transition strata with the

---

[1] *Bridgewater Treatise*, p. 17.

earliest remains of vegetables, so that the evidence of organic remains, as far as it goes, shows the origin of plants and animals to have been contemporaneous : if any creation of vegetables preceded that of animals, no evidence of such an event has yet been discovered by the researches of geology. Still there is, I believe, no sound critical or theological objection to the interpretation of the word 'day' as meaning a long period.'

Archdeacon Pratt also summarily rejects this view as untenable :[1]—

'There is one other class of interpreters, however, with whom I find it impossible to agree,—I mean those who take the six days to be six periods of unknown indefinite length. This is the principle of interpretation in a work on the *Creation and the Fall*, by the Rev. D. Macdonald ; also in Mr. Hugh Miller's posthumous work, the *Testimony of the Rocks*, and also in an admirable treatise on the *Præ-Adamite Earth* in Dr. Lardner's *Museum of Science*. In this last it is the more surprising because the successive chapters are in fact an accumulation of evidence which points the other way, as a writer in the *Christian Observer*, Jan. 1858, has conclusively shown. The late M. D'Orbigny has demonstrated in his *Prodrome de Palæontologie*, after an elaborate examination of vast multitudes of fossils, that there have been at least twenty-nine distinct periods of animal and vegetable existence—that is, twenty-nine creations separated one from another by catastrophes which have swept away the species existing at the time, with a very few solitary exceptions, never exceeding one and a-half per cent. of the whole number discovered which have either survived the catastrophe, or have been erroneously designated. But not a single species of the

---

[1] *Science and Scripture not at Variance,* p. 40, note.

preceding period survived the last of these catastrophes, and this closed the Tertiary period and ushered in the Human period. The evidence adduced by M. D'Orbigny shows that both plants and animals appeared in every one of those twenty-nine periods. The notion, therefore, that the 'days' of Genesis represent periods of creation from the beginning of things is at once refuted. The parallel is destroyed both in the number of the periods (thirty, including the Azoic, instead of six), and also in the character of the things created. No argument could be more complete; and yet the writer of the *Præ-Adamite Earth,* in the last two pages, sums up his lucid sketch of M. D'Orbigny's researches by referring the account in the first chapter of Genesis to the whole creation from the beginning of all things, a *selection* of epochs being made, as he imagines, for the six days or periods.'

In this trenchant manner do theological geologists overthrow one another's theories. However, Hugh Miller was perfectly aware of the difficulty involved in his view of the question, and we shall endeavour to show the reader the manner in which he deals with it.

He begins by pointing out that the families of vegetables and animals were introduced upon earth as nearly as possible according to the great classes in which naturalists have arranged the modern flora and fauna. According to the arrangement of Lindley, he observes —'Commencing at the bottom of the scale we find the thallogens, or flowerless plants, which lack proper stems and leaves—a class which includes all the algæ. Next succeed the acrogens, or flowerless plants that possess both stems and leaves—such as the ferns and their allies. Next, omitting an inconspicuous class, represented by but a few parasitical plants incapable of preservation as fossils, come the endogens— monocotyledonous flowering plants, that include the palms, the liliaceæ, and several other families, all characterized by the parallel venation of their leaves. Next, omitting another inconspicuous tribe, there follows a very important class, the gymnogens—polycotyledonous trees, represented by the coniferæ and cycadaceæ. And last of all come the dicotyledonous exogens—a class to which all our fruit and what are known as our forest trees belong, with a vastly preponderating majority of the herbs and flowers that impart fertility and beauty to our gardens and meadows.' The order in which fossils of these several classes appear in the strata, Hugh Miller states to be as follows :—In the Lower Silurian we find only thallogens, in the Upper Silurian acrogens are added. The gymnogens appear rather prematurely, it might be thought, in the old red sandstone, the endogens (monocotyledonous) coming after them in the carboniferous group. Dicotyledonous exogens enter at the close of the oolitic period, and come to their greatest development in the tertiary. Again, the animal tribes have been introduced in an order closely agreeing with the geological divisions established by Cuvier. In the Silurian beds the invertebrate creatures, the radiata, articulata, and mollusca, appear simultaneously. At the close of the period, fishes, the lowest of the vertebrata, appear : before the old red sandstone period had passed away, reptiles had come into existence ; birds, and the marsupial mammals, enter in the oolitic period ; placental mammals in the tertiary ; and man last of all.

Now, these facts do certainly tally to some extent with the Mosaic account, which represents fish and fowl as having been produced from the waters on the fifth day, reptiles and mammals from the earth on the sixth, and man as made last of all. The agreement, however, is far from exact, as according to geological evidence, reptiles would appear to have existed ages before birds and mammals, whereas here the creation of birds is attributed to the fifth day, that of reptiles to the sixth. There remains, moreover, the insuperable difficulty of the plants and trees being represented as made on the third day—that is, more than an age before fishes and birds; which is clearly not the case.

Although, therefore, there is a superficial resemblance in the Mosaic account to that of the geologists, it is evident that the bare theory that a 'day' means an age or immense geological period might be made to yield some rather strange results. What becomes of the evening and morning of which each day is said to have consisted? Was each geologic age divided into two long intervals, one all darkness, the other all light? and if so, what became of the plants and trees created in the third day or period, when the evening of the fourth day (the evenings, be it observed, precede the mornings) set in? They must have passed through half a seculum of total darkness, not even cheered by that dim light which the sun, not yet completely manifested, supplied on the morning of the third day. Such an ordeal would have completely destroyed the whole vegetable creation, and yet we find that it survived, and was appointed on the sixth day as the food of man and animals. In fact, we need only substitute the word 'period' for 'day' in the Mosaic narrative to make it very apparent that the writer at least had no such meaning, nor could he have conveyed any such meaning to those who first heard his account read.

'It has been held,' says Hugh Miller, 'by accomplished philologists, that the days of Mosaic creation may be regarded without doing violence to the Hebrew language, as successive periods of great extent.'[1] We do not believe that there is any ground for this doctrine. The word 'day' is certainly used occasionally in particular phrases, in an indefinite manner, not only in Hebrew, but other languages. As for instance, Gen. xxxix. 11—'About this time,' Heb. literally,

---

[1] *Testimony*, p. 133.

'about this day.' But every such phrase explains itself, and not only philology but common sense dis-claims the notion, that when 'day' is spoken of in terms like those in the first chapter of Genesis, and described as consisting of an evening and a morning, it can be understood to mean a seculum.

Archdeacon Pratt, treating on the same subject, says (p. 41, note), ' Were there no other ground of objection to this mode of interpretation, I think the wording of the fourth commandment is clearly opposed to it. Ex. xx. 8. 'Remember the Sabbath day to keep it holy. 9. Six days shalt thou labour and do all thy work. 10. But the seventh day is the Sabbath of the Lord thy God. In it thou, shalt not do any work, thou, nor thy son, nor thy daughter, thy man-servant, nor thy maidservant, nor thy cattle, nor thy stranger that is within thy gates. 11. For in six days the Lord made heaven and earth, the sea and all that in them is, and rested the seventh day; wherefore the Lord blessed the Sabbath day and hal-lowed it.'

' Is it not a harsh and forced interpretation to sup-pose that the six days in v. 9 do not mean the same as the six days in v. 11, but that in this last place they mean six periods? In reading through the eleventh verse, it is extremely difficult to believe that the seventh day is a long period, and the sabbath day an ordinary day, that is, that the same word day should be used in two such totally different senses in the same short sentence and without any explanation.'

Hugh Miller saw the difficulty; but he endeavours to escape the consequences of a rigorous application of the periodic theory by modifying it in a peculiar, and certainly ingenious manner. ' Waiving,' he says, ' the question as a philological one, and simply holding with Cuvier, Parkinson, and Silliman, that each of the *six* days of the Mosaic account in the first chapter

R

were what is assuredly meant by the *day*[1] referred to in the second, not natural days but lengthened periods, I find myself called on, as a geologist, to account for but three out of the six. Of the period during which light was created, of the period during which a firmament was made to separate the waters from the waters, or of the period during which the two great lights of the earth, with the other heavenly bodies, became visible from the earth's surface—we need expect to find no record in the rocks. Let me, however, pause for a moment, to remark the peculiar character of the language in which we are first introduced in the Mosaic narrative, to the heavenly bodies —sun, moon, and stars. The moon, though absolutely one of the smallest lights of our system, is described as secondary and subordinate to only its greatest light, the sun. It is the apparent, then, not the actual, which we find in the passage—what *seemed* to be, not what *was;* and as it was merely what appeared to be greatest that was described as greatest, on what grounds are we to hold that it may not also have been what *appeared* at the time to be made that has been described as made? The sun, moon, and stars, may have been created long before, though it was not until this fourth day of creation that they became visible from the earth's surface.'[2]

The theory founded upon this hint is that the Hebrew writer did not state facts, but merely certain appearances, and those not of things which really hap-

---

[1] The expression, Gen. ii. 4, 'In the day that the Lord God created the earth and heaven,' to which Hugh Miller here refers, may possibly mean ' at the time when,' meaning a week, year, or other limited time. But there is not the smallest reason for understanding it to mean 'a *lengthened* period,' *i.e.*, an immense lapse of time. Such a construction would be inadmissible in the Hebrew, or any other language. It is difficult to acquit Hugh Miller of an equivocation here. In real truth, the second narrative is, as we have before observed, of distinct origin from the first, and we incline to the belief that, in this case also, 'day' is to be taken in its proper signification.

[2] *Testimony,* p. 134.

pened, as assumed in the explanation adopted by Archdeacon Pratt, but of certain occurrences which were presented to him in a vision, and that this vision greatly deceived him as to what he seemed to see; and thus, in effect, the real discrepancy of the narrative with facts is admitted. He had in all, seven visions, to each of which he attributed the duration of a day, although indeed each picture presented to him the earth during seven long and distinctly marked epochs. While on the one hand this supposition admits all desirable latitude for mistakes and misrepresentations, Hugh Miller, on the other hand, endeavours to show that a substantial agreement with the truth exists, and to give sufficient reason for the mistakes. We must let him speak for himself. 'The geologist, in his attempts to collate the Divine with the geologic, record, has, I repeat, only three of the six periods of creation to account for[1]—the period of plants, the period of great sea-monsters and creeping things, and the period of cattle and beasts of the earth. He is called on to question his systems and formations regarding the remains of these three great periods, and of them only. And the question once fairly stated, what, I ask, is the reply? All geologists agree in holding that the vast geological scale naturally divides into three great parts. There are many lesser divisions—divisions into systems, formations, deposits, beds, strata; but the master divisions, in each of which we find a type of life so unlike that of the others, that even the unpractised eye can detect the difference, are simply three: the palæozoic, or oldest fossiliferous division; the secondary,

---

[1] A very inadmissible assertion. Any one, be he geologist, astronomer, theologian, or philologist, who attempts to explain the Hebrew narrative, is bound to take it with all that really belongs to it. And in truth, if the fourth day really represented an epoch of creative activity, geology would be able to give some account of it. There is no reason to suppose that any intermission has taken place.

or middle fossiliferous division; and the tertiary, or latest fossiliferous division. In the first, or palæozoic division, we find corals, crustaceans, molluscs, fishes; and in its later formations, a few reptiles. But none of these classes give its leading character to the palæozoic; they do not constitute its prominent feature, or render it more remarkable as a scene of life than any of the divisions which followed. That which chiefly distinguished the palæozoic from the secondary and tertiary periods was its gorgeous flora. It was emphatically the period of plants—'of herbs yielding seed after their kind.' In no other age did the world ever witness such a flora; the youth of the earth was peculiarly a green and umbrageous youth—a youth of dusk and tangled forests, of huge pines and stately araucarians, of the reed-like calamite, the tall tree-fern, the sculptured sigillaria, and the hirsute lepidodendrons. Wherever dry land, or shallow lakes, or running stream appeared, from where Melville Island now spreads out its icy coast under the star of the pole, to where the arid plains of Australia lie solitary beneath the bright cross of the south, a rank and luxuriant herbage cumbered every foot-breadth of the dank and steaming soil; and even to distant planets our earth must have shone through the enveloping cloud with a green and delicate ray. . . . The geologic evidence is so complete as to be patent to all, that the first great period of organized being was, as described in the Mosaic record, peculiarly a period of herbs and trees 'yielding seed after their kind.'

'The middle great period of the geologist—that of the secondary division—possessed, like the earlier one, its herbs and plants, but they were of a greatly less luxuriant and conspicuous character than their predecessors, and no longer formed the prominent trait or feature of the creation to which they belonged. The period had also its corals, its crustaceans, its molluscs, its fishes, and in some one or two exceptional instances, its dwarf mammals. But the grand existences of the age—the existences in which it excelled every other creation, earlier or later—were its huge creeping things—its enormous monsters of the deep, and, as shown by the impressions of their footprints stamped upon the rocks, its gigantic birds. It was peculiarly the age of egg-bearing animals, winged and wingless. Its wonderful *whales*, not however, as now, of the mammalian, but of the reptilian class, —ichthyosaurs, plesiosaurs, and cetosaurs, must have tempested the deep; its creeping lizards and crocodiles, such as the teliosaurus, megalosaurus, and iguanodon—creatures, some of which more than rivalled the existing elephant in height, and greatly more than rivalled him in bulk—must have crowded the plains, or haunted by myriads the rivers of the period; and we know that the foot-prints of at least one of its many birds are of fully twice the size of those made by the horse or camel. We are thus prepared to demonstrate, that the second period of the geologist was peculiarly and characteristically a period of whale-like reptiles of the sea, of enormous creeping reptiles of the land, and of numerous birds, some of them of gigantic size; and in meet accordance with the fact, we find that the second Mosaic period with which the geologist is called on to deal, was a period in which God created the fowl that flieth above the earth, with moving (or creeping) creatures, both in the waters and on land, and what our translation renders great whales, but that I find rendered in the margin great sea-monsters. The tertiary period had also its prominent class of existences. Its flora seems to have been no more conspicuous than that of the present time; its reptiles occupy a very subordinate place; but its beasts of the field were by far the most wonderfully developed, both in size and numbers, that ever appeared on earth. Its mammoths and its mastodons, its rhinoceri and its hippopotami, its enormous dinotherium, and colossal megatherium, greatly more than equalled in bulk the hugest mammals of the present time, and vastly exceeded them in number. * * * 'Grand, indeed,' says an English naturalist, ' was the fauna of the British Islands in these early days. Tigers as large again as the biggest Asiatic species lurked in the ancient thickets; elephants of nearly twice the bulk of the largest individuals that now exist in Africa or Ceylon roamed in herds ; at least two species of rhinoceros forced their way through the primæval forest ; and the lakes and rivers were tenanted by hippopotami as bulky and with as great tusks as those of Africa.' The massive cave-bear and large cave-hyæna belonged to the same formidable group, with at least two species of great oxen (*Bos longifrons* and *Bos primigenius*), with a horse of smaller size, and an elk (*Megaceros Hibernicus*) that stood ten feet four inches in height. Truly this Tertiary age—this third and last of the great geologic periods—was peculiarly the age of great ' beasts of the earth after their kind, and cattle after their kind.' '

Thus by dropping the invertebrata, and the early fishes and reptiles of the Palæozoic period as inconspicuous and of little account, and bringing prominently forward the carboniferous era which succeeded them as the most characteristic feature of the first great division, by classing the great land reptiles of the secondary period with the moving creatures of the waters, (for in the Mosaic account it does not appear that any inhabitants of the land were created on the fifth day), and evading the fact that terrestrial reptiles seem to have preceded birds in their order of appearance upon earth, the geologic divisions are tolerably well assimilated to the third, fifth, and sixth Mosaic days. These things were represented, we are told, to Moses in visionary pictures, and resulted in the short and summary account which he has given.

There is something in this hypothesis very near to

the obvious truth, while at the same time something
very remote from that truth is meant to be inferred.
If it be said the Mosaic account is simply the speculation of some early Copernicus or Newton who
devised a scheme of the earth's formation, as nearly
as he might in accordance with his own observations
of nature, and with such views of things as it was
possible for an unassisted thinker in those days to
take, we may admire the approximate correctness of
the picture drawn, while we see that the writer, as
might be expected, took everything from a different
point of view from ourselves, and consequently represented much quite differently from the fact. But
nothing of this sort is really intended. We are
asked to believe that a vision of creation was
presented to him by Divine power, for the purpose
of enabling him to inform the world of what he had
seen, which vision inevitably led him to give a description which has misled the world for centuries,
and in which the truth can now only with difficulty
be recognised. The Hebrew writer informs us that
on the third day ' the earth brought forth grass, the
herb yielding seed after his kind, and the tree yielding fruit, whose seed was in itself, after his kind;'
and in the 29th verse, that God on the sixth day said,
' Behold, I have given you every herb bearing seed,
which is upon the face of all the earth, and every tree
in the which is the fruit of a tree yielding seed, to you
it shall be for meat. And to every beast of the earth,
and to every fowl of the air, and to everything that
creepeth upon the earth, wherein there is life, I have
given every green herb for meat.' Can it be disputed
that the writer here conceives that grass, corn, and
fruit, were created on the third day, and with a view
to the future nourishment of man and beast? Yet,
according to the vision hypothesis, he must have been
greatly deceived; for that luxuriant vegetation which
he saw on the third day, consisted not of plants des-

tined for the food of man, but for his fuel. It was the
flora of the carboniferous period which he beheld, concerning which Hugh Miller makes the following remark, p. 24 :—'The existing plants whence we derive
our analogies in dealing with the vegetation of this
early period, contribute but little, if at all, to the support of animal life. The ferns and their allies remain
untouched by the grazing animals. Our native club-
mosses, though once used in medicine, are positively
deleterious; the horsetails, though harmless, so abound
in silex, which wraps them round with a cuticle of
stone, that they are rarely cropped by cattle; while
the thickets of fern which cover our hill-sides, and
seem so temptingly rich and green in their season,
scarce support the existence of a single creature, and
remain untouched in stem and leaf from their first
appearance in spring, until they droop and wither
under the frosts of early winter. Even the insects
that infest the herbaria of the botanist almost never
injure his ferns. Nor are our resin-producing conifers,
though they nourish a few beetles, favourites with the
herbivorous tribes in a much greater degree. Judging
from all we yet know, the earliest terrestrial flora may
have covered the dry land with its mantle of cheer-
ful green, and served its general purposes, chemical
and others, in the well-balanced economy of nature;
but the herb-eating animals would have fared but ill,
even where it throve most luxuriantly; and it seems
to harmonize with the fact of its unedible character
that up to the present time we know not that a
single herbivorous animal lived amongst its shades.'
The Mosaic writer is, however, according to the theory,
misled by the mere appearance of luxurious vegetation, to describe fruit trees and edible seed-bearing
vegetables as products of the third day.

Hugh Miller's treatment of the description of the
first dawn of light is not more satisfactory than that
of Dr. Buckland. He supposes the prophet in his

dream to have heard the command ' Let there be light'
enunciated, whereupon ' straightway a grey diffused
light springs up in the east, and casting its *sickly gleam*
over a cloud-limited expanse of steaming vaporous
sea, journeys through the heavens towards the west.
One heavy, sunless day is made the representative of
myriads ; the faint light waxes fainter,—it sinks beneath the dim, undefined horizon.'

We are then asked to imagine that a second and a
third day, each representing the characteristic features
of a great distinctly-marked epoch, and the latter of
them marked by the appearance of a rich and luxuriant
vegetation, are presented to the seer's eye ; but without
sun, moon, or stars as yet entering into his dream.
These appear first in his fourth vision, and then for the
first time we have ' a brilliant day,' and the seer,
struck with the novelty, describes the heavenly bodies
as being the most conspicuous objects in the picture.
In reality we know that he represents them (v. 16) as
having been *made* and *set* in the heavens on that day,
though Hugh Miller avoids reminding us of this.

In one respect the theory of Hugh Miller agrees with
that advocated by Dr. Buckland and Archdeacon Pratt.
Both these theories divest the Mosaic narrative of real
accordance with fact ; both assume that appearances
only, not facts, are described, and that in riddles, which
would never have been suspected to be such, had we
not arrived at the truth from other sources.   It would
be difficult for controversialists to cede more completely
the point in dispute, or to admit more explicitly
that the Mosaic narrative does not represent correctly
the history of the universe up to the time of man.
At the same time, the upholders of each theory see
insuperable objections in details to that of their allies,
and do not pretend to any firm faith in their own.
How can it be otherwise when the task proposed is to
evade the plain meaning of language, and to introduce
obscurity into one of the simplest stories ever told,

for the sake of making it accord with the complex system of the universe which modern science has unfolded? The spectacle of able and, we doubt not, conscientious writers engaged in attempting the impossible is painful and humiliating. They evidently do not breathe freely over their work, but shuffle and stumble over their difficulties in a piteous manner; nor are they themselves again until they return to the pure and open fields of science.

It is refreshing to return to the often-echoed remark, that it could not have been the object of a Divine revelation to instruct mankind in physical science, man having had faculties bestowed upon him to enable him to acquire this knowledge by himself. This is in fact pretty generally admitted; but in the application of the doctrine, writers play at fast and loose with it according to circumstances. Thus an inspired writer may be permitted to allude to the phenomena of nature according to the vulgar view of such things, without impeachment of his better knowledge; but if he speaks of the same phenomena assertively, we are bound to suppose that things are as he represents them, however much our knowledge of nature may be disposed to recalcitrate. But if we find a difficulty in admitting that such misrepresentations can find a place in revelation, the difficulty lies in our having previously assumed what a Divine revelation ought to be. If God made use of imperfectly informed men to lay the foundations of that higher knowledge for which the human race was destined, is it wonderful that they should have committed themselves to assertions not in accordance with facts, although they may have believed them to be true? On what grounds has the popular notion of Divine revelation been built up? Is it not plain that the plan of Providence for the education of man is a progressive one, and as imperfect men have been used as the agents for teaching mankind, is it not to be expected that their teachings should be partial and, to

some extent, erroneous? Admitted, as it is, that
physical science is not what the Hebrew writers, for
the most part, profess to convey, at any rate, that it
is not on account of the communication of such
knowledge that we attach any value to their writings,
why should we hesitate to recognise their fallibility
on this head?

Admitting, as is historically and in fact the case,
that it was the mission of the Hebrew race to lay the
foundation of religion upon the earth, and that Providence used this people specially for this purpose, is it
not our business and our duty to look and see how
this has really been done? not forming for ourselves
theories of what a revelation ought to be, or how we,
if entrusted with the task, would have made one, but
enquiring how it has pleased God to do it. In all his
theories of the world, man has at first deviated widely
from the truth, and has only gradually come to see
how far otherwise God has ordered things than the
first daring speculator had supposed. It has been
popularly assumed that the Bible, bearing the stamp
of Divine authority, must be complete, perfect, and
unimpeachable in all its parts, and a thousand difficulties and incoherent doctrines have sprung out of
this theory. Men have proceeded in the matter of
theology, as they did with physical science before inductive philosophy sent them to the feet of nature,
and bid them learn in patience and obedience the
lessons which she had to teach. Dogma and groundless
assumption occupy the place of modest enquiry after
truth, while at the same time the upholders of these
theories claim credit for humility and submissiveness.
This is exactly inverting the fact; the humble scholar
of truth is not he who, taking his stand upon the
traditions of rabbins, Christian fathers, or schoolmen, insists upon bending facts to his unyielding
standard, but he who is willing to accept such teaching
as it has pleased Divine Providence to afford, without

mŭrmuring that it has not been furnished more copiously or clearly.

The Hebrew race, their works, and their books, are great facts in the history of man ; the influence of the mind of this people upon the rest of mankind has been immense and peculiar, and there can be no difficulty in recognising therein the hand of a directing Providence. But we may not make ourselves wiser than God, nor attribute to Him methods of procedure which are not His. If, then, it is plain that He has not thought it needful to communicate to the writer of the Cosmogony that knowledge which modern researches have revealed, why do we not acknowledge this, except that it conflicts with a human theory which presumes to point out how God ought to have instructed man ? The treatment to which the Mosaic narrative is subjected by the theological geologists is anything but respectful. The writers of this school, as we have seen, agree in representing it as a series of elaborate equivocations—a story which 'palters with us in a double sense.' But if we regard it as the speculation of some Hebrew Descartes or Newton, promulgated in all good faith as the best and most probable account that could be then given of God's universe, it resumes the dignity and value of which the writers in question have done their utmost to deprive it. It has been sometimes felt as a difficulty to taking this view of the case, that the writer asserts so solemnly and unhesitatingly that for which he must have known that he had no authority. But this arises only from our modern habits of thought, and from the modesty of assertion which the spirit of true science has taught us. Mankind has learnt caution through repeated slips in the process of tracing out the truth. The early speculator was harassed by no such scruples, and asserted as facts what he knew in reality only as probabilities. But we are not on that account to doubt his perfect good faith, nor need we attribute to him wilful misrepresentation, or consciousness of asserting that which he knew not to be true. He had seized one great truth, in which, indeed, he anticipated the highest revelation of modern enquiry—namely, the unity of the design of the world, and its subordination to one sole Maker and Lawgiver. With regard to details, observation failed him. He knew little of the earth's surface, or of its shape and place in the universe ; the infinite varieties of organized existences which people it, the distinct floras and faunas of its different continents, were unknown to him. But he saw that all which lay within his observation had been formed for the benefit and service of man, and the goodness of the Creator to his creatures was the thought predominant in his mind. Man's closer relation to his Maker is indicated by the representation that he was formed last of all creatures, and in the visible likeness of God. For ages, this simple view of creation satisfied the wants of man, and formed a sufficient basis of theological teaching, and if modern research now shows it to be physically untenable, our respect for the narrative which has played so important a part in the culture of our race need be in nowise diminished. No one contends that it can be used as a basis of astronomical or geological teaching, and those who profess to see in it an accordance with facts, only do this *sub modo*, and by processes which despoil it of its consistency and grandeur, both which may be preserved if we recognise in it, not an authentic utterance of Divine knowledge, but a human utterance, which it has pleased Providence to use in a special way for the education of mankind.

# TENDENCIES OF RELIGIOUS THOUGHT
# IN ENGLAND, 1688—1750.

THE thirty years of peace which succeeded the Peace of Utrecht (1714), 'was the most prosperous season that England had ever experienced; and the progression, though slow, being uniform, the reign of George II. might not disadvantageously be compared for the real happiness of the community with that more brilliant, but uncertain and oscillatory condition which has ensued. A labourer's wages have never for many ages commanded so large a portion of subsistence as in this part of the 18th century.' (Hallam, *Const. Hist.* ii. 464.)

This is the aspect which that period of history wears to the political philosopher. The historian of moral and religious progress, on the other hand, is under the necessity of depicting the same period as one of decay of religion, licentiousness of morals, public corruption, profaneness of language—a day of 'rebuke and blasphemy.' Even those who look with suspicion on the contemporary complaints from the Jacobite clergy of 'decay of religion' will not hesitate to say that it was an age destitute of depth or earnestness; an age whose poetry was without romance, whose philosophy was without insight, and whose public men were without character; an age of 'light without love,' whose 'very merits were of the earth, earthy.' In this estimate the followers of Mill and Carlyle will agree with those of Dr. Newman.

The Stoical moralists of the second century who witnessed a similar coincidence of moral degradation and material welfare, had no difficulty in connecting them together as effect with cause. ' Bona rerum secundarum optabilia, adversarum mirabilia.' (Seneca, *ad Lucil.* 66.) But the famous theory which satisfied the political philosophers of antiquity, viz., that the degeneracy of nations is due to the inroads of luxury, is laughed to scorn by modern economists. It is at any rate a theory which can hardly be adopted by those who pour unmeasured contempt on the 18th, by way of contrast with the revival of higher principles by the 19th century. It is especially since the High Church movement commenced that the theology of the 18th century has become a byeword. The genuine Anglican omits that period from the history of the Church altogether. In constructing his *Catenæ Patrum* he closes his list with Waterland or Brett, and leaps at once to 1833, when the *Tracts for the Times* commenced—as Charles II. dated his reign from his father's death. Such a legal fiction may be harmless or useful for purposes of mere form, but the facts of history cannot be disposed of by forgetting them. Both the Church and the world of to-day are what they are as the result of the whole of their antecedents. The history of a party may be written on the theory of periodical occultation; but he who wishes to trace the descent of religious thought, and the practical working of the religious ideas, must follow these through all the phases they have actually assumed. We have not yet learnt, in this country, to write our ecclesiastical history on any better footing than that of praising up the party, in or out of the Church, to which we happen to belong. Still further are we from any attempt to apply the laws of thought, and of the succession of opinion, to the course of English theology. The recognition of the fact, that the view of the eternal verities of religion which prevails in any given age is in part determined by the view taken in the age which preceded it, is incompatible with the hypothesis generally prevalent among us as to the mode in which we form our notions of religious truth. Upon none of the prevailing theories as to this mode is a deductive history of theology possible. (1.) The Catholic theory, which is really that of Roman-Catholics, and professedly that of some Anglo-Catholics, withdraws Christianity altogether from human experience and the operation of the ordinary laws of thought. (2.) The Protestant theory of free inquiry, which supposes that each mind takes a survey of the evidence, and strikes the balance of probability according to the best of its judgment—this theory, defers indeed to the abstract laws of logic, but overlooks the influences of education. If, without hypothesis, we are content to observe facts, we shall find that we cannot decline to study the opinions of any age only because they are not our own opinions. There is a law of continuity in the progress of theology which, whatever we may wish, is never broken off. In tracing the filiation of consecutive systems, we cannot afford to overlook any link in the chain, any age, except one in which religious opinion did not exist. Certainly we, in this our time, if we would understand our own position in the Church, and that of the Church in the age, if we would hold any clue through the maze of religious pretension which surrounds us, cannot neglect those immediate agencies in the production of the present, which had their origin towards the beginning of the 18th century.

Of these agencies there are three, the present influence of which cannot escape the most inattentive. 1. The formation and gradual growth of that compromise between Church and State, which is called Toleration, and which, believed by many to be a principle, is a mere arrangement between two principles. But such as it is, it is part of our heritage from the last age, and is the foundation, if foundation it can be called, upon which we still continue to build, as in the late Act for the admission of the Jews to Parliament.  2. — The great rekindling of the religious consciousness of the people which, without the Established Church, became Methodism, and within its pale has obtained the name of the *Evangelical* movement.  However decayed may be the Evangelical party as a party, it cannot be denied that its influence, both on our religious ideas, and on our church life, has penetrated far beyond those party limits.  3. The growth and gradual diffusion through all religious thinking of the supremacy of reason.  This, which is rather a principle, or a mode of thinking, than a doctrine, may be properly enough called *Rationalism*.  This term is used in this country with so much laxity that it is impossible to define the sense in which it is generally intended. But it is often taken to mean a system opposed to revealed religion imported into this country from Germany at the beginning of the present century.  A person, however, who surveys the course of English theology during the eighteenth century will have no difficulty in recognising that throughout all discussions, underneath all controversies, and common to all parties, lies the assumption of the supremacy of reason in matters of religion.  The Kantian Philosophy did but bring forward into light, and give scientific form and a recognised position to, a principle which had long unconsciously guided all treatment of religious topics both in Germany and in England.  Rationalism was not an anti-Christian sect outside the Church making war against religion.  It was a habit of thought ruling all minds, under the conditions of which all alike tried to make good the peculiar opinions they might happen to cherish.  The Churchman differed from the Socinian, and the Socinian from the Deist, as to the number of articles in his creed; but all alike consented to test their belief by the rational evidence for it.  Whether given doctrines or

s

miracles were conformable to reason or not was disputed between the defence and the assault; but that all doctrines were to stand or fall by that criterion was not questioned. The principles and the priority of natural religion formed the common hypothesis on the ground of which the disputants argued whether anything, and what, had been subsequently communicated to man in a supernatural way. The line between those who believed much and those who believed little cannot be sharply drawn. Some of the so-called Deists were, in fact, Socinians; as Toland, who expressly admits all those parts of the New Testament revelation which are, or seem to him, comprehensible by reason. (*Christianity not Mysterious.*) Nor is there any ground for thinking that Toland was insincere in his profession of rational Christianity, as was insinuated by his opponents—*e.g.* Leland. (*View of the Deistical Writers*, vol. i. p. 49.) A more candid adversary, Leibnitz, who knew Toland personally, is 'glad to believe that the design of this author, a man of no common ability, and as I think, a well-disposed person, was to withdraw men from speculative theology to the practice of its precepts.' (*Annotatiunculæ subitaneæ.*) Hardly one here and there, as Hume, professed Rationalism in the extent of Atheism; the great majority of writers were employed in constructing a *via media* between Atheism and Athanasianism, while the most orthodox were diligently 'hewing and chiselling Christianity into an intelligible human system, which they then represented, as thus mutilated, as affording a remarkable evidence of the truth of the Bible.' (*Tracts for the Times*, vol. ii. No. 73.) The title of Locke's treatise, *The Reasonableness of Christianity*, may be said to have been the solitary thesis of Christian theology in England for great part of a century.

If we are to put chronological limits to this system of religious opinion in England, we might, for the

sake of a convenient landmark, say that it came in
with the Revolution of 1688, and began to decline in
vigour with the reaction against the Reform movement
about 1830. Locke's *Reasonableness of Christianity*
would thus open, and the commencement of the *Tracts
for the Times* mark the fall of Rationalism. Not that
chronology can ever be exactly applied to the mutations
of opinion. For there were Rationalists before Locke,
*e.g.* Hales of Eton, and other Arminians, nor has the
Church of England unanimously adopted the principles
of the *Tracts for the Times*. But if we were to follow
up Cave's nomenclature, the appellation *Seculum ra-
tionalisticum* might be affixed to the eighteenth century
with greater precision than many of his names apply
to the previous centuries. For it was not merely that
Rationalism then obtruded itself as a heresy, or obtained a footing of toleration within the Church, but
the rationalizing method possessed itself absolutely of
the whole field of theology. With some trifling exceptions, the whole of religious literature was drawn
in to the endeavour to ' prove the truth' of Christianity.
The essay and the sermon, the learned treatise and
the philosophical disquisition, Addison the polite
writer, and Bentley the classical philologian (Addison :
*Evidences of the Christian Religion*, a posthumous publication. Bentley : *Eight Sermons at Boyle's Lecture*,
1692), the astronomer Newton (*Four Letters, &c.*,
Lond. 1756), no less than the theologians by profession,
were all engaged upon the same task. To one book
of A. Collins, *A Discourse on the Grounds and Reasons
of the Christian Religion*, Lond. 1724, are counted no
less than thirty-five answers. Dogmatic theology had
ceased to exist ; the exhibition of religious truth for
practical purposes was confined to a few obscure
writers. Every one who had anything to say on
sacred subjects drilled it into an array of argument
against a supposed objector. Christianity appeared
made for nothing else but to be ' proved ;' what use to

make of it when it was proved was not much thought about. Reason was at first offered as the basis of faith, but gradually became its substitute. The mind never advanced as far as the stage of belief, for it was unceasingly engaged in reasoning up to it. The only quality in Scripture which was dwelt upon was its 'credibility.' Even the 'Evangelical' school, which had its origin in a reaction against the dominant Rationalism, and began in endeavours to kindle religious feeling, was obliged to succumb at last. It, too, drew out its rational 'scheme of Christianity,' in which the atonement was made the central point of a system, and the death of Christ was accounted for as necessary to satisfy the Divine Justice.

This whole rationalist age must again be subdivided into two periods, the theology of which, though belonging to the common type, has distinct specific characters. These periods are of nearly equal length, and we may conveniently take the middle year of the century, 1750, as our terminus of division. Though both periods were engaged upon the proof of Christianity, the distinction between them is that the first period was chiefly devoted to the internal, the second to the external, attestations. In the first period the main endeavour was to show that there was nothing in the contents of the revelation which was not agreeable to reason. In the second, from 1750 onwards, the controversy was narrowed to what are usually called the 'Evidences,' or the historical proof of the genuineness and authenticity of the Christian records. From this distinction of topic arises an important difference of value between the theological produce of the two periods. A great injustice is done to the 18th century, when its whole speculative product is set down under the description of that Old Bailey theology in which, to use Johnson's illustration, the Apostles are being tried once a week for the capital crime of forgery. This evidential school—the school of Lardner, Paley, and Whately—belongs strictly to the latter half only of the period now under consideration. This school, which treated the exterior evidence, was the natural sequel and supplement of that which had preceded it, which dealt with the intrinsic credibility of the Christian revelation. This historical succession of the schools is the logical order of the argument. For when we have first shown that the facts of Christianity are not incredible, the whole burden of proof is shifted to the evidence that the facts did really occur. Neither branch of the argument can claim to be religious instruction at all, but the former does incidentally enter upon the substance of the Gospel. It may be philosophy rather than theology, but it raises in its course some of the most momentous problems which can engage the human mind. On the other hand, a mind which occupies itself with the 'external evidences' knows nothing of the spiritual intuition, of which it renounces at once the difficulties and the consolations. The supply of evidences in what for the sake of a name may be called the Georgian period (1750-1830), was not occasioned by any demands of controversy. The attacks through the press were nearly at an end, the Deists had ceased to be. The clergy continued to manufacture evidence as an ingenious exercise, a literature which was avowedly professional, a study which might seem theology without being it, which could awaken none of the scepticism then dormant beneath the surface of society. Evidences are not edged tools; they stir no feeling; they were the proper theology of an age, whose literature consisted in writing Latin hexameters. The orthodox school no longer dared to scrutinize the contents of revelation. The preceding period had eliminated the religious experience, the Georgian had lost besides, the power of using the speculative reason.

The historical investigation, indeed, of the *Origines*

of Christianity is a study scarcely second in importance
to a philosophical arrangement of its doctrines.   But
for a genuine inquiry of this nature the English writers
of the period had neither the taste nor the knowledge.
Gibbon alone approached the true difficulties, but met
only with opponents ' victory over whom was a sufficient humiliation.'   (*Autobiography.*)   No Englishman
will refuse to join with Coleridge in ' the admiration '
he expresses ' for the head and heart' of Paley, 'the
incomparable grace, propriety, and persuasive facility
of his writings.'   (*Aids to Reflection,* p. 401.)   But
Paley had unfortunately dedicated his powers to a
factitious thesis ; his demonstration, however perfect,
is in unreal matter.   The case, as the apologists of
that day stated it, is wholly conventional.   The
breadth of their assumptions is out of all proportion
to the narrow dimensions of the point they succeed in
proving.   Of an honest critical enquiry into the origin
and composition of the canonical writings there is but
one trace, Herbert Marsh's Lectures at Cambridge, and
that was suggested from a foreign source, and died
away without exciting imitators.   That investigation,
introduced by a bishop and a professor of divinity, has
scarcely yet obtained a footing in the English Church.
But it is excluded, not from a conviction of its barren-
ness, but from a fear that it might prove too fertile in
results.   This unwholesome state of theological feeling
among us, is perhaps traceable in part to the falsetto
of the evidential method of the last generation.   We
cannot justify, but we may perhaps make our predecessors bear part of the blame of, that inconsistency, which
while it professes that its religious belief rests on historical evidence, refuses to allow that evidence to be
freely examined in open court.

It seems, indeed, a singular infelicity that the construction of the historical proof should have been the
task which the course of events allotted to the latter
half of the 18th century.   The critical knowledge of

antiquity had disappeared from the Universities. The past, discredited by a false conservatism, was regarded with aversion, and the minds of men directed habitually to the future, some with fear, others with hope. 'The disrespect in which history was held by the French *philosophes* is notorious; one of the soberest of them, D'Alembert, we believe, was the author of the wish that all record of past events could be blotted out.' (Mill, *Dissertations*, vol. i. p. 426.) The same sentiment was prevalent, though not in the same degree, in this country. Hume writing to an Englishman in 1756, speaks of 'your countrymen' as 'given over to barbarous and absurd faction.' Of his own history the publisher, Millar, told him he had only sold forty-five copies in a twelvemonth. (*My Own Life*, p. 5.) Warburton had long before complained of the Chronicles published by Hearne that 'there is not one that is not a disgrace to letters; most of them are so to common sense, and some even to human nature.' (Parr's *Tracts, &c.*, p. 109.) The oblivion into which the remains of Christian antiquity had sunk, till disinterred by the Tractarian movement, is well known. Having neither the critical tools to work with, nor the historical materials to work upon, it is no wonder if they failed in their art. Theology had almost died out when it received a new impulse and a new direction from Coleridge. The evidence-makers ceased from their futile labours all at once, as beneath the spell of some magician. Englishmen heard with as much surprise as if the doctrine was new, that the Christian faith, the Athanasian Creed, of which they had come to wish that the Church was well rid, was 'the perfection of human intelligence;' that 'the compatibility of a document with the conclusions of self-evident reason, and with the laws of conscience, is a condition *a priori* of any evidence adequate to the proof of its having been revealed by God,' and that this 'is a principle clearly laid down by Moses and St. Paul;'

lastly, that 'there are mysteries in Christianity, but that these mysteries are reason, reason in its highest form of self-affirmation.' (*Aids to Reflection*, pref. *Lit. Remains*, iii. 293.) In this position of Coleridge, the rationalist theology of England, which was in the last stage of decay and dotage, seemed to recover a second youth, and to revert at once to the point from which it had started a century before.

Should the religious historian then acknowledge that the impatient contempt with which 'the last century' is now spoken of, is justifiable with respect to the later period, with its artificial monotone of proof that is no proof, he will by no means allow the same of the earlier period 1688—1750. The superiority which the theological writing of this period has over that which succeeded it, is to be referred in part to the superiority of the internal, over the external, proof of Christianity, as an object of thought.

Both methods alike, as methods of argumentative proof, place the mind in an unfavourable attitude for the consideration of religious truth. It is like removing ourselves for the purpose of examining an object to the furthest point from which the object is visible. Neither the external nor the internal evidences are properly theology at all. Theology is—1st, and primarily, the contemplative, speculative habit, by means of which the mind places itself already in another world than this; a habit begun here, to be raised to perfect vision hereafter. 2ndly, and in an inferior degree, it is ethical and regulative of our conduct as men, in those relations which are temporal and transitory. Argumentative proof that such knowledge is possible can never be substituted for the knowledge without detriment to the mental habit. What is true of an individual is true of an age. When an age is found occupied in proving its creed, this is but a token that the age has ceased to have a proper belief in it. Nevertheless, there is a difference in this respect be-

tween the sources from which proof may be fetched.
Where it is busied in establishing the 'genuineness
and authenticity' of the books of Scripture, neglecting
its religious lessons, and drawing out instead 'the undesigned coincidences,' Rationalism is seen in its
dullest and least spiritual form. When, on the other
hand, the contents of the Revelation are being freely
examined, and reason as it is called, but really the
philosophy in vogue, is being applied to determine
whether the voice be the voice of God or not, the reasoner is indeed approaching his subject from a false
point of view, but he is still engaged with the eternal
verities. The reason has prescribed itself an impossible task when it has undertaken to prove, instead of
evolve them; to argue instead of appropriate them.
But anyhow, it is handling them; and by the contact
is raised in some measure to the 'height of that great
argument.'

This acknowledgment seems due to the period now
referred to. It is, perhaps, rather thinking of its
pulpit eloquence than its controversies, that Professor
Fraser does not hesitate to call this 'the golden age
of English theology.' (*Essays in Philosophy*, p. 205.)
Such language, as applied to our great preachers, was
once matter of course, but would now hardly be used
by any Anglican, and has to be sought for in the
mouth of members of another communion. The
names which once commanded universal homage
among us—the Souths, Barrows, Tillotsons, Sherlocks,
—excite, perhaps, only a smile of pity. Literary
taste is proverbially inconstant; but theological is still
more so, for here we have no rule or chart to guide
us but the taste of our age. Bossuet, Bourdaloue,
and Massillon have survived a dozen political revolutions. We have no classical theology, though we
have not had a political revolution since 1660. For
in this subject matter the most of Englishmen have
no other standard of merit than the prejudices of sect.

Eminence only marks out a great man for more cordial hatred; every flippant High Church reviewer has learnt to fling at Locke, the father of English Rationalism, and the greatest name among its worthies. Others are, perhaps, only less disliked because less known; '*qui n'a pas de lecteurs, n'a pas d'adversaires.*' The principal writers in the Deistical Controversy, either side of it, have expiated the attention they once engrossed by as universal an oblivion.

The Deistical Controversy, the all-absorbing topic of religious writers and preachers during the whole of this first period, has pretty well-defined limits. Stillingfleet, who died Bishop of Worcester in the last year (1699) of the seventeenth century, marks the transition from the old to the new argument. In the six folios of Stillingfleet's works may be found the latest echoes of the Romanist Controversy, and the first declaration of war against Locke. The Deistical Controversy attained its greatest intensity in the twenties (1720-1740), after the subsidence of the Bangorian controversy, which for a time had diverted attention to itself, and it gradually died out towards the middle of the century. The decay of interest in the topic is sufficiently marked by the fact that the opinions of Hume failed to stimulate curiosity or antagonism. His *Treatise of Human Nature* (1739) 'fell dead-born from the press,' and the only one of his philosophical writings which was received with favour on its first appearance was one on the new topic— *Political Discourses* (1752). Of this he says 'it was the only work of mine which was successful on the first publication, being well received both abroad and at home.' (*My Own Life.*) Bolingbroke, who died in 1751, was the last of the professed Deists. When his works were brought out by his executor, Mallet, in 1754, the interest in them was already gone; they found the public cold or indisposed. It was a rusty blunderbuss, which he need not have been afraid to have discharged himself, instead of 'leaving half-a-crown to a Scotchman to let it off after his death.' (*Boswell*, p. 88.) To talk Deism had ceased to be fashionable as soon as it ceased to attract attention.

The rationalism, which is the common character of all the writers of this time, is a method rather than a doctrine; an unconscious assumption rather than a principle from which they reason. They would, however, all have consented in statements such as the following: Bp. Gibson, *Second Pastoral Letter*, 1730. 'Those among us who have laboured of late years to set up reason against revelation would make it pass for an established truth, that if you will embrace revelation you must of course quit your reason, which, if it were true, would doubtless be a strong prejudice against revelation. But so far is this from being true, that *it is universally acknowledged that revelation itself is to stand or fall by the test of reason*, or, in other words, according as reason finds the evidences of its coming from God to be or not to be sufficient and conclusive, and the matter of it to contradict or not contradict the natural notions which reason gives us of the being and attributes of God.'

Prideaux (Humphrey, Dean of Norwich), *Letter to the Deists*, 1748. 'Let what is written in all the books of the N. T. be tried by that which is the touchstone of all religions, I mean that religion of nature and reason which God has written in the hearts of every one of us from the first creation; and if it varies from it in any one particular, if it prescribes any one thing which may in the minutest circumstances thereof be contrary to its righteousness, I will then acknowledge this to be an argument against us, strong enough to overthrow the whole cause, and make all things else that can be said for it totally ineffectual for its support.'

Tillotson (Archbishop of Canterbury), *Sermons*, vol. iii. p. 485. 'All our reasonings about revelation are necessarily gathered by our natural notions about religion, and therefore he who sincerely desires to do the will of God is not apt to be imposed on by vain pretences of divine revelation; but if any doctrine be proposed to him which is pretended to come from God, he measures it by those sure and steady notions which he has of the divine nature and perfections; he will consider the nature and tendency of it, or whether it be a doctrine according to godliness, such as is agreeable to the divine nature and perfections, and tends to make us like unto God; if it be not, though an angel should bring it, he would not receive it.'

Rogers (John, D.D.), *Sermons at Boyle's Lecture,* 1727, p. 59. 'Our religion desires no other favour than a sober and dispassionate examination. It submits its grounds and reasons to an unprejudiced trial, and hopes to approve itself to the conviction of any equitable enquirer.'

Butler, (Jos., Bp. of Durham),*Analogy, &c.*,pt. 2, ch. 1. 'Indeed, if in revelation there be found any passages, the seeming meaning of which is contrary to natural religion, we may most certainly conclude such seeming meaning not to be the real one.' *Ibid.*, ch. 8 : 'I have argued upon the principles of the fatalists, which I do not believe ; and have omitted a thing of the utmost importance which I do believe : the moral fitness and unfitness of actions, prior to all will whatever, which I apprehend as certainly to determine the divine conduct, as speculative truth and falsehood necessarily determine the divine judgment.'

To the same effect the leading preacher among the Dissenters, James Foster, *Truth and Excellency of the Christian Revelation,* 1731. 'The faculty of reason which God hath implanted in mankind, however it may have been abused and neglected in times past, will, whenever they begin to exercise it aright, enable them to judge of all these things. As by means of this they were capable of discovering at first the being and perfections of God, and that he governs the world with absolute wisdom, equity, and goodness, and what those duties are which they owe to him and to one another, they must be as capable, if they will divest themselves of prejudice, and reason impartially, of rectifying any mistakes they may have fallen into about these important points. It matters not whether they have hitherto thought right or wrong, nor indeed whether they have thought at all; let them but begin to consider seriously and examine carefully and impartially, and they must be able to find out all those truths which as reasonable creatures they are capable of knowing, and which affect their duty and happiness.'

Finally, Warburton, displaying at once his disdain and his ignorance of catholic theology, affirms on his own authority, *Works* iii. p. 620, that 'the image of God in which man was at first created, lay in the faculty of reason only.'

But it is needless to multiply quotations. The received theology of the day taught on this point the doctrine of Locke, as clearly stated by himself. (*Essay*, B. iv. ch. 19. § 4.) 'Reason is natural revelation, whereby the eternal Father of light and fountain of all knowledge communicates to mankind that portion of truth which he has laid within the reach of their natural faculties; revelation is natural reason enlarged by a new set of discoveries communicated by God immediately, which reason vouches the truth of, by the testimony and proofs it gives, that they come from God. So that he that takes away reason to make way for revelation, puts out the light of both, and does much-what the same as if he would persuade a man to put out his eyes the better to receive the remote light of an invisible star by a telescope.'

According to this assumption, a man's religious belief is a result which issues at the end of an intellectual process. In arranging the steps of this process, they conceived natural religion to form the first stage of the journey. That stage theologians of all shades and parties travelled in company. It was only when they had reached the end of it that the Deists and the Christian apologists parted. The former found that the light of reason which had guided them so far indicated no road beyond.' The Christian writers declared that the same natural powers enabled them to recognise the truth of revealed religion. The sufficiency of natural religion thus became the turning point of the dispute. The natural law of right and duty, argued the Deists, is so absolutely perfect that God could not add anything to it. It is commensurate with all the real relations in which man stands. To suppose that God has created artificial relations, and laid upon man positive precepts, is to take away the very notion of morality. The moral law is nothing but the conditions of our actual being, apparent alike to those of the meanest and of the highest capacity. It is inconsistent with this to suppose that God has gone on to enact arbitrary statutes, and to declare them to man in an obscure and uncertain light. This was the ground taken by the great champion of Deism— Tindal, and expressed in the title of the treatise which he published in 1732, when upwards of seventy, *Christianity as old as the Creation; or, the Gospel a Republication of the Religion of Nature.* This was the point which the Christian defenders laboured most, to construct the bridge which should unite the revealed to the natural. They never demur to making the Natural the basis on which the Christian rests, to considering the natural knowledge of God as the starting point both of the individual mind and of the human race. This assumption is necessary to their scheme, in which revelation is an argument addressed to the reason. Christianity is a *résumé* of the knowledge of God already attained by reason, and a disclosure of further truths. These further truths could not have been thought out by reason; but when divinely communicated, they approve themselves to the same reason which has already put us in possession of so much. The new truths are not of another order of ideas, for 'Christianity is a particular scheme under the general plan of Providence,' (*Analogy*, pt. 2, ch. 4,) and the whole scheme is of a piece and uniform. 'If the dispensation be indeed from God, all the parts of it will be seen to be the correspondent members of one entire whole, which orderly disposition of things essential to a religious system will assure us of the true theory of the Christian faith.' (Warburton, *Divine Legation, &c.*, B. ix. Introd. *Works*, vol. iii. p. 600.) 'How these relations are made known, whether by reason or revelation, makes no alteration in the case, because the duties arise out of the relations themselves, not out of the manner in which we are informed of them. (*Analogy*, pt. 2, ch. 1.) 'Those very articles of belief and duties of obedience, which were formerly natural with respect to their manner of promulgation, are now in the declaration of them also supernatural.' (*Ferguson, Reason in Religion*, 1675, p. 29.) The relations to the Redeemer and the Sanctifier are not artificial, but as real as those to the Maker and Preserver, and the obligations arising out of the one set of relations as natural as those arising out of the other.

The deference paid to natural religion is further seen in the attempts to establish *a priori* the *necessity* of a revelation. To make this out it was requisite to show that the knowledge with which reason could supply us was inadequate to be the guide of life, yet reason must not be too much depressed, inasmuch as it was needed for the proof of Christianity. On the one hand, the moral state of the heathen world prior to the preaching of Christianity, and of Pagan and savage tribes in Africa and America now, the superstitions of the most civilized nations of antiquity, the intellectual follies of the wisest philosophers, are exhibited in great detail. The usual arguments of scepticism on the conscious weakness of reason are brought forward, but not pushed very far. Reason is to be humiliated so far as that supernatural light shall be seen to be necessary, but it must retain its competence to judge of the evidence of this supernatural message. Natural religion is insufficient as a light, and a motive to show us our way and to make us walk in it; it is sufficient as a light, and a motive to lead us to revelation, and to induce us to embrace it. How much of religious truth was contained in natural knowledge, or how much was due to supernatural communication, was very variously estimated. Locke, especially, had warned against our liability to attribute to reason much of moral truth that had in fact been derived from revelation. But the uncertainty of the demarcation between the two is only additional proof of the identity of the scheme which they disclose between them. The whole of God's government and dealings with man form one wide-spread and consistent scheme, of which natural reason apprehends a part, and of which Christianity was the manifestation of a further part. Consistently herewith they treated natural religion, not as an historical dispensation, but as an abstract demonstration. There never was a time when mankind had realized or established an actual system of natural religion, but it lies always potentially in his reason. It held the same place as the social contract in political history. The 'original contract' had never had historical existence, but it was a hypothesis necessary to explain the existing fact of society. No society had, in fact, arisen on that basis, yet it is the theoretical basis on which all society can be shown to rest. So there was no time or country where the religion of nature had been fully known, yet the natural knowledge of God is the only foundation in the human mind on which can be built a rational Christianity.

Though not an original condition of any part of mankind, it is an ever-originating condition of every human mind, as soon as it begins to reason on the facts of religion, rendering all the moral phenomena available for the construction of a scientific theory of religion.

In accordance with this view they interpreted the passages in St. Paul which speak of the religion of the heathen; *e.g.*, Rom. ii. 14. Since the time of Augustine (*De Spir. et Lit.* § 27) the orthodox interpretation had applied this verse, either to the Gentile converts, or to the favoured few among the heathen who had extraordinary divine assistance. The Protestant expositors, to whom the words ' do by nature the things contained in the law,' could never bear their literal force, sedulously preserved the Augustinian explanation. Even the Pelagian Jeremy Taylor is obliged to gloss the phrase ' by nature,' thus : ' By fears and secret opinions which the Spirit of God who is never wanting to men in things necessary was pleased to put into the hearts of men.' (*Duct. Dubit.* B. ii. ch. 1, § 3.) The rationalists, however, find the expression ' by nature' in its literal sense exactly conformable to their own views, (Wilkins, *Of Nat. Rel.* ii. c. 9) and have no difficulty even in supposing the acceptableness of these works, and the salvability of those who do them. Burnet on Art. xviii., in his usual confused style of eclecticism, suggests both opinions without seeming to see that they are incompatible relics of divergent schools of doctrine.

Consequent with such a theory of religion was their notion of its practical bearings. Christianity was a republication of the moral law—a republication rendered necessary by the helpless state of moral debasement into which the world was come by the practice of vice. The experience of ages had proved that, though our duty might be discoverable by the light of nature, yet virtue was not able to maintain itself in

T

the world without additional sanctions. The disinterestedness of virtue was here a point much debated.
The Deists, in general, argued from the notion of
morality, that so far as any private regard to my own
interest, whether present or future, influenced my
conduct, so far my actions had no moral worth. From
this they drew the inference that the rewards and
punishments of Christianity—these additional sanctions—could not be a divine ordinance, inasmuch as
they were subversive of morality. The orthodox
writers had to maintain the theory of rewards and
punishments in such a way as not to be inconsistent
with the theory of the disinterestedness of virtue
which they had made part of their theology. Even
here no precise line can be drawn between the Deistical
and the Christian moralists. For we find Shaftesbury
placing in a very clear light the mode in which religious
sanctions do, in fact, as society is constituted, support
and strengthen virtue in the world, though he does
not deny that the principle of virtue in the individual
may suffer from the selfish passion being appealed to
by the hope of reward or the fear of punishment.
(*Characteristicks*, vol. ii. p. 66.) But with whatever
variation in individual disputants, the tone of the discussions is unmistakeable. When Collins was asked,
'Why he was careful to make his servants go to
Church?' he is said to have answered, 'I do it that
they may neither rob nor murder me.' This is but
an exaggerated form of the practical religion of the
age. Tillotson's Sermon (*Works*, vol. iii. p. 43) '*On
the Advantages of Religion to Societies*,' is like Collins'
reply at fuller length. The Deists and their opponents
alike assume that the purpose of the supernatural
interference of the Deity in revelation must have been
to secure the good behaviour of man in this world;
that the future life and our knowledge of it may be a
means to this great end; that the next world, if it
exist at all, bears that relation to the present. We
are chiefly familiar with these views from their having

been long the butt of the Evangelical pulpit, a chief topic in which was to decry the mere ' legal' preaching of a preceding age. To abstain from vice, to cultivate virtue, to fill our station in life with propriety, to bear the ills of life with resignation, and to use its pleasures moderately—these things are indeed not little; perhaps no one can name in his circle of friends a man whom he thinks equal to these demands. Yet the experience of the last age has shown us unmistakeably that where this is our best ideal of life, whether, with the Deists, we establish the obligation of morality on ' independent' grounds; or, with the orthodox, add the religious sanction—in Mr. Mill's rather startling mode of putting it (*Dissertations*, vol. ii. p. 436), 'Because God is stronger than we, and able to damn us if we don't'—it argues a sleek and sordid epicurism, in which religion and a good conscience have their place among the means by which life is to be made comfortable. To accuse the divines of this age of a leaning to Arminianism is quite beside the mark. They did not intend to be other than orthodox. They did not take the Arminian side rather than the Calvinistic in the old conflict or concordat between Faith and Works, between Justification and Sanctification. They had dropt the terminology, and with it the mode of thinking, which the terms implied. They had adopted the language and ideas of the moralists. They spoke not of sin, but of vice, and of virtue, not of works. In the old Protestant theology actions had only a certain exterior relation to the justified man; 'gute fromme Werke machen nimmermehr einen guten frommen Mann, sondern ein guter frommer Mann macht gute Werke.' (*Luther*.) Now, our conduct was thought of, not as a product or efflux of our character, but as regulated by our understanding; by a perception of relations, or a calculation of consequences. This intellectual perception of regulative truth is religious Faith. Faith is no longer the devout condition of the entire inner man. Its dynamic nature, and interior working, are not denied, but they are unknown ; and religion is made to regulate life from without, through the logical proof of the being and attributes of God, upon which an obligation to obey him can be raised.

The preachers of any period are not to be censured for adapting their style of address and mode of arguing to their hearers. They are as necessarily bound to the preconceived notions, as to the language, of those whom they have to exhort. The pulpit does not mould the forms into which religious thought in any age runs, it simply accommodates itself to those that exist. For this very reason, because they must follow and cannot lead, sermons are the surest index of the prevailing religious feeling of their age. When we are reminded of the powerful influence of the pulpit at the Reformation, in the time of the Long Parliament, or at the Methodist revival, it must also be remembered that these preachers addressed a different class of society from that for which our classical pulpit oratory was written. If it could be said that 'Sherlock, Hare, and Gibson preach in vain,' it was because the populace were gone to hear mad Henley on his tub. To charge Tillotson or Foster with not moving the masses which Whitefield moved, is to charge them with not having preached to another congregation than that to which they had to preach. Nor did they preach to empty pews, though their carefully-written 'discourses' could never produce effects such as are recorded of Burnet's extempore addresses, when he 'was often interrupted by the deep hum of his audience, and when, after preaching out the hour-glass, he held it up in his hand, the congregation clamorously encouraged him to go on till the sand had run off once more.' (*Macaulay,* vol. ii. p. 177.) The dramatic oratory of Whitefield could not have sustained its power over the same auditors ; he had a fresh congregation every Sunday. And in the judgment of one quite disposed to do justice to Whitefield there is nothing in his sermons such as are printed. Johnson (ap. *Boswell*) speaking of the comparisons drawn between the preaching in the Church and that of the Methodists to the disadvantage of the former, says, ' I never treated Whitefield's ministry with contempt; I believe he did good. But when familiarity and noise claim the praise due to knowledge, art, and elegance, we must beat down such pretensions.' It is, however, the substance, and not the manner, of the classical sermons of the eighteenth century which is meant, when they are complained of as cold and barren. From this accusation they cannot be vindicated. But let it be rightly understood that it is a charge not against the preachers but against the religious ideas of the period. In the pulpit, the speaker has no choice but to take his audience as he finds them. He can but draw them on to the conclusions already involved in their premises. He cannot supply them with a new set of principles, and alter their fixed forms of thought. The ideas out of which the Protestant or the Puritan movement proceeded were generated elsewhere than in the pulpit.

The Rationalist preachers of the eighteenth century are usually contrasted with the Evangelical pulpit which displaced them. Mr. Neale has compared them disadvantageously with the mediæval preachers in respect of Scripture knowledge. He selects a sermon of the eighteenth and one of the twelfth century; the one by the well-known Evangelical preacher John Newton, Rector of St. Mary Woolnoth; the other by Guarric, Abbot of Igniac. ' In Newton's sermon we find nine references to the Gospels, two to the Epistles, nine to the Prophets, one to the Psalms, and none to any other part of Scripture. In the sermon of Guarric we find seven references to the Gospels, one to the Epistles, twenty-two to the Psalms, nine to the Prophets, and eighteen to other parts of Scripture.

Thus the total number of quotations made by the Evangelical preacher is twenty-one, by Guarric fifty-seven, and this in sermons of about equal length.' (*Mediæval Preaching*, Introd. xxvi.) Mr. Neale has, perhaps, not been fortunate in his selection of a specimen sermon. For having the curiosity to apply this childish test to a sermon of John Blair, taken at random out of his four volumes, I found the number of texts quoted thirty-seven. But, passing this by, Mr. Neale misses his inference. He means to show how much more Scripture knowledge was possessed by the preachers of the 'dark ages.' This is very likely, if familiarity with the mere words of the Vulgate version be Scripture knowledge. But it is not proved by the abstinence of the eighteenth century preacher from the use of Biblical phraseology. The fact, so far as it is one, only shows that our divines understood Scripture differently, some will say better, than the Middle Age ecclesiastic. The latter had, in the mystical theology of the Christian Church, a rich store of religious sentiment, which it was an exercise of their ingenuity to find in the poetical books of the Hebrew canon. Great part of this fanciful allegorizing is lost, apart from the Vulgate translation. But of this the more learned of them were quite aware, and on their theory of Scripture interpretation, according to which the Church was its guaranteed expositor, the verbal meanings of the Latin version were equally the inspired sense of the sacred record. It was otherwise with the English divine of the eighteenth century. According to the then received view of Scripture, its meaning was not assigned by the Church, but its language was interpreted by criticism—*i.e.*, by reason. The aids of history, the ordinary rules of grammar and logic, were applied to find out what the sacred writers actually said. *That* was the meaning of Scripture, the message supernaturally communicated. Where each text of Scripture has but one sense, that sense in which the writer penned it, it can only be cited in that sense without doing it violence. This was the turn by which Selden so discomfited the Puritan divines, who, like the Catholic mystics, made Scripture words the vehicle of their own feelings. ' Perhaps in your little pocket Bibles with gilt leaves the translation may be thus, but the Greek or Hebrew signifies otherwise.' (Whitelocke, Johnson's *Life of Selden*, p. 303.) If the preacher in the eighteenth century had allowed himself to make these allusions, the taste of his audience would have rejected them. He would have weakened his argument instead of giving it effect.

No quality of these ' Discourses ' strikes us more now than the good sense which pervades them. They are the complete reaction against the Puritan sermon of the 17th century. We have nothing far-fetched, fanciful, allegoric. The practice of our duty is recommended to us on the most undeniable grounds of prudence. Barrow had indulged in ambitious periods, and South had been jocular. Neither of these faults can be alleged against the model sermon of the Hanoverian period. No topic is produced which does not compel our assent as soon as it is understood, and none is there which is not understood as soon as uttered. It is one man of the world speaking to another. Collins said of St. Paul, ' that he had a great respect for him as both a man of sense and a gentleman.' He might have said the same of the best pulpit divines of his own time. They bear the closest resemblance to each other, because they all use the language of fashionable society, and say exactly the proper thing. ' A person,' says Waterland, ' must have some knowledge of men, besides that of books, to succeed well here ; and must have a kind of practical sagacity which nothing but the grace of God joined with recollection and wise observation can bring, to be able to represent truths to the life, or to any considerable degree of advantage.'

This is from his recommendatory preface prefixed to an edition of Blair's Sermons (1739); not the Presbyterian Dr. Hugh Blair, but John Blair, the founder and first President of a Missionary College in Virginia, whose 'Sermons on the Beatitudes' were among the most approved models of the day, and recommended by the bishops to their candidates for orders. Dr. Hugh Blair's Sermons, which Johnson thought 'excellently written, both as to doctrine and language,' (ap. *Boswell,* p. 528), are in a different taste—that of the latter half of the century, when solid and sensible reasoning was superseded by polished periods and flowery rhetoric. 'Polished as marble,' says Hugh J. Rose, 'but also as lifeless and as cold.' The sermons which Waterland recommends to young students of divinity comprise Tillotson, Sharp, Calamy, Sprat, Blackhall, Hoadly, South, Claggett, and Atterbury. Of these, 'Sharp's, Calamy's, and Blackhall's are the best models for an easy, natural, and familiar way of writing. Sprat is fine, florid and elaborate in his style, artful in his method, and not so open as the former, but harder to be imitated. Hoadly is very exact and judicious, and both his sense and style just, close, and clear. The others are very sound, clear writers, only Scot is too swelling and pompous, and South is something too full of wit and satire, and does not always observe a decorum in his style.' He advises the student to begin his divinity course with reading-sermons, because 'they are the easiest, plainest, and most entertaining of any books of divinity ; and might be digested into a better body of divinity than any that is yet extant.' (*Advice to a Young Student,* 1730).

Not only the pulpit, but the whole theological literature of the age, takes the same tone of appeal. Books are no longer addressed by the cloistered academic to a learnedly educated class, they are written by popular divines—'men of leisure,' Butler calls them—for the use of fashionable society. There is an epoch in the history of letters when readers and writers change places; when it ceases to be the reader's business to come to the writer to be instructed, and the writer begins to endeavour to engage the attention of the reader. The same necessity was now laid upon the religious writer. He appeared at the bar of criticism, and must gain the wits, and the town. At the debate between the Deists and the Christian apologists the public was umpire. The time was past when Baxter ' talked about another world like one that had been there, and was come as a sort of express from thence to make a report concerning it.' (Calamy, *Life*, i. 220). As the preacher now no longer spake with the authority of a heavenly mission, but laid the state of the argument before his hearers, so philosophy was no longer a self-centered speculation, an oracle of wisdom. The divine went out into the streets, with his demonstration of the being and attributes of God printed on a broadside; he solicits your assent in ' the new court-jargon.' When Collins visited Lord Barrington at Tofts, 'as they were all men of letters, and had a taste for Scripture criticism, it is said to have been their custom, after dinner, to have a Greek Testament laid on the table.' (*Biog. Brit.* Art. 'Barrington.') These discussions were not necessarily unprofitable. Lord Bolingbroke ' was seldom in the company of the Countess of Huntingdon without discussing some topic beneficial to his eternal interests, and he always paid the utmost respect and deference to her ladyship's opinion.' (*Memoirs of Countess of Hunt.*, i. 180.) Bishop Butler gives his clergy hints how to conduct themselves when ' sceptical and profane men bring up the subject (religion) at meetings of entertainment, and such as are of the freer sort; innocent ones, I mean, otherwise I should not suppose you would be present at them.' (*Durham Charge*, 1751). Tindal's reconversion from Romanism is said to have been brought about by the arguments he heard in the

coffee-houses. This anecdote, given in Curll's catch-
penny 'Life,' rests, not on that bookseller's authority,
which is worthless, but on that of the medical man
who attended him in his last illness. It was the same
with the controversy on the Trinity, of which Waterland says, in 1723, that it was 'spread abroad among
all ranks and degrees of men, and the Athanasian
creed become the subject of common and ordinary conversation.' (*Critical Hist. of the Athan. Creed,* Introd.)
The Universities were invaded by the spirit of the age,
and instead of taking students through a laborious
course of philosophy, natural and moral, turned out
accomplished gentlemen upon 'the classics' and a
scantling of logic. Berkeley's ironical portrait of the
modish philosopher is of date 1732. 'Lysicles smiled,
and said he believed Euphranor had figured to himself
philosophers in square caps and long gowns, but thanks
to these happy times, the reign of pedantry was over.
Our philosophers are of a very different kind from those
awkward students who think to come at knowledge
by poring on dead languages and old authors, or by
sequestering themselves from the cares of the world
to meditate in solitude and retirement. They are the
best bred men of the age, men who know the world,
men of pleasure, men of fashion, and fine gentlemen.
EUPH.: I have some small notion of the people you
mention, but should never have taken them for philosophers. CRI.: Nor would any one else till of late.
The world was long under a mistake about the way to
knowledge, thinking it lay through a tedious course
of academical education and study. But among the
discoveries of the present age, one of the principal is
the finding out that such a method doth rather retard
and obstruct, than promote knowledge. LYS.: I will
undertake, a lad of fourteen, bred in the modern way,
shall make a better figure, and be more considered in
any drawing-room, or assembly of polite people, than
one at four-and-twenty, who hath lain by a long time

at school and college. He shall say better things, in a better manner, and be more liked by good judges. EUPH. : Where doth he pick up this improvement? CRI. : Where our grave ancestors would never have looked for it, in a drawing-room, a coffee-house, a chocolate-late-house, at the tavern, or groom-porter's. In these and the like fashionable places of resort, it is the custom for polite persons to speak freely on all subjects, religious, moral, or political. So that a young gentleman who frequents them is in the way of hearing many instructive lectures, seasoned with wit and raillery, and uttered with spirit. Three or four sentences from a man of quality, spoken with a good air, make more impression, and convey more knowledge, than a dozen dissertations in a dry academical way. . . . You may now commonly see a young lady, or a *petit maître* non-plus a divine or an old-fashioned gentleman, who hath read many a Greek and Latin author, and spent much time in hard methodical study.' (*Alciphron*, Dial. i. § 11.)

Among a host of mischiefs thus arising, one positive good may be signalized. If there must be debate, there ought to be fair play; and of this, publicity is the best guarantee. To make the public arbiter in an abstract question of metaphysics is doubtless absurd, yet it is at least a safeguard against extravagance and metaphysical lunacy. The verdict of public opinion on such topics is worthless, but it checks the inevitable tendency of closet speculation to become visionary. There is but one sort of scepticism that is genuine, and deadly in proportion as it is real; that, namely, which is forced upon the mind by its experience of the hollowness of mankind; for ' men may be read, as well as books, too much.' That other logical scepticism which is hatched by over-thinking can be cured by an easy remedy; ceasing to think.

The objections urged against revelation in the course of the Deistical controversy were no chimæras of a sickly brain, but solid charges; the points brought into public discussion were the points at which the revealed system itself impinges on human reason. No time can lessen whatever force there may be in the objection against a miracle; it is felt as strongly in one century as in another. The debate was not frivolous; the objections were worth answering, because they were not pitched metaphysically high. To a platonizing divine they look trivial; picked up in the street. So Origen naturally thought 'that a faith which could be shaken by such objections as those of Celsus was not worth much.' (*Cont. Cels.*, Pref. § 4.) Just such were the objections of the Deists; such as come spontaneously into the thoughts of practical men, who never think systematically, but who are not to be imposed upon by fancies. Persons sneer at the 'shallow Deism' of the last century; and it is customary to reply that the antagonist orthodoxy was at least as shallow. The truth is, the 'shallowness' imputed belongs to the mental sphere into which the debate was for the time transported. The philosophy of the age was not above its mission. 'Philosophy,' thought Thomas Reid, in 1764, 'has no other root but the principles of common sense; it grows out of them, it draws its nourishment from them; severed from this root, its honours wither, its sap is dried up, it dies and rots.' (*Inquiry, &c.*, Intr. § 4.) We, in the present generation, have seen the great speculative movement in Germany die out from this very cause, because it became divorced from the facts on which it speculated. Shut up in the Universities, it turned inwards on itself, and preyed on its own vitals. It has only been neglected by the world, because it first neglected the great facts in which the world has, and feels, an interest.

If ever there was a time when abstract speculation was brought down from inaccessible heights and compelled to be intelligible, it was the period from the

Revolution to the middle of the last century. Closet speculation had been discredited; the cobwebs of scholasticism were exploded; the age of feverish doubt and egotistical introspection had not arrived. In that age the English higher education acquired its practical aim; an aim in which the development of the understanding, and the acquisition of knowledge are considered secondary objects to the formation of a sound secular judgment, of the ' scholar and the gentleman' of the old race of schoolmasters. Burke contrasting his own times with the preceding age ' considered our forefathers as deeper thinkers than ourselves, because they set a higher value on good sense than on knowledge in various sciences, and their good sense was derived very often from as much study and more knowledge, though of another sort.' (*Recollections by Samuel Rogers*, p. 81.)

When a dispute is joined, *e.g.* on the origin and composition of the Gospels, it is, from the nature of the case, confined to an inner circle of Biblical scholars. The mass of the public must wait outside, and receive the result on their authority. The religious public were very reluctant to resign the verse 1 John v. 7, but they did so at last on the just ground that after a philological controversy conducted with open doors, it had been decided to be spurious. No serious man would consider a popular assembly a proper court to decide on the doctrine of transubstantiation, or on the Hegelian definition of God, though either is easily capable of being held up to the ridicule of the half-educated from the platform or the pulpit. It is otherwise with the greater part of the points raised in the Deistical controversy. It is not the speculative reason of the few, but the natural conscience of the many, that questions the extirpation of the Canaanites, or the eternity of hell-torments. These are points of divinity that are at once fundamental and popular. Butler, though not approving ' of entering into an argumentative defence of religion in common conversation,' recommends his clergy to do so from the pulpit on the ground that, 'such as are capable of seeing the force of objections, are capable also of seeing the force of the answers which are given to them.' (*Durham Charge.*) If the philosophic intellect be dissatisfied with the answers which the divines of that day gave to the difficulties started, let it show how, on the rationalist hypothesis, these difficulties are removeable for the mass of those who feel them. The transcendental reason provides an answer which possibly satisfies itself; but to the common reason the answer is more perplexing than the difficulty it would clear.

M. Villemain has remarked in Pascal, 'that foresight which revealed to him so many objections unknown to his generation, and which inspired him with the idea of fortifying and intrenching positions which were not threatened.' The objections which Pascal is engaged with are not only not those of his age, they are not such as could ever become general in any age. They are those of the higher reason, and the replies are from the same inspiration. Pascal's view of human depravity seems to the ordinary man but the despair and delirium of the self-tormenting ascetic. The cynical view of our fallen nature, however, is at least a possible view. It is well that it should be explored, and it will always have its prophets, Calvin or Rochefoucault. But to ordinary men an argument in favour of revelation, founded on such an assumption, will seem to be in contradiction to his daily experience. Pascal's *Pensées* stand alone; a work of individual genius, not belonging to any age. The celebrity which the *Analogy* of Bishop Butler has gained is due to the opposite reason. It is no paradox to say that the merit of the *Analogy* lies in its want of originality. It came (1736) towards the end of the Deistical period. It is the result of twenty years' study—the very twenty years during which the Deistical notions formed the atmosphere which educated people breathed. The objections it meets are not new and unseasoned objections, but such as had worn well, and had borne the rub of controversy, because they were genuine. And it will be equally hard to find in the *Analogy* any topic in reply, which had not been suggested in the pamphlets and sermons of the preceding half century. Like Aristotle's physical and political treatises, it is a *résumé* of the discussions of more than one generation. Its admirable arrangement only is all its own. Its closely packed and carefully fitted order speaks of many years' contrivance. Its substance are the thoughts of a whole age, not barely compiled, but each reconsidered and digested. Every brick in the building has been rung before it has been relaid, and replaced in its true relation to the complex and various whole. In more than one passage we see that the construction of this fabric of evidence, which 'consists in a long series of things, one preparatory to and confirming another from the beginning of the world to the present time,' (*Durham Charge*) was what occupied Butler's attention. 'Compass of thought, even amongst persons of the lowest rank,' (*Pref. to Sermons*), is that form of the reflective faculty to which he is fond of looking both for good and evil. He never will forget that 'justice must be done to every part of a subject when we are considering it.' (*Sermon* iv.) Harmony, and law, and order, he will suppose even where he does not find. The tendency of his reason was that which Bacon indicates; 'the spirit of a man being of an equal and uniform substance doth usually suppose and feign in nature a greater equality and uniformity than is in truth.' (*Advancement of Learning.*) This is, probably, the true explanation of the 'obscurity' which persons sometimes complain of in Butler's style. The reason or matter he is producing is palpable and plain enough. But he is so solicitous to find its due place in the then stage of the argument, so scrupulous to give it its exact weight and no more, so careful in arranging its situation relatively to the other members of the proof, that a reader who does not bear in mind that 'the effect of the whole' is what the architect is preparing, is apt to become embarrassed, and to think that obscurity which is really logical precision.   The generality of men are better qualified for understanding particulars one by one, than for taking a comprehensive view of the whole.   The philosophical breadth which we miss in Butler's mode of conceiving is compensated for by this judicial breadth in his mode of arguing, which gives its place to each consideration, but regards rather the cumulative force of the whole. Many writers before Butler had insisted on this character of the Christian evidences.   Dr. Jenkin, Margaret Professor at Cambridge, whose *Reasonableness and Certainty of the Christian Religion* was the 'Paley' of divinity students then, says, 'there is an excellency in every part of our religion separately considered, but the strength and vigour of each part is in the relation it has to the rest, and the several parts must be taken altogether, if we would have a true knowledge, and make a just estimate of the whole. (*Reasonableness, &c.* Pt. ii. Pref. 1721.)   But Butler does not merely take the hint from others.   It is so entirely the guiding rule of his hand and pen that it would appear to have been forced upon him by some peculiar experience of his own.   It was in society, and not in his study, that he had learned the weight of the Deistical arguments. At the Queen's philosophical parties, where these topics were canvassed with earnestness and freedom, he must have often felt the impotence of reply in detail, and seen, as he says, 'how impossible it must be, in a cursory conversation, to unite all this into one argument, and represent it as it ought.' (*Durham Charge.*) Hence his own labour to work up his materials into a connected framework, a methodized encyclopædia of all the extant topics.

Not that he did not pay attention to the parts. Butler's eminence over his contemporary apologists is seen in nothing more than in that superior sagacity which rejects the use of any plea that is not entitled to consideration singly. In the other evidential books of the time we find a miscellaneous crowd of suggestions of very various value; never fanciful, but often trivial; undeniable, but weak as proof of the point they are brought to prove. Butler seems as if he had sifted these books, and retained all that was solid in them. If he built with brick, and not with marble, it was because he was not thinking of reputation, but of utility, and an immediate purpose. Mackintosh wished Butler had had the elegance and ornament of Berkeley. They would have been sadly out of place. There was not a spark of the littleness of literary ambition about him. 'There was a certain naturalness in Butler's mind, which took him straight to the questions on which men differed around him. Generally it is safer to prove what no one denies, and easier to explain difficulties which no one has ever felt. A quiet reputation is best obtained in the literary quæstiunculæ of important subjects. But a simple and straightforward man studies great topics because he feels a want of the knowledge which they contain. He goes straight to the real doubts and fundamental discrepancies, to those on which it is easy to excite odium, and difficult to give satisfaction; he leaves to others the amusing skirmishing and superficial literature accessory to such studies. Thus there is nothing light in Butler, all is grave, serious, and essential; nothing else would be characteristic of him.' (Bagehot, *Estimates, &c.*, p. 189.) Though he has rifled their books he makes no display of reading. In the *Analogy* he never names the author he is answering. In the *Sermons* he quotes, directly, only Hobbes, Shaftesbury, Wollaston, Rochefoucauld, and Fenelon. From his writings we should infer that his reading was not pro-

U

miscuous, even had he not himself given us to understand how much opportunity he had of seeing the
idleness and waste of time occasioned by light reading.
(*Sermons,* Pref.)

This popular appeal to the common reason of men,
which is one characteristic of the rationalist period,
was a first effort of English theology to find a new
basis for doctrine which should replace those foundations which had failed it. The Reformation had
destroyed the authority of the Church upon which
Revelation had so long rested. The attempt of the
Laudian divines to substitute the voice of the national
Church for that of the Church universal had met with
only very partial and temporary success. When the
Revolution of 1688 introduced the freedom of the press
and a general toleration, even that artificial authority
which, by ignoring non-conformity, had produced an
appearance of unity, and erected a conventional
standard of truth and falsehood, fell to the ground.
The old and venerated authority had been broken by
the Reformation. The new authority of the Anglican
establishment had existed in theory only, and never in
fact, and the Revolution had crushed the theory, which
was now confined to a small band of non-jurors. In
reaction against Anglican ' authority,' the Puritan
movement had tended to rest faith and doctrine upon
the inward light within each man's breast. This
tendency of the *new* Puritanism, which we may call
Independency, was a development of the *old*, purely
scriptural, Puritanism of Presbyterianism. But it
was its natural and necessary development. It was a
consequence of the controversy with the establishment.
For both the Church and Dissent agreed in acknowledging Scripture as their foundation, and the controversy turned on the interpreter of Scripture.
Nor was the doctrine of the inner light, which
individualized the basis of faith, confined to the Nonconformists. It was shared by a section of the Church,

of whom Cudworth is the type, to whom 'Scripture faith is not a mere believing of historical things, and upon artificial arguments or testimonies only, but a certain higher and diviner power in the soul that peculiarly correspondeth with the Deity.' (*Intellectual System,* Pref.) The inner light, or witness of the Spirit in the soul of the individual believer had, in its turn, fallen into discredit through the extravagances to which it had given birth. It was disowned alike by Churchmen and Nonconformists, who agree in speaking with contemptuous pity of the 'sectaries of the last age.' The re-action against individual religion led to this first attempt to base revealed truth on reason. And for the purpose for which reason was now wanted, the higher, or philosophic, reason was far less fitted than that universal understanding in which all men can claim a share. The 'inner light,' which had made each man the dictator of his own creed, had exploded in ecclesiastical anarchy. The appeal from the frantic discord of the enthusiasts to reason must needs be, not to an arbitrary or particular reason in each man, but to a *common* sense, a natural discernment, a reason of universal obligation. As it was to be universally binding, it must be generally recognisable. It must be something not confined to the select few, a gift of the self-styled elect, but a faculty belonging to all men of sound mind and average capacity. Truth must be accessible to 'the bulk of mankind.' It was a time when the only refuge from a hopeless maze, or wild chaos, seemed to be the rational consent of the sensible and unprejudiced. 'Have the bulk of mankind,' writes Locke, 'no other guide but accident and blind chance to conduct them to their happiness or misery? Are the current opinions and licensed guides of every country sufficient evidence and security to every man to venture his great concernments on? Or, can those be the certain and infallible oracles and standards of truth which teach one thing in Christendom, and

another in Turkey? Or shall a poor countryman be
eternally happy for having the chance to be born in
Italy? Or a day labourer be unavoidably lost because
he had the ill-luck to be born in England? How
ready some men may be to say some of these things, I
will not here examine ; but this I am sure, that men
must allow one or other of these to be true, or else
grant that God has furnished men with faculties
sufficient to direct them in the way they should take,
if they will but seriously employ them that way,
when their ordinary vocations allow them the leisure.'
(*Essay,* Book iv. ch. 19, § 3.)

Such an attempt to secure a foundation in a new
consensus will obviously forfeit depth to gain in com-
prehensiveness. This phase of rationalism—' Ration-
alismus vulgaris '—resigns the transcendental, that it
may gain adherents. It wants, not the elect, but all
men. It cannot afford to embarrass itself with the
attempt to prove what all may not be required to
receive. Accordingly there can be no mysteries in Christianity. The word μυστήριον, as Archbishop Whately
points out (*Essays,* 2nd ser., 5th ed., p. 288), always
means in the New Testament not that which is in-
comprehensible, but that which was once a secret,
though now it is revealed it is no longer so. Whately,
who elsewhere (Paley's *Evidences,* new ed.) speaks so
contemptuously of the ' cast-off clothes' of the Deists,
is here but adopting the argument of Toland in his
*Christianity not Mysterious.* (Cf. Balguy, *Discourses,*
p. 237.) There needs no special ' preparation of heart'
to receive the Gospel, the evidences of religion are
sufficient to convince every unprejudiced inquirer.
Unbelievers are blameworthy as deaf to an argument
which is so plain that they cannot but understand it,
and so convincing that they cannot but be aware of
its force. Under such self-imposed conditions religious
proof seems to divest itself of all that is divine, and
out of an excess of accommodation to the recipient

faculty to cease to be a transforming thought. Rationalism can object to the old sacramental system that it
degrades a spiritual influence into a physical effect.
But rationalism itself, in order to make the proof of
revelation universal, is obliged to resolve religion into
the moral government of God by rewards and punishments, and especially the latter. It is this anthropo-
morphic conception of God as the 'Governor of the
universe,' which is presented to us in the theology of
the Hanoverian divines, a theology which excludes on
principle not only all that is poetical in life, but all
that is sublime in religious speculation. 'To degrade
religion to the position of a mere purveyor of motive
to morality is not more dishonourable to the ethics
which must ask, than to the religion which will render
such assistance.' (A. J. Vaughan, *Essays*, vol. 1. p.
61.) It is this character that makes the reading even
of the *Analogy* so depressing to the soul, as Tholuck
(*Vermischte Schriften*, i. 193) says of it 'we weary of
a long journey on foot, especially through deep sand.'
Human nature is not only humbled but crushed. It
is a common charge against the 18th century divines
that they exalt man too much, by insisting on the
dignity of human nature, and its native capacities for
virtue. This was the charge urged against the orthodox by the evangelical pulpit. But only very superficial and incompetent critics of doctrine can suppose
that man is exalted by being thrown upon his moral
faculties. The history of doctrine teaches a very
different lesson. Those periods when morals have
been represented as the proper study of man, and his
only business, have been periods of spiritual abasement
and poverty. The denial of scientific theology, the
keeping in the back-ground the transcendental objects
of faith, and the restriction of our faculties to the
regulation of our conduct, seem indeed to be placing
man in the foreground of the picture, to make human
nature the centre round which all things revolve. But

they do so not by exalting the visible, but by materializing the invisible. 'If there be a sphere of knowledge level to our capacities and of the utmost importance to us, we ought surely to apply ourselves with all diligence to this our proper business, and esteem everything else nothing, nothing as to us, in comparison of it. . . . Our province is virtue and religion, life and manners; the science of improving the temper and making the heart better. This is the field assigned to us to cultivate; how much it has lain neglected is indeed astonishing. . . . He who should find out one rule to assist us in this work would deserve infinitely better of mankind than all the improvers of other knowledge put together.' (*Sermon* xv.) This is the theology of Butler and his contemporaries; a utilitarian theology, like the Baconian philosophy, contemning all employment of mental power that does not bring in fruit. 'Intellectui non plumæ, sed plumbum addendum et pondera,' (Bacon, *Nov. Or.*, i. 104,) might be its device.

In the *Analogy* it is the same. His term of comparison, the 'constitution and course of *nature*,' is not what we should understand by that term; not what science can disclose to us of the laws of the *cosmos*, but a narrow observation of what men do in ordinary life. We see what he means by the 'constitution of things,' by his saying (*Sermon* xv.) that 'the writings of Solomon are very much taken up with reflections upon human nature and human life; to which he hath added, in Ecclesiastes, reflections upon the constitution of things.' In Part i. ch. 3, of the *Analogy*, he compares the *moral* government of God with the *natural*—the distinction is perhaps from Balguy (*Divine Rectitude*, p. 39), that is to say, one part of natural religion with another; for the distinction vanishes, except upon a very conventional sense of the term 'moral.' Altogether we miss in these divines not only distinct philosophical conceptions, but a scientific use of terms. Dr. Whewell considers that Butler shunned 'the appearance of technical terms for the elements of our moral constitution on which he speculated,' and thinks that he 'was driven to indirect modes of expression.' (*Moral Philosophy in England*, p. 109.) The truth is that Butler uses the language of his day upon the topics on which he writes. The technical terms, and strict logical forms, which had been adhered to by the writers, small as well as great, of the 17th century, had been disused as pedantic; banished first from literature, and then from education. They did not appear in style, because they did not form part of the mental habit of the writers. Butler does not, as Dr. Whewell supposes, think in one form, and write in another, out of condescension to his readers. He thinks in the same language in which he and those around him speak. Mr. Hort's remark that 'Butler's writings are stoic to the core in the true and ancient sense of the word' (*Cambridge Essays*, 1856, p. 337) must be extended to their style. The English style of philosophical writing in the Hanoverian period is to the English of the 17th century, as the Greek of Epictetus, Antoninus, or Plutarch, is to that of Aristotle. And for the same reason. The English stoics and their Greek predecessors were practical men who moralized in a practical way on the facts of common life, and in the language of common life. Neither the rhetorical Schools of the Empire, nor the Universities of England, any longer taught the correct use of metaphysical language. To imitate classical Latin was become the chief aim of the University man in his public exercises, and precision of language became under that discipline very speedily a lost art.

Upon the whole, the writings of that period are serviceable to us chiefly as showing what can and what cannot be effected by common-sense thinking in theology. It is of little consequence to inquire whether or not the objections of the Deists and the

Socinians were removed by the answers brought to meet them. Perhaps, on the whole, we might be borne out in saying that the defence is at least as good as the attack; and so, that even on the ground of common reason, the Christian evidences may be arranged in such a way as to balance the common-sense improbability of the supernatural—that 'there are three chances to one for revelation, and only two against it.' (*Tracts for the Times*, No. 85.) Had not circumstances given a new direction to religious interests, the Deistical controversy might have gone on indefinitely, and the 'amœbæan strain of objection and reply, et cantare pares et respondere parati'—have been prolonged to this day without any other result. But that result forces on the mind the suggestion that either religious faith has no existence, or that it must be to be reached by some other road than that of the 'trial of the witnesses.' It is a reductio ad absurdum of common-sense philosophy, of home-baked theology, when we find that the result of the whole is that 'it is safer to believe in a God, lest, if there should happen to be one, he might send us to hell for denying his existence.' (Maurice, *Essays*, p. 236.) If a religion be wanted which shall debase instead of elevating, this should be its creed. If the religious history of the eighteenth century proves anything it is this:—That good sense, the best good sense, when it sets to work with the materials of human nature and Scripture to construct a religion, will find its way to an ethical code, irreproachable in its contents, and based on a just estimate and wise observation of the facts of life, ratified by Divine sanctions in the shape of hope and fear, of future rewards and penalties of obedience and disobedience. This the eighteenth century did and did well. It has enforced the truths of natural morality with a solidity of argument and variety of proof which they have not received since the Stoical epoch, if then. But there its ability ended

When it came to the supernatural part of Christianity its embarrassment began. It was forced to keep it as much in the background as possible, or to bolster it up by lame and inadequate reasonings. The philosophy of common-sense had done its own work; it attempted more only to show, by its failure, that some higher organon was needed for the establishment of supernatural truth. The career of the evidential school, its success and failure,—its success in vindicating the ethical part of Christianity and the regulative aspect of revealed truth, its failure in establishing the supernatural and speculative part, have enriched the history of doctrine with a complete refutation of that method as an instrument of theological investigation.

This judgment, however, must not be left unbalanced by a consideration on the other side. It will hardly be supposed that the drift of what has been said is that common-sense is out of place in religion, or in any other matter. The defect of the eighteenth century theology was not in having too much good sense, but in having nothing besides. In the present day when a godless orthodoxy threatens, as in the fifteenth century, to extinguish religious thought altogether, and nothing is allowed in the Church of England but the formulæ of past thinkings, which have long lost all sense of any kind; it may seem out of season to be bringing forward a misapplication of common-sense in a bygone age. There are times and circumstances when religious ideas will be greatly benefited by being submitted to the rough and ready tests by which busy men try what comes in their way; by being made to stand their trial, and be freely canvassed, coram populo. As poetry is not for the critics, so religion is not for the theologians. When it is stiffened into phrases, and these phrases are declared to be objects of reverence but not of intelligence, it is on the way to become a useless encumbrance, the rubbish of the past, blocking

the road. Theology then retires into the position it
occupies in the Church of Rome at present, an unmean-
ing frostwork of dogma, out of all relation to the actual
history of man. In that system, theological virtue
is an artificial life quite distinct from the moral virtues
of real life. ' Parmi nous,' says Remusat, ' un homme
religieux est trop souvent un homme qui se croit
entouré d'ennemis, qui voit avec défiance ou scandale
les événements et les institutions du siècle, qui se désole
d'être né dans les jours maudits, et qui a besoin d'un
grand fond de bonté innée pour empêcher ses pieuses
aversions de devenir de mortelles haines.' This
system is equally fatal to popular morality and to
religious theory. It locks up virtue in the cloister,
and theology in the library. It originates caste
sanctity, and a traditional philosophy. The ideal of
holiness striven after may once have been lofty, the
philosophy now petrified into tradition may once have
been a vital faith, but now that they are withdrawn
from public life, they have ceased to be social influences.
On the other hand, the eighteenth century exhibits
human attainment levelled to the lowest secular model
of prudence and honesty, but still, such as it was,
proposed to all men as their rule of life. Practical
life as it was, was the theme of the pulpit, the press,
and the drawing-room. Its theory of life was not
lofty, but it was true as far as it went. It did not
substitute a factitious phraseology, the pass-words of
the modern pulpit, for the simple facts of life, but
called things by their right names. ' Nullum numen
habes si sit prudentia' was its motto, not denying the
' numen,' but bringing him very close to the individual person, as his ' moral governor.' The prevailing
philosophy was not a profound metaphysic, but it was
a soundly based arrangement of the facts of society ;
it was not a scheme of the sciences, but a manual for
every-day use. Nothing of the wild spirit of universal
negation which was spread over the Continent fifty

years later belonged to the solid rationalism of this
period. The human understanding wished to be
satisfied, and did not care to believe that of which it
could not see the substantial ground. The reason
was coming slowly to see that it had duties which it
could not devolve upon others ; that a man must think
for himself, protect his own rights, and administer his
own affairs. The reason was never less extravagant
than in this its first essay of its strength. Its demands
were modest, it was easily satisfied ; far too easily, we
must think, when we look at some of the reasonings
which passed as valid.

The habits of controversy in which they lived
deceived the belligerents themselves. The controversial form of their theology, which has been fatal to
its credit since, was no less detrimental to its sound-
ness at the time. They could not discern the line
between what they did, and what they could not,
prove. The polemical temper deforms the books they
have written. Literature was indeed partially refined
from the coarser scurrilities with which the Caroline
divines, a century before, had assailed their Romanist
opponents. But there is still an air of vulgarity about
the polite writing of the age, which the divines adopt
along with its style. The cassocked divine assumes
the airs of the 'roaring blade,' and ruffles it on the
mall with a horsewhip under his arm. Warburton's
stock argument is a threat to cudgel anyone who disputes his opinion. All that can be said is that this
was a habit of treating your opponent which pervaded
society. At a much later period Porson complains,
'In these ticklish times . . . talk of religion it
is odds but you have infidel, blasphemer, atheist, or
schismatic, thundered in your ears; touch upon
politics, you will be in luck if you are only charged
with a tendency to treason. Nor is the innocence of
your intention any safeguard. It is not the publication

that shows the character of the author, but the character of the author that shows the tendency of the publication.' (Luard's 'Porson,' *Camb. Essays,* 1857.) A license of party vituperation in the House of Commons existed, from the time of the opposition to Walpole onwards, which has long been banished by more humane manners. 'The men who took a foremost part seemed to be intent on disparaging each other, and proving that neither possessed any qualification of wisdom, knowledge, or public virtue. . . Epithets of reproach were lavished personally on Lord North, which were applicable only to the vilest and most contemptible of mankind.' (Massey, *Hist. of England,* ii. 218.)

Were this blustering language a blemish of style and nothing more, it would taint their books with vulgarity as literature, but it would not vitiate their matter. But the fault reaches deeper than skin-deep. It is a most serious drawback on the good-sense of the age that it wanted justice in its estimate of persons. They were no more capable of judging their friends than their foes. In Pope's satires there is no medium; our enemies combine all the odious vices, however incongruous; our friends have 'every virtue under heaven.' We hear sometimes of Pope's peculiar 'malignity.' But he was only doing what every one around him was doing, only with a greatly superior literary skill. Their savage invective against each other is not a morally worse feature than the style of fulsome compliment in which friends address each other. The private correspondence of intimate friends betrays an unwholesome insincerity, which contrasts strangely with their general manliness of character. The burly intellect of Warburton displays an appetite for flattery as insatiable as that of Miss Seward and her coterie.

This habit of exaggerating both good and evil the divines share with the other writers of the time. But theological literature, as a written debate, had a form of malignant imputation peculiar to itself. This is one arising out of the rationalistic fiction which both parties assumed, viz., that their respective beliefs were determined by an impartial inquiry into the evidence. The orthodox writers considered this evidence so clear and certain for their own conclusions, that they could account for its not seeming so to others only by the supposition of some moral obliquity which darkened the understanding in such cases. Hence the obnoxious assumption of the divines that the Deists were men of corrupt morals, and the retort of the infidel writers, that the clergy were hired advocates. Moral imputation, which is justly banished from legal argument, seems to find a proper place in theological. Those Christian Deists who, like Toland or Collins, approached most nearly in their belief to Revelation, were treated, not better, but worse, by the orthodox champions ; their larger admissions being imputed to disingenuousness or calculated reserve. This stamp of advocacy which was impressed on English theology at the Reformation—its first work of consideration was an 'Apology'—it has not to this day shaken off. Our theologians, with rare exceptions, do not penetrate below the surface of their subject, but are engaged in defending or vindicating it. The current phrases of 'the bulwarks of our faith,' 'dangerous to Christianity,' are but instances of the habitual position in which we assume ourselves to stand. Even more philosophic minds cannot get rid of the idea that theology is polemical. Theological study is still the study of topics of defence. Even Professor Fraser can exhort us 'that by the study of these topics we might not merely disarm the enemies of religion of what, in other times has been, and will continue to be a favourite weapon of assault, but we might even convert that weapon into an instrument of use in the Christian service.' (*Essays in Philosophy*, p. 4.)   'Modern science,' as it is called, is recommended to the young divine, because in it he may find means of 'confuting infidelity.'

A little consideration will show that the grounds on which advocacy before a legal tribunal rests, make it inappropriate in theological reasoning. It is not pretended that municipal law is coextensive with universal law, and therefore incapable of admitting right on both sides. It is allowed that the natural right may be, at times, on one side, and the legal title on the other; not to mention the extreme case where '*communis error facit jus.*' The advocate is not there to supply all the materials out of which the judge is to form his decision, but only one side of the case. He is the mere representative of his client's interests, and has not to discuss the abstract merits of the juridical point which may be involved. He does not undertake to show that the law is conformable to natural right, but to establish the condition of his client relatively to the law. But the rational defender of the faith has no place in his system for the variable, or the indifferent, or the non-natural. He proceeds on the supposition that the whole system of the Church is the one and exclusively true expression of reason upon the subject on which it legislates. He claims for the whole of received knowledge what the jurist claims for international law, to be a universal science. He lays before us, on the one hand, the traditional canon or symbol of doctrine. On the other hand, he teaches that the free use of reason upon the facts of nature and Scripture is the real mode by which this traditional symbol is arrived at. To show, then, that the candid pursuit of truth leads every impartial intellect to the Anglican conclusion was the task which, on their theory of religious proof, their theology had to undertake. The process, accordingly, should have been analogous to that of the jurist or legislator with regard to the internal evidence, and to that of the judge with regard to the external evidence.

If theological argument forgets the judge and assumes the advocate, or betrays the least bias to one side, the conclusion is valueless, the principle of free inquiry has been violated. Roman Catholic theologians consistently enough teach that 'apologetics' make no part of theology, as usually conducted as replies to special objections urged, but that a true apologetic must be founded (1) on a discovery of the general principle from which the attack proceeds, and (2) on the exhibition, *per contra*, of that general ground-thought of which the single Christian truths are developments. (Hageman, *Die Aufgabe der Catholischen Apologetik.*)

With rare exceptions the theology of the Hanoverian period is of the most violently partisan character. It seats itself, by its theory, in the judicial chair, but it is only to comport itself there like Judge Jefferies. One of the favourite books of the time was Sherlock's *Trial of the Witnesses*. First published in 1729, it speedily went through fourteen editions. It concludes in this way:—

'*Judge.*—What say you? Are the Apostles guilty of giving false evidence in the case of the resurrection of Jesus, or not guilty?

'*Foreman.*—Not guilty.

'*Judge.*—Very well; and now, gentlemen, I resign my commission, and am your humble servant. The company then rose up, and were beginning to pay their compliments to the Judge and the counsel, but were interrupted by a gentleman, who went up to the Judge and offered him a fee. 'What is this?' says the Judge. 'A fee, sir,' said the gentleman. 'A fee to a judge is a bribe,' said the Judge. 'True, sir,' said the gentleman; 'but you have resigned your commission, and will not be the first judge who has come from the bench to the bar without any diminution of honour. Now, Lazarus's case is to come on next, and this fee is to retain you on his side.'

One might say that the apologists of that day had in like manner left the bench for the bar, and taken a brief for the Apostles. They are impatient at the smallest demur, and deny loudly that there is any weight in anything advanced by their opponents. In the way they override the most serious difficulties, they show anything but the temper which is supposed to qualify for the weighing of evidence. The astonishing want of candour in their reasoning, their blindness to real difficulty, the ill-concealed predetermination to find a particular verdict, the rise of their style in passion in the same proportion as their argument fails in strength, constitute a class of writers more calculated than any other to damage their own cause with young ingenuous minds, bred in the school of Locke to believe that ' to love truth for truth's sake is the principal part of human perfection in this world, and the seed-plot of all other virtues. (Locke, æt. 73. *Letter to Collins*.) Spalding has described the moral shock his faith received on hearing an eminent clergyman in confidential conversation with another, who had cited some powerful argument against revelation, say, ' That's truly awkward; let us consider a little how we get out of that;' *wie wir uns salviren*. (*Selbstbiographie*, p. 128.) A truthful mind is a much rarer possession than is commonly supposed, for ' it is as easy to close the eyes of the mind as those of the body.' (Butler, *Sermon* x.) And in this rarity there is a natural limit to the injury which uncandid vindications of revelation can cause. To whatever causes is to be attributed the decline of Deism, from 1750 onwards, the books polemically written against it cannot reckon among them. When Casaubon first visited Paris, and was being shown over the Sorbonne, his guide said, ' This is the hall in which the doctors have *disputed* for 300 years.' ' Aye! and what have they settled?' was his remark.

Some exceptions, doubtless, there are to the incon-

clusiveness of this debate.  Here again the eminent
exception is the *Analogy*.  Butler, it is true, comes
forward not as an investigator, but as a pleader.  But
when we pass from his inferior brethren to this great
master of the art, we find ourselves in the hands of
one who knows the laws of evidence, and carefully
keeps his statements within them.  Butler does not,
like his fellow apologists, disguise the fact that the
evidence is no stronger than it is.  'If it be a *poor*
thing,' to argue in this way, 'the epithet *poor* may be
applied, I fear, as properly to great part, or the whole,
of human life, as it is to the things mentioned.'
(*Analogy*, Part ii. ch. 8.)  Archbishop Whately, defining the temper of the rational theologian, says :—
'A good man will, indeed, wish to find the evidence
of the Christian religion satisfactory ; but a wise man
will not, for that reason, think it satisfactory, but will
weigh the evidence the more carefully on account of
the importance of the question.'  (*Essays*, 2nd series,
p. 24.)  This character Butler's argument exemplifies.
We can feel, as we read, how his judgment must have
been offended in his contemporaries by the dispro-
portion between the positiveness of their assertion
and the feebleness of their argument.  Nor should
we expect that Butler satisfied them.  They thought
him ' a little too little vigorous,' and ' wished he
would have spoke more earnestly.'  (Byrom's *Journal*,
March, 1737.)  Men who believed that they were in
possession of a 'demonstration' of Christianity were
not likely to be satisfied with one who saw so strongly
'the doubtfulness in which things were involved' that
he could not comprehend 'men's being impatient out
of action or vehement in it.'  (*Unpublished Remains*,
*&c.*)  Warburton, who has a proof which ' is very
little short of mathematical certainty, and to which
nothing but a mere physical possibility of the contrary
can be opposed' (*Divine Leg.*, b. i. § 1), was the man
for the age, which did not care to stand higgling with

Butler over the degrees of probability. What could the world do with a man who 'designed the search after truth as the business of my life' (*Correspondence with Dr. Clarke*), and who was so little prepared to dogmatise about the future world that he rather felt that 'there is no account to be given in the way of reason of men's so strong attachments to the present world.' (*Sermon* vii.) Butler's doubtfulness, however, it should be remarked, is not the unsteadiness of the sceptical, but the wariness of the judicial mind; a mind determined for itself by its own instincts, but careful to confine its statements to others within the evidence produced in court. The *Analogy* does not depicture an inward struggle in his own mind, but as 'he told a friend, his way of writing it had been to endeavour to answer as he went along, every possible objection that might occur to any one against any position of his in his book.' (Bartlett's *Life of Butler*, p. 50.) He does not doubt himself, but he sees, what others do not see, the difficulty of proving religion to others. There is a saying of Pitt circulating to the effect that the *Analogy* is 'a dangerous book; it raises more doubts than it solves.' All that is true in this is, that to a mind which has never nourished objections to revelation a book of evidences may be the means of first suggesting them. But in 1736 the objections were everywhere current, and the answers to them were mostly of that truly 'dangerous' sort in which assertion runs ahead of proof. The merit of Butler lies not in the 'irrefragable proof,' which Southey's epitaph attributes to his construction, but in his showing the nature of the proof, and daring to admit that it was less than certain; to own that 'a man may be fully convinced of the truth of a matter and upon the strongest reasons, and yet not be able to answer all the difficulties which may be raised upon it.' (*Durham Charge*, 1751.)

Another, perhaps the only other, book of this

polemical tribe which can be said to have been completely successful as an answer, is one most unlike the
*Analogy* in all its nobler features. This is Bentley's
*Remarks upon a late Discourse of Freethinking, by*
*Phileleutherus Lipsiensis*, 1713. Coarse, arrogant, and
abusive, with all Bentley's worst faults of style and
temper, this masterly critique is decisive. Not, of
course, of the Deistical controversy, on which the critic
avoids entering. The *Discourse of Freethinking* was a
small tract published in 1713 by Anthony Collins.
Collins was a gentleman of independent fortune, whose
high personal character and general respectability
seemed to give a weight to his words, which assuredly
they do not carry of themselves. By freethinking,
he means liberty of thought—the right of bringing
all received opinions whatsoever to the touchstone of
reason. Among the grounds or authorities by which
he supports this natural right, Collins unluckily had
recourse to history, and largely, of course, to the precedent of the Greek philosophers. Collins, who had
been bred at Eton and King's, was probably no worse
a scholar than his contemporary Kingsmen, and the
range of his reading was that of a man who had
made the classics the companions of his maturer years.
But that scholarship which can supply a quotation
from Lucan, or flavour the style with an occasional
allusion to Tully or Seneca, is quite incompetent to
apply Greek or Roman precedent properly to a modern
case. Addison, the pride of Oxford, had done no
better. In his *Essay on the Evidences of Christianity*,
Addison 'assigns as grounds for his religious belief,
stories as absurd as that of the Cocklane ghost, and
forgeries as rank as Ireland's *Vortigern*, puts faith in
the lie about the thundering legion, is convinced that
Tiberius moved the Senate to admit Jesus among the
gods, and pronounces the letter of Agbarus, King of
Edessa, to be a record of great authority.' (Macaulay :
*Essays*.) But the public was quite satisfied with

Addison's citations, in which a public, which had given the victory to Boyle in the *Phalaris* controversy, could hardly suspect anything wrong. Collins was not to escape so easily. The Freethinker flounders hopelessly among the authorities he has invoked. Like the necromancer's apprentice, he is worried by the fiends he has summoned but cannot lay, and Bentley, on whose nod they wait, is there like another Cornelius Agrippa hounding them on and enjoying the sport. Collins's mistakes, mistranslations, misconceptions, and distortions are so monstrous, that it is difficult for us now, forgetful how low classical learning had sunk, to believe that they *are* mistakes, and not wilful errors. It is rare sport to Bentley, this rathunting in an old rick, and he lays about him in high glee, braining an authority at every blow. When he left off abruptly, in the middle of a 'Third Part,' it was not because he was satiated with slaughter, but to substitute a new excitement, no less congenial to his temper—a quarrel with the University about his fees. A grace, voted 1715, tendering him the public thanks of the University, and 'praying him in the name of the University to finish what remains of so useful a work,' could not induce him to resume his pen. The *Remarks of Phileleutherus Lipsiensis*, unfinished though they are, and trifling as was the book which gave occasion to them, are perhaps the best of all Bentley's performances. They have all the merits of the *Phalaris* dissertation, with the advantage of a far nobler subject. They show how Bentley's exact appreciation of the value of terms could, when he chose to apply it to that purpose, serve him as a key to the philosophical ideas of past times, no less than to those of poetical metaphor. The tone of the pamphlet is most offensive, 'not only not insipid, but exceedingly bad-tasted.' We can only say the taste is that of his age, while the knowledge is all his own. It was fair to show that his antagonist undertook ' to interpret the Prophets and Solomon without Hebrew; Plutarch and Zosimus (Collins spells it Zozimus) without Greek; and Cicero and Lucan without Latin.' (*Remarks*, Part i. No. 3.) But the dirt endeavoured to be thrown on Collins will cleave to the hand that throws it. It may be worth mention that this tract of Bentley contains the original of Sidney Smith's celebrated defence of the 'prizes' in the Church. The passage is a favourable specimen of the moral level of a polemic who was accusing his opponent of holding 'opinions the most abject and base that human nature is capable of.' (Letter prefixed to *Remarks*.)

'He can never conceive or wish a priesthood either quieter for him, or cheaper, than that of the present Church of England. Of your quietness himself is a convincing proof, who has writ this outrageous book, and has met with no punishment nor prosecution. And for the cheapness, that appeared lately in one of your parliaments, when the accounts exhibited showed that 6,000 of your clergy, the greater part of your whole number, had, at a middle rate one with another, not 50 pounds a year. A poor emolument for so long, so laborious, so expensive an education, as must qualify them for holy orders. While I resided at Oxford, and saw such a conflux of youth to their annual admissions, I have often studied and admired why their parents would, under such mean encouragements, design their sons for the church; and those the most towardly, and capable, and select geniuses among their children, who must needs have emerged in a secular life. I congratulated, indeed, the felicity of your establishment, which attracted the choice youth of your nation for such very low pay; but my wonder was at the parents, who generally have interest, maintenance and wealth, the first thing in their view, till at last one of your state-lotteries ceased my astonishment. For as in that, a few glittering prizes, 1,000, 5,000, 10,000 pounds among an infinity of blanks, drew troops of adventurers, who, if the whole fund had been equally ticketted, would never have come in ; so a few shining dignities in your church, prebends, deaneries, bishopricks, are the pious fraud that induces and decoys the parents to risk their child's fortune in it.   Everyone hopes his own will get some prize in the church, and never reflects on the thousands of blanks in poor country livings.   And if a foreigner may tell you his mind, from what he sees at home, 'tis this part of your establishment that makes your clergy excel ours [*i. e.*, in Germany, from which *Phileleutherus Lipsiensis* is supposed to write].  Do but once level all your preferments, and you'll soon be as level in your learning.   For, instead of the flower of the English youth, you'll have only the refuse sent to your academies, and those, too, cramped and crippled in their studies, for want of aim and emulation.   So that, if your Freethinkers had any politics, instead of suppressing your whole order, they should make you all alike ; or, if that cannot be done, make your preferments a very lottery in the whole similitude.  Let your church dignities be pure chance prizes, without regard to abilities, or morals, or letters.'  (*Remarks, &c.*, Part ii. § 40.)

It has been mentioned that Bentley does not attempt to reply to the argument of the *Discourse on Freethinking*.  His tactic is to ignore it, and to assume that it is only meant as a covert attack on Christianity ; that Collins is an Atheist fighting under the disguise of a Deist.  Some excuse perhaps may be made for a man nourished on pedagogic latin, and accustomed to launch furious sarcasm at any opponent who betrayed a brutal ignorance of the difference between ' ac ' and ' et.'  But Collins was not a sharper, and would have disdained practices to which Bentley stooped for the sake of a professorship.  When Bentley, in the pride of academic dignity, could thus browbeat a person of Collins's consideration, it was not to be expected that

the inferior fry of Deistical writers,—Toland, a writer
for the press; Tindal, a fellow of a college; or Chubb,
a journeyman glover—met with fairer treatment from
their opponents. The only exception to this is the
case of Shaftesbury, to whom, as well after his death
as in his lifetime, his privileges as a peer seem to have
secured immunity from hangman's usage. He is
simply 'a late noble author.' Nor was this respect
inspired by the Earl's profession of christianity. He
does, indeed, make this profession with the utmost
unreserve. He asserts his 'steady orthodoxy,' and
'entire submission to the truly Christian and Catholic
doctrines of our holy Church, as by law established,'
and that he holds 'the mysteries of our religion even
in the minutest particulars.' (*Characteristicks,*Vol. iii.
p. 315.) But this outward profession would only have
brought down upon any other writer an aggravated
charge of cowardly malice and concealment of Atheism.
If Shaftesbury was spared on account of his rank, the
orthodox writers were not altogether wrong in fasten-
ing upon this disingenuousness as a moral characteristic of their antagonists. The excuse for this want
of manliness in men who please themselves with in-
sinuating unpopular opinions which they dare not
advocate openly, is that it is an injustice perpetrated by
those who have public feeling on their side. 'They
make,' says Mr. Tayler, 'the honest expression of
opinion penal, and then condemn men for disingenuousness. They invite to free discussion, but determine beforehand that only one conclusion can be sound
and moral. They fill the arena of public debate with
every instrument of torture and annoyance for the
feeling heart, the sensitive imagination, and the scrupulous intellect, and then are angry that men do not
rush headlong into the martyrdom that has been prepared for them.' (*Religious Life of England,* p. 282.)

In days when the pillory was the punishment for
common libel, it cannot be thought much that heresy

and infidelity should be punished by public opprobrium. And public abhorrence was the most that a writer against revelation had now to fear.   Mandeville's *Fable of the Bees*, indeed, was presented as a nuisance by the grand jury of Middlesex, in 1723, as were Bolingbroke's collected ' *Works*,' in 1752, and Toland's *Christianity not Mysterious*, in 1699.   We find, too, that Toland had to fly from Dublin, and Collins to go out of the way to Holland, for fear of further consequences. But nothing ever came of these presentments.   The only prosecution for religious libel was that of Woolston, 2 George II., in which the defendant, who was not of sound mind, provoked and even compelled the law officers of the crown to proceed against him, though they were very reluctant to do so.   When thus compelled to declare the law, on this occasion, the Lord Chief Justice (Raymond) ' would not allow it to be doubted that to write against Christianity in general was punishable at common law.'   Yet both then and since, judges and prosecutors have shown themselves shy of insisting upon the naked offence of ' impugning the truth of Christianity.'   That it is an offence at common law, independent of 9 & 10 William III., no lawyer will deny.   But an instinctive sense of the incompatibility of this legal doctrine with the fundamental tenet of Protestant rationalism has always served to keep it in the background.   ' The judges seem to have played fast and loose in this matter, in such sort as might enable the future judge to quote the tolerant or the intolerant side of their doctrine as might prove convenient; and while seemingly disavowing all interference with fair discussion, they still kept a wary hold of the precedents of Hale and Raymond, and of the great arcanum of ' part and parcel;' ' semianimesque micant digiti, ferrumque retractant.'   (*Considerations on the Law of Libel*. By John Search, 1833.)

Whatever excuse the Deistical writers might have

for their insidious manner of writing, it is more to the present purpose to observe that we may draw from it the conclusion that public opinion was throughout on the side of the defenders of Christianity. It might seem almost superfluous to say this, were it not that complaints meet us on every side, which seem to imply the very contrary; that in the words of Mr. Gregory, 'the doctrine of our Church is exploded, and our holy religion become only a name which is everywhere spoken against.' (*Pref. to Beveridge's Private Thoughts*, 1709.) Thirty years later Butler writes, that 'it is come to be taken for granted that Christianity is not so much as a subject of inquiry; but that it is now, at length, discovered to be fictitious. Accordingly they treat it as if in the present age this were an agreed point among all people of discernment, and nothing remained but to set it up as a principal subject of mirth and ridicule, as it were by way of reprisals for its having so long interrupted the pleasures of the world.' (*Advertisement to Analogy*, 1736.) However a loose kind of Deism might be the tone of fashionable circles, it is clear that distinct disbelief of Christianity was by no means the general state of the public mind. The leaders of the Low-church and Whig party were quite aware of this. Notwithstanding the universal complaints of the High-church party of the prevalence of infidelity, it is obvious that this mode of thinking was confined to a very small section of society. The *Independent Whig* (May 4, 1720), in the middle of its blustering and endeavours to terrify the clergy with their unpopularity, is obliged to admit that 'the High-church Popish clergy will laugh in their sleeves at this advice, and think there is folly enough yet left among the laity to support their authority; and will laugh themselves, and rejoice over the ignorance of the Universities, the stupidity of the drunken squires, the pannic of the tender sex, and the never-to-be-shaken constancy of the multitude.'

A still better evidence is the confidence and success with which the writers on the side of Revelation appealed to the popular passions, and cowed their Deistical opponents into the use of that indirect and disingenuous procedure with which they then taunted them.  The clerical sphere was much more a sphere by itself than it has since become.  Notwithstanding the large toleration really practised, strict professional etiquette was still observed in the Church and the Universities.  The horizontal hat, the starched band, and the cassock, were still worn in public, and certain proprieties of outward manner were expected from 'the cloth.'  The violation of these proprieties was punished by the forfeiture of the offenders' prospects of preferment, a point on which the most extreme sensitiveness existed.  In the Balguy and Waterland set an officious spirit of delation seems to have flourished.  The general habit of publicly canvassing religious topics was very favourable to this espionage; as, at the Reformation, the Catholics gathered their best calumnies against Luther from his unreserved 'table-talk.'

It was not difficult to draw the unhappy Middleton into 'unguarded expressions' (Van Mildert, *Life of Waterland,* p. 162); and something which had fallen from Rundle in his younger days was used against him so successfully that even the Talbot interest was able to procure him only an Irish bishoprick.  Lord Chesterfield, seeing what advantage the High-church party derived from this tactic, endeavoured to turn it against them.  He gives a circumstantial account of a conversation with Pope, which would tend to prove that Atterbury was, nearly all his life, a sceptic.  The thing was not true, as Mr. Carruthers has shown (*Life of Pope,* 2nd ed. p. 213), and true or false, the weapon in Chesterfield's hands was pointless.

Though the general feeling of the country was sufficiently decided to oblige all who wished to write against Christianity, to do so under a mask, this was not the case with attacks upon the Clergy. Since the days of the Lollards there had never been a time when the established ministers of religion were held in so much contempt as in the Hanoverian period, or when satire upon churchmen was so congenial to general feeling. This too was the more extraordinary, as there was no feeling against the Church Establishment, nor was non-conformity as a theory ever less in favour. The contempt was for the persons, manners, and character of the ecclesiastics. When Macaulay brought out his portrait of the clergyman of the revolution period, his critics endeavoured to show that that portrait was not true to life. They seem to have brought out the fact that it was pretty fairly true to literature. The difficult point is to estimate how far the satirical and popular literature of any age may be taken as representative of life. Satire to be popular must exaggerate, but it must be exaggeration of known and recognised facts. Mr. Churchill Babington (*Character of the Clergy, &c., considered*, p. 48) sets aside two of Macaulay's authorities, Oldham and T. Wood, because Oldham was an Atheist and Wood a Deist. Admitting that an Atheist and a Deist can be under no obligation to truth, yet a satirist, who intends to be read, is under the most inevitable engagement to the probable. Satire does not create the sentiment to which it appeals. A portrait of the country parson *temp.* George the Second which should be drawn verbatim from the pamphlets of the day would be no more historical, than is that portrait of the begging friar of the sixteenth century which our historians repeat after Erasmus and the *Epistolæ Obscurorum Virorum*. History may be extracted from them, but these caricatures are not themselves history.

One inference which we may safely draw is that public feeling encouraged such representations. It is a symptom of the religious temper of the times, that the same public which compelled the Deist to wear the mask of 'solemn sneer' in his assaults upon Christian doctrine, required no such disguise or reserve when the ministers of the Church were spoken of. Nor does the evidence consist in a few stray extracts from here and there a Deist or a cynic, it is the tone of all the popular writers of that time. The unedifying lives of the clergy are a standard theme of sarcasm, and continue to be so till a late period in the century, when a gradual change may be observed in the language of literature. This antipathy to the clergy visible in the Hanoverian period, admits of comparison with that vein which colours the popular songs of the Wickliffite era. In the fifteenth century, the satire is not indiscriminate. It is against the monks and friars, the bishops and cardinals, as distinct from the 'poor persoun of a toun.' Its point against the organized hypocrisy of the Papal Churchmen is given it by the picture of the ideal minister of 'Christe's Gospel' which always accompanies the burlesque. In the eighteenth century the license of satire goes much beyond this. In the early part of the century we find clerical satire observing to some extent a similar discrimination. The Tory parson is libelled always with an ostentatious reserve of commendation for the more enlightened and liberal Hanoverian, the staunch maintainer of the Protestant succession. This is the tone of the *Independent Whig*, one of the numerous weekly sheets called into being in imitation of the *Tatler*. It was started in 1720, taking for its exclusive theme the clergy, whom it was its avowed object to abuse. A paper came out every Wednesday. It was not a newspaper, and does not deal in libel or personalities, hardly ever mentioning a name, very rarely quoting a fact, but dilating in general terms upon clerical ignorance and bigotry. This dull and worthless trash not only had a considerable circulation at the time, but was reprinted, and passed through several editions in a collected form. The bishops talked of prohibiting it, but, on second thoughts, acted more wisely in taking no notice of it. The only part of the kingdom into which it could not find entrance was the Isle of Man, where the saintly Wilson combined with apostolic virtues much of the old episcopal claims over the consciences of his flock. The *Independent Whig*, though manifestly written by a man of no religion, yet finds it necessary to keep up the appearance of encouraging the 'better sort' of clergy, and affecting to despise only the political priests, the meddling chaplain, the preferment-hunter, the toper, who is notable at bowls, and dexterous at whisk.

As we advance towards the middle of the century, and the French influence begins to mingle with pure English Deism, the spirit of contempt spreads till it involves all priests of all religions. The language now is, 'The established clergy in every country are generally the greatest enemies to all kinds of reformation, as they are generally the most narrow-minded and most worthless set of men in every country. Fortunately for the present times, the wings of clerical power and influence are pretty close trimmed, so that I do not think their opposition to the proposed reformations could be of any great consequence, more of the people being inclined to despise them, than to follow them blindly.' (Burgh, *Political Disquisitions*, 1774.) It was no longer for their vices that the clergy were reviled, for the philosopher now had come to understand that 'their virtues were more dangerous' to society. Strictness of life did but increase the dislike with which the clergyman was regarded; his morality was but double-dyed hypocrisy; religious language from his mouth was methodistical cant. Nor did the orthodox attempt to struggle with this sentiment. They yielded to it, and adopted for their maxim of conduct, 'surtout point de zèle.' Their sermons and pamphlets were now directed against 'Enthusiasm,' which became the bugbear of that time. Every

clergyman, who wished to retain any influence over
the minds of his parishioners, was anxious to vindicate himself from all suspicion of enthusiasm. When
he had set himself right in this respect, he endeavoured to do the same good office for the Apostles.
But if he were not an 'enthusiast,' he was an 'im-
postor.' For every clergyman of the Church had
against him an antecedent presumption as a 'priest.'
It was now well understood, by all enlightened men,
that the whole sacerdotal brood were but a set of im-
postors, who lived by deceiving the people, and who
had invented religion for their own benefit. Natural
religion needed no 'priests' to uphold it; it was
obvious to every understanding, and could maintain
itself in the world without any confraternity sworn to
the secret.

Again came a change. As the Methodist movement gradually leavened the mass beneath, zeal came
again into credit. The old Wickliffite, or Puritan,
distinction is revived between the 'Gospel preachers'
and the 'dumb dogs.' The antipathy to priests was
no longer promiscuous. Popular indignation was
reserved for the fox-hunter and the pluralist; the
Hophni and Phinehas generation; the men, who are
described as 'careless of dispensing the bread of life
to their flocks, preaching a carnal and soul-benumbing
morality, and trafficking in the souls of men by receiving money for discharging the pastoral office in
parishes where they did not so much as look on the
faces of the people more than once a year.' In the
well-known satire of Cowper, it is no longer irreligious
mocking at sacred things under pretence of a virtuous
indignation. It becomes again what it was before
the Reformation—an earnest feeling, a religious sentiment, the moral sense of man; Huss or Savonarola
appealing to the written morality of the Gospel
against the practical immorality consecrated by the
Church.

Something too of the old anti-hierarchical feeling accompanies this revival of the influence of the inferior clergy; a faint reflection of the bitter hatred which the Lollard had borne to pope and cardinal, or the Puritan to 'Prelacy.' The utility of the episcopal and capitular dignities continued to be questioned long after the evangelical parish pastor had re-established himself in the affections of his flock, and 1832 saw the cathedrals go down amid the general approbation of all classes. In the earlier half of the century the reverse was the case. The boorish country parson was the man whose order was despised then, and his utility questioned. The Freethinkers themselves could not deny that the bench and the stalls were graced by some whose wit, reputation, and learning would have made them considerable in any profession. The higher clergy had with them the town and the court, the country clergy sided with the squires. The mass of the clergy were not in sympathy, either politically or intellectually, with their ecclesiastical superiors. The Tory fox-hunter in the *Freeholder* (No. 22.) thinks ' the neighbouring shire very happy for having scarce a Presbyterian in it except the bishop;' while Hickes ' thanks God that the main body of the clergy are in their hearts Jacobites.' The bishops of George the Second deserved the respect they met with. At no period in the history of our Church has the ecclesiastical patronage of the crown been better directed than while it was secretly dispensed by Queen Caroline. For a brief period, liberality and cultivation of mind were passports to promotion in the Church. Nor were politics a hindrance; the queen earnestly pressed an English see upon Bishop Wilson. The corruption which began with the Duke of Newcastle (1746) gradually deepened in the subsequent reign, as political orthodoxy and connexion were made the tests, and the borough-holders divided the dignities of the Church among their adherents.

Of an age so solid and practical it was not to be expected that its theology and metaphysics would mount into the more remote spheres of abstraction. Their line of argument was, as has been seen, regulated by the necessity they laid themselves under of appealing to sound sense and common reason. But not only was their treatment of their topic popular, the motive of their writings was an immediate practical necessity. Bishops and deans might be made for merit, but it was not mere literary merit, classical scholarship, or University distinction. The Deistical controversy did not originate, like some other controversies which have made much noise in their time, in speculative fancy, in the leisure of the cloister, or the college. It had a living practical interest in its complication with the questions of the day. The endeavour of the moralists and divines of the period to rationalize religion was in fact an effort to preserve the practical principles of moral and religious conduct for society. It was not an academical disputation, or a contest of wits for superiority, but a life and death struggle of religious and moral feeling to maintain itself. What they felt they had to contend against was moral depravity, and not theological error ; they wrote less in the interest of truth than in that of virtue. A general relaxation of manners, in all classes of society, is universally affirmed to be characteristic of that time ; and theology and philosophy applied themselves to combat this. A striking instance of this is Bishop Berkeley, the only metaphysical writer of the time, besides Locke, who has maintained a very high name in philosophical history. He forms a solitary—it might seem a singular—exception to what has been said of the prosaic and unmetaphysical character of this moralising age. The two peculiar metaphysical notions which are connected with Berkeley's name, and which, though he did not originate, he propounded with a novelty and distinctness equal to originality, have always ranked as being on the extreme verge of rational speculation, if not actually within the region of unfruitful paradox and metaphysical romance. These two memorable speculations, as propounded by Berkeley in the *Alciphron*, come before us not as a Utopian dream, or an ingenious play of reason, but interwoven in a polemic against the prevailing unbelief. They are made to bend to a most practical purpose, and are Berkeley's contribution to the Deistical controversy. The character of the man, too, was more in harmony with the plain utilitarian spirit of his time than with his own refining intellect. He was not a closet-thinker, like his master Malebranche, but a man of the world and of society, inquisitive and well informed in many branches of practical science. Practical schemes, social and philanthropic, occupied his mind more than abstract thinking. In pushing the received metaphysical creed to its paradoxical consequences, as much as in prescribing 'tar-water,' he was thinking only of an immediate 'benefit to mankind.' He seems to have thought nothing of his argument until he had brought it to bear on the practical question of the day.

Were the 'corruption of manners' merely the complaint of one party or set of writers, a cry of factious Puritanism, or of men who were at war with society, like the Nonjuring clergy, or of a few isolated individuals of superior piety, like William Law, it would be easily explicable. The 'world' at all times, and in all countries, can be described with truth as 'lying in wickedness,' and the rebuke of the preacher of righteousness is equally needed in every age. There cannot be a darker picture than that drawn by the Fathers of the third century of the morals of the Christians in their time. (See passages in Jewel's *Apology*.) The rigorous moralist, heathen or Christian, can always point in sharp contrast the vices and the belief of mankind. But, after making every allowance for the exaggeration of religious rhetoric, and the querulousness of defeated parties, there seems to remain *some* real evidence for ascribing to that age a more than usual moral licence, and contempt of external restraints. It is the concurrent testimony of men of all parties, it is the general strain of the most sensible and worldly divines, prosperous men who lived with this very world they censure, men whose code of morals was not large, nor their standard exacting. To attempt the inquiry what specific evils were meant by the general expressions ' decay of religion' and ' corruption of manners,' the stereotype phrases of the time, is not within the limits of this paper. No historian, as far as I am aware, has attempted this examination ; all have been content to render, without valuation, the charges as they find them. I shall content myself with producing here one statement of contemporary opinion on this point ; for which purpose I select a layman, David Hartley. (*Observations on Man*, vol. ii. p. 441.)

' There are six things which seem more especially to threaten ruin and dissolution to the present States of Christendom.

' 1st. The great growth of atheism and infidelity, particularly amongst the governing parts of these States.

' 2nd. The open and abandoned lewdness to which great numbers of both sexes, especially in the high ranks of life, have given themselves up.

' 3rd. The sordid and avowed self-interest, which is almost the sole motive of action in those who are concerned in the administration of public affairs.

' 4th. The licentiousness and contempt of every kind of authority, divine or human, which is so notorious in inferiors of all ranks.

' 5th. The great worldly-mindedness of the clergy, and their gross neglect in the discharge of their proper functions.

' 6th. The carelessness and infatuation of parents and magistrates with respect to the education of youth, and the consequent early corruption of the rising generation.

'All these things have evident mutual connexions and influences ; and as they all seem likely to increase from time to time, so it can scarce be doubted by a considerate man, whether he be a religious one or no, but that they will, sooner or later, bring on a total dissolution of all the forms of government that subsist at present in the Christian countries of Europe.'

Though there is this entire unanimity as to the fact of the prevailing corruption, there is the greatest diversity of opinion as to its cause. Each party is found in turn attributing it to the neglect or disbelief of the abstract propositions in which its own particular creed is expressed. The Nonjurors and High-Churchmen attribute it to the Toleration Act and the latitudinarianism allowed in high places. One of the very popular pamphlets of the year 1721 was a fast-sermon preached before the Lord Mayor by Edmund Massey, in which he enumerates the evils of the time, and affirms that they 'are justly chargeable upon the corrupt explication of those words of our Saviour, 'My kingdom is not of this world'—*i.e.*, upon Hoadley's celebrated sermon. The latitudinarian clergy divide the blame between the Freethinkers and the Nonjurors. The Freethinkers point to the hypocrisy of the Clergy, who, they say, lost all credit with the people by having preached 'passive obedience' up to 1688, and then suddenly finding out that it was not a scriptural truth. The Nonconformists lay it to the enforcement of conformity and unscriptural terms of communion ; while the Catholics rejoice to see in it the Protestant Reformation at last bearing its natural fruit. Warburton characteristically attributes it to the bestowal of 'preferment' by the Walpole administration. (Dedication to Lord Mansfield, *Works*, ii. 268.) The power of preferment was not under-estimated then. George II. maintained to the last that the growth of Methodism was entirely owing to ministers not having listened to his advice, and 'made White-field a bishop.' Lastly, that everyone may have his say, a professor of moral philosophy in our day is found attributing the same facts to the prevalence of 'that low view of morality which rests its rules upon consequences merely.'

'The reverence which,' says Dr. Whewell, 'handed down by the traditions of ages of moral and religious teaching, had hitherto protected the accustomed forms of moral good, was gradually removed. Vice, and crime, and sin, ceased to be words that terrified the popular speculator. Virtue, and goodness, and purity were no longer things which he looked up to with mute respect. He ventured to lay a sacrilegious hand even upon these hallowed shapes. He saw that when this had been dared by audacious theorists, those objects, so long venerated, seemed to have no power of punishing the bold intruder. There was a scene like that which occurred when the barbarians broke into the Eternal City. At first, in spite of themselves, they were awed by the divine aspect of the ancient magistrates; but when once their leader had smitten one of these venerable figures with impunity, the coarse and violent mob rushed onwards, and exultingly mingled all in one common destruction.' (*Moral Philosophy in England,* p. 79.)

The actual sequence of cause and effect seems, if it be not presumptuous to say so, to be as nearly as possible inverted in this eloquent statement. The licentiousness of talk and manners was not produced by the moral doctrines promulgated; but the doctrine of moral consequences was had recourse to by the divines and moralists as the most likely remedy of the prevailing licentiousness. It was an attempt, well-meant but not successful, to arrest the wanton proceedings of 'the coarse and violent mob.' Good men saw with alarm, almost with despair, that what they

said in the obsolete language of religious teaching was
not listened to, and tried to address the age in plain
and unmistakeable terms. The new theory of consequences was not introduced by 'men of leisure' to
supplant and overthrow a nobler and purer view of
religion and morality, it was a plain fact of religion
stated in plain language, in the hope of deterring the
wicked from his wickedness. It was the address of
the Old Testament prophet, 'Why will ye die, O
house of Israel?' That there is a God and moral
Governor, and that obedience to His commands is
necessary to secure our interests in this world and the
next—if any form of rational belief can control the
actions of a rational being, it is surely this. On the
rationalist hypothesis, the morality of consequences
ought to produce the most salutary effects on the
general behaviour of mankind. This obligation of
obedience, the appeal to our desire of our own welfare,
was the substance of the practical teaching of the age.
It was stated with great cogency of reasoning, and
enforced with every variety of illustration. Put its
proof at the lowest, let it be granted that they did
not succeed in removing all the objections of the
Deistical writers, it must, at least, be allowed that
they showed, to the satisfaction of all prudent and
thinking men, that it was *safer* to believe Christianity
true than not. The obligation to practice in point of
prudence was as perfect as though the proof had been
demonstrative. And what was the surprising result?
That the more they demonstrated the less people believed. As the proof of morality was elaborated and
strengthened, the more it was disregarded, the more
ungodliness and profaneness flourished and grew.
This is certainly not what we should antecedently
expect. If, as Dr. Whewell assumes, and the whole
*doctrinaire* school with him, the speculative belief of
an age determines its moral character, that should be
the purest epoch where the morality of consequences

is placed in the strongest light—when it is most convincingly set before men that their present and future welfare depends on how they act ; that 'all we enjoy, and great part of what we suffer, is placed in our own hands.'

Experience, however, the testimony of history, displays to us a result the very reverse. The experiment of the eighteenth century may .surely be considered as a decisive one on this point. The failure of a prudential system of ethics as a restraining force upon society was perceived, or felt in the way of reaction, by the Evangelical and Methodist generation of teachers who succeeded the Hanoverian divines. So far their perception was just. They went on to infer that, because the circulation of one system of belief had been inefficacious, they should try the effect of inculcating a set of truths as widely remote from the former as possible. Because legal preaching, as they phrased it, had failed, they would essay Gospel preaching. The preaching of justification by works had not the power to check wickedness, therefore justification by faith, the doctrine of the Reformation, was the only saving truth. This is not meant as a complete account of the origin of the Evangelical school. It is only one point of view—that point which connects the school with the general line of thought this paper has been pursuing. Their doctrine of conversion by supernatural influence must on no account be forgotten. Yet it appears that they thought that the channel of this supernatural influence was, in some way or other, preaching. Preaching, too, not as rhetoric, but as the annunciation of a specific doctrine —the Gospel. They certainly insisted on ' the heart' being touched, and that the Spirit only had the power savingly to affect the heart ; but they acted as though this were done by an appeal to the reason, and scornfully rejected the idea of religious education.

It should also be remarked that even the divines of

the Hanoverian school were not wholly blind to some
flaw in their theory, and to the practical inefficacy of
their doctrine. Not that they underrated the force
of their demonstrations. As has been already said,
the greater part of them over-estimated their convinc-
ingness, but they could not but see that they did not,
in fact, convince. When this was forced upon their
observation, when they perceived that an *a priori* demonstration of religion might be placed before a man,
and that he did not see its force, then, inconsequent
with their own theory, they had recourse to the notion
of moral culpability. If a person refused to admit
the evidence for revelation, it was because he did not
examine it with a dispassionate mind. His understanding was biassed by his wishes; some illicit passion he was resolved on gratifying, but which prudence,
forsooth, would not have allowed him to gratify so
long as he continued to believe in a future judgment.
The wish that there *were* no God suggested the thought
that there *is* not. Speculative unbelief is thus asserted to be a consequence of a bad heart: it is the
grounds upon which we endeavour to prove to ourselves and others that the indulgence of our passions
is consistent with a rational prudence. As levelled
against an individual opponent, this is a poor controversial shift. Many of the Deists were men of worth
and probity; of none of them is anything known
which would make them worse men than the average
of their class in life. Mr. Chichester (*Deism compared
with Christianity*, 1821, vol. iii. p. 220) says 'Tindal
was infamous for vice in general;' but I have not
been able to trace his authority for the assertion. As
an imputation, not against individual unbelievers, but
against the competency of reason in general, it may
be true, but is quite inconsistent with the general hypothesis of the school of reasoners who brought it. If
reason be liable to an influence which warps it, then
there is required some force which shall keep this in-

fluence under, and reason alone is no longer the all-
sufficient judge of truth.   In this way we should be
forced back to the old orthodox doctrine of the chronic
impotence of reason, superinduced upon it by the Fall ;
a doctrine which the reigning orthodoxy had tacitly
renounced.

In the Catholic theory the feebleness of Reason is
met half-way and made good by the authority of the
Church.   When the Protestants threw off this
authority, they did not assign to Reason what they
took from the Church, but to Scripture.   Calvin did
not shrink from saying that Scripture ' shone sufficiently by its own light.'   As long as this could be
kept to, the Protestant theory of belief was whole and
sound.   At least it was as sound as the Catholic.   In
both, Reason, aided by spiritual illumination, performs
the subordinate function of recognising the supreme
authority of the Church, and of the Bible, respectively.
Time, learned controversy, and abatement of zeal
drove the Protestants generally from the hardy but
irrational assertion of Calvin.   Every foot of ground
that Scripture lost was gained by one or other of the
three substitutes : Church-authority, the Spirit, or
Reason.   Church-authority was essayed by the Laudian divines, but was soon found untenable, for on
that footing it was found impossible to justify the
Reformation and the breach with Rome.   The Spirit
then came into favour along with Independency.   But
it was still more quickly discovered that on such a
basis only discord and disunion could be reared.   There
remained to be tried Common Reason, carefully distinguished from recondite learning, and not based on
metaphysical assumptions.   To apply this instrument
to the contents of Revelation was the occupation of
the early half of the eighteenth century ; with what
success has been seen.   In the latter part of the century the same Common Reason was applied to the
external evidences.   But here the method fails in a

first requisite—universality ; for even the shallowest
array of historical proof requires some book-learning
to apprehend.   Further than this, the Lardner and
Paley school could not complete their proof satisfactorily, inasmuch as the materials for the investigation
of the first and second centuries of the Christian era
were not at hand.

Such appears to be the past history of the Theory
of Belief in the Church of England.   Whoever would
take the religious literature of the present day as a
whole, and endeavour to make out clearly on what
basis Revelation is supposed by it to rest, whether on
Authority, on the Inward Light, on Reason, on self-
evidencing Scripture, or on the combination of the
four, or some of them, and in what proportions, would
probably find that he had undertaken a perplexing but
not altogether profitless inquiry.

# ON THE INTERPRETATION OF SCRIPTURE.

IT is a strange, though familiar fact, that great differences of opinion exist respecting the Interpretation of Scripture. All Christians receive the Old and New Testament as sacred writings, but they are not agreed about the meaning which they attribute to them. The book itself remains as at the first; the commentators seem rather to reflect the changing atmosphere of the world or of the Church. Different individuals or bodies of Christians have a different point of view, to which their interpretation is narrowed or made to conform. It is assumed, as natural and necessary, that the same words will present one idea to the mind of the Protestant, another to the Roman Catholic; one meaning to the German, another to the English interpreter. The Ultramontane or Anglican divine is not supposed to be impartial in his treatment of passages which afford an apparent foundation for the doctrine of purgatory or the primacy of St. Peter on the one hand, or the three orders of clergy and the divine origin of episcopacy on the other. It is a received view with many, that the meaning of the Bible is to be defined by that of the Prayer-book; while there are others who interpret 'the Bible and the Bible only' with a silent reference to the traditions of the Reformation. Philosophical differences are in the background, into which the differences about Scripture also resolve themselves. They seem to run

up at last into a difference of opinion respecting Revelation itself—whether given beside the human faculties
or through them, whether an interruption of the laws
of nature or their perfection and fulfilment.

This effort to pull the authority of Scripture in
different directions is not peculiar to our own day ;
the same phenomenon appears in the past history of
the Church. At the Reformation, in the Nicene or
Pelagian times, the New Testament was the ground
over which men fought ; it might also be compared
to the armoury which furnished them with weapons.
Opposite aspects of the truth which it contains were
appropriated by different sides. 'Justified by faith
without works' and 'justified by faith as well as works'
are equally Scriptural expressions ; the one has become
the formula of Protestants, the other of Roman
Catholics. The fifth and ninth chapters of the
Romans, single verses such as 1 Corinthians iii. 15,
John iii. 3, still bear traces of many a life-long strife
in the pages of commentators. The difference of
interpretation which prevails among ourselves is partly
traditional, that is to say, inherited from the controversies of former ages. The use made of Scripture
by Fathers of the Church, as well as by Luther and
Calvin, affects our idea of its meaning at the present
hour.

Another cause of the multitude of interpretations
is the growth or progress of the human mind itself.
Modes of interpreting vary as time goes on; they
partake of the general state of literature or knowledge.
It has not been easily or at once that mankind have
learned to realize the character of sacred writings—
they seem almost necessarily to veil themselves from
human eyes as circumstances change; it is the old
age of the world only that has at length understood
its childhood. (Or rather perhaps is beginning to
understand it, and learning to make allowance for its
own deficiency of knowledge ; for the infancy of the

human race, as of the individual, affords but few indications of the workings of the mind within.) More often than we suppose the great sayings and doings upon the earth, 'thoughts that breathe and words that burn,' are lost in a sort of chaos to the apprehension of those that come after. Much of past history is dimly seen and receives only a conventional interpretation, even when the memorials of it remain. There is a time at which the freshness of early literature is lost; mankind have turned rhetoricians, and no longer write or feel in the spirit which created it. In this unimaginative period in which sacred or ancient writings are partially unintelligible, many methods have been taken at different times to adapt the ideas of the past to the wants of the present. One age has wandered into the flowery paths of allegory,

'In pious meditation fancy fed.'

Another has straitened the liberty of the Gospel by a rigid application of logic, the former being a method which was at first more naturally applied to the Old Testament, the latter to the New. Both methods of interpretation, the mystical and logical, as they may be termed, have been practised on the Vedas and the Koran, as well as on the Jewish and Christian Scriptures, the true glory and note of divinity in these latter being not that they have hidden mysterious or double meanings, but a simple and universal one, which is beyond them and will survive them. Since the revival of literature, interpreters have not unfrequently fallen into error of another kind from a pedantic and misplaced use of classical learning; the minute examination of words often withdrawing the mind from more important matters. A tendency may be observed within the last century to clothe systems of philosophy in the phraseology of Scripture. But new wine cannot thus be put 'into old bottles.'

Though roughly distinguishable by different ages, these modes or tendencies also exist together; the remains of all of them may be remarked in some of the popular commentaries of our own day.

More common than any of these methods, and not peculiar to any age, is that which may be called by way of distinction the rhetorical one. The tendency to exaggerate or amplify the meaning of simple words for the sake of edification may indeed have a practical use in sermons, the object of which is to awaken not so much the intellect as the heart and conscience. Spiritual food, like natural, may require to be of a certain bulk to nourish the human mind. But this 'tendency to edification' has had an unfortunate influence on the interpretation of Scripture. For the preacher almost necessarily oversteps the limits of actual knowledge, his feelings overflow with the subject; even if he have the power, he has seldom the time for accurate thought or inquiry. And in the course of years spent in writing, perhaps, without study, he is apt to persuade himself, if not others, of the truth of his own repetitions. The trivial consideration of making a discourse of sufficient length is often a reason why he overlays the words of Christ and his Apostles with commonplaces. The meaning of the text is not always the object which he has in view, but some moral or religious lesson which he has found it necessary to append to it; some cause which he is pleading, some error of the day which he has to combat. And while in some passages he hardly dares to trust himself with the full force of Scripture (Matthew v. 34; ix. 13; xix. 21; Acts v. 29), in others he extracts more from words than they really imply (Matthew xxii. 21; xxviii. 20; Romans xiii. 1; &c.), being more eager to guard against the abuse of some precept than to enforce it, attenuating or adapting the utterance of prophecy to the requirements or to the measure of modern times. Any one who has ever written sermons is aware how hard it is to apply Scripture to the wants of his hearers and at the same time to preserve its meaning.

The phenomenon which has been described in the preceding pages is so familiar, and yet so extraordinary, that it requires an effort of thought to appreciate its true nature. We do not at once see the absurdity of the same words having many senses, or free our minds from the illusion that the Apostle or Evangelist must have written with a reference to the creeds or controversies or circumstances of other times. Let it be considered, then, that this extreme variety of interpretation is found to exist in the case of no other book, but of the Scriptures only. Other writings are preserved to us in dead languages—Greek, Latin, Oriental, some of them in fragments, all of them originally in manuscript. It is true that difficulties arise in the explanation of these writings, especially in the most ancient, from our imperfect acquaintance with the meaning of words, or the defectiveness of copies, or the want of some historical or geographical information which is required to present an event or character in its true bearing. In comparison with the wealth and light of modern literature, our knowledge of Greek classical authors, for example, may be called imperfect and shadowy. Some of them have another sort of difficulty arising from subtlety or abruptness in the use of language; in lyric poetry especially, and some of the earlier prose, the greatness of the thought struggles with the stammering lips. It may be observed that all these difficulties occur also in Scripture; they are found equally in sacred and profane literature. But the meaning of classical authors is known with comparative certainty; and the interpretation of them seems to rest on a scientific basis. It is not, therefore, to philological or historical difficulties that the greater part of the uncertainty in the interpretation of Scripture is to be attributed. No ignorance of Hebrew or Greek is sufficient to account for it. Even the Vedas and the Zendavesta, though beset by obscurities of language probably greater than are found in any portion of the Bible, are interpreted, at least by European scholars, according to fixed rules, and beginning to be clearly understood.

To bring the parallel home, let us imagine the remains of some well-known Greek author, as Plato or Sophocles, receiving the same treatment at the hands of the world which the Scriptures have experienced. The text of such an author, when first printed by Aldus or Stephens, would be gathered from the imperfect or miswritten copies which fell in the way of the editors; after awhile older and better manuscripts come to light, and the power of using and estimating the value of manuscripts is greatly improved. We may suppose, further, that the readings of these older copies do not always conform to some received canons of criticism. Up to the year 1550, or 1624, alterations, often proceeding on no principle, have been introduced into the text; but now a stand is made—an edition which appeared at the latter of the two dates just mentioned is invested with authority; this authorized text is a *pièce de resistance* against innovation. Many reasons are given why it is better to have bad readings to which the world is accustomed than good ones which are novel and strange—why the later manuscripts of Plato or Sophocles are often to be preferred to earlier ones—why it is useless to remove imperfections where perfect accuracy is not to be attained. A fear of disturbing the critical canons which have come down from former ages is, however, suspected to be one reason for the opposition. And custom and prejudice, and the nicety of the subject, and all the arguments which are intelligible to the many against the truth, which is intelligible only to the few, are thrown into the scale to preserve the works of Plato or Sophocles as nearly as possible in the received text.

Leaving the text we proceed to interpret and trans-late. The meaning of Greek words is known with tolerable certainty; and the grammar of the Greek language has been minutely analysed both in ancient and modern times. Yet the interpretation of Sophocles is tentative and uncertain; it seems to vary from age to age: to some the great tragedian has appeared to embody in his choruses certain theological or moral ideas of his own age or country; there are others who find there an allegory of the Christian religion or of the history of modern Europe. Several schools of critics have commented on his works; to the English-man he has presented one meaning, to the Frenchman another, to the German a third; the interpretations have also differed with the philosophical systems which the interpreters espoused. To one the same words have appeared to bear a moral, to another a symbolical meaning; a third is determined wholly by the authority of old commentators; while there is a dis-position to condemn the scholar who seeks to interpret Sophocles from himself only and with reference to the ideas and beliefs of the age in which he lived. And the error of such an one is attributed not only to some intellectual but even to a moral obliquity which pre-vents his seeing the true meaning.

It would be tedious to follow into details the absur-dity which has been supposed. By such methods it would be truly said that Sophocles or Plato may be made to mean anything. It would seem as if some *Novum Organum* were needed to lay down rules of inter-pretation for ancient literature. Still one other sup-position has to be introduced which will appear, perhaps, more extravagant than any which have pre-ceded. Conceive then that these modes of interpreting Sophocles had existed for ages; that great institutions and interests had become interwoven with them, and in some degree even the honour of nations and churches —is it too much to say that in such a case they would be changed with difficulty, and that they would continue to be maintained long after critics and philosophers had seen that they were indefensible?

No one who has a Christian feeling would place classical on a level with sacred literature; and there are other particulars in which the preceding comparison fails, as, for example, the style and subject. But, however different the subject, although the interpretation of Scripture requires 'a vision and faculty divine,' or at least a moral and religious interest which is not needed in the study of a Greek poet or philosopher, yet in what may be termed the externals of interpretation, that is to say, the meaning of words, the connexion of sentences, the settlement of the text, the evidence of facts, the same rules apply to the Old and New Testaments as to other books. And the figure is no exaggeration of the erring fancy of men in the use of Scripture, or of the tenacity with which they cling to the interpretations of other times, or of the arguments by which they maintain them. All the resources of knowledge may be turned into a means not of discovering the true rendering, but of upholding a received one. Grammar appears to start from an independent point of view, yet inquiries into the use of the article or the preposition have been observed to wind round into a defence of some doctrine. Rhetoric often magnifies its own want of taste into the design of inspiration. Logic (that other mode of rhetoric) is apt to lend itself to the illusion, by stating erroneous explanations with a clearness which is mistaken for truth. 'Metaphysical aid' carries away the common understanding into a region where it must blindly follow. Learning obscures as well as illustrates; it heaps up chaff when there is no more wheat. These are some of the ways in which the sense of Scripture has become confused, by the help of tradition, in the course of ages, under a load of commentators.

The book itself remains as at the first unchanged

z

amid the changing interpretations of it. The office of the interpreter is not to add another, but to recover the original one; the meaning, that is, of the words as they first struck on the ears or flashed before the eyes of those who heard and read them. He has to transfer himself to another age; to imagine that he is a disciple of Christ or Paul; to disengage himself from all that follows. The history of Christendom is nothing to him; but only the scene at Galilee or Jerusalem, the handful of believers who gathered themselves together at Ephesus, or Corinth, or Rome. His eye is fixed on the form of one like the Son of man, or of the prophet who was girded with a garment of camel's hair, or of the Apostle who had a thorn in the flesh. The greatness of the Roman Empire is nothing to him; it is an inner not an outer world that he is striving to restore. All the after-thoughts of theology are nothing to him; they are not the true lights which light him in difficult places. His concern is with a book in which as in other ancient writings are some things of which we are ignorant; which defect of our knowledge cannot however be supplied by the conjectures of fathers or divines. The simple words of that book he tries to preserve absolutely pure from the refinements or distinctions of later times. He acknowledges that they are fragmentary, and would suspect himself, if out of fragments he were able to create a well-rounded system or a continuous history. The greater part of his learning is a knowledge of the text itself; he has no delight in the voluminous literature which has overgrown it. He has no theory of interpretation; a few rules guarding against common errors are enough for him. His object is to read Scripture like any other book, with a real interest and not merely a conventional one. He wants to be able to open his eyes and see or imagine things as they truly are.

Nothing would be more likely to restore a natural feeling on this subject than a history of the Interpretation of Scripture. It would take us back to the beginning; it would present in one view the causes which have darkened the meaning of words in the course of ages; it would clear away the remains of dogmas, systems, controversies, which are encrusted upon them. It would show us the 'erring fancy' of interpreters assuming sometimes to have the Spirit of God Himself, yet unable to pass beyond the limits of their own age, and with a judgment often biassed by party. Great names there have been among them, names of men who may be reckoned also among the benefactors of the human race, yet comparatively few who have understood the thoughts of other times, or who have bent their minds to 'interrogate' the meaning of words. Such a work would enable us to separate the elements of doctrine and tradition with which the meaning of Scripture is encumbered in our own day. It would mark the different epochs of interpretation from the time when the living word was in process of becoming a book to Origen and Tertullian, from Origen to Jerome and Augustine, from Jerome and Augustine to Abelard and Aquinas; again making a new beginning with the revival of literature, from Erasmus, the father of Biblical criticism in more recent times, with Calvin and Beza for his immediate successors, through Grotius and Hammond, down to De Wette and Meier, our own contemporaries. We should see how the mystical interpretation of Scripture originated in the Alexandrian age; how it blended with the logical and rhetorical; how both received weight and currency from their use in support of the claims and teaching of the Church. We should notice how the 'new learning' of the fifteenth and sixteenth centuries gradually awakened the critical faculty in the study of the sacred writings; how Biblical criticism has slowly but surely followed in the track of philological and historical (not without a remoter influence

z 2

exercised upon it also by natural science) ; how, too, the form of the scholastic literature, and even of notes on the classics, insensibly communicated itself to commentaries on Scripture. We should see how the word inspiration, from being used in a general way to express what may be called the prophetic spirit of Scripture, has passed, within the last two centuries, into a sort of technical term ; how, in other instances, the practice or feeling of earlier ages has been hollowed out into the theory or system of later ones. We should observe how the popular explanations of prophecy as in heathen (Thucyd. ii. 54), so also in Christian times, had adapted themselves to the circumstances of mankind. We might remark that in our own country, and in the present generation especially, the interpretation of Scripture had assumed an apologetic character, as though making an effort to defend itself against some supposed inroad of science and criticism ; while among German commentators there is, for the first time in the history of the world, an approach to agreement and certainty. For example, the diversity among German writers on prophecy is far less than among English ones. That is a new phenomenon which has to be acknowledged. More than any other subject of human knowledge, Biblical criticism has hung to the past ; it has been hitherto found truer to the traditions of the Church than to the words of Christ. It has made, however, two great steps onward—at the time of the Reformation and in our day. The diffusion of a critical spirit in history and literature is affecting the criticism of the Bible in our own day in a manner not unlike the burst of intellectual life in the fifteenth or sixteenth centuries. Educated persons are beginning to ask, not what Scripture may be made to mean, but what it does. And it is no exaggeration to say that he who in the present state of knowledge will confine himself to the plain meaning of words and the study of their context may know more of the original spirit and intention of the authors of the New Testament than all the controversial writers of former ages put together.

Such a history would be of great value to philosophy as well as to theology. It would be the history of the human mind in one of its most remarkable manifestations. For ages which are not original show their character in the interpretation of ancient writings. Creating nothing, and incapable of that effort of imagination which is required in a true criticism of the past, they read and explain the thoughts of former times by the conventional modes of their own. Such a history would form a kind of preface or prolegomena to the study of Scripture. Like the history of science, it would save many a useless toil; it would indicate the uncertainties on which it is not worth while to speculate further; the byepaths or labyrinths in which men lose themselves; the mines that are already worked out. He who reflects on the multitude of explanations which already exist of the 'number of the beast,' 'the two witnesses,' 'the little horn,' 'the man of sin,' who observes the manner in which these explanations have varied with the political movements of our own time, will be unwilling to devote himself to a method of inquiry in which there is so little appearance of certainty or progress. These interpretations would destroy one another if they were all placed side by side in a tabular analysis. It is an instructive fact, which may be mentioned in passing, that Joseph Mede, the greatest authority on this subject, twice fixed the end of the world in the last century and once during his own lifetime. In like manner, he who notices the circumstance that the explanations of the first chapter of Genesis have slowly changed, and, as it were, retreated before the advance of geology, will be unwilling to add another to the spurious reconcilements of science and revelation. Or to take an example of another kind, the Protestant divine who perceives that the types and figures of the Old Testament are employed by Roman Catholics in support of the tenets of their church, will be careful not to use weapons which it is impossible to guide, and which may with equal force be turned against himself. Those who have handled them on the Protestant side have before now fallen victims to them, not observing as they fell that it was by their own hand.

Much of the uncertainty which prevails in the interpretation of Scripture arises out of party efforts to wrest its meaning to different sides. There are, however, deeper reasons which have hindered the natural meaning of the text from immediately and universally prevailing. One of these is the unsettlement of many questions which have an important but indirect bearing on this subject. Some of these questions veil themselves in ambiguous terms; and no one likes to draw them out of their hiding-place into the light of day. In natural science it is felt to be useless to build on assumptions; in history we look with suspicion on *a priori* ideas of what ought to have been; in mathematics, when a step is wrong, we pull the house down until we reach the point at which the error is discovered. But in theology it is otherwise; there the tendency has been to conceal the unsoundness of the foundation under the fairness and loftiness of the superstructure. It has been thought safer to allow arguments to stand which, although fallacious, have been on the right side, than to point out their defect. And thus many principles have imperceptibly grown up which have overridden facts. No one would interpret Scripture, as many do, but for certain previous suppositions with which we come to the perusal of it. 'There can be no error in the Word of God,' therefore the discrepancies in the books of Kings and Chronicles are only apparent, or may be attributed to differences in the copies. 'It is a thousand times more likely that the interpreter should err

than the inspired writer.' For a like reason the failure
of a prophecy is never admitted, in spite of Scripture
and of history (Jer. xxxvi. 30; Isai. xxiii.; Amos vii.
10—17); the mention of a name later than the supposed age of the prophet is not allowed, as in other
writings, to be taken in evidence of the date (Isaiah
xlv. 1). The accuracy of the Old Testament is measured not by the standard of primeval history, but of
a modern critical one, which, contrary to all probability,
is supposed to be attained; this arbitrary standard
once assumed, it becomes a point of honour or of faith
to defend every name, date, place, which occurs. Or
to take another class of questions, it is said that 'the
various theories of the origin of the three first Gospels
are all equally unknown to the Holy Catholic Church,'
or as another writer of a different school expresses
himself, 'they tend to sap the inspiration of the New
Testament.' Again, the language in which our Saviour
speaks of his own union with the Father is interpreted
by the language of the creeds. Those who remonstrate
against double senses, allegorical interpretations, forced
reconcilements, find themselves met by a sort of pre-
supposition that 'God speaks not as man speaks.'
The limitation of the human faculties is confusedly
appealed to as a reason for abstaining from investigations which are quite within their limits. The suspicion of Deism, or perhaps of Atheism, awaits inquiry. By such fears a good man refuses to be influenced, a philosophical mind is apt to cast them aside
with too much bitterness. It is better to close the
book than to read it under conditions of thought which
are imposed from without. Whether those conditions
of thought are the traditions of the Church, or the
opinions of the religious world—Catholic or Protestant
—makes no difference. They are inconsistent with
the freedom of the truth and the moral character of
the Gospel. It becomes necessary, therefore, to exa-

mine briefly some of these prior questions which lie in the way of a reasonable criticism.

§ 2.

Among these previous questions, that which first presents itself is the one already alluded to—the question of inspiration. Almost all Christians agree in the word, which use and tradition have consecrated to express the reverence which they truly feel for the Old and New Testaments. But here the agreement of opinion ends; the meaning of inspiration has been variously explained, or more often passed over in silence from a fear of stirring the difficulties that would arise about it. It is one of those theological terms which may be regarded as 'great peacemakers,' but which are also sources of distrust and misunderstanding. For while we are ready to shake hands with any one who uses the same language as ourselves, a doubt is apt to insinuate itself whether he takes language in the same senses—whether a particular term conveys all the associations to another which it does to ourselves—whether it is not possible that one who disagrees about the word may not be more nearly agreed about the thing. The advice has, indeed, been given to the theologian that he 'should take care of words and leave things to themselves;' the authority, however, who gives the advice is not good—it is placed by Goethe in the mouth of Mephistopheles. Pascal seriously charges the Jesuits with acting on a similar maxim—excommunicating those who meant the same thing and said another, holding communion with those who said the same thing and meant another. But this is not the way to heal the wounds of the Church of Christ; we cannot thus 'skin and film' the weak places of theology. Errors about words, and the attribution to words themselves of an excessive importance, lie at the root of theological as of other confusions. In theology they are more dangerous than in other sciences, because they cannot so readily be brought to the test of facts.

The word inspiration has received more numerous gradations and distinctions of meaning than perhaps any other in the whole of theology. There is an inspiration of superintendence and an inspiration of suggestion; an inspiration which would have been consistent with the Apostle or Evangelist falling into error, and an inspiration which would have prevented him from erring; verbal organic inspiration by which the inspired person is the passive utterer of a Divine Word, and an inspiration which acts through the character of the sacred writer; there is an inspiration which absolutely communicates the fact to be revealed or statement to be made, and an inspiration which does not supersede the ordinary knowledge of human events; there is an inspiration which demands infallibility in matters of doctrine, but allows for mistakes in fact. Lastly, there is a view of inspiration which recognises only its supernatural and prophetic character, and a view of inspiration which regards the Apostles and Evangelists as equally inspired in their writings and in their lives, and in both receiving the guidance of the Spirit of truth in a manner not different in kind but only in degree from ordinary Christians. Many of these explanations lose sight of the original meaning and derivation of the word; some of them are framed with the view of meeting difficulties; all perhaps err in attempting to define what, though real, is incapable of being defined in an exact manner. Nor for any of the higher or supernatural views of inspiration is there any foundation in the Gospels or Epistles. There is no appearance in their writings that the Evangelists or Apostles had any inward gift, or were subject to any power external to them different from that of preaching or teaching which they daily exercised; nor do they anywhere lead us to suppose that they were free from error or infirmity. St. Paul writes

like a Christian teacher, exhibiting all the emotions
and vicissitudes of human feeling, speaking, indeed,
with authority, but hesitating in difficult cases and
more than once correcting himself, corrected, too, by
the course of events in his expectation of the coming
of Christ. The Evangelist 'who saw it, bare record,
and his record is true : and he knoweth that he saith
true' (John xix. 35). Another Evangelist does not
profess to be an original narrator, but only 'to set
forth in order a declaration of what eye-witnesses had
delivered,' like many others whose writings have not
been preserved to us (Luke i. 1, 2). And the result is
in accordance with the simple profession and style in
which they describe themselves ; there is no appearance, that is to say, of insincerity or want of faith ;
but neither is there perfect accuracy or agreement.
One supposes the original dwelling-place of our Lord's
parents to have been Bethlehem (Matthew ii. 1, 22),
another Nazareth (Luke ii. 4) ; they trace his genealogy
in different ways ; one mentions the thieves blas-
pheming, another has preserved to after-ages the
record of the penitent thief ; they appear to differ
about the day and hour of the Crucifixion ; the
narrative of the woman who anointed our Lord's feet
with ointment is told in all four, each narrative having
more or less considerable variations. These are a few
instances of the differences which arose in the traditions of the earliest ages respecting the history of
our Lord. But he who wishes to investigate the
character of the sacred writings should not be afraid
to make a catalogue of them all with the view of
estimating their cumulative weight. (For it is obvious
that the answer which would be admitted in the case
of a single discrepancy, will not be the true answer
when there are many.) He should further consider that
the narratives in which these discrepancies occur are
short and partly identical—a cycle of tradition beyond
which the knowledge of the early fathers never travels,
though if all the things that Jesus said and did had

been written down, 'the world itself could not have contained the books that would have been written' (John xx. 30; xxi. 25). For the proportion which these narratives bear to the whole subject, as well as their relation to one another, is an important element in the estimation of differences. In the same way, he who would understand the nature of prophecy in the Old Testament, should have the courage to examine how far its details were minutely fulfilled. The absence of such a fulfilment may further lead him to discover that he took the letter for the spirit in expecting it.

The subject will clear of itself if we bear in mind two considerations:—First, that the nature of inspiration can only be known from the examination of Scripture. There is no other source to which we can turn for information; and we have no right to assume some imaginary doctrine of inspiration like the infallibility of the Roman Catholic Church. To the question, ' What is inspiration?' the first answer therefore is, ' That idea of Scripture which we gather from the knowledge of it.' It is no mere *a priori* notion, but one to which the book is itself a witness. It is a fact which we infer from the study of Scripture—not of one portion only, but of the whole. Obviously then it embraces writings of very different kinds—the book of Esther, for example, or the Song of Solomon, as well as the Gospel of St. John. It is reconcileable with the mixed good and evil of the characters of the Old Testament, which nevertheless does not exclude them from the favour of God, with the attribution to the Divine Being of actions at variance with that higher revelation, which he has given of himself in the Gospel; it is not inconsistent with imperfect or opposite aspects of the truth as in the book of Job or Ecclesiastes, with variations of fact in the Gospels or the books of Kings and Chronicles, with inaccuracies of language in the Epistles of St. Paul. For these are all found in Scripture; neither is there any reason why they should not be, except a general impression that Scripture

ought to have been written in a way different from
what it has.  A principle of progressive revelation
admits them all ; and this is already contained in the
words of our Saviour, 'Moses because of the hardness
of your hearts ;' or even in the Old Testament, ' Henceforth there shall be no more this proverb in the house
of Israel.'  For what is progressive is necessarily imperfect in its earlier stages, and even erring to those
who come after, whether it be the maxims of a half-
civilized world which are compared with those of a
civilized one, or the law with the Gospel.  Scripture
itself points the way to answer the moral objections to
Scripture.  Lesser difficulties remain, but only such as
would be found commonly in writings of the same age
or country.  There is no more reason why imperfect
narratives should be excluded from Scripture than
imperfect grammar ; no more ground for expecting
that the New Testament would be logical or Aristotelian
in form, than that it would be written in Attic Greek.

The other consideration is one which has been
neglected by writers on this subject.  It is this—
that any true doctrine of inspiration must conform to
all well-ascertained facts of history or of science.
The same fact cannot be true and untrue, any more
than the same words can have two opposite meanings.
The same fact cannot be true in religion when seen
by the light of faith, and untrue in science when looked
at through the medium of evidence or experiment.
It is ridiculous to suppose that the sun goes round the
earth in the same sense in which the earth goes round
the sun ; or that the world appears to have existed,
but has not existed during the vast epochs of which
geology speaks to us.  But if so, there is no need of
elaborate reconcilements of revelation and science ;
they reconcile themselves the moment any scientific
truth is distinctly ascertained.  As the idea of nature
enlarges, the idea of revelation also enlarges ; it was
a temporary misunderstanding which severed them.
And as the knowledge of nature which is possessed by

the few is communicated in its leading features at least to the many, they will receive with it a higher conception of the ways of God to man. It may hereafter appear as natural to the majority of mankind to see the providence of God in the order of the world, as it once was to appeal to interruptions of it.

It is true that there are a class of scientific facts with which popular opinions on theology often conflict which do not seem to conform in all respects to the severer conditions of inductive science : such especially are the facts relating to the formation of the earth and the beginnings of the human race. But it is not worth while to fight on this debateable ground a losing battle in the hope that a generation will pass away before we sound a last retreat. Almost all intelligent persons are agreed that the earth has existed for myriads of ages; the best informed are of opinion that the history of nations extends back some thousand years before the Mosaic chronology; recent discoveries in geology may perhaps open a further vista of existence for the human species, while it is possible, and may one day be known, that mankind spread not from one but from many centres over the globe; or as others say, that the supply of links which are at present wanting in the chain of animal life may lead to new conclusions respecting the origin of man. Now let it be granted that these facts, being with the past, cannot be shown in the same palpable and evident manner as the facts of chemistry or physiology ; and that the proof of some of them, especially of those last mentioned, is wanting ; still it is a false policy to set up inspiration or revelation in opposition to them, a principle which can have no influence on them and should be rather kept out of their way. The sciences of geology and comparative philology are steadily gaining ground (many of the guesses of twenty years ago have become certainties, and the guesses of to-day may hereafter become so). Shall we peril religion on the possibility of their untruth? on such a cast to stake

the life of man implies not only a recklessness of facts
but a misunderstanding of the nature of the Gospel.
If it is fortunate for science, it is perhaps more fortunate for Christian truth, that the admission of Galileo's discovery has for ever settled the principle of the
relations between them.

A similar train of thought may be extended to the
results of historical inquiries. These results cannot be barred by the dates or narrative of Scripture ;
neither should they be made to wind round into agreement with them. Again, the idea of inspiration must
expand and take them in. Their importance in a
religious point of view is not that they impugn or
confirm the Jewish history, but that they show more
clearly the purposes of God towards the whole human
race. The recent chronological discoveries from
Egyptian monuments do not tend to overthrow revelation, nor the Ninevite inscriptions to support it.
The use of them on either side may indeed arouse a
popular interest in them; it is apt to turn a scientific
inquiry into a semi-religious controversy. And to
religion either use is almost equally injurious, because
seeming to rest truths important to human life on the
mere accident of an archæological discovery. Is it to
be thought that Christianity gains anything from the
deciphering of the names of some Assyrian and Babylonian kings, contemporaries chiefly with the later
Jewish history ? As little as it ought to lose from the
appearance of a contradictory narrative of the Exodus
in the chamber of an Egyptian temple of the year
B.C. 1500. This latter supposition may not be very
probable. But it is worth while to ask ourselves the
question whether we can be right in maintaining any
view of religion which can be affected by such a probability.

It will be a further assistance in the consideration
of this subject, to observe that the interpretation of
Scripture has nothing to do with any opinion respecting its origin. The meaning of Scripture is one

thing; the inspiration of Scripture is another. It is conceivable that those who hold the most different views about the one, may be able to agree about the other. Rigid upholders of the verbal inspiration of Scripture, and those who deny inspiration altogether, may nevertheless meet on the common ground of the meaning of words. If the term inspiration were to fall into disuse, no fact of nature, or history, or language, no event in the life of man, or dealings of God with him, would be in any degree altered. The word itself is but of yesterday, not found in the earlier confessions of the reformed faith; the difficulties that have arisen about it are only two or three centuries old. Therefore the question of inspiration, though in one sense important, is to the interpreter as though it were not important; he is in no way called upon to determine a matter with which he has nothing to do, and which was not determined by fathers of the Church. And he had better go on his way and leave the more precise definition of the word to the progress of knowledge and the results of the study of Scripture, instead of entangling himself with a theory about it.

It is one evil of conditions or previous suppositions in the study of Scripture that the assumption of them has led to an apologetic temper in the interpreters of Scripture. The tone of apology is always a tone of weakness and does injury to a good cause. It is the reverse of 'ye shall know the truth, and the truth shall make you free.' It is hampered with the necessity of making a defence, and also with previous defences of the same side; it accepts, with an excess of reserve and caution, the truth itself, when it comes from an opposite quarter. Commentators are often more occupied with the proof of miracles than with the declaration of life and immortality; with the fulfilment of the details of prophecy than with its life and power; with the reconcilement of the discrepancies in the narrative of the infancy, pointed out by Schleiermacher, than with the importance of the great event of the appearance of the Saviour. ' *To this end was I born and for this cause came I into the world that I should bear witness unto the truth.*' The same tendency is observable also in reference to the Acts of the Apostles and the Epistles, which are not only brought into harmony with each other, but interpreted with a reference to the traditions of existing communions. The natural meaning of particular expressions, as for example : ' Why are they then baptized for the dead' (1 Corinthians xv. 29)? or the words 'because of the angels' (1 Corinthians xi. 10); or, 'this generation shall not pass away until all these things be fulfilled' (Matthew xxiv. 34); or, 'upon this rock will I build my Church (Matthew xvi. 18), is set aside in favour of others, which, however improbable, are more in accordance with preconceived opinions, or seem to be more worthy of the Sacred writers. The language, and also the text, are treated on the same defensive and conservative principles. The received translations of Philippians ii. 6 (' Who, being in the form of God, thought it not robbery to be equal with God'), or of Romans iii. 25 (' Whom God hath set forth to be a propitiation through faith in his blood'), or Romans xv. 6 (' God, even the Father of our Lord Jesus Christ'), though erroneous, are not given up without a struggle ; the 1 Timothy iii. 16, and 1 John v. 7, (the three witnesses), though the first (God manifest in the flesh, ΘΣ for ΟΣ) is not found in the best manuscripts, and the second in no Greek manuscript worth speaking of, have not yet disappeared from the editions of the Greek Testament commonly in use in England, and still less from the English translation. An English commentator who, with Lachman and Tischendorf, supported also by the authority of Erasmus, ventures to alter the punctuation of the doxology in Romans ix. 5 (' Who is over all God blessed for ever') hardly escapes the charge of heresy. That in most of these cases the words referred to have a direct bearing on important contro-

versies is a reason not for retaining, but for correcting
them.

The temper of accommodation shows itself especially
in two ways : first, in the attempt to adapt the truths
of Scripture to the doctrines of the creeds; secondly,
in the adaptation of the precepts and maxims of
Scripture to the language or practice of our own age.
Now the creeds are acknowledged to be a part of
Christianity; they stand in a close relation to the
words of Christ and his Apostles; nor can it be said
that any heterodox formula makes a nearer approach
to a simple and scriptural rule of faith.  Neither is
anything gained by contrasting them with Scripture,
in which the germs of the expressions used in them
are sufficiently apparent.  Yet it does not follow that
they should be pressed into the service of the interpreter.  The growth of ideas in the interval which
separated the first century from the fourth or sixth
makes it impossible to apply the language of the one
to the explanation of the other.  Between Scripture
and the Nicene or Athanasian Creed, a world of the
understanding comes in—that world of abstractions
and second notions; and mankind are no longer at
the same point as when the whole of Christianity was
contained in the words, ' Believe on the Lord Jesus
Christ and thou mayest be saved,' when the Gospel
centred in the attachment to a living or recently departed friend and Lord.  The language of the New
Testament is the first utterance and consciousness of
the mind of Christ ; or the immediate vision of the
Word of life (1 John i. 1) as it presented itself before
the eyes of his first followers, or as the sense of his
truth and power grew upon them (Romans i. 3, 4) ;
the other is the result of three or four centuries of
reflection and controversy.  And although this last
had a truth suited to its age, and its technical expressions have sunk deep into the heart of the human race,
it is not the less unfitted to be the medium by the

help of which Scripture is to be explained. If the occurrence of the phraseology of the Nicene age in a verse of the Epistles would detect the spuriousness of the verse in which it was found, how can the Nicene or Athanasian Creed be a suitable instrument for the interpretation of Scripture? That advantage which the New Testament has over the teaching of the Church, as representing what may be termed the childhood of the Gospel, would be lost if its language were required to conform to that of the Creeds.

To attribute to St. Paul or the Twelve the abstract notion of Christian truth which afterwards sprang up in the Catholic Church, is the same sort of anachronism as to attribute to them a system of philosophy. It is the same error as to attribute to Homer the ideas of Thales or Heraclitus, or to Thales the more developed principles of Aristotle and Plato. Many persons who have no difficulty in tracing the growth of institutions, yet seem to fail in recognising the more subtle progress of an idea. It is hard to imagine the absence of conceptions with which we are familiar; to go back to the germ of what we know only in maturity; to give up what has grown to us, and become a part of our minds. In the present case however the development is not difficult to prove. The statements of Scripture are unaccountable if we deny it; the silence of Scripture is equally unaccountable. Absorbed as St. Paul was in the person of Christ with an intensity of faith and love of which in modern days and at this distance of time we can scarcely form a conception—high as he raised the dignity of his Lord above all things in heaven and earth—looking to him as the Creator of all things, and the head of quick and dead, he does not speak of him as 'equal to the Father,' or 'of one substance with the Father.' Much of the language of the Epistles (passages for example such as Romans i. 2; Philippians ii. 6) would lose their meaning if distri-

buted in alternate clauses between our Lord's humanity
and divinity. Still greater difficulties would be introduced into the Gospels by the attempt to identify them
with the Creeds. We should have to suppose that
He was and was not tempted; that when he prayed
to his Father he prayed also to Himself; that He
knew and did not know 'of that hour' of which He as
well as the angels were ignorant. How could He have
said 'My God, my God, why hast thou forsaken me?'
or 'Father, if it be possible let this cup pass from me.'
How could He have doubted whether 'when the Son
cometh he shall find faith upon the earth?' These
simple and touching words have to be taken out of
their natural meaning and connexion to be made the
theme of apologetic discourses if we insist on reconciling them with the distinctions of later ages.

Neither, as has been already remarked, would the
substitution of any other precise or definite rule of
faith, as for example the Unitarian, be more favourable
to the interpretation of Scripture. How could the
Evangelist St. John have said 'the Word was God,'
or 'God was the Word' (according to either mode of
translating), or how would our Lord Himself have
said, 'I and the Father are one,' if either had meant that
Christ was a mere man, 'a prophet or as one of the
prophets?' No one who takes words in their natural
sense can suppose that 'in the beginning' (John i. 1)
means 'at the commencement of the ministry of Christ,'
or that 'the Word was with God,' only relates 'to the
withdrawal of Christ to commune with God,' or
that 'the Word is said to be God,' in the ironical
sense of John x. 35. But while venturing to turn one
eye on these (perhaps obsolete) perversions of the
meanings of words in old opponents, we must not
forget also to keep the other open to our own. The
object of the preceding remark is not to enter into
controversy with them, or to balance the statements of
one side with those of the other, but only to point out the

error of introducing into the interpretation of Scripture the notions of a later age which is common alike to us and them.

The other kind of accommodation which was alluded to above arises out of the difference between the social and ecclesiastical state of the world, as it exists in actual fact, and the ideal which the Gospel presents to us. An ideal is, by its very nature, far removed from actual life. It is enshrined not in the material things of the external world, but in the heart and conscience. Mankind are dissatisfied at this separation; they fancy that they can make the inward kingdom an outward one also. But this is not possible. The frame of civilization, that is to say, institutions and laws, the usages of business, the customs of society, these are for the most part mechanical, capable only in a certain degree of a higher and spiritual life. Christian motives have never existed in such strength, as to make it safe or possible to entrust them with the preservation of social order. Other interests are therefore provided and other principles, often independent of the teaching of the Gospel, or even apparently at variance with it. 'If a man smite thee on the right cheek turn to him the other also,' is not a regulation of police but an ideal rule of conduct, not to be explained away, but rarely if ever to be literally acted upon in a civilized country; or rather to be acted upon always in spirit, yet not without a reference to the interests of the community. If a missionary were to endanger the public peace and come like the Apostles saying, 'I ought to obey God rather than man,' it is obvious that the most Christian of magistrates could not allow him (say in India or New Zealand) to shield himself under the authority of these words. For in religion as in philosophy there are two opposite poles; of truth and action, of doctrine and practice, of idea and fact. The image of God in Christ is over against the necessities of human nature and the state of man on earth. Our Lord himself recognises this distinction, when he says, 'Of whom do the kings of the earth gather tribute?' and 'then are the children free.' (Matth. xvii. 26.) And again, 'Notwithstanding lest we should offend them,' &c. Here are contrasted what may be termed the two poles of idea and fact.

All men appeal to Scripture, and desire to draw the authority of Scripture to their side; its voice may be heard in the turmoil of political strife; a merely verbal similarity, the echo of a word, has weight in the determination of a controversy. Such appeals are not to be met always by counter-appeals; they rather lead to the consideration of deeper questions as to the manner in which Scripture is to be applied. In what relation does it stand to actual life? Is it a law, or only a spirit? for nations, or for individuals? to be enforced generally, or in details also? Are its maxims to be modified by experience, or acted upon in defiance of experience? Are the accidental circumstances of the first believers to become a rule for us? Is everything, in short, done or said by our Saviour and His Apostles, to be regarded as a precept or example which is to be followed on all occasions and to last for all time? That can hardly be, consistently with the changes of human things. It would be a rigid skeleton of Christianity (not the image of Christ), to which society and politics, as well as the lives of individuals, would be conformed. It would be the oldness of the letter, on which the world would be stretched; not 'the law of the spirit of life' which St. Paul teaches. The attempt to force politics and law into the framework of religion is apt to drive us up into a corner, in which the great principles of truth and justice have no longer room to make themselves felt. It is better, as well as safer, to take the liberty with which Christ has made us free. For our Lord himself has left behind Him words, which contain a principle large enough to admit all the forms of

society or of life ; 'My kingdom is not of this world.'
(John xviii. 36.)   It does not come into collision
with politics or knowledge ; it has nothing to do with
the Roman government or the Jewish priesthood, or
with corresponding institutions in the present day ;
it is a counsel of perfection, and has its dwelling-place
in the heart of man.   That is the real solution of
questions of Church and State ;· all else is relative to
the history or circumstances of particular nations.
That is the answer to a doubt which is also raised
respecting the obligation of the letter of the Gospel
on individual Christians.   But this inwardness of the
words of Christ is what few are able to receive ; it is
easier to apply them superficially to things without,
than to be a partaker of them from within.   And false
and miserable applications of them are often made,
and the kingdom of God becomes the tool of the
kingdoms of the world.

The neglect of this necessary contrast between the
ideal and the actual has had a twofold effect on the
Interpretation of Scripture.   It has led to an unfair
appropriation of some portions of Scripture and an
undue neglect of others.   The letter is in many cases
really or apparently in harmony with existing
practices, or opinions, or institutions.   In other
cases it is far removed from them ; it often seems
as if the world would come to an end before the
words of Scripture could be realized.   The twofold
effect just now mentioned, corresponds to these two
classes.   Some texts of Scripture have been eagerly
appealed to and made (in one sense) too much of ;
they have been taken by force into the service of
received opinions and beliefs ; texts of the other class
have been either unnoticed or explained away.   Consider, for example, the extraordinary and unreasonable
importance attached to single words, sometimes of
doubtful meaning, in reference to any of the following
subjects:—1, Divorce ; 2, Marriage with a Wife's Sister ;

3, Inspiration; 4, the Personality of the Holy Spirit; 5, Infant Baptism; 6, Episcopacy; 7, Divine Right of Kings; 8, Original Sin. There is, indeed, a kind of mystery in the way in which the chance words of a simple narrative, the occurrence of some accidental event, the use even of a figure of speech, or a mistranslation of a word in Latin or English, have affected the thoughts of future ages and distant countries. Nothing so slight that it has not been caught at; nothing so plain that it may not be explained away. What men have brought to the text they have also found there; what has received no interpretation or witness, either in the customs of the Church or in ' the thoughts of many hearts,' is still ' an unknown tongue' to them. It is with Scripture as with oratory, its effect partly depends on the preparation in the mind or in circumstances for the reception of it. There is no use of Scripture, no quotation or even misquotation of a word which is not a power in the world, when it embodies the spirit of a great movement or is echoed by the voice of a large party.

On the first of the subjects referred to above, it is argued from Scripture that adulterers should not be allowed to marry again; and the point of the argument turns on the question whether the words (ἐκτὸς λόγου πορνείας) saving for the cause of fornication, which occur in the first clause of an important text on marriage, were designedly or accidentally omitted in the second (Matth. v. 32.)   'Whosoever shall put away his wife, saving for the cause of fornication, causeth her to commit adultery, and whosoever shall marry her that is divorced committeth adultery;' compare also Mark x. 11, 12).  2. The Scripture argument in the second instance is almost invisible, being drawn from a passage the meaning of which is irrelevant (Lev. xviii. 18.  'Neither shalt thou take a wife to her sister to vex her, to uncover her nakedness beside the other in her lifetime'); and transferred from the Polygamy

360 On the Interpretation of Scripture.

which prevailed in Eastern countries 3000 years ago
to the Monogamy of the nineteenth century and the
Christian Church, in spite of the custom and tradition
of the Jews and the analogy of the brother's widow.
3. In the third case the word (θεόπνευστος) 'given by
inspiration of God' is spoken of the Old Testament,
and is assumed to apply to the New, including that
Epistle in which the expression occurs (2 Tim. iii. 16.)
4. In the fourth example the words used are mysterious (John xiv. 26; xvi. 15), and seem to come out
of the depths of a divine consciousness; they have
sometimes, however, received a more exact meaning
than they would truly bear; what is spoken in a figure
is construed with the severity of a logical statement,
while passages of an opposite tenour are overlooked or
set aside.  5. In the fifth instance, the mere mention
of a family of a jailer at Philippi who was baptized
('he and all his,' Acts xvi. 33), has led to the inference
that in this family there were probably young children,
and hence that infant baptism is, first, permissive,
secondly, obligatory.  6. In the sixth case the chief
stress of the argument from Scripture turns on the
occurrence of the word (ἐπίσκοπος) bishop in the
Epistles to Timothy and Titus, which is assisted by a
supposed analogy between the position of the Apostles
and of their successors; although the term bishop is
clearly used in the passages referred to as well as in
other parts of the New Testament indistinguishably
from Presbyter, and the magisterial authority of
bishops in after ages is unlike rather than like the
personal authority of the Apostles in the beginning
of the Gospel. The further development of Episcopacy
into Apostolical succession has often been rested on
the promise, 'Lo, I am with you alway, even to the
end of the world.'  7. In the seventh case the precepts of order which are addressed in the Epistle to
the 'fifth monarchy men of those days,' are transferred
to a duty of obedience to hereditary princes; the fact

of the house of David, 'the Lord's anointed' sitting on the throne of Israel is converted into a principle for all times and countries. And the higher lesson which our Saviour teaches: 'Render unto Cæsar the things which are Cæsar's,' that is to say, 'Render unto all their due, and to God above all,' is spoiled by being made into a precept of political subjection. 8. Lastly, the justice of God 'who rewardeth every man according to his works,' and the Christian scheme of redemption has been staked on two figurative expressions of St. Paul to which there is no parallel in any other part of Scripture (1 Corinthians xv. 22. 'For as in Adam all die, even so in Christ shall all be made alive,' and the corresponding passage in Romans v. 12); notwithstanding the declaration of the Old Testament as also of the New, 'Every soul shall bear its own iniquity,' and 'neither this man sinned nor his parents.' It is not necessary for our purpose to engage further in the matters of dispute which have arisen by the way in attempting to illustrate the general argument. Yet to avoid misconception it may be remarked that many of the principles, rules, or truths mentioned, as for example, Infant Baptism, or the Episcopal Form of Church Government, have sufficient grounds; the weakness is the attempt to derive them from Scripture.

With this minute and rigid enforcement of the words of Scripture in passages where the ideas expressed in them either really or apparently agree with received opinions or institutions, there remains to be contrasted the neglect, or in some instances the misinterpretation of other words which are not equally in harmony with the spirit of the age. In many of our Lord's discourses he speaks of the 'blessedness of poverty:' of the hardness which they that have riches will experience 'in attaining eternal life.' 'It is easier for a camel to go through a needle's eye,' and 'Son, thou in thy lifetime receivedst thy good things,' and again, 'One thing thou lackest, go sell all that thou hast.'

Precepts like these do not appeal to our own experience of life; they are unlike anything that we see around us at the present day, even among good men; to some among us they will recall the remarkable saying of Lessing,—'that the Christian religion had been tried for eighteen centuries; the religion of Christ remained to be tried.' To take them literally would be injurious to ourselves and to society (at least, so we think). Religious sects or orders who have seized this aspect of Christianity have come to no good, and have often ended in extravagance. It will not do to go into the world saying 'Woe unto you, ye rich men,' or on entering a noble mansion to repeat the denunciations of the prophet about 'cedar and vermillion,' or on being shown the prospect of a magnificent estate to cry out 'Woe unto them that lay field to field that they may be placed alone in the midst of the earth.' Times have altered, we say, since these denunciations were uttered; what appeared to the Prophet or Apostle a violation of the appointment of Providence has now become a part of it. It will not do to make a great supper, and mingle at the same board the two ends of society, as modern phraseology calls them, fetching in 'the poor, the maimed, the lame, the blind,' to fill the vacant places of noble guests. That would be eccentric in modern times, and even hurtful. Neither is it suitable for us to wash one another's feet, or to perform any other menial office, because our Lord set us the example. The customs of society do not admit it; no good would be done by it, and singularity is of itself an evil. Well, then, are the precepts of Christ not to be obeyed? Perhaps in their fullest sense they cannot be obeyed. But at any rate they are not to be explained away; the standard of Christ is not to be lowered to ordinary Christian life, because ordinary Christian life cannot rise, even in good men, to the standard of Christ. And there may be 'standing

among us' some one in ten thousand 'whom we know
not,' in whom there is such a divine union of charity
and prudence that he is most blest in the entire fulfilment of the precept—'Go sell all that thou hast,'—
which to obey literally in other cases would be evil,
and not good. Many there have been, doubtless (not
one or two only), who have given all that they had
on earth to their family or friends—the poor servant
'casting her two mites into the treasury,' denying
herself the ordinary comforts of life for the sake of an
erring parent or brother; that is not probably an uncommon case, and as near an approach as in this life
we make to heaven. And there may be some one or
two rare natures in the world in whom there is such
a divine courtesy, such a gentleness and dignity of
soul, that differences of rank seem to vanish before them, and they look upon the face of others,
even of their own servants and dependents, only
as they are in the sight of God and will be in
His kingdom. And there may be some tender and
delicate woman among us, who feels that she has a
divine vocation to fulfil the most repulsive offices
towards the dying inmates of a hospital, or the soldier
perishing in a foreign land. Whether such examples
of self-sacrifice are good or evil, must depend, not
altogether on social or economical principles, but on
the spirit of those who offer them, and the power
which they have in themselves of 'making all things
kin.' And even if the ideal itself were not carried out
by us in practice, it has nevertheless what may be
termed a truth of feeling. 'Let them that have
riches be as though they had them not.' 'Let the rich
man wear the load lightly; he will one day fold them
up as a vesture.' Let not the refinement of society
make us forget that it is not the refined only who are
received into the kingdom of God; nor the daintiness
of life hide from us the bodily evils of which the rich
man and Lazarus are alike heirs. Thoughts such as

these have the power to reunite us to our fellow-creatures from whom the accidents of birth, position, wealth have separated us; they soften our hearts towards them, when divided not only by vice and ignorance, but what is even a greater barrier, difference of manners and associations. For if there be anything in our own fortune superior to that of others, instead of idolizing or cherishing it in the blood, the Gospel would have us cast it from us; and if there be any-thing mean or despised in those with whom we have to do, the Gospel would have us regard such as friends and brethren, yea, even as having the person of Christ.

Another instance of apparent, if not real neglect of the precepts of Scripture, is furnished by the commandment against swearing. No precept about divorce is so plain, so universal, so exclusive as this; 'Swear not at all.' Yet we all know how the custom of Christian countries has modified this 'counsel of perfection' which was uttered by the Saviour. This is the more remarkable because in this case the precept is not, as in the former, practically impossible of fulfilment or even difficult. And yet in this instance again, the body who have endeavoured to follow more nearly the letter of our Lord's commandment, seem to have gone against the common sense of the Christian world. Or to add one more example : Who, that hears of the Sabbatarianism, as it is called, of some Protestant countries, would imagine that the Author of our religion had cautioned his disciples, not against the violation of the Sabbath, but only against its formal and Pharisaical observance; or that the chiefest of the Apostles had warned the Colossians to 'Let no man judge them in respect of the new moon, or of the sabbath-days.' (ii. 16.)

The neglect of another class of passages is even more surprising, the precepts contained in them being quite practicable and in harmony with the existing state of the world. In this instance it seems as if religious teachers had failed to gather those principles of which they stood most in need. 'Think ye that those eighteen upon whom the tower of Siloam fell?' is the characteristic lesson of the Gospel on the occasion of any sudden visitation. Yet it is another reading of such calamities that is commonly insisted upon. The observation is seldom made respecting the parable of the good Samaritan, that the true neighbour is also a person of a different religion. The words, 'Forbid him not: for there is no man which shall do a miracle in my name, that can lightly speak evil of me,' are often said to have no application to sectarian differences in the present day, when the Church is established and miracles have ceased. The conduct of our Lord to the woman taken in adultery, though not intended for our imitation always, yet affords a painful contrast to the excessive severity with which even a Christian society punishes the errors of women. The boldness with which St. Paul applies the principle of individual judgment, 'Let every man be fully persuaded in his mind,' as exhibited also in the words quoted above, 'Let no man judge you in respect of the new moon, or of the sabbath-days,' is far greater than would be allowed in the present age. Lastly, that the tenet of the damnation of the heathen should ever have prevailed in the Christian world, or that the damnation of Catholics should have been a received opinion among Protestants, implies a strange forgetfulness of such passages as Romans ii. 1-16. 'Who rewardeth every man according to his work,' and 'When the Gentiles, which know not the law, do by nature the things contained in the law,' &c. What a difference between the simple statement which the Apostle makes of the justice of God and the 'uncovenanted mercies' or 'invincible ignorance' of theologians half reluctant to give up, yet afraid to maintain the advantage of denying salvation to those who are '*extra palum Ecclesiæ!*'

The same habit of silence or misinterpretation extends to words or statements of Scripture in which

doctrines are thought to be interested.    When maintaining the Athanasian doctrine of the Trinity, we do
not readily recall the verse, ' of that hour knoweth no
man, no not the Angels of God, *neither the Son,* but the
Father.' (Mark xiii. 32.)  The temper or feeling which led
St. Ambrose to doubt the genuineness of the words
marked in italics, leads Christians in our own day to
pass them over.   We are scarcely just to the Mille-
narians or to those who maintain the continuance of
miracles or spiritual gifts in the Christian Church, in
not admitting the degree of support which is afforded
to their views by many passages of Scripture.   The
same remark applies to the Predestinarian controversy;
the Calvinist is often hardly dealt with, in being
deprived of his real standing ground in the third and
ninth chapters of the Epistle to the Romans.   And the
Protestant who thinks himself bound to prove from
Scripture the very details of doctrine or discipline which
are maintained in his Church, is often obliged to have
recourse to harsh methods, and sometimes to deny appearances which seem to favour some particular tenet of
Roman Catholicism.   (Matthew xvi. 18, 19; xviii. 18; 1
Cor. iii. 15.)   The Roman Catholic, on the other hand,
scarcely observes that nearly all the distinctive articles
of his creed are wanting in the New Testament; the
Calvinist in fact ignores almost the whole of the sacred
volume for the sake of a few verses.   The truth is,
that in seeking to prove our own opinions out of
Scripture, we are constantly falling into the common
fallacy of opening our eyes to one class of facts and
closing them to another.   The favourite verses shine
like stars, while the rest of the page is thrown into
the shade.

Nor indeed is it easy to say what is the meaning of
'proving a doctrine from Scripture.'   For when we
demand logical equivalents and similarity of circumstances, when we balance adverse statements, St.
James and St. Paul, the New Testament with the Old,

it will be hard to demonstrate from Scripture any complex system either of doctrine or practice.    The Bible is not a book of statutes in which words have been chosen to cover the multitude of cases, but in the greater portion of it, especially the Gospels and Epistles, ' like a man talking to his friend.'    Nay, more, it is a book written in the East, which is in some degree liable to be misunderstood, because it speaks the language and has the feeling of Eastern lands.    Nor can we readily determine in explaining the words of our Lord or of St. Paul, how much (even of some of the passages just quoted) is to be attributed to Oriental modes of speech.    Expressions which would be regarded as rhetorical exaggerations in the Western world are the natural vehicles of thought to an Eastern people. How great then must be the confusion where an attempt is made to draw out these Oriental modes with the severity of a philosophical or legal argument ! Is it not such a use of the words of Christ which he himself rebukes when he says, ' It is the spirit that quickeneth, the flesh profiteth nothing.'    (John vi. 52, 63.)

There is a further way in which the language of creeds and liturgies as well as the ordinary theological use of terms exercises a disturbing influence on the interpretation of Scripture.    Words which occur in Scripture are singled out and incorporated in systems like stones taken out of an old building and put into a new one.    They acquire a technical meaning more or less divergent from the original one.    It is obvious that their use in Scripture, and not their later and technical sense, must furnish the rule of interpretation. We should not have recourse to the meaning of a word in Polybius, for the explanation of its use in Plato, or to the turn of a sentence in Lycophron, to illustrate a construction of Æschylus.    It is the same kind of anachronism which would interpret Scripture by the scholastic or theological use of the language of

Scripture. It is remarkable that this use is indeed partial, that is to say it affects one class of words and not another. Love and truth, for example, have never been theological terms; grace and faith, on the other hand, always retain an association with the Pelagian or Lutheran controversies. Justification and inspiration are derived from verbs which occur in Scripture, and the later substantive has clearly affected the meaning of the original verb or verbal in the places where they occur. The remark might be further illustrated by the use of Scriptural language respecting the Sacraments, which has also had a reflex influence on its interpretation in many passages of Scripture, especially in the Gospel of St. John. (John iii. 5; vi. 56, &c.) Minds which are familiar with the mystical doctrine of the Sacraments seem to see a reference to them in almost every place in the Old Testament as well as in the New, in which the words 'water,' or 'bread and wine' may happen to occur.

Other questions meet us on the threshold of a different kind, which also affect therefore the interpretation of Scripture, and demand an answer. Is it admitted that the Scripture has one and only one true meaning? Or are we to follow the fathers into mystical and allegorical explanations? or with the majority of modern interpreters to confine ourselves to the double senses of prophecy, and the symbolism of the Gospel in the law? In either case, we assume what can never be proved, and an instrument is introduced of such subtlety and pliability as to make the Scriptures mean anything—'*Gallus in campanili*,' as the Waldenses described it; 'the weathercock on the church tower,' which is turned hither and thither by every wind of doctrine. That the present age has grown out of the mystical methods of the early fathers is a part of its intellectual state. No one will now seek to find hidden meanings in the scarlet thread of Rahab, or the number of Abraham's followers, or in the little circumstance mentioned after the resurrection of the Saviour that St. Peter was the first to enter the sepulchre. To most educated persons in the nineteenth century, these applications of Scripture appear foolish. Yet it is rather the excess of the method which provokes a smile than the method itself. For many remains of the mystical interpretation exist among ourselves; it is not the early fathers only who have read the Bible crosswise, or deciphered it as a book of symbols. And the uncertainty is the same in any part of Scripture if there is a departure from the plain and obvious meaning. If, for example, we alternate the verses in which our Lord speaks of the last things between the day of judgment and the destruction of Jerusalem; or, in the elder prophecies, which are the counterparts of these, make a corresponding division between the temporal and the spiritual Israel ; or again if we attribute to the details of the Mosaical ritual a reference to the New Testament ; or, once more, supposing the passage of the Red Sea to be regarded not merely as a figure of baptism, but as a pre-ordained type, the principle is conceded ; there is no good reason why the scarlet thread of Rahab should not receive the explanation given to it by Clement. A little more or a little less of the method does not make the difference between certainty and uncertainty in the interpretation of Scripture. In whatever degree it is practised it is equally incapable of being reduced to any rule ; it is the interpreter's fancy, and is likely to be not less but more dangerous and extravagant when it adds the charm of authority from its use in past ages.

The question which has been suggested runs up into a more general one, 'the relation between the Old and New Testaments.' For the Old Testament will receive a different meaning accordingly as it is explained from itself or from the New. In the first case a careful and conscientious study of each one for itself is all that is required ; in the second case the types and

ceremonies of the law, perhaps the very facts and persons of the history, will be assumed to be predestined
or made after a pattern corresponding to the things
that were to be in the latter days. And this question
of itself stirs another question respecting the interpretation of the Old Testament in the New. Is such
interpretation to be regarded as the meaning of
the original text, or an accommodation of it to the
thoughts of other times?

Our object is not to attempt here the determination
of these questions, but to point out that they must be
determined before any real progress can be made or
any agreement arrived at in the interpretation of
Scripture. With one more example of another kind
we may close this part of the subject. The origin of
the three first Gospels is an inquiry which has not
been much considered by English theologians since
the days of Bishop Marsh. The difficulty of the
question has been sometimes misunderstood; the
point being how there can be so much agreement in
words, and so much disagreement both in words and
facts; the double phenomenon is the real perplexity—
how in short there can be all degrees of similarity and
dissimilarity, the kind and degree of similarity being
such as to make it necessary to suppose that large
portions are copied from each other or from common
documents; the dissimilarities being of a kind which
seem to render impossible any knowledge in the
authors of one another's writings. The most probable
solution of this difficulty is that the tradition on which
the three first Gospels are based was at first preserved orally, and slowly put together and written
in the three forms which it assumed at a very early
period, those forms being in some places, perhaps,
modified by translation. It is not necessary to develope this hypothesis farther. The point to be noticed
is, that whether this or some other theory be the true
account (and some such account is demonstrably

necessary), the assumption of such a theory, or rather the observation of the facts on which it rests, cannot but exercise an influence on interpretation. We can no longer speak of three independent witnesses of the Gospel narrative. Hence there follow some other consequences. (1.) There is no longer the same necessity as heretofore to reconcile inconsistent narratives; the harmony of the Gospels only means the parallelism of similar words. (2.) There is no longer any need to enforce everywhere the connexion of successive verses, for the same words will be found to occur in different connexions in the different Gospels. (3.) Nor can the designs attributed to their authors be regarded as the free handling of the same subject on different plans; the difference consisting chiefly in the occurrence or absence of local or verbal explanations or the addition or omission of certain passages. Lastly, it is evident that no weight can be given to traditional statements of facts about the authorship, as, for example, that respecting St. Mark being the interpreter of St. Peter, because the Fathers who have handed down these statements were ignorant or unobservant of the great fact, which is proved by internal evidence, that they are for the most part of common origin.

Until these and the like questions are determined by interpreters, it is not possible that there should be agreement in the interpretation of Scripture. The Protestant and Catholic, the Unitarian and Trinitarian will continue to fight their battle on the ground of the New Testament. The Preterists and Futurists, those who maintain that the roll of prophecies is completed in past history, or in the apostolical age; those who look forward to a long series of events which are yet to come [εἰς ἀφανὲς τὸν μῦθον ἀνενεγκὼν οὐκ ἔχει ἔλεγχον], may alike claim the authority of the Book of Daniel, or the Revelation. Apparent coincidences will always be discovered by those who want to find them. Where there is no critical interpreta-

tion of Scripture, there will be a mystical or rhetorical one. If words have more than one meaning, they
may have any meaning. Instead of being a rule of
life or faith, Scripture becomes the expression of the
ever-changing aspect of religious opinions. The unchangeable word of God, in the name of which we
repose, is changed by each age and each generation
in accordance with its passing fancy. The book in
which we believe all religious truth to be contained,
is the most uncertain of all books, because interpreted
by arbitrary and uncertain methods.

§ 2.

It is probable that some of the preceding statements may be censured as a wanton exposure of the
difficulties of Scripture. It will be said that such
inquiries are for the few, while the printed page lies
open to the many, and that the obtrusion of them
may offend some weaker brother, some half-educated
or prejudiced soul, 'for whom,' nevertheless, in the
touching language of St. Paul, 'Christ died.' A confusion of the heart and head may lead sensitive
minds into a desertion of the principles of the Christian life, which are their own witness, because they
are in doubt about facts which are really external to
them. Great evil to character may sometimes ensue
from such causes. 'No man can serve two' opinions
without a sensible harm to his nature. The consciousness of this responsibility should be always
present to writers on theology. But the responsibility is really two-fold; for there is a duty to speak
the truth as well as a duty to withhold it. The voice
of a majority of the clergy throughout the world, the
half sceptical, half conservative instincts of many lay-
men, perhaps, also, individual interest, are in favour of
the latter course; while a higher expediency pleads that
'honesty is the best policy,' and that truth alone
'makes free.' To this, it may be replied that truth
is not truth to those who are unable to use it; no

reasonable man would attempt to lay before the illiterate such a question as that concerning the origin of the Gospels. And yet it may be rejoined once more, the healthy tone of religion among the poor depends upon freedom of thought and inquiry among the educated. In this conflict of reasons, individual judgment must at last decide. That there has been no rude, or improper unveiling of the difficulties of Scripture in the preceding pages, is thought to be shown by the following considerations :

First, that the difficulties referred to are very well known; they force themselves on the attention, not only of the student, but of every intelligent reader of the New Testament, whether in Greek or English. The treatment of such difficulties in theological works is no measure of public opinion respecting them. Thoughtful persons, whose minds have turned towards theology, are continually discovering that the critical observations which they make themselves have been made also by others apparently without concert. The truth is that they have been led to them by the same causes, and these again lie deep in the tendencies of education and literature in the present age. But no one is willing to break through the reticence which is observed on these subjects ; hence a sort of smouldering scepticism. It is probable that the distrust is greatest at the time when the greatest efforts are made to conceal it. Doubt comes in at the window, when Inquiry is denied at the door. The thoughts of able and highly educated young men almost always stray towards the first principles of things; it is a great injury to them, and tends to raise in their minds a sort of incurable suspicion, to find that there is one book of the fruit of the knowledge of which they are forbidden freely to taste, that is, the Bible. The same spirit renders the Christian minister almost powerless in the hands of his opponents. He can give no true answer to the mechanic or artizan who has either discovered by his mother-wit or who retails at second-hand the objections of critics; for he is unable to look at things as they truly are.

Secondly, as the time has come when it is no longer possible to ignore the results of criticism, it is of importance that Christianity should be seen to be in harmony with them. That objections to some received views should be valid, and yet that they should be always held up as the objections of infidels, is a mischief to the Christian cause. It is a mischief that critical observations which any intelligent man can make for himself, should be ascribed to atheism or unbelief. It would be a strange and almost incredible thing that the Gospel, which at first made war only on the vices of mankind, should now be opposed to one of the highest and rarest of human virtues—the love of truth. And that in the present day the great object of Christianity should be, not to change the lives of men, but to prevent them from changing their opinions; that would be a singular inversion of the purposes for which Christ came into the world. The Christian religion is in a false position when all the tendencies of knowledge are opposed to it. Such a position cannot be long maintained, or can only end in the withdrawal of the educated classes from the influences of religion. It is a grave consideration whether we ourselves may not be in an earlier stage of the same religious dissolution, which seems to have gone further in Italy and France. The reason for thinking so is not to be sought in the external circumstances of our own or any other religious communion, but in the progress of ideas with which Christian teachers seem to be ill at ease. Time was when the Gospel was before the age; when it breathed a new life into a decaying world—when the difficulties of Christianity were difficulties of the heart only, and the highest minds found in its truths not only the rule of their lives, but a well-spring of intellectual delight. Is it to be held a thing impossible that the Christian religion, instead of shrinking into itself, may again embrace the thoughts of men upon the earth? Or is it true that since the Reformation 'all intellect has gone the other way?' and that in Protestant countries reconciliation is as hopeless as Protestants commonly believe to be the case in Catholic.

Those who hold the possibility of such a reconcilement or restoration of belief, are anxious to disengage Christianity from all suspicion of disguise or unfairness. They wish to preserve the historical use of Scripture as the continuous witness in all ages of the higher things in the heart of man, as the inspired source of truth and the way to the better life. They are willing to take away some of the external supports, because they are not needed and do harm; also, because they interfere with the meaning. They have a faith, not that after a period of transition all things will remain just as they were before, but that they will all come round again to the use of man and to the glory of God. When interpreted like any other book, by the same rules of evidence and the same canons of criticism, the Bible will still remain unlike any other book; its beauty will be freshly seen, as of a picture which is restored after many ages to its original state; it will create a new interest and make for itself a new kind of authority by the life which is in it. It will be a spirit and not a letter; as it was in the beginning, having an influence like that of the spoken word, or the book newly found. The purer the light in the human heart, the more it will have an expression of itself in the mind of Christ; the greater the knowledge of the development of man, the truer will be the insight gained into the 'increasing purpose' of revelation. In which also the individual soul has a practical part, finding a sympathy with its own imperfect feelings, in the broken utterance of the Psalmist or the Prophet as well as in the fulness of Christ. The harmony between Scripture and the life of man, in all its stages, may be far greater than appears at present. No one can form any notion from what we see around us, of the power which Christianity might have if it were at one with the conscience of man, and not at variance with his intellectual convictions. There, a world weary of the heat and dust of controversy—of speculations about God and man—weary too of the rapidity of its own motion, would return home and find rest.

But for the faith that the Gospel might win again the minds of intellectual men, it would be better to leave religion to itself, instead of attempting to draw them together. Other walks in literature have peace and pleasure and profit; the path of the critical Interpreter of Scripture is almost always a thorny one in England. It is not worth while for any one to enter upon it who is not supported by a sense that he has a Christian and moral object. For although an Interpreter of Scripture in modern times will hardly say with the emphasis of the Apostle, 'Woe is me, if I speak not the truth without regard to consequences,' yet he too may feel it a matter of duty not to conceal the things which he knows. He does not hide the discrepancies of Scripture, because the acknowledgment of them is the first step towards agreement among interpreters. He would restore the original meaning, because 'seven other' meanings take the place of it; the book is made the sport of opinion and the instrument of perversion of life. He would take the excuses of the head out of the way of the heart; there is hope too that by drawing Christians together on the ground of Scripture, he may also draw them nearer to one another. He is not afraid that inquiries, which have for their object the truth, can ever be displeasing to the God of truth; or that the Word of God is in any such sense a word as to be hurt by investigations into its human origin and conception.

It may be thought another ungracious aspect of the

preceding remarks, that they cast a slight upon the interpreters of Scripture in former ages. The early Fathers, the Roman Catholic mystical writers, the Swiss and German Reformers, the Nonconformist divines, have qualities for which we look in vain among ourselves; they throw an intensity of light upon the page of Scripture which we nowhere find in modern commentaries. But it is not the light of interpretation. They have a faith which seems indeed to have grown dim now-a-days, but that faith is not drawn from the study of Scripture; it is the element in which their own mind moves which overflows on the meaning of the text. The words of Scripture suggest to them their own thoughts or feelings. They are preachers, or in the New Testament sense of the word, prophets rather than interpreters. There is nothing in such a view derogatory to the saints and doctors of former ages. That Aquinas or Bernard did not shake themselves free from the mystical method of the Patristic times, or the Scholastic one which was more peculiarly their own; that Luther and Calvin read the Scriptures in connexion with the ideas which were kindling in the mind of their age, and the events which were passing before their eyes, these and similar remarks are not to be construed as depreciatory of the genius or learning of famous men of old; they relate only to their interpretation of Scripture, in which it is no slight upon them to maintain that they were not before their day.

What remains may be comprised in a few precepts, or rather is the expansion of a single one. *Interpret the Scripture like any other book.* There are many respects in which Scripture is unlike any other book; these will appear in the results of such an interpretation. The first step is to know the meaning, and this can only be done in the same careful and impartial way that we ascertain the meaning of Sophocles or of Plato. The subordinate principles which flow out of this general one will also be gathered from the observation of Scripture. No other science of Hermeneutics is possible but an inductive one, that is to say, one based on the language and thoughts and narrations of the sacred writers. And it would be well to carry the theory of interpretation no further than in the case of other works. Excessive system tends to create an impression that the meaning of Scripture is out of our reach, or is to be attained in some other way than by the exercise of manly sense and industry. Who would write a bulky treatise about the method to be pursued in interpreting Plato or Sophocles? Let us not set out on our journey so heavily equipped that there is little chance of our arriving at the end of it. The method creates itself as we go on, beginning only with a few reflections directed against plain errors. Such reflections are the rules of common sense, which we acknowledge with respect to other works written in dead languages: without pretending to novelty they may help us to 'return to nature' in the study of the sacred writings.

First, it may be laid down that Scripture has one meaning—the meaning which it had to the mind of the prophet or evangelist who first uttered or wrote, to the hearers or readers who first received it. Another view may be easier or more familiar to us, seeming to receive a light and interest from the circumstances of our own age. But such accommodation of the text must be laid aside by the interpreter, whose business is to place himself as nearly as possible in the position of the sacred writer. That is no easy task—to call up the inner and outer life of the contemporaries of our Saviour; to follow the abrupt and involved utterance of St. Paul or one of the old Prophets; to trace the meaning of words when language first became Christian. He will often have to choose the more difficult interpretation (Galatians ii. 20; Romans iii. 15, &c.), and to refuse one more in agreement with received

opinions, because the latter is less true to the style
and time of the author. He may incur the charge of
singularity, or confusion of ideas, or ignorance of Greek,
from a misunderstanding of the peculiarity of the subject in the person who makes the charge. For if it be.
said that the translation of some Greek words is contrary to the usages of grammar (Galatians iv. 13), that
is not in every instance to be denied; the point is
whether the usages of grammar are always observed.
Or if it be objected to some interpretation of Scripture
that it is difficult and perplexing, the answer is—
'that may very well be—it is the fact,' arising out of
differences in the modes of thought of other times, or
irregularities in the use of language which no art of
the interpreter can evade. One consideration should
be borne in mind, that the Bible is the only book in
the world written in different styles and at many
different times, which is in the hands of persons of all
degrees of knowledge and education. The benefit of
this outweighs the evil, yet the evil should be admitted—
namely, that it leads to a hasty and partial interpretation
of Scripture, which often obscures the true one. A sort
of conflict arises between scientific criticism and popular opinion. The indiscriminate use of Scripture has
a further tendency to maintain erroneous readings or
translations; some which are allowed to be such by
scholars have been stereotyped in the mind of the
English reader ; and it becomes almost a political
question how far we can venture to disturb them.

There are difficulties of another kind in many parts
of Scripture, the depth and inwardness of which require a measure of the same qualities in the interpreter
himself. There are notes struck in places, which like
some discoveries of science have sounded before their
time ; and only after many days have been caught up
and found a response on the earth. There are germs
of truth which after thousands of years have never yet
taken root in the world. There are lessons in the

Prophets which, however simple, mankind have not
yet learned even in theory; and which the complexity
of society rather tends to hide; aspects of human life
in Job and Ecclesiastes which have a truth of desolation about them which we faintly realize in ordinary
circumstances. It is, perhaps, the greatest difficulty of
all to enter into the meaning of the words of Christ—
so gentle, so human, so divine, neither adding to them
nor marring their simplicity. The attempt to illustrate
or draw them out in detail, even to guard against their
abuse, is apt to disturb the balance of truth. The
interpreter needs nothing short of 'fashioning' in
himself the image of the mind of Christ. He has to
be born again into a new spiritual or intellectual world,
from which the thoughts of this world are shut out.
It is one of the highest tasks on which the labour of a
life can be spent, to bring the words of Christ a little
nearer the heart of man.

But while acknowledging this inexhaustible or infinite character of the sacred writings, it does not,
therefore, follow that we are willing to admit of hidden
or mysterious meanings in them (in the same way we
recognise the wonders and complexity of the laws of
nature to be far beyond what eye has seen or knowledge reached, yet it is not therefore to be supposed
that we acknowledge the existence of some other laws
different in kind from those we know which are incapable of philosophical analysis). In like manner we
have no reason to attribute to the Prophet or Evangelist any second or hidden sense different from that
which appears on the surface. All that the Prophet
meant may not have been consciously present to his
mind; there were depths which to himself also were
but half revealed. He beheld the fortunes of Israel
passing into the heavens; the temporal kingdom was
fading into an eternal one. It is not to be supposed
that what he saw at a distance only was clearly defined
to him; or that the universal truth which was appear-

ing and reappearing in the history of the surrounding world took a purely spiritual or abstract form in his mind. There is a sense in which we may still say with Lord Bacon, that the words of prophecy are to be interpreted as the words of one 'with whom a thousand years are as one day, and one day as a thousand years.' But that is no reason for turning days into years, or for interpreting the things 'that must shortly come to pass' in the book of Revelation, as the events of modern history, or for separating the day of judgment from the destruction of Jerusalem in the Gospels. The double meaning which is given to our Saviour's discourse respecting the last things is not that 'form of eternity' of which Lord Bacon speaks; it resembles rather the doubling of an object when seen through glasses placed at different angles. It is true also that there are types in Scripture which were regarded as such by the Jews themselves, as for example, the scapegoat, or the paschal lamb. But that is no proof of all outward ceremonies being types when Scripture is silent;—(if we assume the New Testament as a tradition running parallel with the Old, may not the Roman Catholic assume with equal reason a tradition running parallel with the New?) Prophetic symbols, again, have often the same meaning in different places (*e.g.*, the four beasts or living creatures, the colours white or red); the reason is that this meaning is derived from some natural association (as of fruitfulness, purity, or the like); or again, they are borrowed in some of the later prophecies from earlier ones; we are not, therefore, justified in supposing any hidden connexion in the prophecies where they occur. Neither is there any ground for assuming design of any other kind in Scripture any more than in Plato or Homer. Wherever there is beauty and order, there is design; but there is no proof of any artificial design, such as is often traced by the Fathers, in the relation of the several parts of a book, or of

the several books to each other.    That is one of those
mischievous notions which enables us, under the disguise of reverence, to make Scripture mean what we
please.    Nothing that can be said of the greatness or
sublimity, or truth, or depth, or tenderness, of many
passages, is too much.    But that greatness is of a
simple kind; it is not increased by double senses, or
systems of types, or elaborate structure, or design.    If
every sentence was a mystery, every word a riddle,
every letter a symbol, that would not make the Scriptures more worthy of a Divine author; it is a hea-
thenish or Rabbinical fancy which reads them in this
way.    Such complexity would not place them above
but below human compositions in general; for it
would deprive them of the ordinary intelligibleness
of human language.    It is not for a Christian theologian to say that words were given to mankind to
conceal their thoughts, neither was revelation given
them to conceal the Divine.

The second rule is an application of the general
principle; 'interpret Scripture from itself' as in other
respects, like any other book written in an age and
country of which little or no other literature survives,
and about which we know almost nothing except
what is derived from its pages.    Not that all the parts
of Scripture are to be regarded as an indistinguishable
mass.    The Old Testament is not to be identified with
the New, nor the Law with the Prophets, nor the
Gospels with the Epistles, nor the Epistles of St. Paul
to be violently harmonized with the Epistle of St.
James.    Each writer, each successive age, has characteristics of its own, as strongly marked, or more
strongly, than those which are found in the authors
or periods of classical literature.    These differences
are not to be lost in the idea of a Spirit from whom
they proceed or by which they were overruled.    And
therefore, illustration of one part of Scripture by
another should be confined to writings of the same

age and the same authors, except where the writings
of different ages or persons offer obvious similarities.
It may be said further that illustration should be
chiefly derived, not only from the same author, but
from the same writing, or from one of the same period
of his life. For example, the comparison of St. John
and the 'synoptic' Gospels, or of the Gospel of St.
John with the Revelation of St. John, will tend rather
to confuse than to elucidate the meaning of either;
while, on the other hand, the comparison of the
Prophets with one another, and with the Psalms,
offers many valuable helps and lights to the interpreter. Again, the connexion between the Epistles
written by the Apostle St. Paul about the same time
(*e.g.* Romans, 1 and 2 Corinthians, Galatians,—Colossians, Philippians, Ephesians,—compared with Romans,
Colossians,—Ephesians, Galatians, &c.,) is far closer
than of Epistles which are separated by an interval of
only a few years.

But supposing all this to be understood, and that
by the interpretation of Scripture from itself is meant
a real interpretation of like by like, it may be asked,
what is it that we gain from a minute comparison of
a particular author or writing? The indiscriminate
use of parallel passages taken from one end of
Scripture and applied to the other (except so far as
earlier compositions may have afforded the material
or the form of later ones) is useless and uncritical.
The uneducated, or imperfectly educated person who
looks out the marginal references of the English Bible,
imagining himself in this way to gain a clearer insight
into the Divine meaning, is really following the religious associations of his own mind. Even the critical
use of parallel passages is not without danger. For
are we to conclude that an author meant in one place
what he says in another? Shall we venture to mend
a corrupt phrase on the model of some other phrase,
which memory, prevailing over judgment, calls up and

thrusts into the text? It is this fallacy which has filled the pages of classical writers with useless and unfounded emendations.

The meaning of the Canon ' *Non nisi ex Scripturâ Scripturam potes interpretari,*' is only this, ' That we cannot understand Scripture without becoming familiar with it.' Scripture is a world by itself, from which we must exclude foreign influences, whether theological or classical. To get inside that world is an effort of thought and imagination, requiring the sense of a poet as well as a critic—demanding much more than learning a degree of original power and intensity of mind. Any one who, instead of burying himself in the pages of the commentators, would learn the sacred writings by heart, and paraphrase them in English, will probably make a nearer approach to their true meaning that he would gather from any commentary. The intelligent mind will ask its own questions, and find for the most part its own answers. The true use of interpretation is to get rid of interpretation, and leave us alone in company with the author. When the meaning of Greek words is once known, the young student has almost all the real materials which are possessed by the greatest Biblical scholar, in the book itself. For almost our whole knowledge of the history of the Jews is derived from the Old Testament and the Apocryphal books, and almost our whole knowledge of the life of Christ and of the Apostolical age is derived from the New ; whatever is added to them is either conjecture, or very slight topographical or chronological illustration. For this reason the rule given above, which is applicable to all books, is applicable to the New Testament more than any other.

Yet in this consideration of the separate books of Scripture it is not to be forgotten that they have also a sort of continuity. We make a separate study of the subject, the mode of thought, in some degree also of the language of each book. And at length the idea arises in our minds of a common literature, a pervading life, an overruling law. It may be compared to the effect of some natural scene in which we suddenly perceive a harmony or picture, or to the imperfect appearance of design which suggests itself in looking at the surface of the globe. That is to say, there is nothing miraculous or artificial in the arrangement of the books of Scripture; it is the result, not the design, which appears in them when bound in the same volume. Or if we like so to say, there *is* design, but a natural design which is revealed to after ages. Such continuity or design is best expressed under some notion of progress or growth, not regular, however, but with broken and imperfect stages, which the want of knowledge prevents our minutely defining. The great truth of the unity of God was there from the first; slowly as the morning broke in the heavens, like some central light, it filled and afterwards dispersed the mists of human passion in which it was itself enveloped. A change passes over the Jewish religion from fear to love, from power to wisdom, from the justice of God to the mercy of God, from the nation to the individual, from this world to another; from the visitation of the sins of the fathers upon the children, to 'every soul shall bear its own iniquity;' from the fire, the earthquake, and the storm, to the still small voice. There never was a time after the deliverance from Egypt, in which the Jewish people did not bear a kind of witness against the cruelty and licentiousness of the surrounding tribes. In the decline of the monarchy, as the kingdom itself was sinking under foreign conquerors, whether springing from contact with the outer world, or from some reaction within, the undergrowth of morality gathers strength; first, in the anticipation of prophecy, secondly, like a green plant in the hollow rind of Pharisaism,—and individuals pray and commune with God each one for himself. At length the tree of life blossoms; the faith in im-

c c

mortality which had hitherto slumbered in the heart
of man, intimated only in doubtful words (2 Sam. xii.
23; Psalm xvii. 15), or beaming for an instant in
dark places (Job xix. 25), has become the prevailing
belief.

There is an interval in the Jewish annals which we
often exclude from our thoughts, because it has no
record in the canonical writings—extending over about
four hundred years, from the last of the prophets of
the Old Testament to the forerunner of Christ in the
New. This interval, about which we know so little,
which is regarded by many as a portion of secular
rather than of sacred history, was nevertheless as
fruitful in religious changes as any similar period
which preceded. The establishment of the Jewish
sects, and the wars of the Maccabees, probably
exercised as great an influence on Judaism as the
captivity itself. A third influence was that of the
Alexandrian literature, which was attracting the
Jewish intellect, at the same time that the Galilæan
zealot was tearing the nation in pieces with the doctrine
that it was lawful to call 'no man master but God.'
In contrast with that wild fanaticism as well as with
the proud Pharisee, came One most unlike all that had
been before, as the kings or rulers of mankind. In
an age which was the victim of its own passions, the
creature of its own circumstances, the slave of its own
degenerate religion, our Saviour taught a lesson absolutely free from all the influences of a surrounding
world. He made the last perfect revelation of God to
man; a revelation not indeed immediately applicable
to the state of society or the world, but in its truth
and purity inexhaustible by the after generations of
men. And of the first application of the truth which he
taught as a counsel of perfection to the actual circumstances of mankind, we have the example in the Epistles.

Such a general conception of growth or development
in Scripture, beginning with the truth of the Unity

of God in the earliest books and ending with the perfection of Christ, naturally springs up in our minds in
the perusal of the sacred writings. It is a notion of
value to the interpreter, for it enables him at the same
time to grasp the whole and distinguish the parts.
It saves him from the necessity of maintaining that
the Old Testament is one and the same everywhere;
that the books of Moses contain truths or precepts,
such as the duty of prayer or the faith in immortality,
or the spiritual interpretation of sacrifice, which no
one has ever seen there. It leaves him room enough
to admit all the facts of the case. No longer is he
required to defend or to explain away David's imprecations against his enemies, or his injunctions to
Solomon, any more than his sin in the matter of
Uriah. Nor is he hampered with a theory of accommodation. Still the sense of 'the increasing purpose
which through the ages ran' is present to him, nowhere else continuously discernible or ending in a
divine perfection. Nowhere else is there found the
same interpenetration of the political and religious
element—a whole nation, 'though never good for
much at any time,' possessed with the conviction that
it was living in the face of God—in whom the Sun of
righteousness shone upon the corruption of an Eastern
nature—the 'fewest of all people,' yet bearing the
greatest part in the education of the world. Nowhere
else among the teachers and benefactors of mankind
is there any form like His, in whom the desire of the
nation is fulfilled, and 'not of that nation only,' but
of all mankind, whom He restores to His Father and
their Father, to His God and their God.

Such a growth or development may be regarded as
a kind of progress from childhood to manhood. In
the child there is an anticipation of truth; his reason
is latent in the form of feeling; many words
are used by him which he imperfectly understands;
he is led by temporal promises, believing that to be

good is to be happy always; he is pleased by marvels and has vague terrors. He is confined to a
spot of earth, and lives in a sort of prison of sense,
yet is bursting also with a fulness of childish life:
he imagines God to be like a human father, only
greater and more awful; he is easily impressed with
solemn thoughts, but soon 'rises up to play' with
other children. It is observable that his ideas of
right and wrong are very simple, hardly extending to
another life; they consist chiefly in obedience to his
parents, whose word is his law. As he grows older
he mixes more and more with others; first with one
or two who have a great influence in the direction of
his mind. At length the world opens upon him;
another work of education begins; and he learns to
discern more truly the meaning of things and his relation to men in general. (You may complete the
image, by supposing that there was a time in his early
days when he was a helpless outcast 'in the land of
Egypt and the house of bondage'). And as he arrives
at manhood he reflects on his former years, the
progress of his education, the hardships of his infancy,
the home of his youth (the thought of which is inefface-
able in after life), and he now understands that all this
was but a preparation for another state of being, in which
he is to play a part for himself. And once more in age
you may imagine him like the patriarch looking back on
the entire past, which he reads anew, perceiving that
the events of life had a purpose or result which was
not seen at the time; they seem to him bound 'each
to each by natural piety.'

'Which things are an allegory,' the particulars of
which any one may interpret for himself. For the
child born after the flesh is the symbol of the child
born after the Spirit. 'The law was a schoolmaster to
bring men to Christ,' and now 'we are under a schoolmaster' no longer. The anticipation of truth which
came from without to the childhood or youth of the

human race is witnessed to within; the revelation of
God is not lost but renewed in the heart and understanding of the man. Experience has taught us the
application of the lesson in a wider sphere. And
many influences have combined to form the 'after life'
of the world. When at the close (shall we say) of a
great period in the history of man, we cast our eyes
back on the course of events, from the 'angel of his
presence in the wilderness' to the multitude of peoples,
nations, languages, who are being drawn together by
His Providence—from the simplicity of the pastoral
state in the dawn of the world's day, to all the elements
of civilization and knowledge which are beginning to
meet and mingle in a common life, we also understand
that we are no longer in our early home, to which,
nevertheless, we fondly look; and that the end is yet
unseen, and the purposes of God towards the human
race only half revealed. And to turn once more to
the Interpreter of Scripture, he too feels that the
continuous growth of revelation which he traces in
the Old and New Testament, is a part of a larger
whole extending over the earth and reaching to another
world.

§ 3.

Scripture has an inner life or soul; it has also an
outward body or form. That form is language, which
imperfectly expresses our common notions, much more
those higher truths which religion teaches. At the time
when our Saviour came into the world the Greek
language was itself in a state of degeneracy and decay.
It had lost its poetic force, and was ceasing to have
the sway over the mind which classical Greek once
held. That is a more important revolution in the mental
history of mankind, than we easily conceive in modern
times, when all languages sit loosely on thought, and
the peculiarities, or idiosyncrasies of one are corrected
by our knowledge of another. It may be numbered
among the causes which favoured the growth of

Christianity. That degeneracy was a preparation for the Gospel—the decaying soil in which the new elements of life were to come forth—the beginning of another state of man, in which language and mythology and philosophy were no longer to exert the same constraining power as in the ancient world. The civilized portion of mankind were becoming of one speech, the diffusion of which along the shores of the Mediterranean sea made a way for the entrance of Christianity into the human understanding, just as the Roman empire prepared the framework of its outward history. The first of all languages, 'for glory and for beauty,' had become the 'common' dialect of the Macedonian kingdoms; it had been moulded in the schools of Alexandria to the ideas of the East and the religious wants of Jews. Neither was it any violence to its nature to be made the vehicle of the new truths which were springing up in the heart of man. The definiteness and absence of reflectiveness in the earlier forms of human speech, would have imposed a sort of limit on the freedom and spirituality of the Gospel; even the Greek of Plato would have 'coldly furnished forth' the words of 'eternal life.' A religion which was to be universal required the divisions of languages, as of nations, to be in some degree broken down. [' *Pœna linguarum dispersit homines, donum linguarum in unum collegit.*'] But this community or freedom of language was accompanied by corresponding defects; it had lost its logical precision; it was less coherent; and more under the influence of association. It might be compared to a garment which allowed and yet impeded the exercise of the mind by being too large and loose for it.

From the inner life of Scripture it is time to pass on to the consideration of this outward form, including that other framework of modes of thought and figures of speech which is between the two. A knowledge of the original language is a necessary qualification of the Interpreter of Scripture. It takes away at least one chance of error in the explanation of a passage; it removes one of the films which have gathered over the page; it brings the meaning home in a more intimate and subtle way than a translation could do. To this, however, another qualification should be added, which is, the logical power to perceive the meaning of words in reference to their context. And there is a worse fault than ignorance of Greek in the interpretation of the New Testament, that is, ignorance of any language. The Greek Fathers, for example, are far from being the best verbal commentators, because their knowledge of Greek often leads them away from the drift of the passage. The minuteness of the study in our own day has also a tendency to introduce into the text associations which are not really found there. There is a danger of making words mean too much; refinements of signification are drawn out of them, perhaps contained in their etymology, which are lost in common use and parlance. There is the error of interpreting every particle, as though it were a link in the argument, instead of being, as is often the case, an excrescence of style. The verbal critic magnifies his art, which is really great in Æschylus or Pindar, but not of equal importance in the interpretation of the simpler language of the New Testament. His love of scholarship will sometimes lead him to impress a false system on words and constructions. A great critic* who has commented on the three first chapters of the Epistle to the Galatians, has certainly afforded a proof that it is possible to read the New Testament under a distorting influence from classical Greek. The tendency gains support from the undefined feeling that Scripture does not come behind in excellence of language any more than of thought. And if not as in former days, the classic purity of the Greek of the New Testament, yet its certainty and accuracy, the assumption of which,

---

* Herman.

as any other assumption, is only the parent of inaccuracy, is still maintained.

The study of the language of the New Testament has suffered in another way by following too much in the track of classical scholarship. All dead languages which have passed into the hands of grammarians, have given rise to questions which have either no result or in which the certainty; or if certain, the importance of the result, is out of proportion to the labour spent in attaining it. The field is exhausted by great critics, and then subdivided among lesser ones. The subject, unlike that of physical science, has a limit, and unless new ground is broken up, as for example in mythology, or comparative philology, is apt to grow barren. Though it is not true to say that 'we know as much about the Greeks and Romans as we ever shall,' it is certain that we run a danger from the deficiency of material, of wasting time in questions which do not add anything to real knowledge, or in conjectures which must always remain uncertain, and may in turn give way to other conjectures in the next generation. Little points may be of great importance when rightly determined, because the observation of them tends to quicken the instinct of language; but conjectures about little things or rules respecting them which were not in the mind of Greek authors themselves, are not of equal value. There is the scholasticism of philology, not only in the Alexandrian, but in our own times; as in the middle ages, there was the scholasticism of philosophy. Questions of mere orthography, about which there cannot be said to have been a right or wrong, have been pursued almost with a Rabbinical minuteness. The story of the scholar who regretted 'that he had not concentrated his life on the dative case,' is hardly a caricature of the spirit of such inquiries. The form of notes to the classics often seems to arise out of a necessity for observing a certain proportion between the commentary and the text. And the same tendency is noticeable in many of the critical and philological observations which are made on the New Testament. The field of Biblical criticism is narrower, and its materials more fragmentary; so too the minuteness and uncertainty of the questions raised has been greater. For example, the discussions respecting the chronology of St. Paul's life and his second imprisonment: or about the identity of James, the brother of the Lord, or in another department, respecting the use of the Greek article, have gone far beyond the line of utility.

There seem to be reasons for doubting whether any considerable light can be thrown on the New Testament from inquiry into the language. Such inquiries are popular, because they are safe; but their popularity is not the measure of their use. It has not been sufficiently considered that the difficulties of the New Testament are for the most part common to the Greek and the English. The noblest translation in the world has a few great errors, more than half of them in the text; but 'we do it violence' to haggle over the words. Minute corrections of tenses or particles are no good; they spoil the English without being nearer the Greek. Apparent mistranslations are often due to a better knowledge of English rather than a worse knowledge of Greek. It is true that the signification of a few uncommon expressions, *e.g.*, ἐξουσία, ἐπιβαλών, συναπαγόμενοι, κ.τ.λ., is yet uncertain. But no result of consequence would follow from the attainment of absolute certainty respecting the meaning of any of these. A more promising field opens to the interpreter in the examination of theological terms, such as faith (πίστις), grace (χάρις), righteousness (δικαιοσύνη), sanctification (ἁγιασμός), the law (νόμος), the spirit (πνεῦμα), the comforter (παράκλητος), &c., provided always that the use of such terms in the New Testament is clearly separated (1) from their derivation or previous use in Classical or Alexandrian Greek, (2) from their after use in the Fathers and in systems of theology. To which may be added another select class of words descriptive of the offices or customs of the Apostolic Church, such as Apostle (ἀπόστολος), Bishop (ἐπίσκοπος), Elder (πρεσβύτερος), Deacon and Deaconess (ὁ καὶ ἡ διάκονος), love-feast (ἀγάπαι), the Lord's day (ἡ κυριακὴ ἡμέρα), &c. It is a lexilogus of these and similar terms, rather than a lexicon of the entire Greek Testament that is required. Interesting subjects of real inquiry are also the comparison of the Greek of the New Testament with modern Greek on the one hand, and the Greek of the LXX. on the other. It is not likely, however, that they will afford much more help than they have already done in the elucidation of the Greek of the New Testament.

It is for others to investigate the language of the Old Testament, to which the preceding remarks are only in part applicable. [It may be observed in passing of this, as of any other old language, that not the later form of the language, but the cognate dialects, must ever be the chief source of its illustration. For in every ancient language, antecedent or contemporary forms, not the subsequent ones, afford the real insight into its nature and structure. It must also be admitted that very great and real obscurities exist in the English translation of the Old Testament, which even a superficial acquaintance with the original has a tendency to remove.] Leaving, however, to others the consideration of the Semitic languages which raise questions of a different kind from the Hellenistic Greek, we will offer a few remarks on the latter. Much has been said of the increasing accuracy of our knowledge of the language of the New Testament; the old Hebraistic method of explaining difficulties of language or construction, has retired within very narrow limits; it might probably with advantage be confined to still narrower ones—[if it have any place at all except in the Apocalypse or the Gospel of St. Matthew]. There is, perhaps, some confusion between accuracy of our knowledge of language, and the accuracy of language itself; which is also strongly maintained. It is observed that the usages of barbarous as well as civilized nations conform perfectly to grammatical rules; that the uneducated in all countries have certain laws of speech as much as Shakespear or Bacon; the usages of Lucian, it may be said, are as regular as those of Plato, even when they are different. The decay of language seems rather to witness to the permanence than to the changeableness of its structure; it is the flesh, not the bones, that begins to drop off. But such general remarks, although just, afford but little help in determining the character of the Greek of the New Testament, which has of course a certain system, failing in which it would cease to be a language. Some further illustration is needed of the change which has passed upon it. All languages do not decay in the same manner; and the influence of decay in the same language may be different in different countries; when used in writing and in speaking—when applied to the matters of ordinary life and to the higher truths of philosophy or religion. And the degeneracy of language itself is not a mere principle of dissolution, but creative also; while dead and rigid in some of its uses, it is elastic and expansive in others. The decay of an ancient language is the beginning of the construction of a modern one. The loss of some usages gives a greater precision and freedom to others. The logical element, as for example in the Mediæval Latin, will probably be strongest when the poetical has vanished. A great movement, like the Reformation in Germany, passing over a nation, may give a new birth also to its language.

These remarks may be applied to the Greek of the New Testament, which although classed vaguely under the 'common dialect,' has, nevertheless, many features which are altogether peculiar to itself, and such as are found in no other remains of ancient literature.

1. It is more unequal in style even in the same books, that is to say, more original and plastic in one part, more rigid and unpliable in another. There is a want of the continuous power to frame a paragraph or to arrange clauses in subordination to each other, even to the extent to which it was possessed by a Greek scholiast or rhetorician. On the other hand there is a fulness of life, 'a new birth,' in the use of abstract terms which is not found elsewhere, after the golden age of Greek philosophy. Almost the only passage in the New Testament which reads like a Greek period of the time, is the first paragraph of the Gospel according to St. Luke, and the corresponding words of the Acts. But the power and meaning of the characteristic words of the New Testament is in remarkable contrast with the vapid and general use of the same words in Philo about the same time. There is also a sort of lyrical passion in some passages (1 Cor. xiii. ; 2 Cor. vi. 6—10; xi. 21—33) which is a new thing in the literature of the world; to which, at any rate, no Greek author of a later age furnishes any parallel. 2. Though written, the Greek of the New Testament partakes of the character of a spoken language; it is more lively and simple, and less structural than ordinary writing—a peculiarity of style which further agrees with the circumstance that the Epistles of St. Paul were not written with his own hand, but probably dictated to an amanuensis, and that the Gospels also probably originate in an oral narrative. 3. The ground colours of the language may be said to be two ; first, the LXX. which is modified, secondly, by the spoken Greek of eastern countries, and the differences which might be expected to arise between a translation and an original; many Hebraisms would occur in the Greek of a translator, which would never have come to his pen but for the influence of the work which he was translating. 4. To which may be added a few Latin and Chaldee words, and a few Rabbinical

formulæ. The influence of Hebrew or Chaldee in the New Testament is for the most part at a distance, in the background, acting not directly, but mediately, through the LXX. It has much to do with the clausular structure and general form, but hardly anything with the grammatical usage. Philo too, did not know Hebrew, or at least the Hebrew Scriptures, yet there is also a 'mediate' influence of Hebrew traceable in his writings. 5. There is an element of constraint in the style of the New Testament, arising from the circumstance of its authors writing in a language which was not their own. This constraint shows itself in the repetition of words and phrases; in the verbal oppositions and anacolutha of St. Paul; in the short sentences of St. John. This is further increased by the fact that the writers of the New Testament were 'unlearned men,' who had not the same power of writing as of speech. Moreover, as has been often remarked, the difficulty of composition increases in proportion to the greatness of the subject; *e.g.*, the narrative of Thucydides is easy and intelligible, while his reflections and speeches are full of confusion; the effort to concentrate seems to interfere with the consecutiveness and fluency of ideas. Something of this kind is discernible in those passages of the Epistles in which the Apostle St. Paul is seeking to set forth the opposite sides of God's dealing with man, *e.g.*, Romans iii. 1—9; ix., x.; or in which the sequence of the thought is interrupted by the conflict of emotions, 1 Cor. ix. 20; Gal. iv. 11—20. 6. The power of the Gospel over language must be recognised, showing itself, first of all, in the original and consequently variable signification of words (πίστις, χάρις, σωτηρία), which is also more comprehensive and human than the heretical usage of many of the same terms, *e.g.*, γνῶσις (knowledge), σοφία (wisdom), κτίσις (creature, creation); secondly, in a peculiar use of some constructions, such as—δικαιοσύνη

Θεοῦ (righteousness of God), πίστις Ἰησοῦ Χριστοῦ (faith of Jesus Christ), ἐν Χριστῷ (in Christ), ἐν Θεῷ (in God), ὑπὲρ ἡμῶν (for us), in which the meaning of the genitive case or of the preposition almost escapes our notice, from familiarity with the sound of it. Lastly, the degeneracy of the Greek language is traceable in the failure of syntactical power; in the insertion of prepositions to denote relations of thought, which classical Greek would have expressed by the case only; in the omission of them when classical Greek would have required them; in the incipient use of ἵνα with the subjunctive for the infinitive; in the confusion of ideas of cause and effect; in the absence of the article in the case of an increasing number of words which are passing into proper names; in the loss of the finer shades of difference in the negative particles; in the occasional confusion of the aorist and perfect; in excessive fondness for particles of reasoning or inference; in various forms of apposition, especially that of the word to the sentence; in the use, sometimes emphatic, sometimes only pleonastic, of the personal and demonstrative pronouns. These are some of the signs that the language is breaking-up and losing its structure.

Our knowledge of the New Testament is derived almost exclusively from itself. Of the language, as well as of the subject, it may be truly said that what other writers contribute is nothing in comparison of that which is gained from observation of the text. Some inferences which may be gathered from this general fact, are the following:—First, that less weight should be given to lexicons, that is, to the authority of other Greek writers, and more to the context. The use of a word in a new sense, the attribution of a neuter meaning to a verb elsewhere passive, (Romans iii. 9, προεχόμεθα), the resolution of the compound into two simple notions, (Galatians iii. 1, προεγράφη), these, when the context requires it, are not to be set aside by the scholar because sanctioned by no known examples. The same remark applies to grammars as well as lexicons. We cannot be certain that διά with the accusative never has the same meaning as διά with the genitive, (Gal. iv. 13; Phil. i. 15), or that the article always retains its defining power (2 Cor. i. 17; Acts xvii. 1), or that the perfect is never used in place of the aorist (1 Cor. xv. 4; Rev. v. 7, &c.); still less can we affirm that the latter end of a sentence never forgets the beginning (Rom. ii. 17—21; v. 12—18; ix. 22; xvi. 25—27; &c. &c.). Foreign influences tend to derange the strong natural perception or remembrance of the analogy of our own language. That is very likely to have occurred in the case of some of the writers of the New Testament; that there is such a derangement, is a fact. There is no probability in favour of St. Paul writing in broken sentences, but there is no improbability which should lead us to assume in such sentences, continuous grammar and thought, as appears to have been the feeling of the copyists who have corrected the anacolutha. The occurrence of them further justifies the interpreter in using some freedom with other passages in which the syntax does not absolutely break down. When 'confusion of two constructions,' 'meaning to say one thing and finishing with another;' 'saying two things in one instead of disposing them in their logical sequence,' are attributed to the Apostle; the use of these and similar expressions is defended by the fact that more numerous anacolutha occur in St. Paul's writings than in any equal portion of the New Testament, and far more than in the writings of any other Greek author of equal length.

Passing from the grammatical structure, we may briefly consider the logical character of the language of the New Testament. Two things should be here distinguished, the logical form and the logical sequence of thought. Some ages have been remarkable for the former of these two characteristics; they have dealt in opposition, contradiction, climax, pleonasm, reason within reason, and the like; mere statements taking the form of arguments—each sentence seeming to be a link in a chain. In such periods of literature, the appearance of logic is rhetorical, and is to be set down to the style. That is the case with many passages in the New Testament which are studded with logical or rhetorical formulæ, especially in the Epistles of St. Paul. Nothing can be more simple or natural than the object of the writer. Yet 'forms of the schools' appear (whether learnt at the feet of Gamaliel, that reputed master of Greek learning, or not,) which imply a degree of logical or rhetorical training.

The observation of this rhetorical or logical element has a bearing on the Interpretation of Scripture. For it leads us to distinguish between the superficial connexion of words and the real connexion of thoughts. Otherwise injustice is done to the argument of the sacred writer, who may be supposed to violate logical rules, of which he is unconscious. For example, the argument of Rom. iii. 19, may be classed by the logicians under some head of fallacy ('Ex aliquo non sequitur omnis'); the series of inferences which follow one another in Rom. i. 16—18, are for the most part different aspects or statements of the same truth. So in Rom. i. 32 the climax rather appears to be an anticlimax. But to dwell on these things interferes with the true perception of the Apostle's meaning which is not contained in the repetitions of γάρ by which it is hooked together; nor are we accurately to weigh the proportions expressed by his οὐ μόνον— ἀλλὰ καὶ; or πολλῷ μᾶλλον; neither need we suppose that where μὲν is found alone, there was a reason for the omission of δὲ, (Rom. i. 8; iii. 2); or that the opposition of words and sentences is always the opposition of ideas (Rom. v. 7; x. 10). It is true that these and similar forms or distinctions of language, admit of translation into English; and in every case the interpreter may find some point of view in which the simplest truth of feeling may be drawn out in an antithetical or argumentative form. But whether these points of view were in the Apostle's mind at the time of writing may be doubted; the real meaning, or kernel, seems to lie deeper and to be more within. When we pass from the study of each verse to survey the whole at a greater distance, the form of thought is again seen to be unimportant in comparison of the truth which is contained in it. The same remark may be extended to the opposition, not only of words, but of ideas, which is found in the Scriptures generally, and almost seems to be inherent in human language itself. The law is opposed to faith, good to evil, the spirit to the flesh, light to darkness, the world to the believer, the sheep are set ' on his right hand, but the goats on the left.' The influence of this logical opposition has been great and not always without abuse in practice. For the opposition is one of ideas only which is not realized in fact. Experience shows us not that there are two classes of men animated by two opposing principles, but an infinite number of classes or individuals from the lowest depth of misery and sin to the highest perfection of which human nature is capable, the best not wholly good, the worst not entirely evil. But the figure or mode of representation changes these differences of degree into differences of kind. And we often think and speak and act in reference both to ourselves and others, as though the figure were altogether a reality.

Other questions arise out of the analysis of the modes of thought of Scripture. Unless we are willing to use words without inquiring into their meaning, it is necessary for us to arrange them in some relation to our own minds. The modes of thought of the Old Testament are not the same with those of the New, and those of the New are only partially the

same with those in use among ourselves at the present
day. The education of the human mind may be
traced as clearly from the Book of Genesis to the
Epistles of St. Paul, as from Homer to Plato and
Aristotle. When we hear St. Paul speaking of
‘body and soul and spirit,’ we know that such language as this would not occur in the Books of Moses
or in the Prophet Isaiah. It has the colour of a later
age, in which abstract terms have taken the place of
expressions derived from material objects. When we
proceed further to compare these or other words or
expressions of St. Paul with ‘the body and mind,’ or
‘mind’ and ‘matter,’ which is a distinction, not only of
philosophy, but of common language among ourselves,
it is not easy at once to determine the relation between
them. Familiar as is the sound of both expressions,
many questions arise when we begin to compare them.

This is the metaphysical difficulty in the Interpretation of Scripture, which it is better not to ignore,
because the consideration of it is necessary to the
understanding of many passages, and also because it
may return upon us in the form of materialism or
scepticism. To some who are not aware how little
words affect the nature of things it may seem to raise
speculations of a very serious kind. Their doubts
would, perhaps, find expression in some such excla-
mations as the following :—‘ How is religion possible
when modes of thought are shifting? and words
changing their meaning, and statements of doctrine
though ‘starched’ with philosophy, are in perpetual
danger of dissolution from metaphysical analysis ?’

The answer seems to be, that Christian truth is not
dependent on the fixedness of modes of thought. The
metaphysician may analyse the ideas of the mind just
as the physiologist may analyse the powers or parts
of the bodily frame, yet morality and social life still
go on, as in the body digestion is uninterrupted.
That is not an illustration only ; it represents the fact.
Though we had no words for mind, matter, soul,

body, and the like, Christianity would remain the same. This is obvious, whether we think of the case of the poor, who understand such distinctions very imperfectly, or of those nations of the earth, who have no precisely corresponding division of ideas. It is not of that subtle or evanescent character which is liable to be lost in shifting the use of terms. Indeed, it is an advantage at times to discard these terms with the view of getting rid of the oppositions to which they give rise. No metaphysical analysis can prevent ' our taking up the cross and following Christ,' or receiving the kingdom of heaven as little children. To analyse the ' trichotomy' of St. Paul is interesting as a chapter in the history of the human mind and necessary as a part of Biblical exegesis, but it has nothing to do with the religion of Christ. Christian duties may be enforced, and the life of Christ may be the centre of our thoughts, whether we speak of reason and faith, of soul and body, or of mind and matter, or adopt a mode of speech which dispenses with any of these divisions.

Connected with the modes of thought or representation in Scripture, are the figures of speech of Scripture, about which the same question may be asked: ' What division can we make between the figure and the reality ?' And the answer seems to be of the same kind, that ' We cannot precisely draw the line between them.' Language, and especially the language of Scripture, does not admit of any sharp distinction. The simple expressions of one age become the allegories or figures of another; many of those in the New Testament are taken from the Old. But neither is there anything really essential in the form of these figures; nay, the literal application of many of them has been a great stumblingblock to the reception of Christianity. A recent commentator on Scripture appears willing to peril religion on the literal truth of such an expression as ' We shall be caught up to meet the Lord in the air.' Would he be equally ready to stake Christianity on the literal meaning of the words, 'Where their worm dieth not, and the fire is not quenched?'

Of what has been said, this is the sum;—' That Scripture, like other books, has one meaning, which is to be gathered from itself without reference to the adaptations of Fathers or Divines; and without regard to *a priori* notions about its nature and origin. It is to be interpreted like other books, with attention to the character of its authors, and the prevailing state of civilization and knowledge, with allowance for peculiarities of style and language, and modes of thought and figures of speech. Yet not without a sense that as we read there grows upon us the witness of God in the world, anticipating in a rude and primitive age the truth that was to be, shining more and more unto the perfect day in the life of Christ, which again is reflected from different points of view in the teaching of His Apostles.'

§. 4.

It has been a principal aim of the preceding pages to distinguish the interpretation from the application of Scripture. Many of the errors alluded to, arise out of a confusion of the two. The present is nearer to us than the past, the circumstances which surround us pre-occupy our thoughts; it is only by an effort that we reproduce the ideas, or events, or persons of other ages. And thus, quite naturally, almost by a law of the human mind, the application of Scripture takes the place of its original meaning. And the question is, not how to get rid of this natural tendency, but how we may have the true use of it. For it cannot be got rid of, or rather is one of the chief instruments of religious usefulness in the world: 'Ideas must be given through something;' those of religion find their natural expression in the words of Scripture, in the adaptation of which to another state

of life it is hardly possible that the first intention of
the writers should be always preserved. Interpretation is the province of few; it requires a finer perception of language, and a higher degree of cultivation than is attained by the majority of mankind.
But applications are made by all, from the philosopher
reading 'God in History,' to the poor woman who
finds in them a response to her prayers, and the solace
of her daily life. In the hour of death we do not
want critical explanations; in most cases, those to
whom they would be offered are incapable of understanding them. A few words, breathing the sense of
the whole Christian world, such as 'I know that my
Redeemer liveth' (though the exact meaning of them
may be doubtful to the Hebrew scholar); 'I shall go
to him, but he shall not return to me;' touch a chord
which would never be reached by the most skilful exposition of the argument of one of St. Paul's Epistles.

There is also a use of Scripture in education and
literature. This literary use, though secondary to
the religious one, is not unimportant. It supplies a
common language to the educated and uneducated, in
which the best and highest thoughts of both are
expressed; it is a medium between the abstract
notions of the one and the simple feelings of the
other. To the poor especially, it conveys in the form
which they are most capable of receiving, the lesson of
history and life. The beauty and power of speech
and writing would be greatly impaired, if the Scriptures ceased to be known or used among us. The
orator seems to catch from them a sort of inspiration;
in the simple words of Scripture which he stamps
anew, the philosopher often finds his most pregnant
expressions. If modern times have been richer in
the wealth of abstract thought, the contribution of
earlier ages to the mind of the world has not been
less, but, perhaps greater, in supplying the poetry of
language. There is no such treasury of instruments

and materials as Scripture. The loss of Homer, or the loss of Shakespear, would have affected the whole series of Greek or English authors who follow. But the disappearance of the Bible from the books which the world contains, would produce results far greater; we can scarcely conceive the degree in which it would alter literature and language—the ideas of the educated and philosophical, as well as the feelings and habits of mind of the poor. If it has been said, with an allowable hyperbole, that 'Homer is Greece,' with much more truth may it be said, that 'the Bible is Christendom.'

Many by whom considerations of this sort will be little understood, may, nevertheless, recognise the use made of the Old Testament in the New. The religion of Christ was first taught by an application of the words of the Psalms and the Prophets. Our Lord Himself sanctions this application. 'Can there be a better use of Scripture than that which is made by Scripture?' 'Or any more likely method of teaching the truths of Christianity than that by which they were first taught?' For it may be argued that the critical interpretation of Scripture is a device almost of yesterday; it is the vocation of the scholar or philosopher, not of the Apostle or Prophet. The new truth which was introduced into the Old Testament, rather than the old truth which was found there, was the salvation and the conversion of the world. There are many quotations from the Psalms and the Prophets in the Epistles, in which the meaning is quickened or spiritualized, but hardly any, probably none, which is based on the original sense or context. That is not so singular a phenomenon as may at first sight be imagined. It may appear strange to us that Scripture should be interpreted in Scripture, in a manner not altogether in agreement with modern criticism; but would it not be more strange that it should be interpreted otherwise, than in agreement with the ideas of

the age or country in which it was written? The
observation that there is such an agreement, leads to
two conclusions which have a bearing on our present
subject. First, it is a reason for not insisting on the
applications which the New Testament makes of
passages in the Old, as their original meaning.
Secondly, it gives authority and precedent for the use
of similar applications in our own day.

But, on the other hand, though interwoven with
literature, though common to all ages of the Church,
though sanctioned by our Lord and His Apostles, it is
easy to see that such an employment of Scripture is
liable to error and perversion. For it may not only
receive a new meaning; it may be applied in a spirit
alien to itself. It may become the symbol of fanaticism, the cloke of malice, the disguise of policy.
Cromwell at Drogheda, quoting Scripture to his
soldiers; the well-known attack on the Puritans in
the State Service for the Restoration, 'Not every one
that saith unto me, Lord, Lord;' the reply of the
Venetian Ambassador to the suggestion of Wolsey,
that Venice should take a lead in Italy, '*which was
only* the Earth is the Lord's and the fulness thereof,'
are examples of such uses. In former times, it was a
real and not an imaginary fear, that the wars of the
Lord in the Old Testament might arouse a fire in the
bosom of Franks and Huns. In our own day such
dangers have passed away; it is only a figure of
speech when the preacher says, 'Gird on thy sword,
O thou most mighty.' The warlike passions of men
are not roused by quotations from Scripture, nor can
states of life such as slavery or polygamy which
belong to a past age, be defended, at least in England,
by the example of the Old Testament. The danger or
error is of another kind; more subtle, but hardly less
real. For if we are permitted to apply Scripture
under the pretence of interpreting it, the language of
Scripture becomes only a mode of expressing the
public feeling or opinion of our own day. Any

passing phase of politics or art, or spurious philanthropy, may have a kind of Scriptural authority. The words that are used are the words of the Prophet or Evangelist, but we stand behind and adapt them to our purpose. Hence it is necessary to consider the limits and manner of a just adaptation ; how much may be allowed for the sake of ornament · how far the Scripture, in all its details, may be regarded as an allegory of human life — where the true analogy begins—how far the interpretation of Scripture will serve as a corrective to its practical abuse.

Truth seems to require that we should separate mere adaptations, from the original meaning of Scripture. It is not honest or reasonable to confound illustration with argument, in theology, any more than in other subjects. For example, if a preacher chooses to represent the condition of a church or of an individual in the present day, under the figure of Elijah left alone among the idolatrous tribes of Israel, such an allusion is natural enough ; but if he goes on to argue that individuals are therefore justified in remaining in what they believe to be an erroneous communion — that is a mere appearance of argument which ought not to have the slightest weight with a man of sense. Such a course may indeed be perfectly justifiable, but not on the ground that a prophet of the Lord once did so, two thousand five hundred years ago. Not in this sense were the lives of the Prophets written for our instruction. There are many important morals conveyed by them, but only so far as they themselves represent universal principles of justice and love. These universal principles they clothe with flesh and blood ; they show them to us written on the hearts of men of like passions with ourselves. The prophecies, again, admit of many applications to the Christian Church or to the Christian life. There is no harm in speaking of the Church as the Spiritual Israel, or in using the imagery of Isaiah respecting

Messiah's kingdom, as the type of good things to come. But when it is gravely urged, that from such passages as 'Kings shall be thy nursing fathers,' we are to collect the relations of Church and State, or from the pictorial description of Isaiah, that it is to be inferred there will be a reign of Christ on earth—that is a mere assumption of the forms of reasoning by the imagination. Nor is it a healthful or manly tone of feeling which depicts the political opposition to the Church in our own day, under imagery which is borrowed from the desolate Sion of the captivity. Scripture is apt to come too readily to the lips, when we are pouring out our own weaknesses, or enlarging on some favourite theme—perhaps idealizing in the language of prophecy the feebleness of preaching or missions in the present day, or from the want of something else to say. In many discussions on these and similar subjects, the position of the Jewish King, Church, Priest, has led to a confusion, partly caused by the use of similar words in modern senses among ourselves. The King or Queen of England may be called the Anointed of the Lord, but we should not therefore imply that the attributes of sovereignty are the same as those which belonged to King David. All these are figures of speech, the employment of which is too common, and has been injurious to religion, because it prevents our looking at the facts of history or life as they truly are.

This is the first step towards a more truthful use of Scripture in practice—the separation of adaptation from interpretation. No one who is engaged in preaching or in religious instruction can be required to give up Scripture language; it is the common element in which his thoughts and those of his hearers move. But he may be asked to distinguish the words of Scripture from the truths of Scripture—the means from the end. The least expression of Scripture is weighty; it affects the minds of the hearers in a way that no other language can.    Whatever responsibility attaches to idle words, attaches in still greater degree to the idle or fallacious use of Scripture terms.    And there is surely a want of proper reverence for Scripture, when we confound the weakest and feeblest applications of its words with their true meaning—when we avail ourselves of their natural power to point them against some enemy—when we divert the eternal words of charity and truth into a defence of some passing opinion.    For not only in the days of the Pharisees, but in our own, the letter has been taking the place of the spirit ; the least matters, of the greatest, and the primary meaning has been lost in the secondary use.

Other simple cautions may also be added.    The applications of Scripture should be harmonized and, as it were, interpenetrated with the spirit of the Gospel, the whole of which should be in every part ; though the words may receive a new sense, the new sense ought to be in agreement with the general truth. They should be used to bring home practical precepts, not to send the imagination on a voyage of discovery ; they are not the real foundation of our faith in another world, nor can they, by pleasant pictures, add to our knowledge of it.    They should not confound the accidents with the essence of religion—the restrictions and burdens of the Jewish law with the freedom of the Gospel—the things which Moses allowed for the hardness of the heart, with the perfection of the teaching of Christ.    They should avoid the form of arguments, or they will insensibly be used, or understood to mean more than they really do.    They should be subjected to an overruling principle, which is the heart and conscience of the Christian teacher, who indeed ' stands behind them,' not to make them the vehicles of his own opinions, but as the expressions of justice, and truth, and love.

And here the critical interpretation of Scripture

comes in and exercises a corrective influence on its popular use. We have already admitted that criticism is not for the multitude ; it is not what the Scripture terms the Gospel preached for the poor. Yet, indirectly passing from the few to the many, it has borne a great part in the Reformation of religion. It has cleared the eye of the mind to understand the original meaning. It was a sort of criticism which supported the struggle of the sixteenth century against the Roman Catholic Church ; it is criticism that is leading Protestants to doubt whether the doctrine that the Pope is Antichrist, which has descended from the same period, is really discoverable in Scripture. Even the isolated thinker, against whom the religious world is taking up arms, has an influence on his opponents. The force of observations, which are based on reason and fact, remains when the tide of religious or party feeling is gone down. Criticism has also a healing influence in clearing away what may be termed the Sectarianism of knowledge. Without criticism it would be impossible to reconcile History and Science with Revealed Religion ; they must remain for ever in a hostile and defiant attitude. Instead of being like other records, subject to the conditions of knowledge which existed in an early stage of the world, Scripture would be regarded on the one side as the work of organic Inspiration, and as a lying imposition on the other.

The real unity of Scripture, as of man, has also a relation to our present subject. Amid all the differences of modes of thought and speech which have existed in different ages, of which much is said in our own day, there is a common element in human nature which bursts through these differences and remains unchanged, because akin to the first instincts of our being. The simple feeling of truth and right is the same to the Greek or Hindoo as to ourselves. However great may be the diversities of human character,

there is a point at which these diversities end, and
unity begins to appear. Now, this admits of an application to the books of Scripture, as well as to the
world generally. Written at many different times, in
more than one language, some of them in fragments,
they, too, have a common element of which the
preacher may avail himself. This element is twofold, partly divine and partly human; the revelation
of the truth and righteousness of God, and the cry of
the human heart towards Him. Every part of Scripture tends to raise us above ourselves—to give us a
deeper sense of the feebleness of man, and of the
wisdom and power of God. It has a sort of kindred,
as Plato would say, with religious truth everywhere
in the world. It agrees also with the imperfect stages
of knowledge and faith in human nature, and answers
to its inarticulate cries. The universal truth easily
breaks through the accidents of time and place in
which it is involved. Although we cannot apply
Jewish institutions to the Christian world, or venture
in reliance on some text to resist the tide of civilization
on which we are borne, yet it remains, nevertheless, to
us, as well as to the Jews and first Christians, that
'Righteousness exalteth a nation,' and that 'love is
the fulfilling not of the Jewish law only, but of all
law.'

In some cases, we have only to enlarge the meaning
of Scripture to apply it even to the novelties and
peculiarities of our own times. The world changes,
but the human heart remains the same; events and
details are different, but the principle by which they
are governed, or the rule by which we are to act, is
not different. When, for example, our Saviour says,
'Ye shall know the truth, and the truth shall make
you free,' it is not likely that these words would have
conveyed to the minds of the Jews who heard Him
any notion of the perplexities of doubt or inquiry.
Yet we cannot suppose that our Saviour, were He to

come again upon earth, would refuse thus to extend them. The Apostle St. Paul, when describing the Gospel, which is to the Greek foolishness, speaks also of a higher wisdom which is known to those who are perfect. Neither is it unfair for us to apply this passage to that reconcilement of faith and knowledge, which may be termed Christian philosophy, as the nearest equivalent to its language in our own day. Such words, again, as ' Why seek ye the living among the dead?' admit of a great variety of adaptations to the circumstances of our own time. Many of these adaptations have a real germ in the meaning of the words. The precept, ' Render unto Cæsar the things that are Cæsar's, and to God the things that are God's,' may be taken generally as expressing the necessity of distinguishing the divine and human—the things that belong to faith and the things that belong to experience. It is worth remarking in the application made of these words by Lord Bacon, ' Da fidei quæ fidei sunt;' that, although the terms are altered, yet the circumstance that the form of the sentence is borrowed from Scripture gives them point and weight.

The portion of Scripture which more than any other is immediately and universally applicable to our own times is, doubtless, that which is contained in the words of Christ Himself. The reason is that they are words of the most universal import. They do not relate to the circumstances of the time, but to the common life of all mankind. You cannot extract from them a political creed; only, ' Render unto Cæsar the things that are Cæsar's,' and ' The Scribes and Pharisees sit in Moses' seat; whatsoever, therefore, they say unto you do, but after their works do not.' They present to us a standard of truth and duty, such as no one can at once and immediately practise—such as, in its perfection, no one has fulfilled in this world. But this idealism does not interfere with their influence as a religious lesson. Ideals, even though unrealized, have effect on our daily life. The preacher of the Gospel is, or ought to be, aware that his calls to repentance, his standard of obligations, his lamentations over his own shortcomings or those of others, do not at once convert hundreds or thousands, as on the day of Pentecost. Yet it does not follow that they are thrown away, or that it would be well to substitute for them mere prudential or economical lessons, lectures on health or sanitary improvement. For they tend to raise men above themselves, providing them with Sabbaths as well as working days, giving them a taste of 'the good word of God' and of 'the powers of the world to come.' Human nature needs to be idealized; it seems as if it took a dislike to itself when presented always in its ordinary attire; it lives on in the hope of becoming better. And the image or hope of a better life—the vision of Christ crucified—which is held up to it, doubtless has an influence; not like the rushing mighty wind of the day of Pentecost; it may rather be compared to the leaven 'which a woman took and hid in three measures of meal, till the whole was leavened.'

The Parables of our Lord are a portion of the New Testament, which we may apply in the most easy and literal manner. The persons in them are the persons among whom we live and move; there are times and occasions at which the truths symbolized by them come home to the hearts of all who have ever been impressed by religion. We have been prodigal sons returning to our Father; servants to whom talents have been entrusted; labourers in the vineyard inclined to murmur at our lot, when compared with that of others, yet receiving every man his due; well-satisfied Pharisees; repentant Publicans:— we have received the seed, and the cares of the world have choked it—we hope also at times that we have found the pearl of great price after sweeping the house—we are ready like the Good Samaritan to show kindness to all mankind. Of these circumstances of life or phases of mind, which are typified by the parables, most Christians have experience. We may go on to apply many of them further to the condition of nations and churches. Such a treasury has Christ provided us of things new and old, which refer to all time and all mankind—may we not say in His own words—'Because He is the Son of Man?'

There is no language of Scripture which penetrates the individual soul, and embraces all the world in the arms of its love, in the same manner as that of Christ Himself. Yet the Epistles contain lessons which are not found in the Gospels, or, at least, not expressed with the same degree of clearness. For the Epistles are nearer to actual life—they relate to the circumstances of the first believers, to their struggles with the world without, to their temptations and divisions from within—their subject is not only the doctrine of the Christian religion, but the business of the early Church. And although their circumstances are not our circumstances—we are not afflicted or persecuted, or driven out of the world, but in possession of the blessings, and security, and property of an established religion—yet there is a Christian spirit which infuses itself into all circumstances, of which they are a pure and living source. It is impossible to gather from a few fragmentary and apparently not always consistent expressions, how the Communion was celebrated, or the Church ordered, what was the relative position of Presbyters and Deacons, or the nature of the gift of tongues, as a rule for the Church in after ages;—such inquiries have no certain answer, and at the best, are only the subject of honest curiosity. But the words, 'Charity never faileth,' and 'Though I speak with the tongues of men and of angels, and have not charity, I am nothing,'—these have a voice which reaches to the end of time. There are no questions of meats and drinks now-a-days, yet the

noble words of the Apostle remain : ' If meat make
my brother to offend, I will eat no flesh while
the world standeth, lest I make my brother to offend.' Moderation in controversy, toleration towards
opponents, or erring members, is a virtue which has
been thought by many to belong to the development and not to the origin of Christianity, and which
is rarely found in the commencement of a religion.
But lessons of toleration may be gathered from the
Apostle, which have not yet been learned either by theologians or by mankind in general. The persecutions
and troubles which awaited the Apostle, no longer
await us; we cannot, therefore, without unreality,
except, perhaps, in a very few cases, appropriate his
words, ' I have fought the good fight, I have finished
my course, I have kept the faith.' But that other text
still sounds gently in our ears : ' My strength is perfected in weakness,' and ' when I am weak, then am I
strong.' We cannot apply to ourselves the language
of authority in which the Apostle speaks of himself as
an ambassador for Christ, without something like bad
taste. But it is not altogether an imaginary hope
that those of us who are ministers of Christ, may
attain to a real imitation of his great diligence, of his
sympathy with others, and consideration for them—of
his willingness to spend and be spent in his Master's
service.

Such are a few instances of the manner in which
the analogy of faith enables us to apply the words of
Christ and His Apostles, with a strict regard to their
original meaning. But the Old Testament has also
its peculiar lessons which are not conveyed with
equal point or force in the New. The beginnings of
human history are themselves a lesson having a freshness as of the early dawn. There are forms of evil
against which the Prophets and the prophetical spirit
of the Law carry on a warfare, in terms almost too bold
for the way of life of modern times. There, more

plainly than in any other portion of Scripture, is expressed the antagonism of outward and inward, of ceremonial and moral, of mercy and sacrifice. There all the masks of hypocrisy are rudely torn asunder, in which an unthinking world allows itself to be disguised. There the relations of rich and poor in the sight of God, and their duties towards one another, are most clearly enunciated. There the religion of suffering first appears—'adversity, the blessing' of the Old Testament, as well as of the New. There the sorrows and aspirations of the soul find their deepest expression, and also their consolation. The feeble person has an image of himself in the 'bruised reed;' the suffering servant of God passes into the 'beloved one, in whom my soul delighteth.' Even the latest and most desolate phases of the human mind are reflected in Job and Ecclesiastes; yet not without the solemn assertion that 'to fear God and keep his commandments' is the beginning and end of all things.

It is true that there are examples in the Old Testament which were not written for our instruction, and that, in some instances, precepts or commands are attributed to God Himself, which must be regarded as relative to the state of knowledge which then existed of the Divine nature, or given 'for the hardness of men's hearts.' It cannot be denied that such passages of Scripture are liable to misunderstanding; the spirit of the Old Covenanters, although no longer appealing to the action of Samuel, 'hewing Agag in pieces before the Lord in Gilgal,' is not altogether extinguished. And a community of recent origin in America found their doctrine of polygamy on the Old Testament. But the poor generally read the Bible unconsciously; they take the good, and catch the prevailing spirit, without stopping to reason whether this or that practice is sanctioned by the custom or example of Scripture. The child is only struck by the impiety of the children who mocked the

E E

prophet; he does not think of the severity of the punishment which is inflicted on them. And the poor, in this respect, are much like children; their reflection on the morality or immorality of characters or events is suppressed by reverence for Scripture. The Christian teacher has a sort of tact by which he guides them to perceive only the spirit of the Gospel everywhere; they read in the Psalms, of David's sin and repentance; of the never-failing goodness of God to him, and his never-failing trust in Him, not of his imprecations against his enemies. Such difficulties are greater in theory and on paper, than in the management of a school or parish. They are found to affect the half-educated, rather than either the poor, or those who are educated in a higher sense. To be above such difficulties is the happiest condition of human life and knowledge, or to be below them; to see, or think we see, how they may be reconciled with Divine power and wisdom, or not to see how they are apparently at variance with them.

§ 5.

Some application of the preceding subject may be further made to theology and life.

Let us introduce this concluding inquiry with two remarks.

First, it may be observed, that a change in some of the prevailing modes of interpretation is not so much a matter of expediency as of necessity. The original meaning of Scripture is beginning to be clearly understood. But the apprehension of the original meaning is inconsistent with the reception of a typical or conventional one. The time will come when educated men will be no more able to believe that the words, " Out of Egypt have I called my son" (Matth. ii. 15; Hosea xi. 1), were *intended* by the prophet to refer to the return of Joseph and Mary from Egypt, than they are now able to believe the Roman Catholic explanation of Gen. iii. 15, ' Ipsa conteret caput tuum.' They will no more think that the first chapters of Genesis relate the same tale which Geology and Ethnology unfold than they now think the meaning of Joshua x. 12, 13, to be in accordance with Galileo's discovery.

From the circumstance that in former ages there has been a four-fold or a seven-fold Interpretation of Scripture, we cannot argue to the possibility of upholding any other than the original one in our own. The mystical explanations of Origen or Philo were not seen to be mystical; the reasonings of Aquinas and Calvin were not supposed to go beyond the letter of the text. They have now become the subject of apology ; it is justly said that we should not judge the greatness of the Fathers or Reformers by their suitableness to our own day. But this defence of them shows that their explanations of Scripture are no longer tenable ; they belong to a way of thinking and speaking which was once diffused over the world, but has now passed away. And what we give up as a general principle we shall find it impossible to maintain partially, *e. g.*, in the types of the Mosaic Law and the double meanings of prophecy, at least, in any sense in which it is not equally applicable to all deep and suggestive writings.

The same observation may be applied to the historical criticism of Scripture. From the fact that Paley or Butler were regarded in their generation as supplying a triumphant answer to the enemies of Scripture, we cannot argue that their answer will be satisfactory to those who inquire into such subjects in our own. Criticism has far more power than it formerly had ; it has spread itself over ancient, and even modern, history ; it extends to the thoughts and ideas of men as well as to words and facts ; it has also a great place in education. Whether the habit of mind which has been formed in classical studies will not go on to Scripture ; whether Scripture can be made an exception to other ancient writings, now that the nature of both is more understood; whether in the fuller light of history and science the views of the last century will hold out—these are questions respecting which the course of religious opinion in the past does not afford the means of truly judging.

II. It has to be considered whether the intellectual forms under which Christianity has been described may not also be in a state of transition and resolution, in this respect contrasting with the never-changing truth of the Christian life. (1 Cor. xiii. 8.) Looking backwards at past ages, we experience a kind of amazement at the minuteness of theological distinctions, and also at their permanence. They seem to have borne a part in the education of the Christian world, in an age when language itself had also a greater influence than now-a-days. It is admitted that these distinctions are not observed in the New Testament, and are for the most part of a later growth. But little is gained by setting up theology against Scripture, or Scripture against theology; the Bible against the Church, or the Church against the Bible. At different periods either has been a bulwark against some form of error: either has tended to correct the abuse of the other. A true inspiration guarded the writers of the New Testament from Gnostic or Manichean tenets; at a later stage, a sound instinct prevented the Church from dividing the humanity and Divinity of Christ. It may be said that the spirit of Christ forbids us to determine beyond what is written; and the decision of the council of Nicæa has been described by an eminent English prelate as 'the greatest misfortune that ever befel the Christian world.' That is, perhaps, true; yet a different decision would have been a greater misfortune. Nor does there seem any reason to suppose that the human mind could have been arrested in its theological course. It is a mistake to imagine that the dividing and splitting of words is owing to the depravity of the human heart; was it not rather an intellectual movement (the only phenomenon of progress then going on among men) which led, by a sort of necessity, some to go forward to the completion of the system, while it left others to stand aside? A veil was on the human understanding in the great controversies which absorbed the Church in earlier ages; the cloud which the combatants themselves raised intercepted the view. They did not see—they could not have imagined—that there was a world which lay beyond the range of the controversy.

And now, as the Interpretation of Scripture is receiving another character, it seems that distinctions of theology, which were in great measure based on old Interpretations, are beginning to fade away. A change is observable in the manner in which doctrines are stated and defended; it is no longer held sufficient to rest them on texts of Scripture, one, two, or more, which contain, or appear to contain, similar words or ideas. They are connected more closely with our moral nature; extreme consequences are shunned; large allowances are made for the ignorance of mankind. It is held that there is truth on both sides; about many questions there is a kind of union of opposites; others are admitted to have been verbal only; all are regarded in the light which is thrown upon them by church history and religious experience. A theory has lately been put forward, apparently as a defence of the Christian faith, which denies the objective character of any of them. And there are other signs that times are changing, and we are changing too. It would be scarcely possible at present to revive the interest which was felt less than twenty years ago in the doctrine of Baptismal Regeneration; nor would the arguments by which it was supported or impugned have the meaning which they once had. The communion of the Lord's Supper is also ceasing, at least in the Church of England, to be a focus or centre of disunion—

'Our greatest love turned to our greatest hate.'

A silence is observable on some other points of doctrine around which controversies swarmed a generation ago. Persons begin to ask what was the real difference which divided the two parties. They are no longer within the magic circle, but are taking up a position external to it. They have arrived at an age of reflection, and begin to speculate on the action and reaction, the irritation and counter-irritation, of religious forces; it is a common observation that 'revivals are not permanent;' the movement is criticised even by those who are subject to its influence. In the present state of the human mind, any considera· tion of these subjects, whether from the highest or lowest or most moderate point of view, is unfavourable to the stability of dogmatical systems, because it rouses inquiry into the meaning of words. To the sense of this is probably to be attributed the reserve on matters of doctrine and controversy which characterizes the present day, compared with the theological activity of twenty years ago.

These reflections bring us back to the question with which we began—' What effect will the critical interpretation of Scripture have on theology and on life?' Their tendency is to show that the result is beyond our control, and that the world is not unprepared for it. More things than at first sight appear are moving towards the same end. Religion often bids us think of ourselves, especially in later life, as each one in his appointed place, carrying on a work which is fashioned within by unseen hands. The theologian, too, may have peace in the thought that he is subject to the conditions of his age rather than one of its moving powers. When he hears theological inquiry censured as tending to create doubt and confusion, he knows very well that the cause of this is not to be sought in the writings of so-called rationalists or critics who are disliked partly because they unveil the age to itself; but in the opposition of reason and feeling, of the past and the present, in the conflict between the Calvinistic tendencies of an elder generation, and the influences which even in the same family naturally affect the young.

This distraction of the human mind between adverse influences and associations, is a fact which we should have to accept and make the best of, whatever consequences might seem to follow to individuals or Churches. It is not to be regarded as a merely heathen notion that 'truth is to be desired for its own sake even though no 'good' result from it.' As a Christian paradox it may be said, 'What hast thou to do with 'good;' follow thou Me.' But the Christian revelation does not require of us this Stoicism in most cases; it rather shows how good and truth are generally coincident. Even in this life, there are numberless links which unite moral good with intellectual truth. It is hardly too much to say that the one is but a narrower form of the other. Truth is to the world what holiness of life is to the individual—to man collectively the source of justice and peace and good.

There are many ways in which the connexion between truth and good may be traced in the interpretation of Scripture. Is it a mere chimera that the different sections of Christendom may meet on the common ground of the New Testament? Or that the individual may be urged by the vacancy and unprofitableness of old traditions to make the Gospel his own—a life of Christ in the soul, instead of a theory of Christ which is in a book or written down? Or that in missions to the heathen Scripture may become the expression of universal truths rather than of the tenets of particular men or churches? That would remove many obstacles to the reception of Christianity.

Or that the study of Scripture may have a more important place in a liberal education than hitherto? Or that the 'rational service' of interpreting Scripture may dry up the crude and dreamy vapours of religious excitement? Or, that in preaching, new sources of spiritual health may flow from a more natural use of Scripture? Or that the lessons of Scripture may have a nearer way to the hearts of the poor when disengaged from theological formulas? Let us consider more at length some of these topics.

1. No one casting his eye over the map of the Christian world can desire that the present lines of demarcation should always remain, any more than he will be inclined to regard the division of Christians to which he belongs himself, as in a pre-eminent or exclusive sense the Church of Christ. Those lines of demarcation seem to be political rather than religious; they are differences of nations, or governments, or ranks of society, more than of creeds or forms of faith. The feeling which gave rise to them has, in a great measure, passed away; no intelligent man seriously inclines to believe that salvation is to be found only in his own denomination. Examples of this 'sturdy orthodoxy,' in our own generation, rather provoke a smile than arouse serious disapproval. Yet many experiments show that these differences cannot be made up by any formal concordat or scheme of union; the parties cannot be brought to terms, and if they could, would cease to take an interest in the question at issue. The friction is too great when persons are invited to meet for a discussion of differences; such a process is like opening the doors and windows to put out a slumbering flame. But that is no reason for doubting that the divisions of the Christian world are beginning to pass away. The progress of politics, acquaintance with other countries, the growth of knowledge and of material greatness, changes of opinion in the Church of England, the present position

of the Roman Communion—all these phenomena show
that the ecclesiastical state of the world is not destined
to be perpetual. Within the envious barriers which
'divide human nature into very little pieces' (Plato,
*Rep.* iii. 395), a common sentiment is springing up
of religious truth; the essentials of Christianity are
contrasted with the details and definitions of it; good
men of all religions find that they are more nearly
agreed than heretofore. Neither is it impossible that
this common feeling may so prevail over the accidental circumstances of Christian communities, that
their political or ecclesiastical separation may be little
felt. The walls which no adversary has scaled may
fall down of themselves. We may perhaps figure
to ourselves the battle against error and moral evil
taking the place of one of sects and parties.

In this movement, which we should see more clearly
but for the divisions of the Christian world which
partly conceal it, the critical interpretation of Scripture will have a great influence. The Bible will be
no longer appealed to as the witness of the opinions of
particular sects, or of our own age; it will cease to be the
battle field of controversies. But as its true meaning
is more clearly seen, its moral power will also be
greater. If the outward and inward witness, instead
of parting into two, as they once did, seem rather to
blend and coincide in the Christian consciousness, that
is not a source of weakness but of strength. The
Book itself, which links together the beginning and
end of the human race, will not have a less ines-
timable value because the Spirit has taken the place of
the letter. Its discrepancies of fact, when we become
familiar with them, will seem of little consequence in
comparison with the truths which it unfolds. That
these truths, instead of floating down the stream of
tradition, or being lost in ritual observances, have
been preserved for ever in a book, is one of the many
blessings which the Jewish and Christian revelations

have conferred on the world—a blessing not the less real, because it is not necessary to attribute it to miraculous causes.

Again, the Scriptures are a bond of union to the whole Christian world. No one denies their authority, and could all be brought to an intelligence of their true meaning, all might come to agree in matters of religion. That may seem to be a hope deferred, yet not altogether chimerical. If it is not held to be a thing impossible, that there should be agreement in the meaning of Plato or Sophocles, neither is it to be regarded as absurd, that there should be a like agreement in the interpretation of Scripture. The disappearance of artificial notions and systems will pave the way to such an agreement. The recognition of the fact, that many aspects and stages of religion are found in Scripture; that different, or even opposite parties existed in the Apostolic Church; that the first teachers of Christianity had a separate and individual mode of regarding the Gospel of Christ; that any existing communion is necessarily much more unlike the brotherhood of love in the New Testament than we are willing to suppose — Protestants in some respects, as much so as Catholics—that rival sects in our own day—Calvinists and Arminians—those who maintain and those who deny the final restoration of man—may equally find texts which seem to favour their respective tenets (Mark ix. 44—48; Romans xi. 32)—the recognition of these and similar facts will make us unwilling to impose any narrow rule of religious opinion on the ever-varying conditions of the human mind and Christian society.

II. Christian missions suggest another sphere in which a more enlightened use of Scripture might offer a great advantage to the teacher. The more he is himself penetrated with the universal spirit of Scripture, the more he will be able to resist the literal and servile habits of mind of Oriental nations. You cannot transfer

English ways of belief, and almost the history of the
Church of England itself, as the attempt is sometimes
made—not to an uncivilized people, ready like children to receive new impressions, but to an ancient
and decaying one, furrowed with the lines of thought,
incapable of the principle of growth. But you may
take the purer light or element of religion, of which
Christianity is the expression, and make it shine on
some principle in human nature which is the fallen
image of it. You cannot give a people who have
no history of their own, a sense of the importance
of Christianity, as an historical fact : but, perhaps, that
very peculiarity of their character may make them
more impressible by the truths or ideas of Christianity. Neither is it easy to make them understand the growth of Revelation in successive ages—
that there are precepts of the Old Testament which
are reversed in the New—or that Moses allowed many
things for the hardness of men's hearts. They are
in one state of the world, and the missionary who
teaches them is in another, and the Book through
which they are taught, does not altogether coincide
with either. Many difficulties thus arise which we
are most likely to be successful in meeting, when we
look them in the face. To one inference they clearly
point, which is this : that it is not the Book of Scripture which we should seek to give them, to be reve-
renced like the Vedas or the Koran, and consecrated in
its words and letters, but the truth of the Book,
the mind of Christ and His Apostles, in which all
lesser details and differences should be lost and
absorbed. We want to awaken in them the sense
that God is their Father, and they His children ;—
that is of more importance than any theory about the
inspiration of Scripture. But to teach in this spirit,
the missionary should himself be able to separate the
accidents from the essence of religion ; he should be
conscious that the power of the Gospel resides not

in the particulars of theology, but in the Christian life.

III. It may be doubted whether Scripture has ever been sufficiently regarded as an element of liberal education. Few deem it worth while to spend in the study of it the same honest thought or pains which are bestowed on a classical author. Nor as at present studied, can it be said always to have an elevating effect. It is not a useful lesson for the young student to apply to Scripture, principles which he would hesitate to apply to other books; to make formal reconcilements of discrepancies which he would not think of reconciling in ordinary history; to divide simple words into double meanings; to adopt the fancies or conjectures of Fathers and Commentators as real knowledge. This laxity of knowledge is apt to infect the judgment when transferred to other subjects. It is not easy to say how much of the unsettlement of mind which prevails among intellectual young men is attributable to these causes; the mixture of truth and falsehood in religious education, certainly tends to impair, at the age when it is most needed, the early influence of a religious home.

Yet Scripture studied in a more liberal spirit might supply a part of education which classical literature fails to provide. 'The best book for the heart might also be made the best book for the intellect.' The noblest study of history and antiquity is contained in it; a poetry which is also the highest form of moral teaching; there, too, are lives of heroes and prophets, and especially of One whom we do not name with them, because He is above them. This history, or poetry, or biography is distinguished from all classical or secular writings by the contemplation of man as he appears in the sight of God. That is a sense of things into which we must grow as well as reason ourselves, without which human nature is but a truncated, half-educated sort of being. But this sense or consciousness of a Divine presence in the world, which seems to be natural to the beginnings of the human race, but fades away and requires to be renewed in its after history, is not to be gathered from Greek or Roman literature, but from the Old and New Testament. And before we can make the Old and New Testament a real part of education, we must read them not by the help of custom or tradition, in the spirit of apology or controversy, but in accordance with the ordinary laws of human knowledge.

IV. Another use of Scripture is that in sermons, which seems to be among the tritest, and yet is far from being exhausted. If we could only be natural and speak of things as they truly are with a real interest and not merely a conventional one ! The words of Scripture come readily to hand, and the repetition of them requires no effort of thought in the writer or speaker. But, neither does it produce any effect on the hearer, which will always be in proportion to the degree of feeling or consciousness in ourselves. It may be said that originality is the gift of few ; no Church can expect to have, not a hundred, but ten such preachers as Robertson or Newman. But, without originality, it seems possible to make use of Scripture in sermons in a much more living way than at present. Let the preacher make it a sort of religion, and proof of his reverence for Scripture, that he never uses its words without a distinct meaning ; let him avoid the form of argument from Scripture, and catch the feeling and spirit. Scripture is itself a kind of poetry, when not overlaid with rhetoric. The scene and country has a freshness which may always be renewed ; there is the interest of antiquity and the interest of home or common life as well. The facts and characters of Scripture might receive a new reading by being described simply as they are. The truths of Scripture again would have greater reality if divested of the scholastic form in which theology has cast them. The universal and

spiritual aspects of Scripture might be more brought
forward to the exclusion of questions of the Jewish
law, or controversies about the sacraments, or exaggerated statements of doctrines which seem to be at
variance with morality.   The life of Christ, regarded
quite naturally as of one . 'who was in all points
tempted like as we are, yet without sin,' is also the life
and centre of Christian teaching.   There is no higher
aim which the preacher can propose to himself than to
awaken what may be termed the feeling of the presence of God and the mind of Christ in Scripture ;
not to collect evidences about dates and books, or to
familiarize metaphysical distinctions; but to make the
heart and conscience of his hearers bear him witness
that the lessons which are contained in Scripture—
lessons of justice and truth—lessons of mercy and
peace—of the need of man and the goodness of God
to him, are indeed not human but divine.

v. It is time to make an end of this long disquisition
—let the end be a few more words of application to the
circumstances of a particular class in the present age.
If any one who is about to become a clergyman feels
or thinks that he feels that some of the preceding statements cast a shade of trouble or suspicion on his future
walk of life, who, either from the influence of a stronger
mind than his own, or from some natural tendency in
himself, has been led to examine those great questions
which lie on the threshold of the higher study of
theology, and experiences a sort of shrinking or dizzi-
ness at the prospect which is opening upon him ; let
him lay to heart the following considerations :—First,
that he may possibly not be the person who is called
upon to pursue such inquiries.   No man should busy
himself with them who has not clearness of mind
enough to see things as they are, and a faith strong
enough to rest in that degree of knowledge which God
has really given ; or who is unable to separate the truth
from his own religious wants and experiences.   For
the theologian as well as the philosopher has need of

'dry light,' 'unmingled with any tincture of the
affections,' the more so as his conclusions are oftener
liable to be disordered by them. He who is of
another temperament may find another work to do,
which is in some respects a higher one. Unlike
philosophy, the Gospel has an ideal life to offer, not to
a few only, but to all. There is one word of caution,
however, to be given to those who renounce inquiry;
it is that they cannot retain the right to condemn
inquirers. Their duty is to say with Nicodemus,
'Doth the Gospel condemn any man before it hear
him?' although the answer may be only 'Art thou
also of Galilee?' They have chosen the path of
practical usefulness, and they should acknowledge
that it is a narrow path. For any but a 'strong
swimmer' will be insensibly drawn out of it by the
tide of public opinion or the current of party.

Secondly, let him consider that the difficulty is not
so great as imagination sometimes paints it. It is a
difficulty which arises chiefly out of differences of
education in different classes of society. It is a
difficulty which tact, and prudence, and, much more,
the power of a Christian life may hope to surmount.
Much depends on the manner in which things are
said; on the evidence in the writer or preacher of a
real good will to his opponents, and a desire for the
moral improvement of men. There is an aspect of
truth which may always be put forward so as to find
a way to the hearts of men. If there is danger and
shrinking from one point of view, from another, there
is freedom and sense of relief. The wider contemplation of the religious world may enable us to
adjust our own place in it. The acknowledgment of
churches as political and national institutions is the
basis of a sound government of them. Criticism itself is
not only negative; if it creates some difficulties, it does
away others. It may put us at variance with a party or
section of Christians in our own neighbourhood. But
on the other hand, it enables us to look at all men as

they are in the sight of God, not as they appear to
human eye, separated and often interdicted from each
other by lines of religious demarcation, it divides us
from the parts to unite us to the whole. That is a great
help to religious communion. It does away with the
supposed opposition of reason and faith. It throws us
back on the conviction that religion is a personal thing,
in which certainty is to be slowly won and not assumed
as the result of evidence or testimony. It places us, in
some respects (though it be deemed a paradox to say
so), more nearly in the position of the first Christians
to whom the New Testament was not yet given, in
whom the Gospel was a living word, not yet embodied
in forms or supported by ancient institutions.

Thirdly, the suspicion or difficulty which attends
critical inquiries is no reason for doubting their value.
The Scripture nowhere leads us to suppose that the
circumstance of all men speaking well of us is any
ground for supposing that we are acceptable in the
sight of God. And there is no reason why the condemnation of others should be witnessed to by our
own conscience. Perhaps it may be true that, owing
to the jealousy or fear of some, the reticence of others,
the terrorism of a few, we may not always find
it easy to regard these subjects with calmness and
judgment. But, on the other hand, these accidental
circumstances have nothing to do with the question
at issue; they cannot have the slightest influence on
the meaning of words, or on the truth of facts. No
one can carry out the principle that public opinion or
church authority is the guide to truth, when he goes
beyond the limits of his own church or country. That
is a consideration which may well make him pause
before he accepts of such a guide in the journey to
another world. All the arguments for repressing inquiries into Scripture in Protestant countries hold
equally in Italy and Spain for repressing inquiries
into matters of fact or doctrine, and so for denying
the Scriptures to the common people.

Lastly, let him be assured that there is some nobler idea of truth than is supplied by the opinion of mankind in general, or the voice of parties in a church. Every one, whether a student of theology or not, has need to make war against his prejudices no less than against his passions ; and, in the religious teacher, the first is even more necessary than the last. For, while the vices of mankind are in a great degree isolated, and are, at any rate, reprobated by public opinion, their prejudices have a sort of communion or kindred with the world without. They are a collective evil, and have their being in the interest, classes, states of society, and other influences amid which we live. He who takes the prevailing opinions of Christians and decks them out in their gayest colours—who reflects the better mind of the world to itself—is likely to be its favourite teacher. In that ministry of the Gospel, even when assuming forms repulsive to persons of education, no doubt the good is far greater than the error or harm. But there is also a deeper work which is not dependent on the opinions of men in which many elements combine, some alien to religion, or accidentally at variance with it. That work can hardly expect to win much popular favour, so far as it runs counter to the feelings of religious parties. But he who bears a part in it may feel a confidence, which no popular caresses or religious sympathy could inspire, that he has by a Divine help been enabled to plant his foot somewhere beyond the waves of time. He may depart hence before the natural term, worn out with intellectual toil ; regarded with suspicion by many of his contemporaries ; yet not without a sure hope that the love of truth, which men of saintly lives often seem to slight, is, nevertheless, accepted before God.

F F

# NOTE ON BUNSEN'S BIBLICAL RESEARCHES.

SINCE the Essay on Bunsen's Biblical Researches was in type, two
more parts of the '*Bible for the People*' have reached England.
One includes a translation of Isaiah, but does not separate the
distinguishable portions in the manner of Ewald, or with the freedom which the translator's criticisms would justify. The other
part comprehends numerous dissertations on the Pentateuch, entering largely on questions of its origin, materials, and interpretation. There seems not an entire consistency of detail in these
dissertations, and in the views deducible from the author's Egypt,
but the same spirit and breadth of treatment pervade both. The
analysis of the Levitical laws, by which the Mosaic germs are distinguished from subsequent accretions, is of the highest interest.
The Ten Plagues of Egypt are somewhat rationalistically handled,
as having a true historical basis, but as explicable by natural
phenomena, indigenous to Egypt in all ages. The author's tone
upon the technical definition of miracles, as distinct from great
marvels and wonders, has acquired a firmer freedom, and would
be represented by some among ourselves as 'painfully sceptical.'
But even those who hesitate to follow the author in his details
must be struck by the brilliant suggestiveness of his researches,
which tend more and more, in proportion as they are developed, to
justify the presentiment of their creating a new epoch in the
science of Biblical criticism.

R. W.

THE END.